"*40 Questions About the Great Com*
pastor, professor, or student who ca
a biblical scholar, missiologist, and seminary president join forces to answer every question you've ever asked—or never asked—about our Lord's parting commission to his disciples. Substantive, lucid, and compelling. Buy this book now!"

—Bruce Ashford, Southeastern Baptist Theological Seminary

"The church has one job. It is called the Great Commission. Every Christian soldier should know the who, the what, the why, and the where of the marching orders left by our Lord and Commander-in-Chief, and this book does just that in an engaging and encouraging way. Read it and then get on with it!"

—James Merritt, The Southern Baptist Theological Seminary

"This book is a succinct and at the same time wide-ranging exposition of the commission of Jesus given to the disciples and thus to the church to proclaim the gospel far and wide. The authors elucidate the meaning of key passages in Scripture and thus present the geographical scope, the theological content, and important historical parameters of the mission of the church. This book deserves to be read by every Christian believer committed to the glory of God in all the world and to the proclamation of the gospel of Jesus Christ."

—Eckhard J. Schnabel, Gordon-Conwell Theological Seminary

"*40 Questions About the Great Commission* is a book that gets to the very heart of the Christian faith. Jesus's last words to his disciples on a mountain in Galilee changed the course of human history. Christians today need to reflect on these important words and their implications for our lives. Akin, Merkle, and Robinson challenge us all to consider the comprehensive meaning of the Great Commission and the role we might play in God's overarching mission in the world."

—Paul Akin, Dean, The Southern Baptist Theological Seminary

"I'm grateful for this book. Not only do I believe that the church needs a renewed commitment to the Great Commission, but it also needs men like Danny Akin, Ben Merkle, and George Robinson to lead the way. I know these men, and they are much more than scholars who write about this important topic; they are practitioner-scholars who have given their lives to help their neighbors and the nations know about Christ. This work is a unique academic resource that also informs, inspires, challenges, and convicts the reader. It is a resource that I will keep near."

—Chuck Lawless, Southeastern Baptist Theological Seminary

"This is a book on the Great Commission from every conceivable angle. The more I read it, the more excited I became. The writing is clear and concise. The arguments are compelling. The implications are inspiring. This is a book for anyone who wants to obey Jesus's final command to make disciples of the nations."

—Steve Addison,
author of *The Rise and Fall of Movements: A Roadmap for Leaders*

"Excellent! Simply excellent! Akin, Merkle, and Robinson have produced a comprehensive, scholarly, yet, easy-to-understand work for the Church. Biblical, inspirational, and practical! The authors dig deeply into the Great Commission mine and, page-after-page, keep bringing up gold!"

—J. D. Payne, Samford University

"This is a very comprehensive book that brings clarity on the Great Commission theologically, historically, and with practical implications for the local church. Every follower of Jesus Christ should be equipped with the principles in this book in order to obey the Great Commission. We are entrenched in a battle for the souls of our family, friends, and neighbors; the tools and principles presented in this book are proven to aid in expanding God's kingdom, until there is no place left where the gospel of Jesus Christ has not been preached (Romans 15:23). For me, greater than the book itself are the men who wrote it—men who are impacting the spread of the gospel by not only 'knowing,' but 'being' and doing Great Commission activities. These are men to follow as they make disciples of the nations!"

—Jeff Sundell, Chief Strategy Officer, E3 Partners
and cofounder of the "No Place Left" movement

"This book is a comprehensive study on the Great Commission (Matthew 28:18–20 and related texts) and its multiple dimensions/aspects (i.e., what, who, why, where, when and how). It is organized in five parts (in content) and 40 questions (in format). It includes exegetical study of texts, historical review of the topic, and practical application. At the end of each question, there are reflection questions for discussion. This book is recommended for all those who are interested in the topic of the Great Commission and ready to carry it out in practical ways."

—Enoch Wan, Western Seminary

40 QUESTIONS ABOUT
The Great Commission

Daniel L. Akin
Benjamin L. Merkle
George G. Robinson

Benjamin L. Merkle, Series Editor

Kregel
Academic

Also Available in the 40 Questions Series

40 Questions About Baptism and the Lord's Supper
John S. Hammett

40 Questions About Christians and Biblical Law
Thomas R. Schreiner

40 Questions About Church Membership and Discipline
Jeremy M. Kimble

40 Questions About Creation and Evolution
Kenneth D. Keathley, Mark F. Rooker

40 Questions About Elders and Deacons
Benjamin L. Merkle

40 Questions About Interpreting the Bible
Robert L. Plummer

40 Questions About Salvation
Matthew Barrett

40 Questions About the End Times
Eckhard Schnabel

40 Questions About the Historical Jesus
C. Marvin Pate

40 Questions About Angels, Demons, and Spiritual Warfare
John R. Gilhooly

40 Questions About Heaven and Hell
Alan W. Gomes

40 Questions About Calvinism
Shawn D. Wright

40 Questions About the Great Commission
© 2020 Daniel L. Akin, Benjamin L. Merkle, and George G. Robinson

Published by Kregel Academic, an imprint of Kregel Publications, 2450 Oak Industrial Dr. NE, Grand Rapids, MI 49505-6020.

This book is a title in the 40 Questions Series edited by Benjamin L. Merkle.

The Hebrew font, NewJerusalemU, and the Greek font, GraecaU, are available from www.linguistsoftware.com/lgku.htm, +1-425-775-1130.

ISBN 978-0-8254-4448-7

Printed in the United States of America

20 21 22 23 24 / 5 4 3 2 1

"Dedicated to all the faithful missionaries who have and who continue to labor among the nations to make known the gospel of the Lord Jesus. May their tribe increase until our King returns in glory. And to those who are yet to join them, may this book encourage you along that path."

Contents

Introduction / 9
Abbreviations / 13

Part 1: General Questions about the Great Commission
 1. What Is the Great Commission? / 17
 2. To Whom Was the Great Commission Given? / 23
 3. What Does the Great Commission Imply Regarding Other Religions? / 29
 4. How Does the Great Commission Relate to the Great Commandment? / 37
 5. When Will the Great Commission Be Fulfilled? / 45

Part 2: Historical Questions about the Great Commission
 6. Where Do We Stand in Relation to Fulfilling the Great Commission?? / 55
 7. How Has the Great Commission Been Interpreted in History? / 63
 8. Who Are the Great Commission Heroes of the Church's First 1,000 Years? / 71
 9. Who Are the Great Commission Heroes of the Church's Second 1,000 Years? / 79
 10. How Have Missionary Movements and Conferences Impacted the Great Commission? / 87
 11. What Are Some Excellent Quotes Regarding the Great Commission? (Part 1) / 97
 12. What Are Some Excellent Quotes Regarding the Great Commission? (Part 2) / 111

Part 3: Exegetical Questions about the Great Commission
 13. How Does Matthew 28:16–18 Relate to the Great Commission? / 127
 14. What Is the Main Command of the Great Commission? / 133
 15. What Is the Meaning of "All Nations"? / 141
 16. Should the Verb "Go/Going" Be Understood as a Command? / 147
 17. How Do Baptism and Teaching Relate to the Great Commission? / 155
 18. What Is a Summary of Jesus's Commands for His Disciples? / 161
 19. What Is the Meaning of "I Am with You Always, to the End of the Age"? / 169

Part 4: Biblical-Theological Questions about the Great Commission

Section A: Questions Related to the Various Versions of the Great Commission

20. What Is the Contribution of Mark's Version of the Great Commission? / 177
21. What Is the Contribution of Luke's Version of the Great Commission? / 183
22. What Is the Contribution of John's Version of the Great Commission? / 191
23. What Is the Contribution of Acts' Version of the Great Commission? / 199

Section B: Questions Related to Biblical Theology and the Great Commission

24. How Does the Great Commission Relate to God's Creation Order in Genesis? / 207
25. How Does the Old Testament Relate to the Great Commission? / 219
26. How Do the Major Themes in Matthew Relate to the Great Commission? / 225
27. How Does Jesus's Life and Mission Relate to the Great Commission? / 231
28. How Does the Great Commission Relate to Jesus's Second Coming? / 239
29. How Does the Book of Acts Relate to the Great Commission? / 247
30. How Do Paul's Epistles Relate to the Great Commission? / 253
31. How Do the General Epistles Relate to the Great Commission? / 261

Part 5: Practical-Missiological Questions about the Great Commission

32. How Does the Bible Display the Gospel to Advance the Great Commission? / 269
33. What Is the Responsibility of Each Christian to the Great Commission? / 275
34. What Is the Responsibility of the Local Church to the Great Commission? / 283
35. Does the Great Commission Involve Social Action? / 289
36. What Are Some Helpful Prayer Resources? / 295
37. What Are Some Helpful Mobilization Resources? / 303
38. How Should the Great Commission Influence Our Mission Strategy? / 311
39. Is It Possible to Overemphasize the Great Commission? / 319
40. How Should We Preach the Great Commission? / 325

Select Bibliography / 333
Appendix A: 6 Seasons of God's Kingdom Strategy / 335
Appendix B: Sermon on Matthew 28:16–20—The Great Commission &
         William Carey: A Passionate Global Vision / 343
Scripture Index / 353

Introduction

In 1991 I (George) was standing at a university bus stop, disillusioned with life and looking for purpose or meaning. Another student approached me that day and offered me hope, pointing me toward the purpose he had found in following Jesus. I knew about Jesus from Sunday school where my sweet grandmas had taken me as a child. But I didn't know Jesus. I had yet to surrender to him in such a way as to find that he *is* the meaning of life. The friend who shared Jesus with me on that day had been compelled to share the gospel with me, not because he was a trained minister. He wasn't. Rather, he shared with me on that day out of the overflow of his own relationship with God and in obedience to Jesus's final command—the Great Commission. Just over a week later that good news would penetrate my heart and begin to shape my life as it had his. I very quickly came to understand that the gospel saves us from sin, for God, into the church, and onto his mission. And I have invested the past twenty-seven years of my life growing in that understanding and the obedience that Jesus commissioned me to.

Each of the three authors of this book has our own story of how we first encountered the good news of the gospel and then embraced the mission that is inextricably tied to it. That mission is summarized potently in Jesus's famous last words found in Matthew 28:18–20. This book is devoted to our and your deeper understanding and obedience to those words. At the time we were writing, all three of us served in varying capacities at Southeastern Seminary, where the motto is well known: "Every classroom is a Great Commission classroom." From our college business and literature courses to our graduate counseling, biblical languages, and missions courses, each one is devoted to helping our students maximize their effectiveness in making reproducing disciples among their neighbors and the nations.

But my own journey in Great Commission obedience didn't begin in a seminary classroom. It started on the university campus, while I was a student learning to live on mission. And then it developed more while I was a public school teacher. Eventually I did end up in a seminary classroom, followed by overseas missionary service. My employment has changed through the years, as has my geographic location. But my mission has not. The moment I embraced the gospel of Jesus, I inherited the mission of Jesus! And that should be true in your life and the lives of all Christians. Our prayer is that this book won't simply be read, but lived—that you, the reader, will embrace the mission of Jesus and continue to grow in your effectiveness wherever God sends you.

Toward that end, this book has been organized into five parts addressing various aspects of the Great Commission. Parts 1 and 2 were authored by Daniel Akin and answer general and historical questions, respectively. There you will find well-researched answers related to the audience and implications of the Great Commission as well as how we measure progress, how others have understood the mission, and several chapters devoted to "heroes" and the inspiring things that they said. Parts 3 and 4 were authored, with the exception of questions 15 and 24 (Robinson), by Ben Merkle. Part 3 zooms in like a microscope, and is devoted to exegetical questions digging deep into the precise wording of Great Commission-related Scriptures, what they say and mean, and what the implications for various understandings may be. Part 4 then pans out like a telescope, addressing the broader biblical and theological issues of the various iterations of the Great Commission in each of the Gospels and Acts and then how the mission is situated in the Bible. Part 5, authored by George Robinson, addresses issues related to the practical-missiological application of the Great Commission. If the first four parts aim to inform the head and motivate the heart, this final part aims to animate the hands toward Great Commission obedience. What we do with what we know matters.

As I write this short introduction, the weight of what is at stake is staring me in the face. In my office when I look in one direction I see a photo of a man I'll call "Rashid." The photo was taken more than a decade ago in an Asian village. I first visited Rashid's country a few years earlier and worked with some courageous men and women who had been persecuted for their faith in Christ. One night, while I was sleeping in one of the leaders' homes, I faced serious spiritual warfare in the form of a dream wherein I was attacked for my faith. When I woke, I lay paralyzed in fear. A few days later, when I got on the flight leaving that country, I had decided I was never going back. I wouldn't have told anyone that, but I was unsettled. About six months later I was asked to come back and train a few dozen indigenous leaders, and I reluctantly agreed. Less than two weeks before my trip, one of the local leaders was killed for his faith. I faced a serious dilemma as to whether or not I should proceed with the trip as planned. The local leaders persisted and I reluctantly went. The courage and faith of those men and women in the face of persecution emboldened me! They understood what was at stake and kept sharing the gospel and making disciples in spite of it.

Fast-forward a year and I was back in that land working in an area that, to our knowledge, heretofore had never been evangelized. As we prayer-walked through the area, asking God to give us an open door for the gospel, a man who in my estimation epitomized what a terrorist would look like came out and invited us into his home. I nervously and prayerfully received his hospitality. But I was honestly fearing that my earlier dream would come true right then and there. Rashid asked me what brought us to his village and I sheepishly replied, "I am a follower of Jesus and he sent me here." Rashid's eyes widened and he became very animated and loud. The lump in my throat grew even larger . . . until he shared that someone had started to share the message of Jesus with him decades earlier, and he had rejected that message and refused to listen. But recently, he went on, he had been having dreams and Jesus would come to him saying, "Follow me!" Rashid told me the dreams always ended the same—with him replying, "Jesus, I don't know the way." And then Jesus would say, "I will send someone to show you the way." Wide-eyed, Rashid blurted out, "Tell me how to follow Jesus! Tell me what I must do!" For the next several hours we laid out the gospel, which both he and his wife responded to in repentance and faith. Then we started entry-level discipleship, explaining the importance of the Bible, baptism, worship, and prayer. We gave him a Bible and he said, "If Jesus said to make disciples, then I will need more of these." As we walked away planning follow-up with him, Rashid went house to house through his village, telling his neighbors to come hear the greatest news he'd ever heard! A week later he was baptized, and a year later a missionary to that land said Rashid had won many of his neighbors to Christ and that they were studying the Bible and worshipping together in his home! Great Commission obedience, even when it's with fear and hesitancy, can lead to stories like that.

So when I'm sitting in my office looking in one direction, I see Rashid. But when I look in the other direction, there's a window. And outside of that window is a broken world filled with people who need the hope of the gospel—people like I was, at that bus stop nearly three decades ago. People like Rashid. People like you once were. This book is a feeble attempt to help you to go to those people with head, heart, and hands readied to make disciples who reproduce.

It is for God's glory, our joy, and the good of the nations.

Abbreviations

BDAG	W. Bauer, F. W. Danker, W. F. Arndt, and F. W. Gingrich. *Greek-English Lexicon of the New Testament and Other Early Christian Literature.* 3rd ed. Chicago: University of Chicago Press, 2000.
BECNT	Baker Exegetical Commentary on the New Testament
BSAC	*Bibliotheca Sacra*
CNTC	Calvin's New Testament Commentaries
EBC	Expositor's Bible Commentary
EDT	*Evangelical Dictionary of Theology*
ICC	International Critical Commentary
ISBE	*International Standard Bible Encyclopedia*
JSNT	*Journal for the Study of the New Testament*
LCC	Library of Christian Classics
Louw & Nida	Johannes P. Louw and Eugene A. Nida. *Greek-English Lexicon of the New Testament Based on Semantic Domains,* 2 vols. New York: United Bible Societies, 1988.
NACSBT	NAC Studies in Bible and Theology
NICNT	New International Commentary on the New Testament
NIGTC	New International Greek Testament Commentary
NIDNTTE	*New International Dictionary of New Testament Theology and Exegesis*
NSBT	New Studies in Biblical Theology
NTC	New Testament Commentary
OTL	Old Testament Library
PNTC	Pillar New Testament Commentary
REDS	Reformed Exegetical Doctrinal Studies
ResQ	*Restoration Quarterly*
STR	*Southeastern Theological Review*
TDNT	Theological Dictionary of the New Testament
TNTC	Tyndale New Testament Commentary
TrinJ	*Trinity Journal*
TynBul	*Tyndale Bulletin*
WBC	Word Biblical Commentary
WTJ	*Westminster Theological Journal*
ZECNT	Zondervan Exegetical Commentary on the New Testament

PART 1

General Questions about the Great Commission

What Is the Great Commission?

In the last chapter of Matthew, almost all modern English translations place a subheading before Jesus's last words to his disciples: "The Great Commission." If one looks above Mark 16:14, the label occurs again in many English Bibles as well.[1] Many Christians today are familiar with the term. It appears as the theme or title of countless blogs, articles, books, conferences, and sermons. Subheadings and titles like these are helpful because they summarize what passages are teaching. This chapter will explore the meaning of the title "Great Commission," where it originated, and where and why it appears in Scripture.

The History of the "Great Commission"

Who coined the label "Great Commission" is not certain. Because the phrase is so common today, it is difficult to decipher the history of the title. An author or speaker may refer to someone in history as teaching about the Great Commission even if that historical person did not use the title. For example, many rightly refer to William Carey (1761–1834), the father of the modern missionary movement, as writing about the Great Commission in his work *An Enquiry into the Obligation of Christians to Use Means for the Conversion of the Heathens*. Although Carey's teaching is congruent with much of our understanding about the Great Commission today, he never used the expression in his famous mission treatise.[2] Another difficulty, as David Wright reveals, is that "commission" is a common enough noun and "great" is also so common

---

1. The English Standard Version (ESV), the Christian Standard Bible (CSB), and the New King James Version (NKJV) all place the same header in Mark 16 that occurs in Matthew 28. In the New American Standard Bible (NASB), the heading "The Disciples Commissioned" appears instead of "The Great Commission." In the New International Version (NIV), there is no heading above the verse.
2. Timothy C. Tennent, *Invitation to World Missions: A Trinitarian Missiology for the Twenty-First Century* (Grand Rapids: Kregel, 2010), 127.

of a descriptor that the phrase "great commission" appears in a general sense long before its modern restricted use.[3]

Timothy Tennent says the expression seems to first appear in print in 1889 when Eugene Stock published his three-volume work, *History of the Church Mission Society*.[4] Robbie Castleman writes that it is possible that the Dutch missionary Justinian von Welz (1621–1688) created the label.[5] But, Malcom Yarnell argues that the earliest identification of Matthew 28:18–19 as the Great Commission appears in Francis Johnson's 1595 work *A treatise of the ministry of the Church of England*.[6] Johnson describes the passage with adjectives, calling it the "last and great commission."[7] Yarnell further argues that Benjamin Keach, a seventeenth-century particular Baptist, is the first to repeatedly develop "the idea that Matthew 28:16–20 is the Great Commission from which the Christian churches should live their lives."[8] However, Johnson's and Keach's understanding still differ from the full modern idea of the Great Commission as a title for Matthew 28:16–20 as the missionary mandate.

Although the history of the phrase is not easy to sort, many Christians have adopted the phrase and continue to use it today. Some argue that Hudson Taylor (1832–1905), missionary to China, popularized the use of the label.[9] Taylor is often attributed with the now famous quote, "The Great Commission is not an option to be considered; it is a command to be obeyed." A source that confirms

---

3. David F. Wright, "The Great Commission and the Ministry of the Word: Reflections Historical and Contemporary on Relations and Priorities," *Scottish Bulletin of Evangelical Theology* 25, no. 2 (September 2007): 153. Wright provides a helpful survey and assessment of works that use the words "great commission" in his article.

4. Tennent, *Invitation*, 127.

5. Robbie F. Castleman, "The Last Word: The Great Commission: Ecclesiology," *Themelios* 32, no. 3 (April 2007): 68. Unfortunately, Castleman does not reference what part of Welz's work led her to this conclusion.

6. Malcom Yarnell, "Enduring Submission to the Great Commission," *Love Each Stone*, August 29, 2007, http://loveeachstone.blogspot.com/2007/08/rogers-yarnell-dialogue-on-great_30.html.

7. Francis Johnson, *A Treatise of the Ministry of the Church of England* (1595), 32.

8. Yarnell, "Enduring Submission to the Great Commission." Here is Keach's quote in full: "Sir, All that are to be baptized, are, by virtue of the great Commission of our Saviour, to be first taught and made Disciples by teaching; and take heed you add not to his Word, nor attempt to invert the Order of the Charter and gracious Grant of the King of Heaven and Earth" (Benjamin Keach, *The Rector Rectified and Corrected, or, Infant-Baptism Unlawful: Being a Sober Answer to a Late Pamphlet Entituled an Argumentative and Practical Discourse of Infant-Baptism, Published by Mr. William Burkit, Rector of Mildin in Suffolk: Wherein All His Arguments for Pedo-Baptism Are Refuted and the Necessity of Immersion, I.e. Dipping, Is Evidenced, and the People Falsly Called Anabaptists Are Cleared from Those Unjust Reproaches and Calumnies Cast Upon Them: Together with a Reply to the Athenian Gazette Added to Their 5th Volume About Infant-Baptism: With Some Remarks Upon Mr. John Flavel's Last Book in Answer to Mr. Philip Cary* [London: John Harris, 1692], 78).

9. Castleman, "The Last Word," 68.

the attribution, however, does not exist.[10] Whether Taylor popularized the term cannot be known with certainty, given the dearth of information. But we do know that either during or shortly after Taylor's life, the term became popular. As Wright concludes "it was not until the last decades of the nineteenth century, or even perhaps the earliest years of the twentieth, that Matthew 28:18–20 came to be conventionally referred to as 'the Great Commission.'"[11]

Why Matthew 28:18–20 Is the "Great Commission"

It is important to consider why Matthew 28:18–20 has this title, its full meaning, and what other passages the title fits. What has prompted writers to label it a "commission," and what is it that makes this commission so "great"?[12] Why is it not—as others have asked—for example, called the Great *Command*, the Great *Declaration*, or the Great *Suggestion*? There are several reasons. First, Jesus's words are not a declaration or a suggestion, because Jesus commands his disciples with the authority of the Creator and Sovereign Lord. He sends out his disciples with "all authority in heaven and on earth." His words require a response. The Greek aorist participle *poreuthentes* should not be translated with a relaxed idea ("as you go") but with an imperatival force ("Go!").[13] In fact, each participle in this passage (going, baptizing, and teaching) has an imperatival force.[14] The disciples must obey Jesus's words.

Second, Jesus's words are also more than a command. A command is an authoritative order that can be positive or negative. For example, "feed the hungry" and "do not murder" are commands, but they are not commissions. In a commission, one is sent with another's authority to fulfill a task or mission. Artists are commissioned to produce a painting, and ships are commissioned to deploy in service. The one commissioned has the power and authority to act for the one sending them. With his final words, Jesus sends out his disciples to participate in God's mission with his authority and with the power of the Holy Spirit. This is why many have correctly labeled Matthew 28:18–20 as a "commission." God, through Christ, has sent his followers to participate in his mission by making disciples of all nations.

Before asking why this commission is so great, it is important to understand that the Great Commission is only a part, albeit a crucial part, of all that

---

10. Mitzi J. Smith and Jayachitra Lalitha, *Teaching All Nations: Interrogating the Matthean Great Commission* (Minneapolis: Fortress, 2014), 58; Wright also makes a similar point ("The Great Commission and the Ministry of the Word," 156–57).
11. Wright, "The Great Commission and the Ministry of the Word," 132.
12. This wording of the second question comes from Kevin DeYoung and Greg Gilbert, *What Is the Mission of the Church? Making Sense of Social Justice, Shalom, and the Great Commission* (Wheaton, IL: Crossway, 2011), 40.
13. See Question 16.
14. The imperatival force of "going" (Go!) is stronger than that of the other two participles ("baptizing" and "teaching"). See Question 17.

God is doing. From the entire story of the Bible, the grand redemptive story, we see that there is a larger *missio dei*, a Latin phrase meaning the "mission of God." From the opening line of "In the beginning" to the closing "Amen," the Bible tells the story of God's mission to redeem humanity and creation. As Christopher Wright says, "*The whole Bible is itself a 'missional' phenomenon. . . .* The Bible renders to us the story of God's mission through God's people in their engagement with God's world for the sake of the whole of God's creation."[15] Mission is ultimately about what God is doing, which is not limited to what man does. The Great Commission is man's role in God's greater work. God is working to bring all creation back to himself, but he gives a specific command within that greater work for his people to proclaim the gospel of Jesus. As Kevin DeYoung and Greg Gilbert write, "There are certain things that God intends to do one day that we are to have no part in. . . . [T]here were also certain elements of Jesus' mission during his first coming that were unique to him. We have no part, for example in dying for the sins of the world."[16] Our role is to be a witness of God's mission in Christ. We understand the Great Commission best then if we understand it as part of God's mission. John Massey summarizes it well: "'Mission' is, therefore, God's work in the world; the church serves as a sign and instrument for that mission."[17]

If the Great Commission is only a part of God's mission, then what makes it "great"? First, Robert Plummer answers, "Jesus commissions [the disciples] with language that draws a parallel to his own mission" (John 20:21).[18] The God of all creation is at work in his mission to restore the world and mankind to himself, and he allows his followers to play a part in that mission, a role that parallels the Son of God himself. The Great Commission is our Spirit-empowered work in God's mission. Second, what makes this commission even more important, as DeYoung and Gilbert demonstrate, is its "strategic placement" at the very end of Matthew to climax all that has occurred prior, and its ability to sum up the major themes of the Gospel.[19] D. A. Carson agrees: "The Great Commission is not simply tacked on at the end of the Gospel of Matthew. Rather, it brings to a climax one of the themes that drives through the entire book."[20] The Great Commission completes Matthew's teaching that Jesus came to save (Matt. 1:21). Third, these words are also Jesus's final words

---

15. Wright, "The Great Commission and the Ministry of the Word," 22 (emphasis added).
16. DeYoung and Gilbert, *What Is the Mission of the Church?*, 42.
17. John Massey, "The Missionary Mandate of God's Nature," in *Missiology: An Introduction to the Foundations, History, and Strategies of World Missions*, ed. John Mark Terry (Nashville: B&H Academic, 2015), 102.
18. Robert L. Plummer, "The Great Commission in the New Testament," *SBTJ* 9, no. 4 (2005): 7.
19. DeYoung and Gilbert, *What Is the Mission of the Church?*, 43–44.
20. D. A. Carson, "Conclusion: Ongoing Imperative for World Mission," in *The Great Commission: Evangelicals and the History of World Missions*, eds. Martin I. Klauber and Scott M. Manetsch (Nashville: B&H, 2008), 178.

to his apostles before he leaves them. As a result, they carry extra power and importance. Last words are meant to be lasting words. Finally, Ed Stetzer also says, "At this moment the mission shifts in Jesus' words from a centripetal mission—*up to* Jerusalem—to a centrifugal mission—go therefore *out from* this place."[21] The expanded scope of worldwide evangelism is what makes this commission great.

When we place Matthew 28:18–20 in the context of God's mission and Matthew's structure, we can see why many have labeled it the *Great Commission*. In it, we reach the top of a mountain, literally and figuratively, seeing all that Christ has done for mankind and all that Christ will do.[22] We also see our glorious, life-encompassing marching orders from our Savior.

The Great Commission or Great Commissions?

When Eugene Stock uses the title "Great Commission" in his work, he referred to all the gospel mandates rather than Matthew alone.[23] Matthew 28:18–20 is a crucial part of the Great Commission. But, our understanding of the "Great Commission" must broaden beyond Matthew's final verses. Mark 13:10,[24] Luke 24:46–49, John 20:19–23, and Acts 1:8 each record commissions by Jesus to spread the gospel.[25] Although these passages differ in their specific focus, they all capture the command for Christians to spread the gospel. And all but John specifically reference bringing the gospel to the nations/world.[26] Timothy Tennent is right then when he says that there are actually Great Commissions (plural) in the Bible and that each adds to the collective force of the Great Commission (singular).[27] The benefit of expanding the title to include all of these passages is

---

21. Ed Stetzer, "To Our Neighbors and the Nations," in *Finish the Mission: Bringing the Gospel to the Unreached and Unengaged*, eds. John Piper and David Mathis (Wheaton, IL: Crossway, 2012), 125 (emphasis original).
22. Interestingly, many key events in Matthew's Gospel take place on a mountain, including the giving of the Great Commission. The climactic temptation (4:8–11), the Sermon on the Mount (5–7), the Transformation (17:1), the Olivet Discourse (24–25), and the Great Commission (28:16–20) all occur on a mountain.
23. Tennent, *Invitation*, 127.
24. Mark 14:9 also mentions the prediction of the gospel going out into the whole world. The passage typically labeled in Mark as the Great Commission, Mark 16:15–20, is a part of the longer ending to Mark's Gospel (Mark 16:9–20), which scholars almost unanimously agree is a latter addition to the book (R. T. France, *The Gospel of Mark*, NIGTC [Grand Rapids: Eerdmans, 2002], 685–88).
25. Technically, Mark 13:10 and Luke 24:46–49 are predictions of the fulfillment of the Great Commission. Nonetheless, we should read them with the other texts as implicit commissions for the church.
26. One can interpret an implicit direction in Jesus sending us to the nations because Jesus's followers have a parallel mission to his. John also records Jesus giving the disciples the Holy Spirit, which correlates well with the teaching in Acts 1:8 that the reception of the Spirit begins the commission to all of the world (cf. Acts 2:1–4).
27. Tennent, *Invitation*, 128.

that it allows the title to carry the unique contribution of each book, and it highlights the truth that this theme is important to all of the New Testament.

Robert Plummer argues that the Great Commission also appears implicitly in Paul's writings. Paul commands in Philippians 2:16 "to hold out the word of life";[28] he encourages the Thessalonians because the word was going out from them everywhere (1 Thess. 1:8); and he commands the church to imitate him, which has an evangelistic component (1 Cor. 4:16).[29] The Great Commission is present throughout the New Testament. It reaches its fulfillment as we move toward the *eschaton* (Rev. 5; 7). Its presence should not surprise us because God's mission is central to the story of the whole Bible. We should expect to see our role in it in multiple locations.

Summary

The title "Great Commission" is not in the original New Testament manuscripts, but it faithfully captures the heart of Jesus's words, just like the word "Trinity" faithfully captures the Bible's understanding of God's being, character, and identity. Jesus has sent his disciples to continue his mission and to be witnesses to the great work that God is accomplishing. One day God will complete his mission and his followers will enter into God's perfect rest to enjoy him forever. Until then, we have work to do!

REFLECTION QUESTIONS

1. Where does the Great Commission fit into the overall story of the Bible?

2. How does Jesus's commission in the New Testament differ from God's commands to Israel in the Old Testament?

3. Reread the passages this chapter gives as being a part of the Great Commission. What does each contribute?

4. How does placing the Great Commission within God's larger mission give us a proper perspective?

5. In what ways is Jesus's life on earth an example for our work in the Great Commission?

---

28. Plummer acknowledges that the translation of this verse is debated ("The Great Commission in the New Testament," 8).
29. Ibid.

To Whom Was the Great Commission Given?

Whose task the Great Commission is has not always been agreed upon in church history. Some argue that Jesus commissioned only the original eleven apostles, who fulfilled the work in the first generation of the church.[1] Others argue that Jesus's words are still binding on every believer. This chapter will investigate upon whom Jesus' words are binding. The answer to the question "To whom is the Great Commission given?" is threefold. Jesus gave the Great Commission to the apostles, to each individual Christian, and to the church.

Jesus Gave the Great Commission to the Apostles

That Jesus gave the Great Commission to the apostles is clear. In Matthew's account, Jesus spoke the Great Commission to the eleven disciples (Matt. 28:16). The disciples were the immediate audience of Jesus's commission, and the book of Acts records the continuing efforts of the church to complete it. In Acts 1:8, Jesus tells his apostles that they will be his witnesses "in Jerusalem, in all Judea and Samaria, and to the end of the earth." By the time we reach Acts 9:31, the apostles and other believers have proclaimed the gospel in Jerusalem, Galilee, and Samaria. The church continued to grow as the gospel went to the rest of the known world (Acts 13–28). By the end of Acts, the gospel had spread to modern-day Turkey, Greece, and Rome through Paul's ministry. From Rome, Paul hoped to continue to Spain (Rom. 15:24).

Now, Acts is silent with respect to the ministries of most of the apostles. It primarily highlights the spread of the gospel to the "remotest parts of the

---

1. For an overview of early ideas about the Great Commission, see David F. Wright, "The Great Commission and the Ministry of the Word: Reflections Historical and Contemporary on Relations and Priorities," *Scottish Bulletin of Evangelical Theology* 25, no. 2 (September 2007): 132–57.

earth" through the ministry of Paul and his three missionary journeys. It is not likely, however, that all the other apostles remained in Jerusalem and the surrounding areas. We can be confident that they too spread the gospel abroad. Early traditions of the church even testify to the missionary efforts of the apostles reaching the known world, from Rome to India.[2]

Jesus Gave the Great Commission to Every Disciple

The apostles held a unique role as pioneers of the Great Commission. Indeed, the gospel spread across the known world within the first generation of the church because of their influence and ministry. However, the Great Commission was not limited to those on the mountain in Galilee. The eleven apostles physically heard the words of Jesus, but they and the early church understood the Great Commission to extend to all who would be followers of Jesus. Again, the book of Acts testifies to this truth, recording the missionary work of Phillip (Acts 8), Barnabas (Acts 13–14), Silas (Acts 15:40), Timothy (Acts 16:3), Priscilla and Aquila (Acts 18:2–3, 18), and Apollos (Acts 18:24–27), to note some of the more prominent personalities.

There are two primary reasons for concluding that Jesus envisioned the Great Commission continuing beyond the lifetimes of his original apostles. First, Jesus tells them that they are to make disciples, baptize them, and then teach them to observe all that Jesus commanded them. This observance to Jesus's commands would include the command to make disciples. D. A. Carson says that Jesus does not say to his apostles, "[teach] them to obey everything I have commanded you, except for this commandment to make disciples. Keep their grubby hands off that one, since it belongs only to you, my dear apostles."[3] Elsewhere he adds, "The injunction is given at least to the Eleven, but to the Eleven in their own role as disciples (28:16). Therefore, they are paradigms for *all* disciples. . . . It is binding on all Jesus' disciples to make others what they themselves are—disciples of Christ."[4] Jesus's command was that these first disciples were to make new disciples who would repeat the

---

2. See Bryan M. Litfin, *After Acts: Exploring the Lives and Legends of the Apostles* (Chicago: Moody, 2015); Davis also points out that the apocryphal book the Acts of Thomas, a third-century text, describes the apostles dividing the world amongst themselves and going to the region that God gave to them (John Jefferson Davis, "'Teaching Them to Observe All That I Have Commanded You': The History of the Interpretation of the 'Great Commission' and Implications for Marketplace Ministries," *Evangelical Review of Theology* 25, no. 1 [January 1, 2001]: 69). Whether or not these traditions are true, the point is that the early church left a legacy of valuing and being committed to the Great Commission.

3. D. A. Carson, "Ongoing Imperative for World Mission," in *The Great Commission: Evangelicals and the History of World Missions*, eds. Martin I. Klauber and Scott M. Manetsch (Nashville: B&H, 2008), 179.

4. D. A. Carson, "Matthew," in *Matthew & Mark*, rev. ed., EBC, eds. Tremper Longman and David E. Garland (Grand Rapids: Zondervan, 2010), 666.

discipleship process. Disciple-making of the nations was not the unique stewardship of the apostles. They were to teach others to do the same.

Second, Jesus's promise at the end of the commission extends beyond the lifetime of the apostles. Jesus says, "And remember, I am with you always, to the end of the age" (Matt. 28:20). This statement alone decisively proves that the Great Commission is for the whole church, for the whole period between the two advents of our Lord. The end of the age has not yet come. It is exegetically logical to conclude that Jesus's promise is still in effect and will remain so until he returns. Jesus's disciples today still possess the promise of the presence of Christ as they labor to make disciples of all nations. Christ was with his disciples in those early days as they preached the gospel, made disciples, and planted churches. And Christ's presence is with his disciples now as they continue to do the same.

Disciple-making is the call of every believer. Charles Spurgeon made it clear, "Every Christian . . . is either a missionary or an imposter."[5] Likewise, David Platt captures this idea well in his commentary on Matthew 28:16–20: "This is a costly command directing every Christian to go, baptize, and make disciples of all nations. . . . To be a disciple is to make disciples. Scripture knows nothing of disciples who aren't making disciples."[6] It is the responsibility and privilege of every Christian to participate in God's mission. It is a corporate mission in which everyone has a role. This will not look the same for every disciple of Christ. Just as Paul describes the church as one body with many members and many gifts united by one Spirit (1 Cor. 12:12–31), God has united his many and diverse people around his one mission to use their unique, Spirit-empowered gifts to complete it.

Each disciple may not fulfill every aspect of the Great Commission. Some may be more gifted in evangelism, some in teaching, and some in service to the body. In the same way, not every Christian must go to the nations. Some send, others go. But on a fundamental level, every Christian must bear witness to the gospel and make disciples. J. C. Ryle makes this point powerfully when he writes, "Let us never forget that this solemn injunction is still in full force. It is still the bounden duty of every disciple of Christ to do all he can in person, and by prayer, to make others acquainted with Jesus."[7]

Every individual Christian must be able to honestly answer the following questions: In what ways am I contributing toward the Great Commission? How am I, as a disciple, actively serving the church's mission? In what ways am I using my time, my gifts, my skills, and my resources to engage in Great Commission work? Everyone who is called to be Christ's disciple is also called

5. C. H. Spurgeon, *The Metropolitan Tabernacle Pulpit*, vol. 54 (Pasadena, TX: Pilgrim Publications, 1978), 476.

6. David Platt, *Christ-Centered Exposition: Exalting Jesus in Matthew* (Nashville: B&H, 2013), 375.

7. J. C. Ryle, *Expository Thoughts on Matthew* (Carlisle, PA: The Banner of Truth Trust, 2001), 410.

to obey Christ's command to make disciples. Each Christian must bear witness to the gospel of Jesus Christ and contribute to the Great Commission (see Question 33).

Jesus Gave the Great Commission to the Church

The Great Commission is for all believers. However, this truth should not lead us to interpret the Great Commission too individualistically. As one pastor says, "a *primarily* individualistic application of this command is more a product of our Western culture than from a natural reading of the text."[8] Instead, we should understand the Great Commission as Christ's commission to his newly formed church. Earlier in Matthew, Jesus promised that he would build his church and that the gates of hell would not prevail against it (Matt. 16:18). Then, we see the church as the one sending out Paul and Barnabas on their missionary journey (Acts 13). Later, they return to the church to report their work (Acts 14:27–28). In this light, the Great Commission is Christ's final marching orders to his church. He does not send out maverick missionaries but believers intimately attached to a local church.

Mark Dever argues that the Great Commission is principally a command to make disciples and plant churches. He writes, "The Great Commission is normally fulfilled through planting and growing local churches. Churches fulfill the Great Commission through planting more churches."[9] Church planting is precisely what takes place in the book of Acts. The apostles and other believers go from place to place, evangelizing, making disciples, and planting churches. These churches then become the sending hubs for further mission work. The Great Commission needs a local church environment to fulfill the activities that Christ calls his disciples to do. It cannot be detached from the church. Again, Dever is helpful on this point:

> So think once more of the four commands of the Great Commission: go, make disciples, baptize, and teach. Who does all this? Who sends out the going Christians to make disciples? The local church. And who names them as disciples by baptizing them, and then helps them to grow by teaching them? The local church does. The local church is the normal means God has given us to fulfill the Great Commission.[10]

---

8. Ryan King, "The Great Commission: Fulfilled by Churches and for Churches," *9Marks*, n.d., https://www.9marks.org/article/the-great-commission-fulfilled-by-churches-and-for-churches.

9. Mark Dever, *Understanding the Great Commission* (Nashville, TN: B&H, 2016), 2.

10. Ibid., 4–5.

The church is the environment in which disciples are made, baptized, and taught. The church is also the primary entity for training, equipping, and sending disciples to make new disciples and plant new churches. The Great Commission is the church's mission (see Question 34).

Summary

The apostles were the original pioneers of the Great Commission. They were the first to make disciples of the nations, and they established the first churches across the known world. But, the Great Commission is Christ's commission to his church today as well. Christ's promise to be with his church, even to the end of the age, clearly and powerfully implies that this command is still in effect. This mission incorporates every disciple of Christ and requires each to contribute their gifts and resources. This is our assignment while we are on this earth. This will be the church's assignment until Christ returns.

REFLECTION QUESTIONS

1. In what ways is your church currently taking part in the Great Commission at home and abroad?

2. What are some ways you and your church can be more committed to the Great Commission?

3. How are believers able to make disciples better as part of the church than as individuals alone?

4. Why is Jesus's promise "I am with you always, to the end of the age" important?

5. If every disciple of Jesus is called to fulfill the Great Commission, will every disciple participate in the same way? Why or Why not?

What Does the Great Commission Imply Regarding Other Religions?

Jesus teaches in the Great Commission that his followers are to make disciples of all nations. It is reasonable, however, to believe that almost every person in Jesus's day already followed a religion. Everyone already worshipped their own god or gods. Although many in the West claim to be areligious, including agnostics and atheists (belief systems that we would argue are still forms of faith), the majority of the world today is still religious.[1] Therefore, Jesus's words provoke asking how Christians should interact with other religions. In other words, should Christians evangelize and try to make disciples of Buddhists, Hindus, Jews, Muslims, Animists, or the many other world religions? This chapter will answer this question by examining four implications of the Great Commission for other religions.[2]

Implication #1: Other Religions Do Not Have Leaders with Divine Authority

Almost every religion has someone whom its followers hold as the source of ultimate truth.[3] There is no shortage of spiritual teachers who claim to be God or speak on behalf of God. However, the Great Commission implies that

---

1. According to the Pew Research Center, the religiously affiliated currently make up the largest percentage of the world population, a group that will continue to grow in number because those religiously unaffiliated will shrink in percentage of the global population by 2060. "The Changing Global Religious Landscape," *Pew Research Center's Religion & Public Life Project*, April 5, 2017, http://www.pewforum.org/2017/04/05/the-changing-global-religious-landscape.
2. For an in-depth look at how Christians should relate to other religions, see Terry Muck and Frances Adeney, *Christianity Encountering World Religions: The Practice of Mission in the Twenty-First Century* (Grand Rapids: Baker Academic, 2009).
3. A notable exception would be Hinduism, which does not have a single founder or god.

Jesus has sole, divine authority in spiritual matters. When he says, "All authority in heaven and on earth has been given to me," he makes a sweeping claim (Matt. 28:18). Jesus claims the authority of the one who created the world.[4] "In heaven and on earth" is a phrase that encompasses all creation. Nothing limits Jesus's authority. As Abraham Kuyper says, "There is not a square inch in the whole domain of our human life of which Christ, who is Sovereign over all, does not cry: Mine!"[5]

This authority that Jesus possesses comes from God the Father (cf. John 3:35; 17:2; 20:21; Dan. 7:14).[6] On what basis can Jesus claim to receive such authority. when other leaders claim they too were sent by God? The early church father Jerome answers our question when he says, "Authority has been given to him who a little earlier was crucified, who was buried in a tomb, who lay there dead, who afterward was resurrected."[7] As Ephesians 1:20–22 confirms, when Christ was raised from the dead, God the Father placed him "far above every rule and authority and power and dominion, and above every name that is named, not only in this age but also in the one to come." When Jesus commands his disciples in the Great Commission, he does so with the authority of one who was raised from the dead.

Jesus's resurrection-powered, all-encompassing authority implies that he has authority above other religious teachers. It is common to hear some compare Jesus with other religious teachers as if they are equal. However, he does not share authority with Buddha, Confucius, Muhammad, or any other proclaimed god or religious leader. Therefore, Christians should obey Jesus's calling to make disciples of other nations despite what other religious leaders might say or teach. Other religious leaders may teach good ideas, give commands, or offer reward, but Jesus claims universal authority. The Great Commission compels Christians to listen to and follow him alone. His resurrection from the dead is proof that Jesus has authority over all things.

The apostles' interaction with Jewish leaders in Acts 4 exemplifies Christ's authority above other leaders. Acts 4:2 records that the Jewish leaders were "greatly annoyed" when Peter and John preached about Jesus and the resurrection, and they threatened them to stop speaking so the message would not spread (vv. 4:17–18). Peter and John respond that they follow another

---

4. The rest of the New Testament also declares Jesus's supreme authority: every knee will bow before him (Phil. 2:9–10), he is the head over all rule and authority (Col. 2:10), he owns all things (John 3:35), he has authority over all flesh (John 17:2), and he is the Lord of lords and King of kings (Rev. 17:14).

5. Abraham Kuyper and James D. Bratt, *Abraham Kuyper: A Centennial Reader* (Grand Rapids: Eerdmans, 1998), 488.

6. There is a very strong connection between this claim of Jesus in the Great Commission and the Ancient of Days passages in Daniel 7.

7. Jerome and Thomas P. Scheck, *Commentary on Matthew*, The Fathers of the Church, vol. 117 (Washington, DC: Catholic University of America Press, 2008), 327.

authority; saying, "Whether it is right in the sight of God for us to listen to you rather than to God, you must judge, for we cannot but speak of what we have seen and heard" (4:19–20). Because they were commissioned by Jesus's creation-wide authority, no other leader could stop them.

Implication #2: Other Religions Cannot Offer Genuine Salvation

Jesus's universal authority is clear in his commission to his disciples to preach the gospel and make more disciples from Jerusalem to the ends of the earth (Acts 1:8). This mission necessarily includes evangelizing people of all other religions. It requires that anyone trusting a source of ultimate truth other than Jesus must abandon it and follow Christ. The Great Commission implies that the disciples of Jesus carry the only true message of salvation. This is clearly witnessed by the words of Jesus (John 14:6), Peter (Acts 4:12), and Paul (1 Tim. 2:5).

In the Gospel of John, Jesus tells his disciples that he is preparing a place for them so that they may be where he is (John 14:2–3). In response, the apostle Thomas declares, "Lord, we do not know where you are going. How can we know the way?" (John 14:5). Jesus's answer to Thomas is paramount to the Christian faith. He says, "I am the way, and the truth, and the life. No one comes to the Father except through me" (John 14:6). Here, Jesus claims to be the exclusive path to God and eternal life. Carson rightly states that "[Jesus] does not mean for a moment to suggest that Christianity is merely one more religion amongst many. They are ineffective in bringing people to the true God. *No-one*, Jesus insists, *comes to the Father except through me.* That is the necessary stance behind all fervent evangelism."[8] This point is even more clear when John states the purpose of his book. He says, "these are written so that you may believe Jesus is the Christ, the Son of God, and that by believing you may have life in his name" (John 20:31). In other words, "Not all roads lead to possession of eternal life. Jesus is the God-appointed way."[9] Peter, likewise, summarizes this truth when he addresses a Jewish council: "This Jesus is the stone that was rejected by you, the builders, which has become the cornerstone. And there is salvation in no one else, for there is no other name under heaven given among men by which we must be saved" (Acts 4:11–12). Paul rounds out this trio of witnesses in an exhortation to pray for all people. He reminds Timothy, his young son in the ministry, in 1 Timothy 2:5, "For there is one God and one mediator between God and men, the man Christ Jesus." There are not many or several mediators. There is only one, and his name is Jesus.

---

8. D. A. Carson, *The Gospel according to John*, reprint ed. (Grand Rapids: Eerdmans, 1990), 491–92 (emphasis original).
9. Tokunboh Adeyemo, ed., *Africa Bible Commentary* (Grand Rapids: Zondervan, 2006), 1283.

If eternal life and relationship with God comes only through faith in Jesus, then any religion that does not preach salvation through the life, death, and resurrection of Jesus Christ will not save. The Great Commission shows that other religions are ineffective ways to interpret truth and meaning in life. The Great Commission is built upon the principle of exclusive faith in Christ as God, Savior, and King as the only effective means to know God. To say it differently, if faith in Jesus Christ is not the single way to be saved, then the Great Commission is irrelevant. However, because Jesus is God and because he was raised from the dead, it is imperative for his disciples to persuade others to abandon their false religions and turn to Christ to be saved. It is the necessary and loving thing to do.

Objections to Implication #2

The claim that salvation is found exclusively in Christ arouses many objections by those who do not believe any religion should make such audacious claims. Every possible objection cannot be addressed here, but two are particularly common. First, some argue that when Christians evangelize other religions, they are engaging in a form of colonialism, paternalism, or cultural imperialism. Missionaries, they claim, wrongly impose their culture upon another's and destroy cultural differences. At the very least, the argument continues, missionaries are creating unnecessary political or military tension by claiming and spreading a foreign religion.[10]

It is right and necessary for Christians to acknowledge the faults of past missionaries who confused Western civilization and cultural practices with being a Christian.[11] It is also important to be aware that Western missionaries can create unhelpful economic and relational dependence today. However, these sad truths should be balanced with how Christian missionaries also have blessed other cultures.[12] In Robert Woodbury's groundbreaking study, he found that "areas where Protestants missionaries have a significant

---

10. See Michael W. Goheen, Cindy Kiple, and Beth Hagenberg, *Introducing Christian Mission Today: Scripture, History and Issues* (Downers Grove, IL: IVP Academic, 2014), 333–34. For a more in-depth study on this topic, see Stephen Neill, *Colonialism and Christian Missions* (New York: McGraw-Hill, 1966); Andrew N. Porter, *Religion versus Empire? British Protestant Missionaries and Overseas Expansion, 1700–1914* (Manchester: Manchester University Press, 2004); Andrew N. Porter, *The Imperial Horizons of British Protestant Missions, 1880–1914*, Studies in the History of Christian Missions (Grand Rapids: Eerdmans, 2003).

11. As Borthwick writes, "Crosscultural missionaries went out to present Christ, but they often were unaware of the cultural and nationalistic biases that they carried with them" (Paul Borthwick, *Western Christians in Global Mission: What's the Role of the North American Church?* [Downers Grove, IL: InterVarsity, 2012], 118).

12. As Lamin O. Sanneh demonstrates, through translation work, Christian missionaries have preserved and given value to indigenous languages and art forms, began vernacular renewal, and encouraged indigenous ascendancy (*Translating the Message: The Missionary Impact on Culture*, American Society of Missiology 13 [Maryknoll, NY: Orbis, 1989], 124–25).

presence in the past are on average more economically developed today, with comparatively better health, lower infant mortality, lower corruption, greater literacy, higher educational attainment (especially for women), and more robust membership in nongovernmental associations."[13] Still, what is most important is that the Great Commission itself does not call for Jesus's disciples to discard cultural differences or impose beliefs coercively.[14] The early church began in the Middle East, and it thrived in Asia and Africa before moving into the West. Even now, Christianity is so widespread that no single location can claim to be the center of Christianity.[15] As the apostles realized in the Jerusalem council (Acts 15), the beauty of the Great Commission is that it calls people of all nations and cultures to follow Christ while retaining cultural elements that do not contradict the gospel message and biblical revelation.

Second, others object to this exclusive claim by arguing that no religion has complete knowledge of God. Many argue that various religions simply perceive of the one God or gods differently. Each has a portion of the truth, while none has all the truth. Therefore, followers of various religions should be tolerant and accepting of all beliefs. There is a popular parable about blind men describing parts of an elephant that attempts to illustrates how all religions have a partial knowledge of God.[16] The moral of the parable is that no man can claim to have superior knowledge because he cannot see the whole elephant. His knowledge is partial. By analogy and application, each religion has limited knowledge of God and cannot claim their religion is superior to any other.

While there are many faults with these claims, it is sufficient to observe two fundamental errors. First, Christianity is not unique in its claim to universal truth or exclusive salvation. As apologist Douglas Groothuis writes, "While religions involve many elements related to morality, ritual, experience

---

13. Andrea Palpant Dilley, "The World the Missionaries Made," *Christianity Today* 58, no. 1 (February 1, 2014): 39.

14. Goheen keenly observes that Islam and Christianity differ here regarding whether the religion should be forced or coerced (Goheen, Kiple, and Hagenberg, *Introducing Christian Mission Today*, 338).

15. "Global Christianity—a Report on the Size and Distribution of the World's Christian Population," *Pew Research Center's Religion & Public Life Project*, December 19, 2011, http://www.pewforum.org/2011/12/19/global-christianity-exec. See also, Philip Jenkins, *The New Faces of Christianity: Believing the Bible in the Global South* (New York: Oxford University Press, 2008).

16. As the parable goes, several blind men are feeling an elephant. One man feels its tusk, another feels its tail, another feels its leg, and still another feels its hide. The one who felt the tusk says the elephant is like a snake. The one who felt his tail describes it as a rope, the one who felt its leg says it is like a tree trunk, and the one felt its ear says it is like a fan. Although the parable seems persuasive at first, many have pointed out that the inherent fault with the parable is that someone can see the whole elephant and have full knowledge of reality.

and so on, all world religions make truth claims about ultimate reality. . . . Religious founders, whether Buddha or Jesus or Muhammad, purport to have received knowledge of objective truth—truth that all need to know in order to find spiritual liberation."[17] Many religions are exclusive in some form. For example, the first pillar of Islam (the Shahadah), which all Muslims must recite states, "There is no God but Allah and Muhammad is his prophet." Even nonreligious people believe their ideas are universally true.

Second, all religions differ in many essential beliefs, which negates the idea that Christianity teaches the same truth as other religions. Jews claim that Jesus was only a man. Muslims believe Jesus was only a prophet. Buddhists believe he is an enlightened one. Hindus believe he is a holy man and wise teacher. Each of these views differs from the biblical presentation of Jesus as the Son of God. D. A. Carson rightly declares that it is not enough for Muslims to see Jesus as a prophet because they do not regard him as the greatest prophet; it is not enough for Hindus to consider Jesus as divine because they do not believe that only he is divine; it is not enough for Buddhists to believe Jesus is enlightened because they do not believe that salvation is found only in him; and it is not enough that Jesus was a Jew because Jews do not regard him as God.[18] Beyond their views about Jesus, a deeper study of the beliefs of the major world religions demonstrates that each religion differs in its fundamental worldviews. Each differs in how it describes the problem in humanity, the solution to that problem, and the truths of ultimate reality.[19] In sum, neither of these objections negate what the Great Commission implies and the rest of Scripture confirms: Jesus alone offers genuine salvation.

Implication #3: Followers of Other Religions Need to Hear the Gospel of Christ

Because there is no salvation outside of Christ, Christians must proclaim the gospel to all peoples of every religion. Salvation comes through the preaching of the word (Rom. 10:9–17; 1 Cor. 1:21). Christians should be willing to leave everything to follow Christ. Examples of this implication can be seen in how the first participants in the Great Commission, the apostles, addressed other religions. In Acts 2, Peter preaches to citizens of many nations (Acts 2:8–11), telling them to turn to Christ and be saved. Likewise, Paul reasoned with the people of Athens and called them to stop following idols and believe in Jesus (Acts 17:16). The Athenians were "very religious," but Paul preaches to them the one true God (Acts 17:23–24). To both Jews and

---

17. Douglas R. Groothuis, *Christian Apologetics: A Comprehensive Case for Biblical Faith* (Downers Grove, IL: IVP Academic, 2011), 569.

18. D. A. Carson, "Conclusion: Ongoing Imperative for World Mission," in *The Great Commission: Evangelicals and the History of World Missions*, eds. Martin I. Klauber and Scott M. Manetsch (Nashville: B&H, 2008), 180.

19. Groothuis, *Christian Apologetics*, 569–70.

Gentiles, the apostles preached the gospel in hopes that they would believe in Christ. Jesus tells his disciples to go because all people need to come.[20]

Implication #4: Other Religions Do Not Provide Infallible Books to Know the One True God

If Christ alone possesses divine authority, and if he is the only source for true salvation and eternal life, then are other religions completely devoid of truth? Can Western Christians or new Christians with a Hindu or Muslim background learn from other religious books? Many in the West, who desire to be spiritual but reject a structured religion, take a cafeteria approach by selecting various spiritual practices and adapting or appropriating what appeals to them. Others might simply use non-Christian books to help them know the God of the Bible in different or new ways. The Great Commission implies, however, that the Christian Scriptures are the only means of special revelation since it is Jesus's teaching that his disciples are to follow and observe. The Scriptures are the only inspired authority that allows us to know God personally and to know how to live as he expects. They alone are backed by the authority of Jesus and his commission to teach all that he commanded.

This implication does not mean that everything taught in Christianity is unique. The practice of fasting appears in other religions. And, we hope that every religion teaches that murder is wrong. Nor does it mean that nothing can be learned from other religions. Some ethical claims in Christianity appear in other religions.[21] Arthur Holmes reminds us, "All truth is God's truth wherever it be found."[22] There must be, as Timothy Tennent encourages, a balance between two extremes of broad condemnation and naïve acceptance.[23]

---

20. This discussion naturally causes many to ask what happens to those who do not hear the gospel message. In short, the Bible teaches that God has revealed himself via general revelation in nature (Rom. 1) and conscience (Rom. 2), and that he has revealed himself in special revelation in Christ and the Scriptures. General revelation can condemn, but it cannot save (Rom. 1:20). Only the special revelation of the gospel of Jesus Christ can bring a person into a right relationship with God. To be clear, God judges no one for what they do not know. Those who die without hearing the gospel are condemned for their rejection of general revelation not special revelation. That is why we send missionaries. We must get the saving special revelation of the gospel to the nations so that they can be saved. Carly F. H. Henry is right, "The gospel is only good news if it gets there in time." For more information on this, see ibid., 585–98; Keith Johnson, "Christian Theology of Religions," in *Missiology: An Introduction to the Foundations, History, and Strategies of World Missions*, ed. John Mark Terry (Nashville: B&H Academic, 2015), 373.
21. Johnson, "Christian Theology of Religions," 370–72.
22. Arthur F. Holmes, *All Truth Is God's Truth* (Grand Rapids: Eerdmans, 1977), 8.
23. Timothy C. Tennent, *Theology in the Context of World Christianity: How the Global Church Is Influencing the Way We Think About and Discuss Theology* (Grand Rapids: Zondervan, 2007), 68. Tennent provides three guidelines for using nonbiblical texts. Nonbiblical texts should be used for evangelistic outreach, as a corroborative witness to a biblical message, and any nonbiblical text should be reoriented in a new christocentric setting (ibid., 71–72).

He argues that even though non-Christian books may "be true, insightful, inspirational, and even spiritually edifying, they cannot be regarded as inspired or revelatory since they lack the proper Christological and ecclesiological context."[24]

Summary

Christians are commanded to share the good news about Jesus to all the nations. They are given the mandate to urge people to repent of their sins and trust in Jesus alone, since he alone has made satisfaction for sins. Consequently, such a mandate implies that (1) other religions do not have leaders with divine authority—only Jesus has all authority under heaven and earth; (2) other religions cannot offer genuine salvation—there is salvation in no other name; (3) followers of other religions need to hear the gospel of Christ—they cannot believe in him whom they have not heard; and (4) other religions do not provide infallible books to know the one true God—we must teach them to obey all things that Jesus taught his disciples.

REFLECTION QUESTIONS

1. What does it look like for Christians to persuade others to follow Jesus while respecting cultural differences?

2. With so many religions, can Christians have confidence that what the Bible says is true?

3. How does Christianity differ from other religions?

4. Why is belief in Jesus necessary to receive salvation?

5. What are ways today in which missionaries are able to benefit other cultures like missionaries in the past?

---

24. Ibid., 73–74.

How Does the Great Commission Relate to the Great Commandment?

Loving God and participating in his mission form the backbone of Christian practice. Both the Great Commandment and the Great Commission are essential in the life of the church. These two central tenets of Jesus's teaching are inseparably linked. They complement one another. In order to understand the proper relationship between the Great Commission and the Great Commandment, we must first understand the Great Commandment in its own right. Therefore, this chapter will begin by considering the Great Commandment, including how loving God relates to loving neighbor. The second section then will consider how the Great Commandment and the Great Commission are related to one another.

Understanding the Great Commandment

The Great Commandment commonly refers to Jesus's statement "You shall love the Lord your God with all of your heart and with all of your soul and with all of your mind" (Matt. 22:37), as recorded in Matthew 22:37–40, Mark 12:29–31, and Luke 10:24–27.[1] Jesus quotes Deuteronomy 6:4–5, and follows the Great Commandment with a secondary and related command, "You shall love your neighbor as yourself" (Matt. 22:39), a quote from Leviticus 19:18. To unpack the Great Commandment and its relationship to the Second Great Commandment, we will consider the motivation for loving God, and the relationship between love for God and love for neighbor.[2]

---

1. The Synoptic accounts vary, but in a complementary fashion. For a detailed outline of the differences and similarities, see Wendell Lee Willis, "Three Perspectives on the Great Commandment," *ResQ* 57, no. 3 (2015): 173–78.
2. There is some diversity as to whether the term "Great Commandment" refers solely to "love the Lord your God," or includes both "love the Lord your God" and "love your neighbor as yourself." This chapter views those commands as distinct, yet inseparably linked. Thus,

The command for God's people to love God with all their heart, soul, and mind begins with God's love for them. In this instance, God's love for his people surfaces from the covenant context of his command. By quoting from Deuteronomy, Jesus places his command in the context of God's covenant with his people. Deuteronomy is introduced as a covenantal document that recounts God's acts for and requirements of his people.[3] According to Peter J. Gentry and Stephen J. Wellum, "At the heart of covenant . . . is a relationship between parties characterized by faithfulness and loyalty in love."[4] When God commands his people to love him he does so after having initiated the covenant with his loving faithfulness. In application to Jesus's New Testament recapitulation of the Great Commandment, Robert Stein comments, "Like all such commands, this command is not understood as a means for entering into a covenantal relationship with God but rather as a stipulation deriving from and resulting from such a covenantal relationship."[5] Stein encourages readers to remember that God's commands to his people begin with God's own love expressed through his covenant faithfulness. Stein further points out the theological reality that humanity's love for God is always a response to God's love for humanity. John sums up the idea when he exhorts the church, "We love because he first loved us" (1 John 4:19).

As God reveals his love for his people, they should rightfully respond with love for him that permeates the whole of their beings. Walter Brueggemann argues that even the use of the word "love" in Deuteronomy 6:5 "means to acknowledge the covenant Lord (covenant partner) and so to honor obligations that belong to the covenant."[6] The type of love expressed toward God in Deuteronomy 6:5 and by Jesus in the Gospels is a covenantal love offered to the covenant-keeping God. The proper response to God's covenant faithfulness is to love him in covenant faithfulness and with the whole of one's being. Craig Blomberg explains this type of love as "wholehearted devotion to God with every aspect of one's being, from whatever angle one chooses to consider

---

the term "Great Commandment" and "First Great Commandment" refer specifically to "love the Lord your God." The term "Second Great Commandment" refers to "love your neighbor as yourself." The term "Great Commandments" refers to both of these commands.

3. Eugene H. Merrill summarizes the covenantal context in Deuteronomy 5:1–11:32, saying, "This central division of the book opens with an explanation of the need for covenant renewal and an exhortation for that people to take it seriously. . . . The nature of the relationship between Yahweh and Israel consists fundamentally of the recognition that God is one (6:4–5) and that his people, if they are to enjoy the benefits of the ancient patriarchal promises, must serve him with undivided loyalty and faithfulness" (*Deuteronomy*, NAC 4 [Nashville: B&H, 1994], 41).

4. Peter J. Gentry and Stephen J. Wellum, *God's Kingdom through God's Covenants: A Concise Biblical Theology* (Wheaton, IL: Crossway, 2015), 54.

5. Robert H. Stein, *Mark*, BECNT (Grand Rapids: Baker Academic, 2008), 561.

6. Walter Brueggemann, "The First Great Commandment," *J. Preachers* 34, no. 4 (2011): 12.

it—emotionally, volitionally, or cognitively."[7] Love for God is all-consuming. It springs up from deep within one's being and overflows into every channel of one's life.

Out of the overflow of love for God comes the Second Great Commandment, to "love your neighbor as yourself" (Matt. 22:39; Mark 12:31). Textually, the Synoptic Gospels differ slightly in their accounts.[8] Even so, they each intimately connect love for God with love for neighbor. As Blomberg says, "Divine love issues into interpersonal love."[9] David Bosch calls love of neighbor the "litmus test for love of God."[10] The theme of loving one's neighbor as a result of loving God consistently appears across the Scriptures.[11] The apostle John wrote it plainly, "If anyone says, 'I love God,' and hates his brother, he is a liar; for he who does not love his brother whom he has seen cannot love God whom he has not seen" (1 John 4:20). Loving God with the whole of one's being necessarily overflows into love of one's neighbor and drives the church's participation in the Great Commission.

The Great Commandment and the Great Commission

Love for God in response to God's love for us provides the primary motivation for the church's participation in his mission. The Great Commandment precedes and fuels the Great Commission, and the Great Commission is the natural outgrowth of the Great Commandment. They are interdependent. Participation in the Great Commission is an upward expression of the believer's love for God, and the outward overflow of that love for God to the world (the Great Commandment).

---

7. Craig L. Blomberg, *Matthew*, NAC 22 (Nashville: B&H, 1992), 335.
8. In the Markan account, Jesus knits the command to "love the Lord your God" (Mark 12:30) and to "love your neighbor as yourself" (Mark 12:31) by referring to them as one singular commandment in verse 31, "indicating that the first command necessarily includes this [the second] one" (Willis, "Three Perspectives on the Great Commandment," 176). In the Matthean account, he separates the two commands completely, noting that to "love the Lord your God" (Matt. 22:37) is the "first and greatest commandment" (Matt. 22:38), but the "second is like it" (Matt. 22:39). In Matthew, the commands are distinct and yet the command to "love the Lord your God" is "all inclusive," subsuming the command to "love your neighbor as yourself" (ibid.). Though Matthew and Mark make the connection in slightly different ways, each of them makes plain that love of neighbor is predicated on and intimately connected to loving God with the whole of ones being.
9. Blomberg, *Matthew*, 335.
10. David Jacobus Bosch, *Transforming Mission: Paradigm Shifts in Theology of Mission*, twentieth anniversary ed. (Maryknoll, NY: Orbis, 2011), 67.
11. Darrell L. Bock explains the greater connection, saying, "The NT elsewhere connects displaying love for one's neighbor to devotion to God. Paul's greetings often link faith toward God and love for the saints (Col 1:3–5; Philem 6; 1 Thess. 1:3). . . . Other texts closely link love toward God or Jesus and love for one another (John 13:34–35; 15:9–12; 1 Peter 2:17; 1 John 4:11). To do the law means, in essence, to love. To live by the Spirit means to love and do righteousness" (*Luke*, BECNT 3 [Grand Rapids: Baker, 1994], 1025).

God is a missional God, and to love him with the whole of one's being must include participating in his mission in the world. "Missions exists because God exists."[12] God himself is the driving and motivating force behind the Christian mission. The Great Commission was not created by the church. The source is in the very heart of God. At the center of the gospel is an invitation to participate in the communion of the triune God from whom the mission flows. In participating in the communion of the Trinity through union with Christ, the believer expresses love for God by joining in his work in the world. Kevin Vanhoozer says, "The mission of the church is to join in the triune mission." He continues, "The life of the church is to participate in and display that same love that the Father has for the Son, and that same obedience that the Son shows the Father."[13] Through loving God, participating in the communion of the Trinity, and displaying that love to the world, the church joins in God's mission.

Thus, the believer offers love back to God through active obedience. In Jesus's own words, "If you love me, you will keep my commandments" (John 14:15). J. Andrew Kirk notes, "Love is not a concept that can be understood theoretically. To be appreciated it has to be seen in action."[14] The church receives the love of God through his actions toward us, communicated most fully through the life, death, and resurrection of Jesus. In response, we express our love for him through our actions, which includes making disciples of all nations. One cannot love God with the whole of his being and not actively obey his command to "Go . . . and make disciples" (Matt. 28:19). To disobey is to actively rebel against the very communion into which Christ has welcomed the church.

The love we express upward to God in obedience to the Great Commandment flows outward toward our neighbor. Thus, the Great Commandment fuels the Great Commission by motivating our love for one another. Augustine explores this idea in "Of the Morals of the Catholic Church."[15] For Augustine, love for God must overflow to love for neighbor, and love for neighbor must include leading one's neighbor to love God. Augustine puts it this way:

> He [Jesus] says then that the second precept is, "Thou shall love thy neighbor as thyself." Now you love yourself suitably

---

12. Keith Whitfield, "The Triune God: The God of Mission," in *Theology and Practice of Mission: God, the Church, and the Nations,* ed. Bruce Riley Ashford (Nashville: B&H Academic, 2011), 17. G. William Schweer argues a similar point, saying, "The missionary mandate is a revelation of God's inner being" ("The Missionary Mandate of God's Nature," in *Missiology: An Introduction to the Foundations, History, and Strategies of World Missions,* eds. John Mark Terry, Ebbie C. Smith, and Justice Anderson [Nashville: B&H, 1998], 97).

13. Kevin J. Vanhoozer, *The Drama of Doctrine: A Canonical-Linguistic Approach to Christian Theology* (Louisville: Westminster John Knox, 2005), 72.

14. J. Andrew Kirk, *What Is Mission? Theological Explorations* (Minneapolis: Fortress, 2000), 28.

15. The term "catholic" here refers to the universal church.

when you love God better than yourself. What, then, you aim at in yourself you must aim at in your neighbor, namely, that he may love God with a perfect affection. For you do not love him as yourself, unless you try to draw him to that good which you are yourself pursuing.[16]

Augustine intimately links the Great Commandment and the Great Commission, almost as a chain reaction. For Augustine, a Christian who loves God with all of his heart, soul, mind, and strength will inevitably love his neighbor as himself. Since he loves himself by loving God completely, he loves his neighbor by leading him to love God too.

The natural means by which believers lead their neighbors to love God involves both proclamation of the gospel and discipleship. Troy L. Bush comments that loving one's neighbor usually means involvement in his life and context, but he concludes, "Always, though, we must preach the Gospel."[17] Owing largely to the missional nature of God, our love for our neighbor is most accurately expressed when we invite them into union with Christ so that they can enjoy communion with the Trinity along with us. In fact, one would be hard pressed to think of something more unloving than withholding the gospel from our neighbor, and denying them the opportunity to "glorify God and to enjoy him forever."[18] As a result, the church should live missionally, "being intentional and deliberate about reaching others."[19] Again, we see the Great Commission is the necessary outflow of the Great Commandment.

Teaching one's neighbor to love God with his whole being means believers must love their neighbors holistically. John Stott and Christopher Wright agree with Augustine that love for neighbor must certainly include evangelism and the Great Commission. In their words, "How can we possibly claim to love him [his neighbor] if we know the gospel but keep it from him?"[20] At the same time, they continue on saying, "Equally, however, if we truly love our neighbor we shall not stop with evangelism. Our neighbor is neither a bodyless soul that we should love only his soul, nor a soulless body that we should care for its welfare alone nor even a body-soul isolated from society."[21]

---

16. Augustine, "Of the Morals of the Catholic Church," in *Nicene and Post-Nicene Christianity*, ed. Philip Schaff (1867; repr., Peabody, MA: Hendrickson, 2012), 55.
17. Troy L. Bush, "The Great Commission and the Urban Context," in *The Great Commission Resurgence: Fulfilling God's Mandate in Our Time*, eds. Charles E. Lawless, et al. (Nashville: B&H Academic, 2010), 314.
18. John Whitecross and Westminster Assembly, eds., *The Shorter Catechism Illustrated* (Vestavia Hills, AL: Solid Ground Christian Books, 2003), 7.
19. Ed Stetzer, *Planting Missional Churches: Planting a Church That Is Biblically Sound and Reaching People in Culture* (Nashville: B&H, 2006), 19.
20. John R. W. Stott and Christopher J. H. Wright, *Christian Mission in the Modern World* (Downers Grove, IL: InterVarsity, 2015), 29.
21. Ibid.

Stott and Wright's ground for this interpretation is primarily in the Johannine commission (John 20:21).[22] Because Jesus sends his disciples as the Father sent him, Stott and Wright conclude, "Our understanding of the church's mission must be deduced from our understanding of the Son."[23] As the Son came caring for people's needs, and proclaiming the kingdom, so the church must both proclaim the gospel and care for people's practical needs. When the Great Commission is fueled by the Great Commandment, the church is keenly aware of the primary mandate to make disciples who love God with their whole being. At the same time, the church must also be concerned with loving their whole person, just as the Son has loved them.[24]

Summary

Clearly, the Great Commandment and the Great Commission are interdependent. Love for God directed upward naturally and joyfully overflows outward to love for neighbor. Love for neighbor must include engaging others with the gospel, leading them to love God as well. In considering the Great Commandment and the Great Commission, David Wheeler and Vernon Whaley conclude that worship expressed as love for God "is a passionate response to the heart cry of God that includes active participation in the Great Commission."[25] Wheeler and Whaley summarize the chain reaction expressed above. The force of God's love for humanity compels the church to respond by returning love to God, which overflows into love for neighbor. These two loves in the life of those who follow Christ drive participation in the Great Commission. Without love for God, there can be no righteous motivation for participation in his mission. Out of love for God, Christians join him in his mission in the world and love him all the more. Looking at the intersection of the Great Commandment and the Great Commission provides yet another angle through which to see that "the Christian faith . . . is intrinsically missional."[26]

---

22. They write, "The crucial form in which the Great Commission has been handed down to us (though it is the most neglected because it is the most costly) is the Johannine" (ibid., 23).
23. Ibid.
24. There are many discussions surrounding the relationship between compassion ministries and how they relate to the Great Commission. The intention in this chapter is not to resolve the precise relationship between practical, compassion ministries, and the ministry of proclamation. Rather, the intention is to acknowledge that both are necessary in some capacity, and that they must be intimately linked to one another as a result of the Great Commandments. For further reading on seeking balance, see Michael David Sills, *Changing World, Unchanging Mission: Responding to Global Challenges* (Downers Grove, IL: InterVarsity, 2015), 107–26.
25. David A. Wheeler and Vernon M. Whaley, *The Great Commission to Worship: Biblical Principles for Worship-Based Evangelism* (Nashville: B&H Academic, 2011), 22.
26. Bosch, *Transforming Mission*, 8.

REFLECTION QUESTIONS

1. How would God's command to love others be different if it was not preceded by his covenant love for us?

2. What does it mean to love God and love neighbor?

3. Are the ways your culture talks about love similar or different to how the Bible speaks about love?

4. What will happen if believers pursue the Great Commission without it being an expression of their love for God?

5. This chapter teaches that fully loving one's neighbor means caring for both their soul and their body. Which type of care are you more likely to focus on?

When Will the Great Commission Be Fulfilled?

Since the time Jesus gave the Great Commission almost two thousand years ago, his followers have been making disciples (albeit not consistently). The gospel has spread to every continent and almost every geographic and political nation. Millions upon millions of people have turned to follow Christ. Because such a length of time has passed and so many have professed faith, it is natural to ask when Christians can expect to finish the task of making disciples of all nations. In other words, when will the Great Commission be fulfilled? This chapter will explore whose assignment it is to fulfill the Great Commission, what it means to fulfill it, and whether the Church can calculate its progress to finishing it.

Did the Disciples Complete the Great Commission?[1]

The common opinion from the early church, through the Reformation and up until the eighteenth century, was that Jesus gave the Great Commission to the apostles and that they completed the task in the first century.[2] This opinion remained common because interpretations of Matthew 28 revolved around theological and ecclesiastical controversies such as baptism, the Trinity, and Christ's deity.[3] According to this thinking, the Great Commission is a finished, not unfulfilled, task.

---

1. See Questions 2 and 7 for more on to whom Jesus gave the Great Commission and how the church has historically interpreted the Great Commission.
2. See the discussion in Question 7.
3. John Jefferson Davis, "'Teaching Them to Observe All That I Have Commanded You:' The History of the Interpretation of the 'Great Commission' and Implications for Marketplace Ministries." *Evangelical Review of Theology,* January 1, 2001; see also Timothy C. Tennent, *Invitation to World Missions: A Trinitarian Missiology for the Twenty-First Century* (Grand Rapids: Kregel, 2010), 66–67.

Many scholars, however, have correctly argued that the Great Commission is the ongoing task of the whole church, not the task of the apostles alone. For example, Robert Plummer says, "The commission to the apostles explicitly indicates that the apostles are to teach their converts to 'obey everything' that Jesus had commanded them—apparently including this Great Commission as well."[4] Likewise, John Piper states it well about Matthew 28:20 when he says, "If the sustaining promise is expressed in terms that endure to the end of the age, we may rightly assume that the command to make disciples also endures to the end of the age."[5] Thus, the Great Commission remains to be fulfilled.

The Great Commission Will Be Completed by the Church

To know when the Great Commission will be fulfilled requires knowing what counts as finishing the task, *who* we are to reach, and *what* we are to do. In Matthew 28:19, Jesus describes *who* we are to reach. He commissions the apostles to make disciples "of all nations" (Greek *panta ta ethnē*). Likewise, Luke uses a variation of the same words when he writes, "the forgiveness of sins should be proclaimed in his name *to all nations,* beginning from Jerusalem" (Luke 24:47, emphasis added). Some scholars understand the Greek phrase *panta ta ethnē* in a negative, restricted sense, which gives the phrase the meaning "to all the Gentiles" as opposed to the Jews.[6] This is a legitimate interpretation in some contexts like Matthew 25:32. However, translating *ethnē* as "Gentiles" in Matthew 28 would place the focus of Jesus's words on reaching every Gentile individual. Aside from the unlikeliness of a commission to reach every person, evidence heavily leans toward understanding the passage as "all the nations (people groups)."[7] As R. T. France writes, the "emphasis falls positively on the universal scope of Jesus' mission rather than negatively on 'Gentiles' as opposed to Jews."[8] The task of the Great Commission then is to bring the gospel "to all nations."

Although the English word "nations" often connotes the idea of political or geographical nations, this understanding does not fit Matthew 28. Modern labels of political and geographic nations are simply inadequate to define the word.[9] Tennent demonstrates that Jesus could have used several other words like kingdom (*basilea*), territory (*chōra*), or country (*agros*) to emphasize

---

4. Robert L. Plummer, "The Great Commission in the New Testament," *SBTJ* 9, no. 4 (2005): 4–5.
5. John Piper, *Let the Nations Be Glad! The Supremacy of God in Missions*, 3rd ed. (Grand Rapids: Baker Academic, 2010), 182.
6. Douglas R. A. Hare and Daniel J. Harrington, "Make Disciples of All the Gentiles (Mt 28:19)," *CBQ* 37, no. 3 (July 1975): 359–69.
7. Piper, *Let the Nations Be Glad*, 189.
8. R. T. France, *The Gospel according to Matthew*, NICNT (Grand Rapids: Eerdmans, 1985), 1114.
9. Tennent notes that before the 1970s, many mainline churches were downsizing their missionary efforts because they believed the Great Commission was a geographic challenge and that this task was completed (*Invitation*, 357).

geography.[10] Instead, Jesus uses the Greek word *ethnē*, which more properly refers to "peoples" or "people groups" distinguished by cultural, ethnic, and linguistics differences. Therefore, one should understand the task of the Great Commission as making disciples of all peoples (see Question 15).

In the same passages, Jesus tells us *what* we are to do: make disciples, baptize, and teach others to obey Jesus's commands. Fulfilling the Great Commission then is more than evangelism. As Bruce Ashford summarizes, "Our Mission is to teach people the saving words of God and to baptize them into local communities of believers—churches!—that will equip them to bring the whole of their lives into line with God's intentions for them."[11] To fulfill the Great Commission is to make disciples among all peoples who follow Jesus with their whole life.

Future Fulfillment of the Great Commission

If the church's task is to make disciples of all peoples who follow Jesus with their whole life, when will Christians complete it? Before delving into specifics, there is some broad agreement about if and when the task of Great Commission will be completed. First, because Jesus sends with "all authority in heaven and on earth," it ensures the task can and will be completed. As David Mathis writes, "Christ Jesus now rules the whole universe (our little globe included) with the very sovereignty of God, ensuring the success of his global mission."[12] The apostle John confirms the surety of its completion when he affirms that God will have people from every tribe, language, people, and nation worship him in his eternal kingdom (Rev. 5:9; 7:9; 14:6; 15:4). One day, God will reverse the spreading out of the languages at the tower of Babel by uniting all ethnicities and languages around the salvation of Christ.[13] John's vision also confirms that the Great Commission will be fulfilled when Christ returns. At the end of time, God will have made a diverse people, one from all peoples of the world. Until then, Christians can know that the task is still unfinished.

Can We Calculate Our Progress in the Great Commission?

That the Great Commission will be fulfilled when Christ returns is certain. The next question one may ask is whether Christians can calculate their progress. Can Christians use Jesus's reference to "all nations" in Matthew 28:19 and his promise in Matthew 24:14 ("And this gospel of the kingdom will be proclaimed throughout the whole world as a testimony to all nations [*panta ta ethnē*], and then the end will come") to calculate how much work is left to do?

---

10. Ibid., 358.

11. Daniel L. Akin and Bruce Riley Ashford, *I Am Going* (Nashville: B&H, 2016), 15.

12. John Piper and David Mathis, eds., *Finish the Mission: Bringing the Gospel to the Unreached and Unengaged* (Wheaton, IL: Crossway, 2012), 13.

13. J. Daniel Hays, *From Every People and Nation: A Biblical Theology of Race* (Downers Grove, IL: IVP Academic, 2003), 115, 129, 165.

There are massive complexities regarding how to interpret Matthew 24:14 and the rest of the chapter.[14] Setting these complexities aside, could one still calculate the Great Commission's progress if Matthew 24:14 is a prediction of God's people fulfilling it? One might be tempted to answer yes given the numerous occasions where numbers on the world's people groups are connected to talk about the Great Commission. If "all the nations" means all peoples, then research on people groups could be a measuring device for our progress.[15] By numbering how many people groups exist in the world and assessing how many are still unreached, one could better determine the progress toward fulfilling the Great Commission. The current number of people groups listed in the world varies between 11,774[16] and 16,962,[17] depending upon what factors (country boundaries, language, ethnicity, etc.) one uses to count. Out of these peoples, the number of unreached peoples—people groups that contain less than two percent evangelical Christians—is approximately seven thousand.[18] Is reaching these unreached people groups the last barrier to finishing the mission?

There are too many difficulties with applying the people-groups figures as a progress meter for the Great Commission. First, the number of people groups changes regularly, which prevents it from being a reliable measurement.[19] Second, as Piper writes, God probably did not intend our precise definition of people groups. He states, "The point of Matthew 24:14 . . . is

---

14. Matthew 24 is one the most hotly debated chapters in the whole Gospel. Scholars differ over whether Jesus is speaking about events in the past, the future, or both the past and future. Some argue that all or most of the events that Jesus describes occurred in the first century and climax with the destruction of Jerusalem and the temple in A.D. 70; some divide the chapter between the past historical destruction (24:1–35) and future coming of Jesus (24:36–25:46); some argue that the events will primarily or solely occur in the future when Jesus returns; and still others believe that Jesus describes both the destruction of Jerusalem and his future return (David L. Turner, *Matthew*, BECNT [Grand Rapids: Baker Academic, 2008], 566–67). One can also understand Jesus's reference to "all nations" in Matthew 28:20 and 24:14 as general terminology about the expansion of God's kingdom rather than as literal criteria for mission work. From this perspective, Jesus is speaking about the universal scope of the disciple's task (France, *The Gospel according to Matthew*, 1114). See also the discussion on Matthew 24 in Question 28.

15. A people group is "the largest group within which the gospel can spread as a church planting movement without encountering barriers of understanding or acceptance" (Tennent, *Invitation*, 360). Many mission organizations like the International Mission Board use people group information to aid their efforts.

16. https://www.imb.org/research/people-groups.

17. https://joshuaproject.net.

18. *Global Status of Evangelical Christianity: January 2018* (International Mission Board, January 2018), 3, http://grd.imb.org/wp-content/uploads/documents/gsec-files/2018-01_GSEC_Overview.pdf.

19. From the time of Timothy Tennent's writing of *Invitation to World Missions* in 2010, the Joshua Project's number of people groups increased from 16,304 to 16,962, and the IMB's number increased from 11,571 to 11,744.

not that we should reach all the nations as we understand them and then stop. The point rather is that as long as the Lord has not returned, there must be people groups to reach, and we should keep on reaching them."[20] Moreover, the Bible does not say whether "all nations" means all peoples that have existed in history or those at a specific point in history. Neither does it tell us what counts as having evangelized or reached the nations. One must remember that the marker of a reached people group (2 percent evangelical Christian) is a sociological, not a biblical, guide. Finally, Jesus himself says in Matthew 24:36, "concerning that day [the day of his return] and hour no one knows, not even the angels of heaven, nor the Son, but the Father only." We would do well to take Jesus's statement seriously as we pursue the fulfilling of the Great Commission.

Research on people groups is crucial for missions, but it cannot function as a countdown for Christ's return. Neither does Jesus intend for Christians to try to calculate it. Rather, the focus of the Great Commission is that Jesus sends out believers to those peoples that are outside of Jerusalem and Judea in worldwide evangelism and disciple-making. As Jeffrey Brawner writes, "The job of the church is not to 'finish the task' in mission. Christ will finish the task. Instead, the church's purpose is to strive to reach the current generation for Christ and lay the foundation for other generations to know him as well."[21]

Should then we cease to use the people group models in our mission strategy? Not at all! They are a helpful tool in many ways. They help the church to know who still needs to hear the gospel so that Christians can "preach the gospel, not where Christ has already been named" (Rom. 15:20). They reveal the barriers (economic, social, political, religious, etc.) that prevent the gospel from spreading. And, they help the church to focus its efforts on places that have the most need.

Nevertheless, simply "reaching" people with the good news of the gospel is not the fulfillment of the Great Commission. The Great Commission is more comprehensive in scope and involves not only evangelism, but discipleship, healthy church formation, and local ownership of the missionary task.

---

20. Piper, *Let the Nations Be Glad*, 212. See also Ralph D. Winter and Bruce A. Koch, "Finishing the Task: The Unreached Peoples Challenge," in *Perspectives on the World Christian Movement: A Reader*, eds. Ralph D. Winter and Steven C. Hawthorne, 4th ed. (Pasadena, CA: William Carey Library, 2009), 533, "Who are these peoples? Jesus did not provide a list of the peoples. He did not define the idea of peoples with precise detail. What matters most is not that the peoples can be definitively identified and *counted*, but that God has given us a task that can be *completed*." None of these authors make Christ's return imminent upon reaching all people groups either.
21. Jeffrey Brawner, "Finishing the Task: A Balanced Approach," in *Missiology: An Introduction to the Foundations, History, and Strategies of World Missions*, rev. ed., ed. John Mark Terry (Nashville: B&H, 2015), 573.

Evangelism is important and urgent, but maturing disciples (teaching and observing), forming healthy churches, and training pastors and leaders are all a part of the Great Commission. Our goal is not to figure out when the task will be finished. Our goal is to be faithful to spread the gospel and make disciples. George Ladd wisely says,

> Someone else will say, "How are we to know when the mission is completed? How close are we to the accomplishment of the task? Which countries have been evangelized and which have not? How close are we to the end? Does this not lead to date-setting?"
>
> I answer, I do not know. God alone knows the definition of terms. I cannot precisely define who "all the nations" are. . . . He alone . . . will know when that objective has been accomplished. But I do not need to know. I only know one thing: Christ has not yet returned; therefore the task is not yet done. When it is done, Christ will come. Our responsibility is not to insist on defining the terms of our task; our responsibility is to complete it. So as long as Christ does not return, our work is undone. Let us get busy and complete our mission.[22]

Summary

Our Great Commission task is to make sure everyone has an opportunity to hear the gospel, knowing that Jesus's resurrection confirms that the end result of all nations worshiping God is sure. We should long for all peoples to know Jesus and to see our work on earth complete. And, we should use our life as best as we can to pursue that end. However, God is in charge of his mission and he alone knows exactly when it will be fulfilled. He began it, and he will finish it. We can praise God that he would use us in it.

REFLECTION QUESTIONS

1. Why should Christians not concern themselves with determining when the Great Commission will be completed?

2. Does the Great Commission feel like an overwhelming task to you? What in Scripture can encourage you that it will be completed?

---

22. George Eldon Ladd, *The Gospel of the Kingdom: Scriptural Studies in the Kingdom of God* (Grand Rapids: Eerdmans, 1959), 136–37.

3. Can Christians who do not move overseas still participate in the Great Commission? How?

4. How does it make you feel that God has entrusted his mission to the church?

5. If the Great Commission includes making disciples, how does this change how we approach cross-cultural missions?

PART 2

Historical Questions about the Great Commission

Where Do We Stand in Relation to Fulfilling the Great Commission?

When James Fraser (1886–1938) was a student at London University, he received a booklet that would change his life. The year was 1906. Rather than pursuing a career as an engineer and concert pianist, he would leave Great Britain as a missionary to the Lisu people group in western China. The booklet was entitled *Do Not Say*, and the words that gripped Fraser's heart still have force today:

> "Go ye into all the world and preach the Gospel to every creature." More than half the people in the world have never heard the Gospel yet. A command has been given. It has not been obeyed. What are we to say to this? Surely it concerns us Christians very seriously. For we are the people who are responsible. . . .
>
> If our Master returned to-day to find millions of people un-evangelized, and looked, as of course He would look, to *us* for an explanation, I cannot imagine what explanation we should have to give.
>
> Of one thing I am certain—that most of the excuses we are accustomed to make with such good conscience *now*, we should be wholly ashamed of *then*.[1]

Missiologists and on-the-ground missionaries speak of "The Unfinished Task."[2] It is a painful and honest recognition that the Great Commission of our

---

1. James Heywood Horsburgh, *"Do Not Say": Or, the Church's Excuses for Neglecting the Heathen* (Chicago: F. H. Revell, 1892), 8, 10. See also Eileen Fraser Crossman, *Mountain Rain* (Singapore: Overseas Missionary Fellowship, 1985), 4.
2. See, e.g., http://www.missionfrontiers.org/issue/article/an-overview-of-the-unfinished-task; http://www.affinity.org.uk/foundations-issues/issue-73-exploring-the-unfinished-task-priorities-for-mission-locally-and-globally. Robert Speer used this phrase in his

Lord Jesus (Matt. 28:16–20; Acts 1:8) has not and is not being fulfilled. Fraser read in 1906 that half the world had not heard the gospel. Today, with all our numbers, technology, and dollars, things have not changed (percentage-wise). With the world population passing 7.6 billion (2018), approximately 4 billion do not have adequate opportunity to hear the gospel.[3] Is it possible we are actually losing ground?

Making disciples, planting healthy and indigenous churches, and training leaders among all people groups of the world are still the keys to fulfilling the Great Commission. In answering the question "Where do we stand in relation to fulfilling the Great Commission?" we need to trace the historic advance of the gospel since its inception and consider the current status of evangelical Christianity among all people groups of the world. There are, however, two difficulties with such a task. The first difficulty concerns how to define progress and determine what counts as fulfilling the Great Commission.[4] The second difficulty is that as soon as you print any sort of data regarding population and people groups, it is already outdated. Figures change daily. One can reference any previous work on the Great Commission's status to see that this is the case. We acknowledge these difficulties and present in this chapter current figures on the spread of the gospel among people groups in order to display the gospel's movement around the world, to highlight the need for more missionaries, and to motivate and encourage future work.

Global Status of Evangelical Christianity in 2018[5]

The Global Research Division of the International Mission Board (IMB) has created a scale called the Global Status of Evangelical Christianity (GSEC), which measures the spread of the gospel among people groups.

---

book *The Unfinished Task of Foreign Missions* (New York: Fleming H. Revell, 1926). Ralph Winter popularized it in "Missions Frontiers" and other publications of the US Center for World Missions.

3. For an illuminating glance at the need for missions, see the International Mission Board's "The Unfished Task Clock–Population Clock" at http://grd.center/portals/0/unfinished-task.htm.

4. See the previous chapter's discussion.

5. *Global Status of Evangelical Christianity: January 2018* (International Mission Board, January 2018), 1–2, http://grd.imb.org/wp-content/uploads/documents/gsec-files/2018-01_GSEC_Overview.pdf.

GSEC Level	People Groups	Population	GSEC Description
0	401	9,268,915	No evangelical Christians or churches. No access to major evangelical print, audio, visual, or human resources.
1	4,507	919,049,170	Less than 2 percent evangelical Christians. Some evangelical resources available, but no active church planting within the last two years.
2	1,754	1,864,236,850	Less than 2 percent evangelical Christians. Initial (localized) church planting within past two years.
3	377	1,556,532,600	Less than 2 percent evangelical Christians. Widespread church planting within past two years.
4	1,370	573,549,895	Greater than or equal to 2 percent evangelical Christians.
5	1,479	1,952,468,945	Greater than or equal to 5 percent evangelical Christians.
6	1,856	561,860,765	Greater than or equal to 10 percent evangelical Christians.
Total	**11,744**	**7,436,967,140**	

As of January 2018, there are 11,744 people groups around the world with a total world population of more than 7.4 billion. A people group is the largest group within which the gospel can spread without encountering barriers of understanding or acceptance. Of these 11,744 people groups, 7,053 are unreached (GSEC Level 0 to 3) with a total population of 4.3 billion. A people group is considered unreached when there is no indigenous community of believing Christians able to engage this people group with church planting. After two millennia, more than half of the world's total population are still waiting to hear the gospel in their heart language. And, for some in the unreached category, prospects for hearing the gospel are even more bleak.

The majority of these unreached people groups reside in the 10/40 window, "the rectangular area of North Africa, the Middle East and Asia approximately between 10 degrees north and 40 degrees north latitude."[6] According to the Joshua Project, this area contains the top one hundred of the world's unreached people groups by population. Many of these peoples still do not have a Bible translation in their own language. This area is one of the most important for current and future missions.

Of those unreached people groups, approximately 3,180 are unengaged. A people group is unengaged when there is no church planting strategy, consistent with evangelical faith and practice, underway. In other words, there is no missionary activity within those groups at this time. Making disciples and forming healthy churches are the keys to establishing an indigenous, an effective, and a multiplying presence among these people groups. The total population of these unengaged unreached people groups stands at 223.8 million, representing just under three percent of the world's total population.

Now, this is not to say advances have not taken place since Pentecost and the birth of the church. The charts below contain information that is both encouraging and discouraging. What has happened in the last century regarding the spread of Islam is particularly disconcerting.

The Progress of Major World Religions by Population Percentage[7]

World Religions	1800	1900	2015	2050
Christians	22.68%	34.44%	31–32%	31–35%
Muslims	10.01%	12.37%	23–24%	28–29%
Hindus	11.95%	12.53%	13–15%	12–14%
Buddhists	7.58%	7.84%	6–7%	5–6%

---

6. "What Is the 10/40 Window?," *Joshua Project*, n.d., https://joshuaproject.net.
7. Figures taken from Todd M. Johnson and Gina A. Zurlo, eds., *World Religion Database* (Leiden/Boston: Brill, accessed March 2018); Todd M. Johnson and Peter F. Crossing, "Christianity 2014: Independent Christianity and Slum Dwellers," *International Bulletin of Missionary Research* 31, no. 1 (April 21, 2014): 29; "Global Christianity—a Report on the Size and Distribution of the World's Christian Population," *Pew Research Center's Religion & Public Life Project*, December 19, 2011, http://www.pewforum.org/2011/12/19/global-christianity-exec. The percentage range for 2015 and 2050 is due to the different calculations by Pew Research and the World Religion Database. To understand why they differ, see *Center for the Study of Global Christianity*, http://www.gordonconwell.edu/ockenga/research/documents/CSGCPewResponse.pdf.

Top Five Populations of Christians by Region[8]

	1900	2015	2050
1	Eastern Europe	South America	Eastern Africa
2	Western Europe	Northern America	South America
3	Northern America	Eastern Africa	Middle Africa
4	Southern Europe	Eastern Europe	Northern America
5	North Europe	Central America	Western Africa

Top Five Populations of Christians by Country[9]

	1900	2015	2050
1	United States	United States	United States
2	Russia	Brazil	China
3	Germany	China	Brazil
4	France	Mexico	Nigeria
5	United Kingdom	Russia	Congo DR

In A.D. 100, there were already one million Christians in the world (0.6% of the world's population of 181.5 million).[10] Shortly after William Carey wrote *An Inquiry into the Obligations of Christians* in 1792, Christianity had grown to 204.9 million people (22.68% of the world's population of 903.6 million).[11] As of 2015, there were an estimated 2.2–2.4 billion Christians in the world (31–32% of the world's population of 7.2 billion).[12] Although Christianity has

---

8. Todd M. Johnson and Brian J. Grim, eds., *World Christian Database* (Leiden/Boston: Brill, accessed March 2018). For these charts, a "Christian" is one who self-identifies as such and includes nominal and nonpracticing Christians.
9. Ibid.
10. David B. Barrett, *World Christian Encyclopedia: A Comparative Study of Churches and Religions in the Modern World,* A.D. *1900–2000* (Oxford: Oxford University Press, 1982), 3.
11. Johnson and Crossing, "Christianity 2014: Independent Christianity and Slum Dwellers," 29.
12. "The Changing Global Religious Landscape," *Pew Research Center's Religion & Public Life Project,* April 5, 2017, accessed December 13, 2017, http://www.pewforum.org/2017/04/05/the-changing-global-religious-landscape.

grown in number, it has maintained a stable percentage of the total world population over the last century. Clearly there is still work to be done. But there are challenges to completing "The Unfinished Task."

There are at least four challenges to fulfilling the Great Commission. First, the rise of "the nones" has increased to 16 percent of the world's population as of 2015.[13] The "nones" are people who identify themselves as atheists, agnostics, or with no particular religion, a group. This group is significantly growing in the West, and the influence of secularism is a clear reality in our day. To deny secularism's impact is simply not tenable.[14]

Second, the rapid growth of Islam will be a major challenge to world evangelism. According to Pew Research, Islam is growing at a faster rate than Christianity and should grow by 70 percent between 2015 and 2060.[15] Christianity, in contrast, should increase by 34 percent. In 2015, there were 1.8 billion followers of Islam and 2.3 billion followers of Christianity. At present trends, Islam will grow to 2.9 billion by 2060 and Christianity will reach 3 billion. Islam will surpass Christianity by 2075. Pew demonstrates that Islam's growth is, in large part, due to Muslims having more children

---

13. Pew Research does note that while those in "the nones" category will grow to 1.20 billion in 2060, they will be outpaced by the growth of other religious groups and the world population, causing them to shrink in percentage to 13 percent ("Why People with No Religion Are Projected to Decline as a Share of the World's Population," *Pew Research Center*, April 7, 2017, http://www.pewresearch.org/fact-tank/2017/04/07/why-people-with-no-religion-are-projected-to-decline-as-a-share-of-the-worlds-population). This percentage means around 1.17 billion people reject any type of religion.

14. In 2012, a Pew report revealed that "one of five Americans is now 'unaffiliated' and disconnected from any church or organized faith. More shocking is the fact that fully one in three Americans under age 30 report themselves as unaffiliated. 'In the last five years alone, the unaffiliated have increased from just over 15% to just under 20% of all U.S. adults,' the report reveals. Of the unaffiliated, about 13 million Americans (about 6%) identify as atheists or agnostics, with another 33 million (14%) simply claiming no affiliation. The unaffiliated are not church shopping, according to the researchers. Instead, these Americans say they are very comfortable being disconnected from any church or organized faith." Albert Mohler Jr. notes, "The unaffiliated are not openly hostile to churches or religious institutions, but they are not planning to join one. Most are not atheists or agnostics, and many follow some religious practice such as meditation, but they do not see themselves as meaningfully connected to any faith commitment. . . . As older Americans pass from the scene, they are replaced by a generation that is markedly less likely to affiliate with a church or religious tradition. One in three young adults [those under 30] have no religious affiliation, while only one in ten adults aged 65 and older identify themselves that way" ("The Great Clarification: Fuzzy Fidelity and the Rise of the Nones," October 16, 2012, http://albertmohler.com/2012/10/16/the-great-clarification-fuzzy-fidelity-and-the-rise-of-the-nones.

15. "The Changing Global Religious Landscape." It should be noted that the growth of Islam includes all children born to Muslim fathers and that social forces very strongly discourage leaving Islam. Thus, though nominalism exists, it is not readily measurable. In addition, Christianity, at least in theory, only grows through conversion. These factors are not accounted for in Barrett's stats.

than Christians. Demographics are not on our side when it comes to our challenge from Islam.

Third, Christian missions can be extremely dangerous. The majority of IMB missionaries are serving in security level three areas, countries that are antagonistic to missionaries and the gospel.[16] The IMB releases no public information on these missionaries due to security. but news cycles confirm this danger with stories of persecuted house churches in China and Nigeria, the imprisonment of Iranian pastors, and heinous attacks against Coptic Christians in Egypt.

Despite these challenges, Christians can have hope of fulfilling the Great Commission. Many people have received the Bible in their own language for the first time, previously unreached people groups have received the gospel, and Christians have a greater ability to reach the nations now than at any time in Christian history. Having this great missions force assumes, of course, that everyone is involved in finishing the task. Perhaps the promise also should be seen as a challenge. Also, the rise of Christianity in the Global South and its participation in the Great Commission are causes for excitement, hope, and rejoicing. In the twentieth century, all of the top five Christian regions and countries were either European or in the West. Today, however, most of world's Christian population has shifted to Africa, South America, and East Asia. We praise God that many of these countries like Palestine, Brazil, and South Korea are also now some of the top missionary-sending countries.[17]

Summary

The statistical information in this chapter reveals that the remaining task is huge. However, it also shows how the gospel has spread from a tiny room of only a few in Jerusalem to billions of men and women in almost every country across the world. God has been building his kingdom among the nations. And he has promised that all nations will worship him in his heavenly kingdom. So, while there are challenges facing the church in fulfilling the Great Commission, the church has unprecedented opportunities, and thus should have unparalleled hope as well.

---

16. International Mission Board (SBC), *2017 Annual Personnel Report: Executive Summary*, February 2018, 2.
17. Melissa Steffan, "The Surprising Countries Most Missionaries Are Sent From and Go To," News & Reporting, *Christianity Today*, http://www.christianitytoday.com/news/2013/july/missionaries-countries-sent-received-csgc-gordon-conwell.html. Palestine sends the largest number of missionaries per million in population. Brazil sends the second most total missionaries. And South Korea sends the fifth most missionaries per million church members.

REFLECTION QUESTIONS

1. Do the above figures encourage or discourage you? Why?

2. What does the shift of Christianity from the West to the South and East mean for world evangelism?

3. Do you know what people groups live around you? How might your church begin to pray and engage these groups? Visit peoplegroups.info to help you get started.

4. How can you incorporate prayer for unreached peoples into your daily life?

5. Why should the growth of Islam and the danger of missions not deter Christians from engaging unreached peoples?

QUESTION 7

How Has the Great Commission Been Interpreted in History?

What comes to mind when one thinks of the "Great Commission"? For many, the term conjures up images of going overseas, strange culture, mission conventions, Bible schools, or preachers proclaiming a sermon about Matthew 28:18–20.[1] While many modern readers recognize the Great Commission passages as foundational mission texts, historical interpretations of these passages have not always stressed this emphasis. The prevalent missional tone found in today's contemporary understanding of these texts has evolved over time. This chapter will give an overview of major historical interpretations of the Great Commission passages.

First, the Great Commission will be defined. After that, a brief overview of historical interpretations will be discussed, focusing on interpretations from pre-Reformation scholars, Reformation scholars, those who first used the term "Great Commission," Modern Missions Movement theologians, historical critical scholars, twentieth-century missiologists, and finally, global Christians. The major focus of the historical interpretations will center around Matthew's commission passage. This chapter represents only an overview of some major interpretations. Even within specific time-frames, such as the Reformation or Modern Missions Movement, other less prevalent interpretations were also present.

---

1. Some shorten this pericope to include only Matthew 28:19–20, leaving out verse 18, "All authority in heaven and on earth is given to me." Timothy Tennent points out that this verse is essential for the theological foundation of the Great Commission, because it is the proclamation of who Jesus is. Tennent states, "Jesus' *being* precedes the church's *doing*" (Timothy C. Tennent, *Invitation to World Missions: A Trinitarian Missiology for the Twenty-First Century*, Invitation to Theological Studies Series [Grand Rapids: Kregel, 2010], 137).

What Is the Great Commission?

While many immediately correlate the Great Commission to the passage in Matthew 28:18–20, other scholars point out that the Great Commission has a much fuller meaning located in the multiple commissioning passages of the gospel writers (Matt. 28:18–20; Mark 13:10; 16:14–18; Luke 24:44–49; John 20:19–23; and Acts 1:7–8). Timothy Tennent states, "The term is identified specifically with Matthew 28:18–20 and, unfortunately, is frequently treated as an isolated pericope, separated from the rest of the gospel, as well as the larger biblical context of the *missio dei*."[2] To Tennent, and we would agree, the full meaning of the Great Commission is missed when only one passage is isolated from the biblical canon. Like a diamond held up to the light, each version of the commission illustrates a slightly different facet of Jesus's plan and heart for the nations.

Historical Interpretations of the Great Commission

Before at least the seventeenth century, the Matthew text was largely ignored when discussing the church's missional assignment. In the early church, the writers had other needs that occupied their attention and took precedence. During an age when church fathers wrestled with defining the doctrines of the faith, this passage was often source material for theological debates over topics such as baptism and the Trinity. Augustine used the Matthew text as theological evidence for the Trinity.[3] Gregory Nazianzen used the passage to implement a threefold liturgical baptism, and Basil and Gregory of Nyssa held a similar view.[4] Tennent considers this early doctrinal emphasis as one barrier to the Matthean text's missiological interpretation.[5] During the Middle Ages, many scholars debated to whom the commission was given. Medieval Catholics largely viewed the commission as binding to the apostles and those who followed them.

---

2. Ibid., 127. Wright argues that the entire Bible should be read through a "missional hermeneutic," rather than basing our understanding of mission from a single (or several) texts (Christopher J. H. Wright, *The Mission of God: Unlocking the Bible's Grand Narrative* [Downers Grove, IL: IVP Academic, 2006]).

3. Augustine, "On the Trinity 15.51," in *Basic Writings of Saint Augustine*, ed. Whitney J. Oates, 2nd ed., vol. 2 (New York: Random House, 1948); T. Fomberg, "Matthew and His Readers: Some Examples from the History of Interpretation," *Theology and Life* 22 (1999): 142. Augustine, however, still had a missionary concern that the gospel be preached in Africa where it had not yet been preached (John Jefferson Davis, "'Teaching Them to Observe All That I Have Commanded You': The History of the Interpretation of the 'Great Commission' and Implications for Marketplace Ministries," *Evangelical Review of Theology* [January 1, 2001]: 68–69).

4. Frederick Norris, "Gregory Nazianzen: Constructing and Constructed by Scripture," in *The Bible in Greek Christian Antiquity*, vol. 1, ed. Paul Bowers (Notre Dame, IN: University of Notre Dame Press, 1997), 150. For more information about early church father interpretations, see Davis, "Teaching Them to Observe All That I Have Commanded You."

5. Tennent, *Invitation to World Missions*, 451.

Bishops, due to their belief in apostolic succession, were the rightful heirs of the apostles and the ones who carried on the apostles' mission.[6]

The Reformers balked at the Catholic interpretation of the Matthew passage. Even though scholars historically did not interpret the Matthew passage missionally, they did believe in mission or missions. They simply looked to other biblical passages for support.[7] They claimed that the mandate was given to and already completed by Jesus's original disciples.[8] It had no bearing on the contemporary church. Douglas McLain Shaw points out that neither John Calvin nor Martin Luther saw the Matthew text as a missional commandment for their generation, albeit for different reasons. Luther believed the apostolate referred only to the original disciples, even though the mandate was still valid. For Luther, those in the apostolate took the gospel to all the world. In discussing Mark 16:15, Luther states, "But they [the apostles] had a command and were ordained and called and sent to preach the Gospel. . . . Since then, however, no one has had this general apostolic command."[9] The mandate itself could be carried out by church leaders through the teaching and baptizing of their *own* congregations.[10] Calvin, on the other hand, believed both the apostolate and the commission had ended.[11] In the years following the Reformation, many held to Calvin's and Luther's interpretations of the Great Commission passage. Shaw reports that one school in 1652 even "warned of anarchy among churches if every preacher were to abandon his pulpit to go out into the world to preach the gospel."[12] However, although the Reformers' view was prevalent, it was not all-encompassing. Hadrian Saravia and Justinian von Welz are two Protestant scholars of the time who believed Matthew 28:18–20 was a missional passage for current believers.[13]

---

6. Fomberg, "Matthew and His Readers," 143. Fomberg also claims that even Christopher Columbus referenced the Matthew text, proclaiming that the apostles had taken the gospel to the three known areas of the world (Africa, Europe, and Asia) and that it was now time for Christendom to take the gospel to the fourth, newly discovered realm (ibid., 143).

7. For an example, see the story of Luther's interpretation of Psalm 117 in Martin Luther, *Selected Psalms III*, vol. 14, Luther's Works (St. Louis: Concordia, 1958), 9; Tennent, *Invitation to World Missions*, 451.

8. Douglas McClain Shaw, "The Great Commission in Protestant Missionary Apologetics" (Dissertation, New Orleans Baptist Theological Seminary, 1986). For a concise overview of views from the Reformation to 1791, see the Introduction of Douglas Mclain Shaw's dissertation. Shaw covers Luther, Calvin, Bucer, Saravia, Gerhard, Huernius, Voetius, von Weltz, Horbeeck, the Puritans, Millar, and Spangenberg.

9. Martin Luther, *Selected Psalms II*, vol. 13, Luther's Works (St. Louis: Concordia, 1956), 64.

10. Ibid., 13:64–65; Shaw, "The Great Commission in Protestant Missionary Apologetics," 15–16.

11. For examples, see Jean Calvin, *Calvin's Institutes*, abridged ed. Donald K. McKim (Louisville: Presbyterian Publishing Corporation, 2001), 132–33. Also see Shaw, "The Great Commission in Protestant Missionary Apologetics," 20.

12. Shaw, "The Great Commission in Protestant Missionary Apologetics," 28.

13. David Hesselgrave, "Great Commission," eds. A. Scott Moreau, et al., *Evangelical Dictionary of World Missions* (Grand Rapids: Baker, 2000), 413. For a brief overview of these two

The Anabaptists stand out as a notable exception to the predominant interpretation of the commission by the Reformers. They viewed it as a command for the current church. Franklin Littell writes, "No words of the Master were given more serious attention by His Anabaptist followers than the Great Commission" and later "The Anabaptists were among the first to make the commission binding upon all church members."[14] The Matthean text, while missional, was also an important text in their emphasis on believer's baptism.[15] Anabaptist Menno Simons writes, "Here we have the Lord's commandment concerning baptism, as to when according to the ordinance of God it shall be administered and received; namely, that the Gospel must first be preached, and then those baptized who believe it."[16] Abraham Friesen claims the Anabaptist interpretation of the Great Commission is built upon Erasmus's interpretation of Matthew 28, in which the humanist links the Matthew passage to the baptismal passages in Acts.[17] Some scholars, however, find his argument dubious.[18]

In a watershed moment in mission history, William Carey published his *Enquiry into the Obligation of Christians to Use Means for the Conversion of the Heathens*. It claimed that, contrary to popular opinion, the Great Commission was given to all believers. In it, he admits that the commission (mainly Mark 16:15, with some emphasis on Matthew 28:18–20) was given to the original disciples. He then gives three reasons why they are binding to both the disciples and the contemporary church.[19] If the command to make disciples is not valid, he suggests, neither is the command to baptize. Also, those in Christian history who have preached the gospel did so without God's authority. Finally, if the command is not valid, neither is his promise to be with the disciples. He also suggests that since the apostles did not complete the task, this commission applied not only to the original disciples, but also to the current believers. He states, "Some attempts are still being made, but they are inconsiderable in

---

scholars' works, see Shaw, "The Great Commission in Protestant Missionary Apologetics," 23, 28. Shaw references Saravia's treatise, Hadrianus Saravia, *De Diversis Ministrorum Evangelii Gradibus, Sicut a Domini Fuerunt Instituti* (Frankfurt, 1591). Also see David F. Wright, "The Great Commission and the Ministry of the Word: Reflections Historical and Contemporary on Relations and Priorities," *Scottish Bulletin of Evangelical Theology* 25, no. 2 (Fall 2007): 145–47.

14. Franklin H. Littell, *Origins of Sectarian Protestantism* (New York: MacMillan, 1964), 110, 112.
15. Abraham Friesen, *Erasmus, the Anabaptists, and the Great Commission* (Grand Rapids: Eerdmans, 1998), 54.
16. Menno Simons, *The Complete Writings of Menno Simons: C.1496–1561*, ed. J. C. Wenger (Scottdale, PA: Herald, 1986), 120.
17. Friesen, *Erasmus, the Anabaptists, and the Great Commission*, 44.
18. Howard Louthan, "Erasmus, the Anabaptists and the Great Commission," *The Mennonite Quarterly Review* 74, no. 3 (July 2000): 484.
19. William Carey, *An Enquiry into the Obligations of Christians to Use Means for the Conversion of the Heathens*, ed. John L. Pretlove (Dallas: Criswell, 1988), 5.

comparison with what might be done if the whole body of Christians entered heartily into the spirit of the divine command on this subject."[20] This understanding of the Great Commission launched the modern mission movement and captured the hearts and imaginations of voluntary missions agencies and missionaries for years.[21]

During the early 1900s, various authors questioned the authenticity of the Matthew commissioning passage. To these scholars, the passage was nothing more than a summary sentence put back in the document by zealous disciples. Adolf von Harnack doubted that the commission actually came from Jesus. This global mandate, he contested, could not be the words of Jesus because the rest of the gospel paints him as an obvious Jewish nationalist with little concern for the world.[22] To him, it had to be the words of the disciples inserted into the gospel. David Hesselgrave points out that Harnack had a change of heart. He writes, "In later life, he found it to be only a fitting conclusion to that Gospel." He further adds that the commission is "so magnificent that it would be difficult to say anything more meaningful and complete in an equal number of words."[23]

Another shift in the interpretation of Matthew 28:18–20 occurred in the 1950s when Donald McGavran altered the prevailing definition of *nations* in the Matthew text. He shifted from a political-geographic understanding of nations to the idea of "peoples," which he claimed better represented the original Greek word *ethne*.[24] To him, peoples included "clans, tribes, castes."[25] Another turning point occurred in a 1974 conference, when Ralph Winter pushed against the prevailing idea that cross-cultural missions were no longer needed because "Christians have now fulfilled the Great Commission in at least a geographical sense."[26] Building upon the Greek translation of "peoples" (*ethne*), Winter stressed the reality of "2387 million who are not within the range of the ordinary evangelism of any Christian congregation—people who

---

20. Ibid., 2.
21. Interestingly, Shaw claims that the Mark 16 commission was Carey's primary text and the more often quoted passage during the early years of the modern mission movement (Shaw, "The Great Commission in Protestant Missionary Apologetics," 51, 83.
22. Adolf von Harnack, *The Mission and Expansion of Christianity in the First Three Centuries*, vol. 1, ed. James Moffat, trans. James Moffat (New York: G. P. Putnam's Sons, 1908), 38–41; Shaw, "The Great Commission in Protestant Missionary Apologetics," 86–87.
23. David J. Hesselgrave, "Great Commission," in *Evangelical Dictionary of World Missions*, ed. A. Scott Moreau (Grand Rapids: Baker Academic, 2000), 414.
24. Donald A. McGavran, *The Bridges of God: A Study in the Strategy of Missions* (Eugene, OR: Wipf & Stock, 2005), 14.
25. Ibid., 1.
26. Ralph D. Winter, "The New Macedonia: A Revolutionary New Era in Mission Begins," in *Perspectives on the World Christian Movement: A Reader*, eds. Ralph D. Winter and Steven C. Hawthorne, 4th ed. (Pasadena, CA: William Carey Library, 2009), 339.

require cross cultural evangelism."[27] He later builds his argument on an exposition of Acts 1:8, where he claims that "Jerusalem, Judea, and Samaria" pertain to cultural distance, not geographical difference.[28]

Today, majority world voices are also joining the swelling chorus of Great Commission interpretations. Some Chinese believers use the Great Commission as the foundation for their "Back to Jerusalem Movement," claiming that the gospel spreads west, lapping the earth, and will one day return to Jerusalem. Based on this interpretation of the Great Commission, these Chinese Christians believe that it is their duty to continue the westward march of the gospel.[29]

Great Commission obedience in the East has paved the way for the blossoming of majority world churches (i.e., churches in what has been known as developing countries). These churches no longer view themselves as only the recipients of the message of the Great Commission, but those commanded to carry it out. Joe Kapolyo, an African scholar, states,

> For too long we [the African church] have been recipients of the benefits of the gospel, and with few exceptions most of our church communities do not anticipate, let alone participate in, mission. We do not see it as our duty to go and spread the good news to people within our own countries, or to people beyond the borders of our own countries. . . . We must repent of this sin and take up his call to make disciples of all nations.[30]

Summary

Throughout history, the interpretation of the Great Commission has ebbed and flowed, often colored by current cultural settings. While the missional impetus of the Great Commission has at times been overlooked or assigned to someone else, there can be little doubt that the text calls believers from all ages to make disciples of all nations through the authority and promised presence of the Lord Jesus Christ. Christopher Wright states, "The Great Commission is the command of the new covenant."[31] All those who enter into the new covenant are responsible for carrying out the command of the King.

---

27. Ralph Winter, "The Highest Priority, Cross Cultural Evangelism," *The Ralph D. Winter Research Center*, http://dev.ralphdwinter.org/lausanne_1974.html.

28. Winter, "The New Macedonia," 342–43.

29. "A Captivating Vision: Why Chinese House Churches May Just End Up Fulfilling the Great Commission," *Christianity Today* 48, no. 4 (April 2004): 84.

30. Joe Kapolyo, "Matthew 28:16–20," in *Africa Bible Commentary* (Grand Rapids: Zondervan, 2010), 1196.

31. Wright, *The Mission of God*, 354.

REFLECTION QUESTIONS

1. How did the concerns and culture of past Christians shape their interpretation of the Great Commission? What does this teach us about how we interpret the Bible?

2. Do early interpretations of a fulfilled Great Commission mean that Christians before William Carey did not participate in missions?

3. How did William Carey's interpretation of Matthew 28:18–20 change the church's understanding?

4. Which interpretations of the Great Commission from Christian history have you heard before? Has this chapter changed how you interpret Matthew 28:18–20?

5. What is the difference between understanding the Great Commission as a command to go to all geographical or political nations versus going to all peoples?

Who Are the Great Commission Heroes of the Church's First 1,000 Years?

The first millennium of church history witnessed the massive expansion of Christianity from Judea, Samaria, and to the uttermost parts of the earth (Acts 1:8).[1] As individual Christians shared their faith with others, and as they planted churches across the known world, the church expanded. The book of Acts records the initial expansion as the gospel spreads from Jerusalem to Rome. However, gospel expansion did not end with the close of the first century. It continued to spread with significant advance. The church father Eusebius of Caesarea (A.D. 263–339) provides a helpful witness to this when he writes,

> Most of the disciples of that time . . . first fulfilled the Saviour's command and distributed their goods among the needy, and then, entering upon long journeys, performed the work of evangelists, being eager to preach everywhere to those who had not yet the word of faith and to pass on the writing of the divine Gospels. As soon as they had only laid the foundations of the faith in some foreign lands, they appointed others as pastors and entrusted to them the nurture of those who had recently been brought in, but they themselves went on to other lands and peoples with the grace and co-operation of God, for a great many marvelous miracles of the divine spirit were still being worked by them at that time, so that whole

---

1. For an extensive treatment of the spread of Christianity provided in a biographical format, consult the fine work by Ruth Tucker, *From Jerusalem to Irian Jaya: A Biographical History of Christian Missions* (Grand Rapids: Zondervan, 2004). The book is well written and nearly five hundred pages in length.

multitudes of men at the first hearing eagerly received within their souls the religion of the Creator of the universe.[2]

What follows in this chapter and the next is what we are calling "Great Commission heroes." The list is by no means exhaustive. No doubt there are many unsung heroes of whom we have no historical information at all. Still, we will look at some of those who took the Great Commission to heart and are examples of valuable efforts at spreading the gospel and making disciples of Jesus Christ among the nations.

The Apostle Paul (c. 5–67)

Any list of Great Commission heroes in the early church must begin with the apostle Paul. He is probably the greatest Christian missionary who ever lived. His methods and strategies are foundational. He was known as the apostle to the Gentiles. The New Testament records his missionary labors throughout Europe and Asia Minor. Paul completed at least three missionary journeys, which are recorded in the book of Acts. There is also evidence that Paul continued his missionary travels after his Roman imprisonment, perhaps making it to Spain.[3] It is impossible to know how many churches Paul planted, but according to the New Testament, we know that he started churches in the major provinces of Galatia, Asia, Achaia, Macedonia, and Crete.

The apostle Paul was most likely single (1 Cor. 7:7–8), and gave his whole life to making disciples through the preaching of the gospel. It was Paul's pattern to go to major cities, to preach first in the local synagogue of a given region, and then to expand his preaching ministry to Gentiles. This was his approach, for example, in Ephesus (Acts 18–19). It could be said that the book of Romans, Paul's masterful letter, is a missionary fundraising letter with a lengthy introduction. Paul asked for help as he aimed to take the gospel to Spain (Rom. 15:24, 28). We do not know if he ever got there. Nonetheless, the apostle Paul is a Great Commission hero.[4] In many ways the Great Commission became the personal mission statement of Paul's life. His life was bent on finding "a wide door of effective work" wherever he went (1 Cor. 16:9). The missiologist Roland Allen states well the impact of the apostle,

---

2. Eusebius, *Ecclesiastical History*, Books 1–5 (The Fathers of the Church, Volume 19), trans. Roy J. Deferrari, *The Fathers of the Church: A New Translation* (Washington, DC: Catholic University of America Press, 2005), 200–201.
3. Andreas J. Köstenberger, L. Scott Kellum, and Charles L. Quarles, *The Cradle, the Cross, and the Crown: An Introduction to the New Testament*, 2nd ed. (Nashville: B&H Academic, 2016), 473.
4. We should not ignore the work of Peter, Barnabas, Silas, Timothy, Apollos, or Priscila and Aquila recorded in Acts.

In little more than ten years St. Paul established the Church in four provinces of the Empire, Galatia, Macedonia, Achaia and Asia. Before A.D. 47 there were no Churches in these provinces; in A.D. 57 St. Paul could speak as if his work there was done. . . . This is truly an astonishing fact. That Churches should be founded so rapidly, so securely, seems to us today, accustomed to the difficulties, the uncertainties, the failures, the disastrous relapses of our own missionary work, almost incredible. Many missionaries in later days have received a larger number of converts than St. Paul; many have preached over a wider area than he; but none has so established Churches. We have long forgotten that such things could be . . . . To-day if a man ventures to suggest that there may be something in the methods by which St. Paul attained such wonderful results worthy of our careful attention, and perhaps of our imitation, he is in danger of being accused of revolutionary tendencies.[5]

Ordinary and Unknown Great Commission Heroes

Most historians of the early church agree that the primary way by which the gospel spread in the early church was through the ordinary witness of God's people. Edward Engelbrecht writes,

By the year 250, Christianity had spread to the limits of the known world. We hear legends about it in England, but know little more. We hear about it in areas of the east of Armenia, even in India and China, but know almost nothing about it. Two facts, however, become clear. First, the Church spread rapidly over a wide geographical area, increasing phenomenally in numbers at the same time. Second, this work was done by ordinary Christians. We know of no missionary societies; we hear nothing of organized effort. Wherever Christians went doing their regular tasks, the pagan saw a different kind of individual and heard about "the Savior."[6]

With very little organized mission activity, the gospel spread throughout the world. This was largely due to the efforts of Christians who took the final

---

5. Roland Allen, *Missionary Methods: St. Paul's or Ours, a Study of the Church in the Four Provinces* (London: Scott, 1913), 3–4.
6. Edward A. Engelbrecht, ed., *The Church from Age to Age: A History from Galilee to Global Christianity* (St. Louis: Concordia, 2011), 13.

marching orders of the Savior, the Great Commission, seriously. Church historian Stephen Neill says it well,

> What is clear is that every Christian was a witness. Where there were Christians, there would be a living, burning faith, and before long an expanding Christian community. In later times, great Churches were much set on claiming apostolic origin—to have an apostle as founder was a recognized certificate of respectability. But in point of fact few, if any, of the great Churches were really founded by apostles. Nothing is more notable than the anonymity of the early missionaries. . . . That was the greatest glory of the Church of those days. The Church was the body of Christ, indwelt by his Spirit; and what Christians had begun to do, that the Church would continue to do, through all the days and unto the uttermost parts of the earth until his unpredictable but certain, coming again.[7]

The primary way by which the gospel spread throughout world was through the everyday evangelistic efforts of ordinary Christians. The Great Commission was not the stewardship of a select few; it was part of the communal awareness of the entire body of Christ.

Addai (c. 2nd century)

Also known as Thaddaeus, Addai is called the "Apostle to Edessa," what is today northeast Turkey. He is honored as the "first missionary to cross the Roman border into the principalities of Edessa."[8]

Gregory Thaumaturgus (c. 213–270)

This missionary, also known as Gregory of Neocaserea, was born around A.D. 213 in Pontus. He converted to Christianity through the witness of Origen (c. 185–254) at Caesarea in Palestine. He is famous for his missions work in the region of Cappadocia, where he saw many people convert to Christianity. Many believed that Gregory could work miracles, and these supernatural displays often yielded credibility to his message. Engelbrecht writes,

> At daybreak, men, women, and children suffering from demon possession and disease would gather at his door. As

---

7. Stephen Neill and Owen Chadwick, *A History of Christian Missions* (New York: Penguin, 1990), 22–23.
8. Samuel Hugh Moffett, "Addai," in *Biographical Dictionary of Christian Missions*, ed. Gerald H. Anderson (New York: Macmillan, 1998), 5.

he healed these people, he would talk to them about the Gospel, advise them about their troubles, and discuss with them various religious problems. Gregory of Nyssa wrote that is was "above all for this that he drew many numbers to hear his preaching. . . . His discourse would astonish their hearing, and the wonders he performed would astonish their sight."[9]

Perhaps Gregory's most famous convert was Macrina, who was the grandmother of the great fourth-century theologians Gregory of Nyssa and Basil of Caesarea. H. Leclercq, in *The Catholic Encyclopedia*, notes, "From an ancient source we learn a fact that is at once a curious coincidence, and throws light on his missionary zeal; whereas he began with only seventeen Christians, at his death there remained but seventeen pagans in the whole town of Caesarea."[10]

Ulfilas (c. 311–383)

Ulfilas was consecrated by Eusebius of Nicomedia as a bishop to the Goths in A.D. c. 341. Tucker calls him "one of the greatest foreign missionaries of the early church."[11] He ministered for forty years among his people (his father was a Goth) with significant success amidst persecution. He translated the Scriptures into the Gothic language. Neill notes, "This was the first time that a language of Northern Europe became a literary language."[12] Unfortunately, however, he appears to have affirmed a "mild form of Arianism."[13]

Patrick of Ireland (c. 389–461)

Little is known for certain about St. Patrick, and many myths and legends abound regarding his life and ministry. What is known is that Patrick brought the gospel to Ireland. Adrian Hastings writes, "It was, nevertheless, from the mid-fifth-century British Church of which we know so little that Patrick came to become the evangelist of Ireland—the first major advance in the West beyond what had once been the empire."[14] He was known as the

---

9. Eusebius Pamphilus, *Eusebius' Ecclesiastical History: Complete and Unabridged*, updated ed., trans. C. F. Cruse (Peabody, MA: Hendrickson, 1998), 12.
10. H. Leclercq, "Gregory of Neocaesarea," in *The Catholic Encyclopedia*, ed. Charles George Herbermann (London: Universal Knowledge Foundation, 1913), 15.
11. Tucker, *From Jerusalem to Irian Jaya*, 35.
12. Neill and Chadwick, *A History of Christian Missions*, 49.
13. Tucker, *From Jerusalem to Irian Jaya*, 36. Arianism, based on the teachings of Arius (c. 250–336), denies the deity of Jesus Christ. Instead, Arians affirm that Jesus was created by the Father and therefore is subordinate to him.
14. Adrian Hastings, *A World History of Christianity* (Grand Rapids: Eerdmans, 1999), 58.

apostle of Ireland, and did more to evangelize the region in the fifth century than any other person. Ruther Tucker notes, "by 447, after fifteen years of preaching, much of Ireland had been evangelized."[15]

Columba (521–597)

Columba was an Irish missionary to the Scots. Taking twelve monks with him, he established a monastic missions center on the Island of Iona, near the coast of Scotland. Tucker notes, "[The center] provided training for evangelists who were then sent out to preach the gospel, build churches, and establish more monasteries."[16] Columba was interested in making the Bible available. Florence Scott informs us, Columba himself is said to have written out more than three hundred copies of the Vulgate and Psalter.[17] At his death he was copying the Psalms. Columba's influence would extend to other parts of the British Isles, Europe, and Iceland. He was known as "the Apostle of the Western Isles" and "the Moses of Iona."[18]

Augustine of Canterbury (d. 604)

Considered the "Apostle to the English" and not to be confused with the famous Augustine of Hippo (354–430), Augustine of Canterbury was a sixth-century missionary to Britain who served as the first Bishop of Canterbury. Augustine received a charge in 596 by Pope Gregory (c. 540–604) to take a team of monks to evangelize Britain. When he arrived in England, most of his mission work was done among pagans in southern England. His missionary activity saw remarkable fruit, including the conversion of the king and queen of Kent. Once the king and queen were converted, thousands of others joined them in believing the gospel, and Christianity was born in England. Neill notes that ten thousand Saxons were baptized the year the king was converted.[19]

Alopen (c. 635)

Alopen is the first known missionary to China, arriving during the Tang Dynasty. Sent from the Nestorian Church, he exclusively is known from what is called the "Nestorian Monument," which describes his arrival in the Chinese capital of Chang-an. Neill notes, "The monument is universally accepted as genuine. It dates from the year 781."[20] He was received by the emperor and allowed to evangelize. Although his work was

---

15. Tucker, *From Jerusalem to Irian Jaya*, 39.
16. Ibid., 41.
17. Florence R. Scott, "Columba," in *Evangelical Dictionary of World Missions*, eds. A. Scott Moreau, et al. (Grand Rapids: Baker, 2000), 211.
18. Ibid.
19. Neill and Chadwick, *A History of Christian Missions*, 59.
20. Ibid., 82.

met with opposition, he went on to establish the Christian faith, which would survive for more than two centuries.[21] The church would disappear (c. 907), and for the next three hundred years we have no written record of Christianity in China.[22]

Boniface (Winfrid) (c. 675–754)

Born in England, he went to Germany to conduct mission work. Called "the greatest of all missionaries of the Dark Ages," and "the Apostle of Germany," he would serve among the Germanic tribes for forty years.[23] He became famous and advanced the cause of Christianity by chopping down the sacred oak tree at Geismar in Hesse, which was dedicated to the thunder god Thor. Neill notes, "The Germans were convinced that anyone who infringed the sacredness of the sanctuary would be destroyed by the gods; Boniface affirmed that he would be unscathed. The oak was felled; nothing happened. The watchers were at once convinced that Boniface was right, and that the God he proclaimed was really stronger than the gods of their fathers. With the wood of the tree Boniface built a chapel in honour of St. Peter."[24] Thousands were baptized following this event. Boniface also moved against the tide of the times in his recruitment of women in the work of missions. Staunchly devoted to the Roman Church, he clashed with Celtic and French missionaries. In 753, he went to Holland to work among the unevangelized Frisians. There he and fifty assistants were martyred by a company of armed and hostile pagans.[25]

Cyril (c. 827–869) and Methodius (c. 815–885)

Cyril and Methodius were brothers who ministered among Slavs. Moreau, Corwin, and McGee say they are, "among the greatest missionaries," noting they "envisioned the creation of an alphabet for translating the Scriptures and liturgical texts from Greek into Slavonic."[26] Called the "Apostles to the Slavs," they began their work in Moravia in 862. They immediately began the task of translating the Bible into Slavic in 863. Following the death of his brother, Methodius continued working among the Slavs, although it was not without opposition.

---

21. Ibid.
22. Samuel Hugh Moffett, "Alopen," in *Biographical Dictionary of Christian Missions,* ed. Gerald H. Anderson (New York: Macmillan, 1998), 14.
23. Neill and Chadwick, *A History of Christian Missions,* 64.
24. Ibid., 65.
25. Tucker, *From Jerusalem to Irian Jaya,* 48–49.
26. Moreau, Corwin, and McGee, *Introducing World Missions,* 101.

Summary

The growth of the church in the first millennium was a global phenomenon.[27] Faithful men and women[28] from numerous nationalities and ethnicities brought the gospel to the farthest reaches of the earth. Although many more missionaries could be listed, and there are no doubt many that only God knows, these heroes of the faith continue the cloud of witnesses (Heb. 11) that point our eyes to the worthiness of our Christ and the privilege of being used by him.

REFLECTION QUESTIONS

1. Does anything surprise you about the missionaries of the first one thousand years?

2. Why is remembering missionaries of the past important?

3. What are the similarities and differences between missionaries of the past and missionaries today?

4. Are missionaries a special class of Christians? Why or why not?

5. What can we learn from these past missionaries?

---

27. For more on the global spread of Christianity during this time, see Robert Louis Wilken, *The First Thousand Years: A Global History of Christianity* (New Haven, CT: Yale University Press, 2012).

28. Although the majority of well-known missionaries are men, we would be remiss to not acknowledge the efforts that women played in the spread of Christianity. For more on this, see Lynn H. Cohick and Amy Brown Hughes, *Christian Women in the Patristic World: Their Influence, Authority, and Legacy in the Second through Fifth Centuries* (Grand Rapids: Baker Academic, 2017); see also Mary T. Malone, *Women & Christianity*, vol. 1 (Maryknoll, NY: Orbis, 2001).

Who Are the Great Commission Heroes of the Church's Second 1,000 Years?

The second millennium of the church features countless missionaries who embraced the Great Commission call and dedicated their lives to advance the gospel in unreached places all over the world. Many endured hardship, bore much fruit, and left legacies worthy of admiration. The list for this time period is much larger than those considered in question 8, especially following the time of the Reformation and launch of the modern missionary movement. Out of necessity, we can only consider a select number.

Ramon Lull (c. 1232–c. 1316)

Born in 1232 on an island off the coast of Spain, Lull died of wounds from stoning. He grew up in a Christian family, but lived a pagan, hedonistic lifestyle. He was converted and felt a call by God to missionary service in his early thirties. Lull learned Arabic, renounced his worldly possessions, and traveled to North Africa on four separate occasions to preach the gospel to Muslims. Lull saw little fruit in his own missionary activities, but his work demonstrated a shift away from Christian advance by the sword toward Christian advance by preaching and apologetics.

Lull was also one of the first to outline a clear missionary method for reaching the lost. Stephen Neil says of Lull, "Ramón Lull must rank as one of the greatest missionaries in the history of the Church. Others were filled with an equally ardent desire to preach the Gospel to the unbelievers, and if necessary to suffer for it; it was left to Lull to be the first to develop a theory of missions—not merely to wish to preach the Gospel, but to work out in careful detail how it was to be done."[1]

---

1. Stephen Neill and Owen Chadwick, *A History of Christian Missions* (New York: Penguin, 1990), 114–15.

John Eliot (1604–1690)

Born in England and ordained in the Anglican Church, Eliot is often called the "Apostle to the Indians." He zealously embraced the task of reaching Native Americans for Christ. He poured himself into studying their language and preached the gospel to them. Eliot eventually led around 3,600 Native Americans to Christ and began training some of them to serve as ministers.[2] He began translating the Bible into their "Moheecan" language, but King Philip's War in 1675 destroyed much of his work.

Elliot made disciples in the midst of great trials and warfare, and did so faithfully until his death at the age of eighty-five. Ruth Tucker notes, "Although much of Eliot's work was ravaged by the devastation of war, his example as an evangelist and Bible translator paved the way for further missionary efforts among the natives."[3]

Count Nicolaus von Zinzendorf (1700–1760)

Founder and leader of the Moravians, this German Lutheran was only ten when he determined that he would give his life to evangelizing the nations. With five other boys, he founded the "Order of the Grain of Mustard Seed." United by prayer, "They purposed to witness to the power of Jesus Christ, to draw other Christians together in fellowship, to help those who were suffering for their faith, and to carry the gospel of Christ overseas."[4] They were the first student-led missions group about which we know.

In God's providence, they would leave taking the gospel to Greenland, the West Indies, North America, Central America, and Africa. Concerning the Moravian movement, Neil writes, "Under the leadership of Zinzendorf this small Church was seized with a missionary passion which has never left it. The Moravians have tended to go to the most remote, unfavourable, and neglected parts of the surface of the earth. Many of the missionaries have been quite simple people, peasants and artisans; their aim has been to live the Gospel, and so to commend it to those who have never heard it."[5] Tucker calls Zinzendorf "one of the greatest missionary statesman of all times and the individual who did the most to advance the cause of Protestant missions during the course of the eighteenth century. . . . [H]e launched a world-wide missionary movement that set the stage for William Carey and the 'Great Century' of missions that would follow."[6]

2. Ibid., 192.
3. Ruth Tucker, *From Jerusalem to Irian Jaya: A Biographical History of Christian Missions* (Grand Rapids: Zondervan, 2004), 79.
4. David Howard, "Student Power in World Missions," in *Perspectives on the World Christian Movement: A Reader*, eds. Ralph D. Winter and Steven C. Hawthorne, 4th ed. (Pasadena, CA: William Carey Library, 2009), 305.
5. Neill and Chadwick, *A History of Christian Missions*, 202.
6. Tucker, *From Jerusalem to Irian Jaya*, 69–70.

George Liele (1750–1820)

Liele,[7] a black man and former slave, was the first American Baptist missionary, predating William Carey by more than ten years.[8] If Carey is the father of the modern mission movement and Judson is the father of the American missionary movement, perhaps we should acknowledge Liele as "the grandfather"! Born in Virginia, Liele was converted when he was twenty-three years old and pursued a new calling to ministry after gaining his freedom. Liele started the first African Baptist Church in North America as a bivocational pastor. Additionally, he preached to slaves on plantations from Georgia to South Carolina for two years before sailing to Kingston, Jamaica as an indentured servant—Liele had to borrow money so he and his family could make the journey. Liele baptized five hundred persons and established a strong and vibrant church in Kingston. He also faced imprisonment because of his preaching. In 1814, there were approximately eight thousand Baptists in Jamaica. Eighteen years later, in 1832, there were twenty thousand Baptists in Jamaica. Clarence Wagner comments on Liele's influence, saying that the "black Baptist heritage stems from the seeds planted by him in the soils of difficulty in America, Jamaica and Africa."[9]

William Carey (1761–1834)

Carey was born in England and died in India. Prior to serving overseas, he was a poor shoemaker and a pastor of two small congregations. During his pastorate, he became convicted that the Great Commission was the church's primary calling and responsibility. Known as the "Father of the Modern Missions," Carey catalyzed the missionary wave of the nineteenth century. He wrote *An Enquiry into the Obligation of Christians to Use Means for the Conversion of the Heathens* to argue that worldwide missions was a central task of the church. Carey undercut the common belief of the time that the Great Commission only applied to the original apostles. His passion and arguments for the Great Commission also overcame opposition by some of the existing clergy.[10]

The Baptist Missionary Society sent Carey as one of its first missionaries. He sailed for India in 1793 and served there for about forty years. He translated the Bible into many languages, including Bengali and Sanskrit. He established a church in Serampore, and baptized new converts into that existing church. He trained national believers to serve as church planters. Moreover, Carey was also influential in areas of social justice in India, speaking out against infanticide and the burning of widows. Tucker well notes, "Carey, more than

---

7. Also sometimes spelled "Leile."
8. This section borrows heavily from my previous work, Daniel L. Akin, *10 Who Changed the World* (Nashville: B&H, 2012), 85–101.
9. Clarence M. Wagner, *Profiles of Black Georgia Baptists* (Gainesville, GA: Wagner, 1980), 4.
10. John Ryland Sr. responded to Carey saying, "Young man, sit down. When God please to convert the heathen, He will do it without your aid or mine" (Timothy George, *Faithful Witness: The Life & Mission of William Carey* [Birmingham, AL: New Hope, 1991], 53).

any other missionary of this period, stirred the imagination of the Christian world and showed by his own example what could be done in a wide variety of ways to further the cause of world evangelism."[11]

Adoniram Judson (1788–1850) and the Boardmans

Born in 1788 in Massachusetts, Judson and his first wife Ann arrived in Burma in 1813. Their teammates, George and Sarah Boardman, arrived in Burma around 1826. Judson and Ann labored for seven years without seeing anyone come to faith. However, their pioneering work in Burma eventually saw tens of thousands come to faith in Christ. During his time, Judson worked to translate the New Testament into Burmese. However, he was interrupted when war broke out in Burma. Under the suspicion that he was a foreign spy for Great Britain, he spent seventeen months in prison under extremely rough conditions, surviving only by the aid of his wife, who visited daily and brought provisions for him. After his release, Judson once again poured himself into the mission work.

A major breakthrough came when the Boardmans brought a former murderer named Ko Tha Byu, whom Judson led to faith, to help evangelize the Karen people. After hearing the gospel, a movement broke out and thousands of Karens professed faith in Christ. Today some estimate there are more than 600,000 Baptist believers in modern Myanmar. Both Ann Judson and George Broadman would die on the mission field, and Adoniram Judson would eventually marry Sarah. She would also die later after becoming gravely ill. Judson went on to marry Emily Chubbuck. Just four year later he would die from tuberculosis.[12]

Hudson Taylor (1832–1905)

Hudson Taylor was born in Yorkshire, England and died in China. His father was a Methodist preacher who stoked in him a passion for missions. Taylor pioneered missionary efforts to reach the vast interior of China. He formed the China Inland Mission (CIM)—today it is known as OMF International. This new society was distinct in that it was interdenominational, drew missionary recruits from the lower classes, was headquartered in China, required the adoption of Chinese apparel for missionaries, and primarily sought to spread the gospel across the many inland provinces.

Several decades after the inception of the CIM, it had placed more than six hundred missionaries across nearly all of the interior provinces of China.

---

11. Tucker, *From Jerusalem to Irian Jaya*, 122.
12. More on the Judsons can be found in Akin, *10 Who Changed the World*, 13–27; The classic missionary biography on the Judsons remains Courtney Anderson, *To the Golden Shore: The Life of Adoniram Judson* (Valley Forge, PA: Judson, 1987). For more on the legacy and sacrifice of Judson's three wives, see Arabella W. Stuart, *Lives of the Three Mrs. Judsons* (n.c.: ValdeBooks, 2010).

Also, Taylor's emphasis on adopting indigenous dress, his example of mobilizing missionaries to live in unreached places, and his single-minded devotion to evangelizing the lost all left an indelible mark on missions. Concerning Taylor's work, Tucker says, "Few missionaries in the nineteen centuries since the apostle Paul have had a wider vision and have carried out a more systematic plan of evangelizing a broad geographical area than did James Hudson Taylor."[13]

Ludwig Nommensen (1834–1918)

This little-known missionary was born in a Danish-controlled area of Europe that is now part of modern Germany. He served on the island of Sumatra in Indonesia, and Neil calls him, "one of the most powerful missionaries of whom we have record anywhere."[14] His labors on the island of Sumatra in Indonesia sparked a movement that led to more than 100,000 people turning to Christ.

He ministered to the Batak people, whose strong communal nature made it difficult for individuals to turn from their ancestral beliefs and embrace Christianity. However, several of the tribal chiefs professed faith in Christ, and they began leading their own people to Jesus. In 1866, there were only fifty-two known Christians among the Batak people. By 1911, the number of Batak Christians had grown to 103,525.[15] Nommensen labored to furnish the new Batak church with trained, indigenous pastors and leaders. Echoing the words of Neil, Werner Raupp says, "Nommenson may have been one of the most successful missionaries ever to preach the gospel."[16]

Charlotte "Lottie" Moon (1840–1912)

Pioneer missionary work was often not an option for single women due to the mindset of the day. However, women provided vital support on the home front for missionary efforts. And, the obstacles that women had to overcome highlight even more the effort and sacrifice of single women who went overseas.[17] Charlotte (Lottie) Diggs Moon represents this type of sacrifice. Moon was born 1840 in Virginia. Moon served as a missionary for almost forty years, mostly in China. A strong and independent woman, she never married, and would often preach due to the absence of men on the field.

Moon exemplified the fierce determination and faithfulness of the single women who followed God's call to the foreign mission field in the nineteenth

---

13. Tucker, *From Jerusalem to Irian Jaya*, 186, 200–201.
14. Neill and Chadwick, *A History of Christian Missions*, 295.
15. Ibid., 296.
16. John D. Woodbridge, ed., *Ambassadors for Christ: Distinguished Representatives of the Message throughout the World*, illustrated ed. (Chicago: Moody, 1994), 146.
17. For more on the work of women in missionary efforts, see "Single Women: 'Second-Class Citizens'," in Tucker, *From Jerusalem to Irian Jaya*, 231–54.

century. After she encountered restrictions imposed on her as a female by the mission organization, she moved to a rural village where she would have greater opportunity to carry out evangelistic ministry. Moon evangelized and helped establish a local church. In the years that followed, the Chinese pastor of the church led over a thousand people to embrace Christianity. Moon also established a missionary offering that has since channeled billions of dollars toward international mission work. She died in 1912 in Japan on board a ship. She weighed a mere fifty pounds. Of her life and missionary service, fellow missionary T. W. Ayers said, "[Lottie Moon] is one woman who will have her crown covered with stars. She is one of the most unselfish saints God ever made."[18]

Eliza Davis-George (1879–1979)

Before Lottie Moon, "The first single American woman (not widowed) to serve as a foreign missionary was Betsy Stockton, a black woman and former slave who went to Hawaii in 1823."[19] After Moon, the Baptist missionary Eliza Davis-George displayed a similar fervor and sacrifice as she faced the burden of being both black and a woman. George was born into an enslaved family; however, she was able to earn a teacher's certificate and teach for five years. One morning, while praying during a morning devotion, her "heart was suddenly filled with an overwhelming desire to see her brothers and sisters in Africa. . . . As clearly as if she were there, she saw Africans passing before the judgment seat of Christ, weeping and moaning, 'But no one ever told us You died for us.'"[20] So, in 1913, "Mother George" sailed to Liberia, Africa where she worked as a missionary until she was ninety.

While in Africa, she evangelized throughout the area and established an academy for boys.[21] She experienced financial trouble when two separate conventions discontinued support for her, but she nonetheless persisted in the work, bringing many to faith. Before she died, the Eliza Davis-George Baptist Association had established almost thirty churches in Africa.[22] One man said of his encounter with George, "Her ministry was vast. She was almost blind. She walked with a walking stick. She had a large tropical cancer on her leg, and she was still pressing the claims of Christ."[23]

---

18. Lottie Moon, *Send the Light: Lottie Moon's Letters and Other Writings*, ed. Keith Harper (Macon, GA: Mercer University Press, 2002), 447.
19. Tucker, *From Jerusalem to Irian Jaya*, 232. For more on Stockton, see Alice T. Ott, "The 'Peculiar Case' of Betsey Stockton: Gender, Race and the Role of an Assistant Missionary to the Sandwich Islands (1822–1825)," *Studies in World Christianity* 21, no. 1 (2015): 4–19.
20. Lorry Lutz, *When God Says Go: The Amazing Journey of a Slave's Daughter* (Grand Rapids: Discovery House, 2002), 40.
21. Ruth Tucker, *Extraordinary Women of Christian History* (Grand Rapids: Baker, 2016), 137.
22. Ibid., 138.
23. "Eliza Davis George," Malachi Project, n.d., https://www.ihopkc.org/malachiproject/biography/eliza-george.

Jim (1927–1956) and Elizabeth (1926–2015) Elliot

Perhaps no life, short as it was, has done more to inspire missionary service in the last one hundred years than that of Jim Elliot. Elliot was only twenty-nine when he was martyred, along with five male companions, by Auca Indians in Ecuador in 1956. His wife Elizabeth, who continued for a time as a missionary to the tribe who killed her husband, popularized his story in *Shadow of the Almighty* (1989). Jim met Elizabeth at Wheaton College, and together they would go to Ecuador. Jim Elliot's life has inspired many, but perhaps no statement has inspired more men and women to go to the nations than Jim's October 28, 1949 journal entry: "He is no fool who gives what he cannot keep to gain that which he cannot lose."[24]

Summary

Like the first millennium, the second one thousand years of the church brims with men and women that exemplify a life sacrificed for Christ. More could be said about mission heroes like Bill Wallace, John and Betty Stam, James Fraser, Amy Carmichael, Betha Smith, Samuel Zwemer, Robert and Mary Moffat, Amanda Berry Smith, David Brainerd, John Nevius, David Livingstone, John Patton, and many others who served our Lord Jesus faithfully. As the church embarks on a third millennium, may Christ raise more sacrificial and Spirit-empowered missionary heroes from across the globe to proclaim the gospel of Jesus where it has not yet been proclaimed.

REFLECTION QUESTIONS

1. What is it that makes these missionaries Great Commission heroes?

2. How can you know whether God is calling you to become a cross-cultural missionary?

3. What can we learn from these missionaries?

4. Do you think the sacrifices that many of these missionaries endured was worth it? Why?

5. Which missionary do you most identify with? Why?

---

24. Elisabeth Elliot, *Shadow of the Almighty: The Life and Testament of Jim Elliot* (Peabody, MA: Hendrickson, 2008), 108.

How Have Missionary Movements and Conferences Impacted the Great Commission?

At times, the church has forgotten its calling in the Great Commission. At other times, it has pursued the Great Commission through political or other inappropriate means. God, however, will not allow sin to stop or negate his mission. By his grace, there have been movements in history where Christians have awakened to their calling to bring the gospel to all nations. As Christians have pursued this call to cross-cultural missions, they have positively (and sometimes negatively) impacted the Great Commission through their effort. This chapter will review some of the major missionary movements and conferences in Christian history to see how they have impacted the Great Commission. Space constraints prevent discussion on every movement and conference, but the following section will provide a small window into this history.

Missionary Movements

Early Church
    "From its inception, Christianity has been a missionary religion."[1] This missionary religion began to take form when Christ commissioned his apostles to take the gospel "to the ends of the earth" (Acts 1:8). Paul recounts how the gospel spread into all the world (Rom. 1:8; 16:19; Col. 1:23: 1 Thess. 1:8), and tradition claims that the apostles spread the gospel from Spain to India

---

1. John Mark Terry, "The Ante-Nicene Church on Mission," in *Discovering the Mission of God: Best Missional Practices for the 21st Century*, eds. Mike Barnett and Robin Martin (Downers Grove, IL: IVP Academic, 2012), 212.

(see Question 2). The apostles, however, did not work alone. The spread of the early church is indebted to the work of ordinary Christians, the Priscillas and Aquilas of the first and second century. They, with the apostles, show that the Great Commission has always been a global enterprise, that it is the task of the whole church, and that persecution is often a fuel, not a threat, to it (cf. Acts 11:19–26). The early church's work also reveals that the death and resurrection of Jesus is the Great Commission's central message and point of unity (cf. Acts 2; 17:18, 32). In sum, the early church set the standard and goal for the coming centuries of missions.

Monastics

The medieval period often evokes images of a dark age and reclusive men hiding amidst caves in the desert. Yet, Scott Sunquist asserts that the Christian mission in the fourth to fifteenth centuries stayed alive through monastic movements.[2] He writes, "Monasticism began to be transformed from spiritual renewal and a school of personal holiness with limited missional concern to a missional community designed for holiness and service to others."[3] As monasticism spread further East from its origins in Syria and Persia, monks would build monasteries along the main trading route, the Silk Road. These monasteries benefited the Great Commission through their holistic efforts. They often helped equip the church through education in the Scriptures, they functioned as centers of refuge and care for the surrounding areas, and they were missionary posts to evangelize unbelievers and spread the gospel into new places.

An example of the monastic missionaries is the Nestorian monks like Alopen, who brought the gospel to China as early as 635.[4] Similarly, monks like Patrick of Ireland (c. 389–461), Colomba (c. 521–597), Augustine of Canterbury (d. 604), and Boniface (c. 675–754) evangelized vast swaths of Western Europe. What makes these mission efforts so impactful is that they not only spread the gospel from Ireland to China, they also were committed to contextualizing the gospel for the present culture.[5] Unfortunately, many of the same monasteries that positively impacted the Great Commission

---

2. Scott Sunquist, *Understanding Christian Mission: Participation in Suffering and Glory* (Grand Rapids: Baker Academic, 2013), 30.

3. Ibid., 32.

4. We know of Alopen through the Nestorian Stele, a nine-foot monument in Xián, the capital of China during the T'ang dynasty, that describes the story of the Nestorian mission by Alopen. See Timothy C. Tennent, *Invitation to World Missions: A Trinitarian Missiology for the Twenty-First Century* (Grand Rapids: Kregel, 2010), 238; see also John Mark Terry and Robert L. Gallagher, *Encountering the History of Missions: From the Early Church to Today*, Encountering Mission (Grand Rapids: Baker Academic, 2017), 32–37. It should be noted that Nestorianism (wrongly) denies the hypostatic union of Christ, affirming the distinction between his two natures.

5. Tennent, *Invitation*, 239.

later became centers of domination in the Crusades due to corruption by political power and money.[6]

Reformers

After Monasticism, we can see a focus on doctrine within the context of the Great Commission in some of the Protestant Reformers.[7] Many Protestants at the time believed that the apostles completed the Great Commission. However, a movement developed among them that gave theological and doctrinal girth for those obeying the Great Commission. One of the ways this doctrinal foundation arose was through the work of John Calvin (1509–1564). Calvin started the Academy of Geneva to educate students in preaching and theology. Evangelism was important to the school, but Calvin emphasized the importance of "pastor-missionaries" who could train others in Reformed doctrine.[8]

The Academy had a global impact. Students came from across Europe to be trained. Then they returned to their countries to preach and teach. Calvin's focus on building upon evangelism by training ministers to lead, teach, and plant churches positively affected immediate and later Protestant missions. One example of this impact is the training of French immigrants who came to Geneva as refugees before returning to France as pastor-missionaries. After 142 missionaries returned, Protestant churches in France grew from five underground groups to 2,150 churches in seven years.[9] The flourishing of missionaries from Geneva represents the impact that robust doctrine can have in the Great Commission.

Moravians

A key figure in the Moravian movement was Count Nicholas von Zinzendorf (1700–1764), whom J. Herbert Kane calls "the greatest missionary statesmen of the eighteenth century."[10] During persecution, Moravians (then known as Unity of the Brethren) gathered at Zinzendorf's estate in Hernnhut for refuge. While there, a revival among the group caused an explosion outward into worldwide evangelism that eventually saw

---

6. Sunquist, *Understanding Christian Mission*, 36–38.
7. Timothy Tennent writes that "Sixteenth-century Protestantism did not produce any missionaries. It was the advent of Pietism two centuries later that produced the first Protestant missionaries, Bartholomew Ziegen Balg and Henry Plutschau" (*Invitation*, 248). Tennent has a point because the missionary movement in Pietism differed greatly from the movement among the Reformers. However, Calvin believed the gospel should spread across Europe, and he worked to send pastors to the nations. Because of this work, we believe it is proper to call the Reformer's work a missionary movement.
8. Terry and Gallagher, *Encountering*, 130, 137.
9. Ibid., 138.
10. J. Herbert Kane, *Understanding Christian Missions*, 4th ed. (Grand Rapids: Baker, 1974), 173.

hundreds of missionaries across North and South America, the Caribbean, Africa, the Middle East, and India.[11]

In addition to sending a massive missionary force, the Moravians prioritized the power of prayer for world evangelism. Timothy Tennent praises their ability to maintain a prayer vigil for every hour of the day for more than one hundred years, saying, "The entire 'great century' of Protestant missions was birthed out of the fervent prayers of the Moravians at Hernhut."[12] The Moravians were among the first to recognize that all Christians were to be in missionary work,[13] and they emphasised that preaching in missions should focus on the atoning death of Christ.[14] They were also the example that William Carey used to awaken Protestantism to its missionary responsibility and spur the beginning of the Great Century of missions.[15]

The Great Century (1792–1910)

Tennent captures the impact of the modern missionary movement when he says, "Never before had so many Christians moved to so many vast and remote parts of the globe and communicated the gospel across so many cultural boundaries."[16] It is not the numbers alone that made this period so impactful. Rather, it is also the practical developments in missions. Due to William Carey's An Enquiry, missionary societies arose. These societies both launched and served as "the practical engine for missionary mobilization throughout the period. . . . [They] made the 'Great Century' possible."[17] In addition to these new societies, Christians also emphasized indigenous church planting, vernacular Bible translations, faith missions, and female missionaries.[18] These new strategies, resources, and workers impassioned and empowered thousands of hearts for the Great Commission.

During the Great Century, there was also a movement among African Americans to evangelize the States, the Caribbean Islands, and the continent of Africa. During the late eighteenth and early nineteenth century, a "back to Africa" movement led to overseas missionary work among African Americans.[19] Missionaries like George Liele went to Jamaica, while others like Lott Carey served in Liberia.[20] Although they faced intense prejudice

---

11. Tennent, Invitation, 249.
12. Ibid.
13. Ibid., 250.
14. Terry and Gallagher, Encountering, 220.
15. Ibid.
16. Tennent, Invitation, 256–57.
17. Ibid., 263–64.
18. For more on each of these, see ibid., 255–83; Terry and Gallagher, Encountering, 258–73.
19. David Killingray, "The Black Atlantic Missionary Movement and Africa, 1780s–1920s," Journal of Religion in Africa 33, no. 1 (2003): 6.
20. Lott Carey, who is sometimes referred to as the "other Carey" due to the similarity of his last name with William Carey, was born on a slave plantation in Charles City County, VA. After

and racism (e.g., lower pay, less benefits, longer service periods, and shorter furloughs), African American men and women persevered in their calling.[21] They were able to spread the gospel, present a more positive image of Africa, provide valuable information on African society, and contribute to social and political reform.[22]

Another significant movement that began in the Great Century is the Student Volunteer Movement for Foreign Missions (SVM). The SVM began in 1886 at a summer conference in Mount Hermon, Massachusetts when, during the conference, Robert Wilder led fellow students interested in missions to pray and to invite delegates to speak on the topic of missions.[23] By 1896, the SVM had become an official missions society that operated in all major American and Canadian universities, calling thousands of university students to pledge their lives for world missions.[24] When they joined, students would pledge, "It is my purpose, if God permit, to become a foreign missionary."[25] These university students went out with an evangelistic zeal founded upon the deity and authority of Christ and with a sense of the urgency of missions that "was inextricably bound to the last commands of Jesus Christ."[26] By the end of the movement, more than twenty thousand students had joined the SVM, bringing a new wave of young missionaries to the field.

Conferences

The end of the "Great Century" marks the beginning of a new era in missions. From this point forward, world mission conferences and evangelical mission conferences are the prominent features on the landscape of mission

---

purchasing his freedom, Carey began preaching the gospel to his fellow African Americans, and he would eventually travel to Africa with the Baptist Board of Foreign Missions to preach the gospel. Carey served for only eight years in Africa, but his life continued to impact the work being done there (Mark Sidwell, "Lott Carey," in *Profiles of African-American Missionaries*, eds. Robert J. Stevens and Brian Johnson [Pasadena, CA: William Carey Library, 2012], 47–51). For a list of more biographical works and other resources, see Sylvia M. Jacobs, "Black Americans and the Missionary Movement in Africa: A Bibliography," in *Black Americans and the Missionary Movement in Africa: A Bibliography*, ed. Sylvia M. Jacobs (Westport, CT: Praeger, 1982), 229–37.

21. Killingray, "The Black Atlantic Missionary Movement and Africa, 1780s–1920s," 18.
22. Jacobs, "The Impact of Black American Missionaries in Africa," 225.
23. Michael Parker, *The Kingdom of Character: The Student Volunteer Movement for Foreign Missions (1886-1926)* (Lanham, MD: American Society of Missiology and University Press of America, 1998), 1–3. For the role that women played in the SVM, see Thomas Russell, "Can the Story Be Told Without Them? The Role of Women in the Student Volunteer Movement," *Missiology* 17, no. 2 (April 1989): 159–75.
24. Ben Harder, "The Student Volunteer Movement for Foreign Missions and Its Contribution to 20th Century Missions," *Missiology* 8, no. 2 (April 1980): 142.
25. Parker, *The Kingdom of Character*, 14–15.
26. Harder, "The Student Volunteer Movement for Foreign Missions," 142.

thought and effort.[27] Although each differed in design and focus, every world mission conference had seven things in common. Every conference was certain of God's calling to engage in mission, had a desire to pass certainty of this calling to all Christians, hoped for awakening and revival of the church, desired to newly discover God's grace and power for the world, desired to face the challenges of their time, devoted space to Bible study and analysis of world events, and finally, had a willingness to learn.[28]

In 1910, the first world mission conference occurred in Edinburgh, Scotland. The conference brought Christians from mission societies around the world to address current issues and challenges in missions. Prior to this point, Christians had not gathered in such a way to focus on the Great Commission. This global unity began what many call a modern ecumenical movement. Tennent says, "Never again could the Western church think honestly about the Christian movement in isolation from vibrant currents of indigenous Christianity around the world."[29] The conference also chose to gather delegates from mission societies, as opposed to churches, which introduced a new structure that prioritized the efforts of those already engaged in missions.[30]

Edinburgh 1910 committed to deep research and analysis of current missionary issues prior to and following the conference.[31] According to Norman Thomas, the genius of Edinburgh was that it was able to both inspire and educate for missions as well as thoroughly study the vital questions of mission thought and action.[32] What also caused the conference to be so impactful was its creation of the Continuation Committee, which Kane says is the "most significant thing to come out of Edinburgh."[33] The committee committed to ongoing research after the conference, which led to academic studies and journals like the *International Review of Missions*, a journal that continues to produce scholarly work on missions.

After Edinburgh, world mission conferences like Tambaram 1939 underscored the importance of including young churches. Here also are the "first stirrings of the keyword 'indigenization.'"[34] Charles Forman argues that the call to educate indigenous leadership is "the most widely adopted and

---

27. Local mission conferences occurred prior to this point; however, these conferences did not take place on an ecumenical scale like those in Edinburgh and following.
28. Wolfgang Günther, "The History and Significance of World Mission Conferences in the 20th Century," *International Review of Mission* 92, no. 367 (October 2003): 521–23.
29. Tennent, *Invitation*, 283.
30. Ibid., 282.
31. These include issues such as the relationship of missions to non-Christians and the government as well as how to prepare missionaries and create unity around missions.
32. Norman E. Thomas, "World Mission Conferences: What Impact Do They Have?," *International Bulletin of Missionary Research* 20, no. 4 (October 1996): 151.
33. Kane, *Understanding Christian Missions*, 179.
34. Günther, "The History and Significance of World Mission Conferences," 527.

influential new program to emerge from any world mission conference."[35] The conference also had people from countries that were currently at war work together, proving that the Great Commission can and should surmount the political agendas of governments.

Another conference—this time in Willingen, Germany 1952—sought to answer how missions could be justified, asking whether Christians should participate in missions at all. Willingen delegates grounded missions in the Triune God and affirmed Christian participation. Wolfgang Gunther observes that the conference recognized that "mission is not founded on human intention, nor is the church the foundation of mission. Mission comes from God himself."[36] The conclusions at Willingen eventually led to the use of the phrase *missio dei* (Latin: mission of God), a regular and crucial theological concept in missions today.[37]

World mission conferences continued into the twenty-first century. Thomas suggests eight positive impacts came from them: "uniting in prayer, broadening *koinonia*, networking for mission, training for ecumenical leadership, inspiring for world evangelization, transforming mission theology, deepening analysis of mission context, and envisioning new wineskins."[38] However, not every conference positively impacted the Great Commission. After 1961, most world missions conferences focused on inspiration and experience rather than study and consultation of mission issues. This focus disabled attendees from impacting anyone outside of the conference attendees.[39] Also, despite the numerous addresses on Western imperialism and a western-centric theology in missions, significant change did not always occur. Moreover, the conferences did not always retain the evangelistic priority of Edinburgh. Whitby 1947 widened the definition of evangelism beyond what the Scriptures describe, which diminished evangelistic activity.[40] Finally, later conferences let theological disagreements and preferences create disunity and separation over the Great Commission. A disagreement over the balance of evangelism and social action at the Bangkok 1973 conference resulted in the departure of evangelicals from broader ecumenical gatherings.[41]

---

35. Charles W. Forman, "Response to Norman Thomas," *International Bulletin of Missionary Research* 20, no. 4 (October 1996): 156.
36. Günther, "The History and Significance of World Mission Conferences," 529.
37. The conference did not use these exact words, but they cleared the path for others to develop the concept. For an insightful work on this topic, see Christopher J. H. Wright, *The Mission of God: Unlocking the Bible's Grand Narrative* (Downers Grove, IL: IVP Academic, 2006).
38. Thomas, "World Mission Conferences," 149; For a helpful assessment of Thomas's article, see Forman, "Response to Norman Thomas."
39. Thomas, "World Mission Conferences," 148.
40. Terry and Gallagher, *Encountering*, 303.
41. Prior to this separation, the relationship between evangelicals and the ecumenical movement had already waned due to concerns of liberal theology, which caused evangelicals to leave the International Missionary Council (IMC) in 1961 when it joined the World

Despite the separation, the resulting evangelical conferences positively impacted the Great Commission in several ways. Most notable is the Lausanne movement. In particular, the conference in Lausanne, Switzerland 1974 prioritized the importance of evangelism, returning to the precedent of Edinburgh 1910, and resulted in the formation of the Lausanne Committee for World Evangelization. The Lausanne Covenant was also drafted there, providing a theological foundation for much of the succeeding evangelical mission work in the following decades. One of the major contributions of Lausanne was an understanding and prioritization of missions to unreached people groups. This concept fundamentally changed how evangelicals focus their efforts in the Great Commission. Forman places Lausanne 1974 with Edinburgh 1910 as one of the most impactful of all the mission conferences.[42] After Lausanne, subsequent iterations in Manila, Philippines 1989 and Cape Town, South Africa 2010 brought together larger and more diverse gatherings of evangelical Christians.[43] Additionally, the concept of the "10/40 window" was popularized through the spread of Lausanne's influence. This concept identified those areas between ten degrees and forty degrees north in latitude between western Africa and Eastern Asia as the densest concentration of lostness with the fewest missionaries. Although not without fault, the evangelical conferences effectively united around bringing the gospel to all nations and overcoming missiological issues.

Summary

These are not the only missionary movements in Christian history. We could still mention others like the missionary movements by the Jesuits and Methodists and the current global movement. Beyond their impact to the Great Commission, those who remembered the call of our Lord Jesus to make disciples of all nations have made some of the most important contributions in Christian history. Only when the church remembers this call will it continue to positively impact Christ's kingdom. The final marching orders of King Jesus must be obeyed until his return.

Council of Churches (WCC), the major institution of the ecumenical movement. Tennent helpfully clarifies that evangelicals were not unconcerned with social action, but that the difference is one of emphasis. He points out how the Lausanne Covenant addresses social action in article five (*Invitation*, 391–92). Likewise, the World Mission conferences also mention evangelism in their articles, but emphasize social issues.

42. Forman, "Response to Norman Thomas," 156.

43. Many regularly refer to Cape Town 2010 as one of the most representative gatherings of evangelical Christians. See, for example, John W. Kennedy, "Most Diverse Gathering Ever," *Christianity Today*, September 29, 2010, http://www.christianitytoday.com/ct/2010/september/34.66.html. The most ecumenical of the four largest mission conferences in 2010 (Edinburgh, Tokyo, Cape Town, and Boston) was Edinburgh because it also included Catholics and Orthodox Christians. Allen Yeh, *Polycentric Missiology: 21st-Century Mission from Everyone to Everywhere* (Downers Grove, IL: IVP Academic, 2016), 94.

REFLECTION QUESTIONS

1. What were the catalysts that started the various missionary movements?

2. Should Christians expect missionary movements like those in the past to happen today? What can Christians learn from the past to pursue a modern missionary movement?

3. How should we describe attention to the Great Commission during the Reformation?

4. Is it important to have unity in missions among various Christian denominations?

5. How should Christians think and feel about the missionary efforts that had both negative and positive impacts on the Great Commission?

What Are Some Excellent Quotes Regarding the Great Commission? (Part 1)

Great missionary quotes and statements have been used by God to humble his people and move them to action. They serve at least two important services. First, they reveal an internal impulse in the missionaries themselves that give us insight into what gripped their souls and compelled them to go to the nations. Second, they inspire the church of the Lord Jesus to go to and pursue our Lord's final marching orders, because the task is not completed. We go until Christ returns in glory, and only then does our task come to an end.

There is a measure of frustration in tracking down and citing great missions declarations. There are so many to choose from, and so many lack documentation! To remedy this first problem, we have dedicated two chapters. Concerning the latter we have: (1) provided documentation when we can locate it, and (2) included significant statements that seem certain to have come from particular individuals, while noting that the source of the statement is unknown to us.[1] This chapter will include quotations from those born before the twentieth century, and the following chapter will include quotations from those born in the twentieth century.

---

1. Though footnotes are used throughout this book, these two chapters detailing great missions statements use in-text citations in parentheses, prefaced by a brief description of the missionary. We deemed this more helpful. For a 352-page resource on great missionary quotes, see Marvin J. Newell, *Expect Great Things* (Pasadena, CA: William Carey Library, 2013). A number of quotes here can be found in Newell's work; however, many citations do not lead directly to an original, reliable source. Many quotations without a parenthetical reference are from Newell.

John Calvin (1509–1564)

- "Seeing that God has given us such a treasure and so inestimable a thing as His Word, we must employ ourselves as much as we can, that it may be kept safe and sound and not perish. And let every man be sure to lock it up securely in his own heart. But it is not enough to have an eye to his own salvation, but the knowledge of God must shine generally throughout the whole world" (prayer following sermon on 1 Timothy 2:3).

- "The Lord orders the ministers of the gospel to go far out to scatter the teaching of salvation throughout all the regions of the earth" (quoted in Timothy George, *Faithful Witness: The Life and Mission of William Carey* [Downers Grove, IL: IVP, 1992], 93).

Nicolaus von Zinzendorf (1700–1760). Bishop of the Moravian Church. Religious and social reformer, devout Lutheran, and missions mobilizer. Called by some "the real father of missions."

- "I have but one passion: It is [Christ], it is [Christ alone]. The world is the field and the field is the world; and henceforth that country shall be my home where I can be most used in winning souls for Christ."

- "These wounds were meant to purchase me. These drops of blood were shed to obtain me. I am not my own today. I belong to another. I have been bought with a price. And I will live every moment of this day so that the Great Purchaser of my soul will receive the full reward of His suffering" (SermonIndex.net).

- "I am destined to proclaim the message, unmindful of personal consequences to myself" (ibid.).

- "Missions, after all, is simply this: Every heart with Christ is a missionary, every heart without Christ is a mission field" (ibid.).

- "Preach the gospel, die and be forgotten" (ibid.).

David Brainerd (1718–1747). Missionary to the American Indians. Major influence on the modern missionary movement.

- "I exceedingly longed, that God would get to himself a name among the heathen. . . . I cared not where or how I lived, or what hardship I went through, so that I could but gain souls to Christ (David

Brainerd, *Memoirs of Rev. David Brainerd: Missionary to the Indians of North America*, ed. J. M. Sherwood [New York: Funk & Wagnalls, 1884], 111).

- "I declare, now I am dying, I would not have spent my life otherwise for the whole world" (ibid., 312).

- "We should always look upon ourselves as God's servants, placed in God's world to do his work; and accordingly labor faithfully for Him" (ibid., 85).

George Liele (c. 1750–1828). First African American to be ordained, and Baptist missionary to Jamaica. Born a slave and later freed, he precedes William Carey to the mission field by a decade. The "grandfather of modern missions"!

- "I requested of my Lord and Master to give me a work, I did not care how mean it was, only to try and see how good I would do it" (Edward Holmes, Jr., "George Liele: Negro Slavery's Prophet of Deliverance," *Baptist History and Heritage* 1 [August 1965]: 28).

Andrew Fuller (1754–1815). English Baptist pastor who assisted William Carey in launching the modern missions movement.

- "I have found the more I do for Christ, the better it is with me. I never enjoyed so much the pleasures of religion, as I have within the last two years, since we have engaged in the Mission business. Mr. Whitfield [*sic*] used to say, 'the more a man does for God, the more he may'" (quoted in Peter J. Morden, *Offering Christ* [Carlisle, UK, Paternoster, 2003], 167).

William Carey (1761–1834). Father of the modern missionary movement. Served in India from 1793–1834 where he died. He never returned to England once he sailed for India.

- "Expect great things. Attempt great things" (later tradition added "from God" and "for God" to capture the intended meaning; quoted in George, *Faithful Witness*, 32).

- "This commission [Matt. 28:18–20] was as extensive as possible, and laid them under obligation to disperse themselves into every country to the habitable globe, and preach to all the inhabitants, without exception or limitation" (William Carey, *An Enquiry into the Obligations of Christian to Use Means for the Conversion of the Heathens* [Dallas: Criswell Publications, 1988], 4).

- "I question whether all are justified in staying here, while so many are perishing without means of grace in other lands" (ibid., 56).

- "When I am gone, say nothing about Dr. Carey. Speak about Dr. Carey's Savior" (George, *Faithful Witness*, xii).

- "I care not where or how I lived, or what hardships I went through, so that I could but gain souls for Christ. While I was asleep I dreamed of these things, and when I awoke the first thing I thought of was this great work. All my desire was for the conversion of the heathen, and all my hope was in God" (ibid., 45).

Henry Martyn (1781–1812). Missionary to India and Persia for only six years. Died at age thirty-one on the mission field from fever, and probably tuberculosis. Buried in Tocat, Turkey.

- "Now let me burn out for God" (upon arrival to Calcutta in April 1806; "Henry Martyn forsook all for Christ," Christianity.com).

- "The spirit of Christ is the spirit of missions. The nearer we get to Him, the more intensely missionary we become."

- "If [Christ] has work for me to do, I cannot die" (Henry Martyn, *Journal and Letters of the Rev. Henry Martyn*, ed. Samuel Wilberforce [New York: M. W. Dodd, 1851], 460).

- "I see no business in life except the work of Christ" (John Hall, *The Life of Rev. Henry Martyn* [Philadelphia: American Sunday School Union, 1831], 45).

Adoniram Judson (1788–1834). American missionary to Burma (modern Myanmar). Buried two wives and several infant children. Suffered many hardships but bore much fruit in his labors for Christ. Called "the apostle of the love of Christ in Burma."

- "The motto of every missionary, whether preacher, printer or schoolmaster, ought to be 'Devoted for life'" (Courtney Anderson, *To the Golden Shore: The Life of Adoniram Judson* [Boston: Little, Brown and Company, 1956], 409).

- "There is a love that never fails. If I had not felt certain that every additional trial was ordered by infinite love and mercy, I could not have survived my accumulated sufferings" (Eugene Myers Harrison, *Giants of the Missionary Trail: The Life Stories of Eight Men Who Defied Death and Demons* [Chicago: Scripture Press, 1954], available online at http://www.wholesomewords.org/missions/giants/biojudson2.html).

- "How do Christians discharge this trust committed to them? . . . They let three fourths of the world sleep the sleep of death, ignorant of the simple truth that a Savior had died for them. Content if they can be useful in the little circle of their acquaintances, they quietly sit and see whole nations perish for the lack of knowledge" (Anderson, *To The Golden Shore*, 63–64).

- "Endeavor to rejoice in every loss and suffering incurred for Christ's sake and the gospel's, remembering that though, like death, they are not to be willfully incurred, yet, like death, they are great gain" (Edward Judson, *The Life of Adoniram Judson* [New York: Anson D. F. Randolph and Co., 1883], 315).

Harriet Newell (1793–1812). Part of the first group of missionaries to leave America (excluding George Liele) and go overseas. She would die at the age of nineteen, shortly after giving birth to her daughter who died on her fifth day. She never made it to the missions field.

- "O that I had a thousand pious relatives well-calculated for the important station of missionaries . . . . I would say to them, 'Go, and let the destitute millions of Asia and Africa know there is compassion in the hearts of Christians. Tell them of the love of Jesus and the road to bliss on high'" (Harriet Newell, *Delighting in Her Heavenly Bridegroom: The Memoirs of Harriet Newell, Teenage Missionary Wife*, ed. Jennifer Adams [Forest, VA: Corner Pillar Press, 2011], 124).

- "I think I am willing to bear whatever God sees fit to lay upon me. Let my dear Heavenly Father inflict the keenest anguish, I will submit, for He is infinitely excellent and can do nothing wrong" (ibid., 86).

- "Providence now gives me an opportunity to go myself to the heathen. Shall I refuse the offer? Shall I love the glittering toys of this dying world so well, that I cannot relinquish them for God? Forbid it heaven! Yes, I will go. However weak and unqualified I am, there is an all-sufficient Saviour ready to support me. In God alone is my hope. I will trust His promises and consider it one of the highest privileges that could be conferred upon me to be permitted to engage in His glorious service among the wretched inhabitants of India" (ibid., 124).

- "Tell them—*assure* them, that I approve on my dying bed the course I have taken. *I have never repented leaving all for Christ*" (ibid., 209).

Robert Moffat (1795–1883). Scottish missionary to Africa. Father-in-law of David Livingstone.

- "Oh, that I had a thousand lives, and a thousand bodies! All of them should be devoted to no other employment but to preach Christ to these degraded, despised, yet beloved mortals."

David Livingstone (1813–1873). Explorer and medical missionary to southern Africa; later moved throughout the continent and died in Zambia from malaria.

- "If you have men, who will only come if they know there is a good road, I don't want them. I want men who will come if there is no road at all."

- "I place no value on anything I have or may possess except in relation to the kingdom of Christ."

- "If a commission by an earthly king is considered an honor, how can a commission by a Heavenly King be considered a sacrifice?"

- "God had an only Son and he was a missionary. A poor, poor example of him I am. But in this work I now live. And in this work, I wish to die."

- "Shall I tell you what sustained me amidst the toil, the hardship, and loneliness of my exiled life? It was the promise, 'Lo, I am with you always, even unto the end'" (Basil Matthews, *Livingstone the Pathfinder* [Missionary Movement of the United States and Canada, 1912], 136).

John Paton (1824–1907). Scottish missionary to the New Hebrides. Lost his wife and his newborn son in the first months he was there.

- Response to criticism about going to the New Hebrides where cannibals had murdered and eaten two missionaries: "Mr. Dickson, you are advanced now, and your own prospect is soon to be laid in the grave, there to be eaten by worms; I confess to you, that if I can but live and die serving and honoring the Lord Jesus, it makes no difference to me whether I am eaten by Cannibals or by worms; for in the Great Day my resurrection body will arise as fair as yours in the likeness of our risen Redeemer" (David Sills, *The Missionary Call* [Chicago: Moody, 2008], 188).

William Booth (1829–1912). Founder of the Salvation Army and a British Methodist preacher.

- "'Not called!' did you say? 'Not heard the call,' I think you should say. Put your ear down to the Bible, and hear Him bid you go and pull sinners out of the fire of sin. Put your ear down to the burdened, agonized heart of humanity, and listen to its pitiful wail for help. Go stand by the gates of hell, and hear the damned entreat you to go to their father's house and bid their brothers and sisters and servants and masters not to come there. Then look Christ in the face—whose mercy you have professed to obey—and tell Him whether you will join heart and soul and body and circumstances in the march to publish His mercy to the world."

Hudson Taylor (1832–1905). British missionary to China and founder of China Inland Mission. Served fifty-one years in China. A radical faith missionary.

- "The Great Commission is not an option to be considered; it is a command to be obeyed."

- "God's work done in God's way will never lack God's supply."

- "God uses men who are weak and feeble enough to lean on Him."

- "Brother, if you would enter that Province, you must go forward on your knees."

- "It will not do to say that you have no special call to go. . . . [W]ith these facts before you and with the command of the Lord Jesus to go and preach the gospel to every creature, you need rather to ascertain whether you have a special call to stay at home."

- "I have found that there are three stages in every great work of God; first, it is impossible, then it is difficult, then it is done."

- "Would that God would make hell so real to us that we cannot rest; heaven so real that we must have men there; Christ so real that our supreme motive and aim shall be to make the Man of Sorrows the Man of Joy by the conversion to him of many."

- "If I had 1,000 lives, I'd give them all for China."

- "Unless there is the element of extreme risk in our exploits for God, there is no need for faith."

- "It is always helpful to us to fix our attention on the God-ward aspect of Christian work; to realize that the work of God does not mean so much man's work for God, as God's own work through man" (J. Hudson Taylor, *Hudson Taylor* [Minneapolis: Bethany House, 1987], 7–8).

- "The less I spent on myself, the more I gave to others, the fuller of happiness and blessing did my soul become" (Howard Taylor and George Verwer, *Hudson Taylor's Spiritual Secret* [Chicago: Moody, 2009], 27).

- "Is anything of value in Christ's service which costs little?"

- "We did not come to China because missionary work here was either safe or easy, but because He has called us. We did not enter upon our present positions under a guarantee of human protection, but relying on the promise of His presence. The accidents of ease or difficulty, of apparent safety or danger, of man's approval or disapproval, in no wise affect our duty. Should circumstances arise involving us in what may seem special danger, we shall have grace, I trust, to manifest the depth and reality of our confidence in Him, and by faithfulness to our charge to prove that we are followers of the Good Shepherd who did not flee from death itself."

Charles Spurgeon (1834–1892). "The Prince of Preachers." British Baptist and pastor of the Metropolitan Tabernacle in London. Prolific author, evangelical Calvinist, and supporter of missions.

- "Every Christian . . . is either a missionary or an imposter" (C. H. Spurgeon, *The Metropolitan Tabernacle Pulpit*, vol. 54 [Pasadena, TX: Pilgrim Publications, 1978], 476).

- "If God calls you to be a missionary, don't stoop to be a king" (also attributed to Thomas Carlyle, G. K. Chesterton, and Jordan Groom).

- "I remember one who spoke on the missionary question one day saying, 'The great question is not, "Will not the heathen be saved if we do not send them the gospel?" but "Are we saved ourselves if we do not send them the gospel?"'"

- "If there be any one point in which the Christian church ought to keep its fervor at a white heat, it is concerning missions to the heathens. If there be anything about which we cannot tolerate lukewarmness, it is in the matter of sending the gospel to a dying world" (C. H. Spurgeon, *The Metropolitan Tabernacle Pulpit*, vol. 14 [Pasadena, TX: Pilgrim Publications, 1982], 220).

- "You will never make a missionary of the person who does no good at home. . . . He that will not serve the Lord in the Sunday-school at home, will not win children to Christ in China" (C. H. Spurgeon, *The Metropolitan Tabernacle Pulpit*, vol. 34 [Pasadena, TX: Pilgrim Publications, 1974], 522).

- "If I was saved by a simple gospel, then I am bound to preach that same gospel till I die, so that others too may be saved by it. When I cease to preach salvation by faith in Jesus, put me in a lunatic asylum, for you may be sure that my mind is gone" (C. H. Spurgeon, *The Metropolitan Tabernacle Pulpit*, vol. 26 [Pasadena, TX: Pilgrim Publications, 1980], 391).

- "If sinners be damned, at least let them leap to hell over our bodies; and if they will perish, let them perish with our arms about their knees. . . . [L]et no one go there unwarned and unprayed for" (C. H. Spurgeon, *The Metropolitan Tabernacle Pulpit*, vol. 7 [Pasadena, TX: Pilgrim Publications, 1979], 11).

Lottie Moon (1840–1912). Single woman missionary to China. Southern Baptists take an annual missions offering in her name.

- "I do not believe that any trouble comes upon us unless it is needed, and it seems to me that we ought to be just as thankful for sorrow as for joys" (Catherine Allen, *The New Lottie Moon Story*, 2nd ed. [Birmingham, AL: Woman's Missionary Union, 1980], 48).

- "As I wander from village to village, I feel it is no idle fancy that the Master walks beside me, and I hear His voice saying gently; I am with you always, even unto the end" (Keith Harper, *Send the Light: Lottie Moon's Letters and Other Writings* [Macon, GA: Mercer University Press, 2002], 89).

- "Let not the heathen sink down into eternity without one opportunity to hear that blessed Gospel" (ibid., 17).

- "I have a firm conviction that I am immortal till my work is done" (Allen, *The New Lottie Moon Story*, 294).

- "If you really love the work, it will atone for all you give up, and when your work is ended and you go Home, to see the Master's smile and hear his voice of welcome will more than repay your toils amid the heathen" (Harper, *Send the Light*, 216).

Ion (John) Keith-Falconer (1856–1887). Scottish missionary and Arabic scholar. World cycling champion, 1878. Died of malaria at age thirty-two in Yemen, where he was buried.

- "I have but one candle of life to burn, and I would rather burn out in a land filled with darkness than in a land flooded with light."

- "While vast continents are shrouded in darkness the burden of proof lies upon you to show that the circumstances in which God has placed you were meant by God to keep you out of the foreign mission field."

C. T. Studd (1860–1931). Missionary to China, India, Sudan, and the Belgian Congo. Died and buried in the Congo.

- "Some wish to live within the sound of a chapel bell; I want to run a rescue mission within a yard of hell."

- "Had I cared for the comments of people, I should never have been a missionary."

- "If Jesus Christ be God and died for me, then no sacrifice can be too great for me to make for Him."

- "How little chance the Holy Ghost has nowadays. The churches and missionary societies have so bound him in red tape that they practically ask Him to sit in a corner while they do the work themselves."

- "Christ wants not nibblers of the possible, but grabbers of the impossible."

Amy Carmichael (1867–1951). Irish missionary to India for fifty-five years without furlough. Opened an orphanage. Severely injured in a fall and was mostly bedridden for the last two decades of her life. Prolific writer.

- "You can give without loving. But you cannot love without giving."

- "All along, let us remember we are not asked to understand, but simply to obey" (quoted in Elizabeth Elliot, *Keep a Quiet Heart* [Ann Arbor, MI: Vine Books, 1995], 57).

- "Missionary life is simply a chance to die."

Eleanor Chestnut (1868–1905). Medical missionary to China. Martyred on October 28, 1905.

- "Being in doubt, I say Lord, make it plain!
  Which is the true, safe way? Which would be in vain?
  I am not wise to know, Not sure of foot to go,
  My blind eyes cannot see What is so clear to Thee;
  Lord, make it clear to me.
  Being perplexed, I say, Lord make it right!
  Night is as day to Thee, Darkness as light.
  I am afraid to touch Things that involve so much;
  My trembling hand may shake,
  My skill-less hand may break—Thine can make no mistake."

James Fraser (1886–1938). Accomplished concert pianist and honors student in engineering at the University of London. Left those career opportunities to be a missionary to the Lisu peoples in western China. The "prayer missionary."

- "A command has been given: 'Go ye into all the world and preach the Gospel to every creature.' It has not been obeyed. More than half the people in the world have never yet heard the Gospel. What are we to say to this? Surely it concerns us Christians very seriously. For we are the people who are responsible. . . . If our Master returned today to find millions of people un-evangelised, and looked as of course He would look, to us for an explanation, I cannot imagine what explanation we should have to give. . . . Of one thing I am certain—that most of the excuses we are accustomed to make with such good conscience now, we should be wholly ashamed of then" ("Do Not Say," quoted in Eileen Crossman, *Mountain Rain* [Singapore: OMF, 1982], 4).

- "Solid, lasting missionary work is done on our knees" (ibid., 58).

- "We are, as it were, God's agents—used by him to do his work not ours. We do our part, and then can only look to him, with others, for his blessings. . . . I believe it will only be known on the last day how much has been accomplished in missionary work by the prayers of earnest believers at home" (James Fraser, *Prayer of Faith* [Littleton, CO: OMF, 2008], 11).

• "The Gospel of a broken heart begins the ministry of bleeding hearts. As soon as we cease to bleed we cease to bless. We must bleed if we would be ministers of the Saving Blood" (Crossman, *Mountain Rain*, 147).

William Borden (1887–1913). Died at age twenty-five in Egypt on his way to China to share the gospel with Muslims. Yale graduate and heir to a family fortune.

• "No reserves. No retreats. No regrets" (famously said to have been written in his Bible but it has not be discovered by any biographers).

Oswald Smith (1889–1986). Canadian pastor, author, and missions advocate. Preached more than twelve thousand sermons and wrote thirty-five books.

• "We talk of the Second Coming; half the world has never heard of the first."

• "The supreme task of the Church is the evangelization of the world."

• "No one has the right to hear the gospel twice, while there remains someone who has not heard it once."

• "The mission of the church is missions."

• "If God wills the evangelization of the world, and you refuse to support missions, then you are opposed to the will of God."

• "Any church that is not seriously involved in helping fulfill the Great Commission has forfeited its biblical right to exist."

William Cameron Townsend (1896–1982). Founder of Wycliffe Bible Translators and Summer Institute of Linguistics.

• "The greatest missionary is the Bible in the mother tongue. It needs no furlough and is never considered a foreigner."

REFLECTION QUESTIONS

1. Which quote do you find most helpful? Why?

2. What are some of the common themes among each missionary's statements?

3. Do any of these quotes change how you previously thought about missions?

4. Why does the church benefit from knowing the missionary quotes of the past?

5. Do any of these statements challenge you? How so?

What Are Some Excellent Quotes Regarding the Great Commission? (Part 2)

Whereas the previous chapter included quotations from those born before the twentieth century, this chapter includes quotations from those born in the twentieth century.

Eric Liddell (1902–1945). Born to missionary parents in China, he would die as a missionary there as well in a Japanese prison camp. Gold medalist in the 1924 Olympics in Paris. Became famous through the 1982 movie *Chariots of Fire*.

- "I believe it is God's will that the whole world should be without any barriers of race, colour, class, or anything else that breaks the spirit of fellowship" (Eric Liddell, *The Disciplines of the Christian Life* [London: SCPK, 2009], 38).

- "God's will is only revealed to us step by step. He reveals more as we obey what we know. Surrender means we are prepared to follow his will step by step as it is revealed to us, no matter what" (ibid., 77).

- "We are all missionaries. . . . Wherever we go we either bring people nearer to Christ or we repel them from Christ. We are working for the great kingdom of God—the time when all people will turn to Christ as their leader, and will not be afraid to own him as such" (quoted in Dave McCasland, *Eric Liddell: Pure Gold* [Oxford: Lion Hudson, 2012], 163).

- "Jesus came to proclaim the kingdom of God, to offer its blessings to those who would take heed, and to instruct people in its obligations and responsibilities. When he left, he committed to the church the duty of carrying on this work. The church is his voice in the world announcing the good news about God, calling men everywhere to repent and inviting them to enter the kingdom. Every individual in the church shares this responsibility. We are called to witness. Are we doing it?" (Liddell, *Disciplines of the Christian Life*, 125).

John Oswald Sanders (1902–1992). General director of China Inland Mission, later called Overseas Missionary Fellowship (1954–1969). Wrote more than forty books.

- "It is always true in the work of evangelization that the present can never anticipate the future, and the future can never replace the past. What is to be done in soul saving must be done by that generation" (Patrick Cate, *Through God's Eyes* [Pasadena, CA: William Carey Library, 2003], 120).

- "If this indeed is the present condition and future prospect of the heathen—and Scripture seems to offer no alternative—and if the Church of Christ has in her charge the message which alone can transform these tragic 'withouts' into the possession of 'the unsearchable riches of Christ,' then how urgent is the missionary enterprise. And how great the tragedy if we fail to proclaim it" (*What of Those Who Have Never Heard* [Crowborough, East Sussex, UK: Highland Books, 1986], 124).

- "It is conceivable that God might have ordained to preach the gospel directly to man through dreams, visions, and revelations. But as a matter of fact he has not done this, but rather has committed the preaching to man, telling them to go and disciple all nations. The responsibility lies squarely on our shoulders" (Cate, *Through God's Eyes*, 33).

- "Before we can conquer the world, we must first conquer the self" (J. Oswald Sanders, *Spiritual Leadership* [Chicago, IL: Moody, 2007], 52.

- "The frontiers of the kingdom of God were never advanced by men and women of caution" (ibid., 128).

- "Jesus drank a cup of wrath without mercy, that we might drink a cup of mercy without wrath."

- "There is no conceivable situation in which it is not safe to trust God."

- "Ambition that centers on the glory of God and welfare of the church is a mighty force for good." (*Earthen Vessels* [Grand Rapids, MI: Discovery House, 2015], 96).

John (1907–1934) and Betty (1906–1934) Stam. Missionary couple to China, martyred on December 8, 1934 by beheading. Betty was twenty-eight and John was twenty-seven. Left behind a baby daughter, who miraculously survived.

- "The faithfulness of God is the only certain thing in the world today. We need not fear the results of trusting Him" (John) (Mrs. Howard Taylor, *To Die Is Gain: The Triumph of John and Betty Stam* [Denton, TX: Westminster Resources, 2004], 55).

- "Lord, I give up all my own plans and purposes all my own desires and hopes and accept Thy will for my life. I give myself, my life, my all utterly to Thee to be Thine forever. Fill me and seal me with Thy Holy Spirit. Use me as Thou wilt, send me where Thou wilt and work out Thy whole will in my life at any cost now and forever" (Betty) (Carl Stam, "John and Betty Stam," CarlStam.org, http://www.carlstam. org/familyheritage/jbstam.html, accessed May 2, 2017).

- "I would sooner be the most humble Christian, than have all a man could want of earthly things and yet be without Christ. . . . Oh, He is a wonderful Savior and Lord, and a wonderful Master to work for" (John) (Taylor, *To Die Is Gain*, 17).

- "We have been guilty of acting more like the beleaguered garrison of a doomed fortress than like soldiers of our ever-conquering Christ. . . . Shall we beat a retreat, and turn back from our high calling in Christ Jesus; or dare we advance at God's command, in face of the impossible? . . . Let us remind ourselves that the Great Commission was never qualified by clauses calling for advance only if funds were plentiful and no hardship or self-denial involved. On the contrary, we are told to expect tribulation and even persecution, but with it victory in Christ. . . . The Faithfulness of God is the only certain thing in the world today. We need not fear the result of trusting him" (John) (ibid., 54–56).

- "Does it not thrill our hearts to realize that we do not go forward in our own strength? Think of it, God Himself is with us for our Captain! The Lord of hosts is present in person on every field of conflict, to encourage us and fight with us. With such a Leader, who never lost a battle, or deserted a soldier in distress, or failed to get through the needed supplies, who would not accept the challenge to go forward, 'bearing precious seed'?" (John) (ibid.).

Bill Wallace (1908–1951). Medical missionary to China. Martyred.

- "Since my senior year in high school, I have felt God would have me be a medial missionary, and to that end I have been preparing" (Jesse Fletcher, *Bill Wallace of China* [Nashville: B&H, 1996], 17).

- "You may ask why do I want to go to China . . . and there spend my life and energy. You might say there is much to be done in this country and many have said you can do a lot of good here. Why should I go when there are such hardships and inconveniences? The only answer I have is that it is God's plan that I go" (ibid., 7).

- "I want to go to China because someone has prayed . . . and God heard these prayers and has answered as he always does when God's people pray. I would rather be going out as God's missionary this morning than anything else in the world" (ibid.).

J. Herbert Kane (1910–1988). Missionary to China, missions professor at Trinity Evangelical Divinity School (1967–80). Productive and influential missiologist.

- "David Livingstone said, 'God had only one Son and He made that Son a missionary.' Every missionary follows in the steps of the Son of God, who visited this planet two thousand years ago on a mission of redemption. . . . The worldwide mission of the Christian church is rooted in the Incarnation and is part of God's redemptive purpose for the world'" (J. Herbert Kane, *Understanding Christian Missions*, 4th ed. [Grand Rapids: Baker, 1974], 15).

- "God is a missionary God. The Bible is a missionary book. The gospel is a missionary message. The church is a missionary institution. And, when the church ceases to be missionary minded, it has denied its faith and betrayed its trust" (*The Making of a Missionary*, 2nd ed. [Grand Rapids: Baker, 1987], 1).

- "Missionaries have always been apostles of love. Count Zinzendorf, the greatest missionary statesman of the eighteenth century, said: 'I have one passion, it is He and He alone.' Hudson Taylor, who gave fifty years to the service of Christ in China, said: 'If I had a thousand lives, I'd give them all to China.' Alexander Mackay, writing to the Church Missionary Society, said: 'My heart burns for the deliverance of Africa.' Melville Cox died after being in Liberia only four months. His last words were: 'Let a thousand fall before Africa be given up.' Henry Martyn on his arrival in India said, "Now let me burn out for God.' All these men were, like Paul, constrained by the love of Christ (2 Cor. 5:14) and they literally burned themselves out for God and man" (Kane, *Understanding Christian Missions*, 34).

- "The Great Commission then, is based on the supremacy and sovereignty of Jesus Christ, the Son of God, who in the Incarnation became the Son of Man, that through His death and resurrection He might become the Savior and Sovereign of the world. He is not only the Head of the church and the Lord of the harvest; He is also the Lord of history, the King of the nations, and the Arbiter of human destiny. Sooner or later all men must come to terms with Him. He and He alone has the right to demand universal allegiance" (ibid., 123).

Carl F. H. Henry (1913–2003). Theologian and first editor-in-chief of *Christianity Today*. Prolific author, including his magisterial six-volume work *God, Revelation and Authority*.

- "The Gospel is only good news if it gets there in time" (quoted in Gregory Thornbury, *Recovering Classic Evangelicalism: Applying the Wisdom and Vision of Carly F. H. Henry* [Wheaton, IL: Crossway, 2013], 175).

Darlene Diebler Rose (1917–2004). Missionary to Papua New Guinea. Imprisoned in Japanese prison camp for four years during World War II. Husband Russell died during this time. Later remarried and returned to New Guinea to continue missions work.

- "When I took my eyes off the circumstances that were overwhelming me, over which I had no control, and looked up, my Lord was there, standing on the parapet of heaven looking down. Deep in my heart He whispered, 'I'm here. Even when you don't see Me, I'm here. Never for a moment are you out of My sight'" (Darlene Deibler Rose, *Evidence Not Seen* [New York: Harper One, 1988], 46).

- "Lord, I will go anywhere with You, no matter what it cost" (ibid., 46).

- "My ignorance of the future held no cause for anxiety, for my spirit witnessed within me that God was and would be in control" (ibid., 135).

- "So tenderly my Lord wrapped His strong arms of quietness and calm about me. I knew they could lock me in, but they couldn't lock my wonderful Lord out. Jesus was there in the cell with me" (ibid., 126).

John R. W. Stott (1921–2011). Pastor-theologian, worldwide evangelical church leader, and missions advocate.

- "The highest of all missionary motives is neither obedience to the Great Commission (important as that is), nor love for sinners who are alienated and perishing (strong as that incentive is, especially when we contemplate the wrath of God . . .), but rather zeal-burning and passionate zeal for the glory of Jesus Christ. . . . Only one imperialism is Christian, however, and that is concern for His Imperial Majesty Jesus Christ, and for the glory of his empire or kingdom" (John R. W. Stott, *Romans* [Downers Grove, IL: InterVarsity, 1994], 53).

- "The Church is under orders. The risen Lord has commanded it to 'go,' to 'preach' to 'make disciples'; and that is enough. The Church engages in evangelism today, not because it wants to or because it chooses to or because it likes to, but because it has been told to. Evangelistic inactivity is disobedience. It is right, therefore, to go back to the very beginning and re-examine the Church's marching orders" (John R. W. Stott, "The Great Commission," *Christianity Today* [April 26, 1968]: 3).

- "We need to become global Christians with a global vision, for we have a global God" (John R. Stott, "The Living God Is a Missionary God," in *Perspective on the World Christian Movement*, 4th ed., eds. Ralph D. Winter and Steven C. Hawthorne [Pasadena, CA: William Carey Library, 2013], 9).

- "His authority on earth allows us to dare to go to all the nations. His authority in Heaven gives us our only hope of success. And His presence with us leaves us no other choice."

Nate Saint (1923–1956). Martyred missionary to the Auca Indians in Ecuador. Killed with four other missionary companions.

- "People who do not know the Lord ask why in the world we waste our lives as missionaries. They forget that they too are expending their lives and when the bubble has burst they will have nothing of eternal significance to show for the years they have wasted" (Russell T. Hitt,

Jungle Pilot: The Life and Witness of Nate Saint [Grand Rapids, MI: Discovery House, 1959], 158).

- "The way I see it, we ought to be willing to die. In the military, we were taught that to obtain our objectives we had to be willing to be expendable. Missionaries must face that same expendability" (Marvin J. Newell, *Expect Great Things* [Pasadena, CA: Williams Carey Library, 2013], 51).

David Hesselgrave (1924–present). Missionary to Japan for twelve years. Professor emeritus of missions at Trinity Evangelical Divinity School. A major voice in missiological studies.

- "Unfortunately, evangelicals in mission still tend to proceed as though their major problems are methodological. They are not. They are theological. It would be to their everlasting credit if evangelicals would devote themselves, their organizations and their conferences to frequent and thorough studies of the Christian mission as set forth in the biblical text. By its very nature, biblical mission entails clear biblical priorities. When we set agendas in accordance with human preferences and interests, the idea that we either have, or obey, a Great Commission is belied. When we redefine mission so as to encompass anything and everything the church and believers actually do, or even ought to do, we surrender the distinctive priorities of the Christian mission and risk assignment of the word to the terminological dustbin. Rather than setting still newer agendas as some are already doing, evangelicals should first set the boundaries of evangelical mission" (David J. Hesselgrave, "Evangelical Mission in 2001 and Beyond—Who Will Set the Agenda?" pre-publication of TWF article, email attachment, April 5, 2001).

Jim Elliot (1927–1956). Missionary to the Auca Indians in Ecuador. Martyred at age twenty-nine with four missionary companions.

- "Oh that God would make us dangerous" (Elisabeth Elliot, *Shadow of the Almighty: The Life and Testament of Jim Elliot* [San Francisco: Harper and Row, 1989], 79).

- "Surely those who know the great passionate heart of Jehovah must deny their own loves to share in the statement of His. . . . American believers have sold their lives to the service of Mammon, and God has his rightful way of dealing with those who succumb to the spirit of Laodicea" (ibid., 132).

- "Prayed a strange prayer today. I covenanted with my Father that He would do either of two things—either glorify Himself to the utmost in me, or slay me. By His grace I shall not have His second best. For He heard me, I believe, so that now I have nothing to look forward to but a life of sacrificial sonship (that's how thy Savior was glorified, my soul) or heaven soon. Perhaps tomorrow. What a prospect!" (*The Journals of Jim Elliot* [Grand Rapids: Revell, 2002], 97).

- "Father, take my life, yea, my blood if thou wilt, and consume it with Thine enveloping fire. I would not save it, for it is not mine to save. Have it, Lord, have it all. Pour out my life as an oblation for the world. Blood is only of value as it flows before thine altar" (ibid.).

- "Forgive me for being so ordinary while claiming to know so extraordinary a God" (ibid., 98).

- "Remember you are immortal until your work is done. But don't let the sands of time get into the eyes of your vision to reach those who still sit in darkness. They simply must hear" (Elliot, *Shadow of the Almighty*, 81).

- "Missionaries are very human folks, just doing what they are asked. Simply a bunch of nobodies trying to exalt Somebody" (ibid., 46).

- "He is no fool who gives what he cannot keep to gain that which he cannot lose" (*Journals of Jim Elliot*, 174).

David Bosch (1929–1992). Well-known missiologist and theologian. Authored *Transforming Mission: Paradigm Shifts in Theology of Missions.*

- "Mission is . . . seen as a movement from God to the world; the Church is viewed as an instrument for that mission. There is a church because there is mission, not vice versa" (David Bosch, *Transforming Mission: Paradigm Shifts in Theology of Mission* [Maryknoll, NY: Orbis, 1991], 400. This quote is a paraphrase of the words of Anna Marie Aagaard).

- "Mission is, quite simply, the participation of Christians in the liberating mission of Jesus (Hering 1980:78), wagering on a future that verifiable experience seems to belie. It is the good news of God's love, incarnated in the witness of a community, for the sake of the world" (ibid., 532).

- "Mission [is] understood as being derived from the very nature of God. It [is] thus put in the context of the doctrine of the Trinity, not of ecclesiology or soteriology. The classical doctrine of the *missio Dei* as God the Father sending the Son, and God the Father and the Son sending the Spirit [is] expanded to include yet another 'movement': Father, Son, and Holy Spirit sending the church into the world" (ibid., 390).

Adrian Rogers (1931–2005). Pastor of Bellevue Baptist Church (1972–2005) in Memphis, Tennessee, and three-time president of the Southern Baptist Convention.

- "There is no omission in the Great Commission" (Adrian Rogers, *Adrianisms* [New York: Innovo Publishing, 2015], 337).

John Piper (1946–present). Pastor of Bethlehem Baptist Church in Minneapolis, Minnesota from 1980–2013. Leader of Desiring God Ministries (desiringgod.org) and influential missions advocate.

- "I'm convinced that a great missionary movement will begin not with a new focus on the world but with a new vision of God—and then the world" (John Piper, "Hallowed Be Thy Name: In All the Earth," *Desiring God*, November 4, 1984, https://www.desiringgod.org/messages/hallowed-be-thy-name-in-all-the-earth).

- "Missions is not the ultimate goal of the church. Worship is. Missions exists because worship doesn't. Worship is ultimate, not missions, because God is ultimate, not man. When this age is over, and the countless millions of the redeemed fall on their faces before the throne of God, missions will be no more. It is a temporary necessity. But worship abides forever. Worship, therefore, is the fuel and goal of missions. It's the goal of missions because in missions we simply aim to bring the nations into the white-hot enjoyment of God's glory. The goal of missions is the gladness of the peoples in the greatness of God. . . . Missions begins and ends in worship" (John Piper, *Let the Nations Be Glad*, rev. and exp. [Grand Rapids: Baker, 2003], 17).

- "Missions is not a recruitment project for God's labor force. It is a liberation project from the heavy burdens and hard yokes of other gods (Matt. 11:28–30)" (ibid., 36).

- "When missions moves forward by prayer, it magnifies the power of God. When it moves by human management, it magnifies man" (ibid., 67).

- "Persecution can have harmful effects on the church, but prosperity it seems is even more devastating to the mission God calls us to" (ibid., 95).

- "God's will for missions is that every people group be reached with the testimony of Christ and that a people be called out for his name from all the nations" (ibid., 157).

- "If you love the glory of God, you cannot be indifferent to missions. This is the ultimate reason Jesus Christ came into the world" (ibid., 208).

- "If you love what Jesus Christ came to accomplish, you love missions" (ibid.).

- "There is a world of difference in a church 'having' a missionary and a church 'sending' a missionary" (ibid., 237).

- "Not every Christian is called to be a missionary, but every follower of Christ is called to be a world Christian. A world Christian is someone who is so gripped by the glory of God and the glory of his global purpose that he chooses to align himself with God's mission to fill the earth with the knowledge of his glory as the waters cover the sea (Hab. 2:14). Everything a world Christian does is with a view to the hallowing of God's name and the coming of God's kingdom among all the peoples of the earth. The burning prayer of the world Christian is, 'Let the peoples praise you, O God; let all the peoples praise you!' (Ps. 67:3). So whether we are those who send or those who go, let us glory in the supremacy of God in missions, and let us link arms together as we join in the refrain of old, 'Let the nations be glad!'" (ibid., 234; statement is by Tom Steller, Pastor for Leadership Development, Bethlehem Baptist Church).

- "The resurrection of Christ the King is God's open declaration that he lays claim on every person and tribe and tongue and nation" ("Worship the Risen Christ," desiringgod.org, 4/3/83).

Gailyn Van Rheenen (1946–present). Facilitator of church planting and renewal at Mission Alive. Missionary to East Africa for fourteen years. Taught missions and evangelism at Abilene Christian University for seventeen years.

- "Mission is the very lifeblood of the church. As the body cannot survive without blood, so the church cannot survive without mission. Without blood the body dies; without mission the church dies. As the physical body becomes weak without sufficient oxygen-carrying red blood cells, so the church becomes anemic if it does not express its faith. The church . . . establishes its rationale for being—its purpose for existing—while articulating its faith. An unexpressed faith withers. A Christian fellowship without mission loses its vitality. Mission is the force that gives the body of Christ vibrancy, purpose, and direction. When the church neglects its role as God's agent for mission, it is actually neglecting its own lifeblood" (Gailyn Van Rheenen, *Missions: Biblical Foundations and Contemporary Strategies* [Grand Rapids, MI: Zondervan, 2014], 31).

Larry Poston (1952–present). Professor of religion at Nyack College. Served with Greater European Mission.

- "There are no closed countries if you do not expect to come back" (Larry Poston, Evangelical Missiological Society national meeting, Nov. 15, 2000).

Daniel L. Akin (1957–present). President of Southeastern Baptist Theological Seminary (2004–present). Missions advocate. Author of *Ten Who Changed the World* and *I Am Going.*

- "Missions and theology must always go together. You cannot be a great missionary without also being a great theologian. And, you cannot be a great theologian without being a great missionary."

- "The greatest theologian who ever lived was also the greatest missionary who ever lived. His name was Jesus. And, the greatest Christian theologian who ever lived was also the greatest Christian missionary who ever lived. His name was Paul."

- "The person who has Jesus plus nothing actually has everything. And, the person who has everything minus Jesus actually has nothing. This is why we must go, to give them Jesus."

- "The question we should be asking is not, 'Lord, should I go?' The question we should be asking is, 'Lord, why should I stay?'"

David Platt (1978–present). Pastor and former president of the International Mission Board of the Southern Baptist Convention. Author of *Radical* and *Radical Together*, and coauthor (with Francis Chan) of *Follow Me.*

- "Six thousand people groups are unreached for a reason—they're hard to reach. All the easy ones have already been evangelized. These people groups are dangerous to reach. These people groups don't want to be reached, and anyone who tries to reach them with the gospel will most certainly be met with suffering and affliction" (David Platt, "Why the Great Commission Is Great," in *God's Love Compels Us*, eds. D. A. Carson and Kathleen Nielson [Wheaton, IL: Crossway, 2015], 33).

- "A materialistic world will not be won to Christ by a materialistic church."

- "We owe Christ to the world—to the least person and to the greatest person, to the richest person and to the poorest person, to the best person and to the worst person. We are in debt to the nations" (David Platt, *Radical: Taking Your Faith Back from the American Dream* [Colorado Springs: Multnomah, 2010], 74).

- "The beauty of the gospel creates a burden for mission" (David Platt, "Our Obligation to the Unreached Part 2," sermon, Birmingham, AL, August 24, 2014).

- "When will the concept of unreached peoples become intolerable to the church?" (David Platt, *Counter Culture*, rev. ed. [Carol Stream, IL: Tyndale, 2017], 272).

- "Every saved person this side of heaven owes the gospel to every lost person this side of hell" (Platt, *Radical*, 74).

- "God blesses his people with extravagant grace so they might extend his extravagant glory to all peoples on the earth" (ibid., 69).

- "Making disciples by going, baptizing, and teaching people the Word of Christ and then enabling them to do the same thing in other people's lives—this is the plan God has for each of us to impact nations for the glory of Christ" (ibid., 103).

- "Why are so many supposed Christians sitting on the sidelines of the church, maybe even involved in the machinery of the church, but not wholeheartedly, passionately, sacrificially, and joyfully giving their lives to making disciples of all the nations? Could it be because so many people in the church have settled for superficial religion instead of supernatural regeneration?" (David Platt and Francis Chan, *Follow Me* [Carol Stream, IL: Tyndale, 2013], 69).

- "'God loves me' is not the essence of biblical Christianity. . . . 'God loves me,' so that I might make him—his ways, his salvation, his glory, and his greatness—known among all nations. . . . We are not the end of the gospel; God is. . . . We have received salvation so that his name will be proclaimed in all nations. God loves us for his sake in the world. To disconnect God's blessing from God's global purpose is to spiral downward into unbiblical, self-saturated Christianity that missed the point of God's grace" (Platt, *Radical*, 70–71).

- "Today more than a billion people in the world live and die in desperate poverty. They attempt to survive on less than a dollar per day. If I am going to address urgent spiritual need by sharing the gospel of Christ or building up the body of Christ around the world, then I cannot overlook dire physical need in the process" (ibid., 108–9).

- "When God chose to bring salvation to you and me, he did not send gold or silver, cash or check. He sent himself—the Son. If we are going to accomplish the global purpose of God, it will not be primarily through giving our money, as important as that is. It will happen primarily through giving of ourselves" (ibid., 198).

- "Going starts where we live, but it doesn't stop there. . . . If there are a billion people who have never heard the gospel and billions of others who still have not received the gospel, then we have an obligation to go to them. This is not an option. This is a command, not a calling. What is the matter of calling is where we will go and how long we will stay. We will not all go to the same places, and we will not all stay the same length of time. But it is clearly the will of God for us to take the gospel to the nations" (ibid., 200).

Unknown Origin or Source

- "The reason some folks don't believe in missions is that the brand of religion they have isn't worth propagating."

- "Only as the church fulfills her missionary obligation does she justify her existence on earth."

REFLECTION QUESTIONS

1. Which quote do you find most helpful or encouraging? Why?

2. What are some of the common themes among each missionary's statements?

3. Do any of these quotes change how you previously thought about missions?

4. Why does the church benefit from knowing the missionary quotes of the past?

5. Do any of these statements challenge you? How so?

PART 3

Exegetical Questions
about the Great Commission

How Does Matthew 28:16–18 Relate to the Great Commission?

Matthew 28:16–20 represents the climactic conclusion of Matthew's account of Jesus's life and ministry, providing the final charge of what would continually ring in the ears of the disciples. After the resurrection, Mary Magdalene and the other Mary went to the tomb, only to be confronted by an angel who informed them that Jesus was not there but was raised from the dead. The angel further instructed them to tell the disciples what they had witnessed. On their way to convey the good news to the disciples, the women encountered Jesus who instructed them to tell his disciples to go to Galilee. In verse 16 we are then informed that the disciples made it to Galilee to the mountain where Jesus told them to wait. By using repetition, Matthew emphasized the importance of the disciples going to Galilee and the message that Jesus desired to share with them there.

First, the angel relayed the message to the women (v. 7), then Jesus himself reiterated the message to them (v. 10), and finally Matthew reported that the disciples were in Galilee when Jesus met them (v. 16). Thus, it is obvious that something very important was going to take place there. But where exactly does the Great Commission begin? Usually, it is thought to start at verse 19: "Go therefore and make disciples . . . ." But what about verse 18 ("All authority in heaven and on earth has been given to me")? Should this verse be regarded as part of the Great Commission, or merely as a precursor to the commission?

Matthew 28:16–17

Before we formally discuss the role of verse 18, it will be helpful to analyze verses 16–17 to see what function these verses play in Matthew's discourse. We are told in verse 16 that "the eleven disciples went to Galilee, to the mountain to which Jesus had directed them." The mention of only eleven disciples

is a stark reminder of Judas's betrayal. And although their Messiah was crucified, they still obediently followed Jesus's orders and came to Galilee (26:32;
cf. 28:7, 10). Interestingly, Jesus's ministry ended in the same place it began—
Galilee. In Matthew 4:15–16, Matthew quotes Isaiah 9:1–2 which mentions
"Galilee of the Gentiles" (*Galilaia tōn ethnōn*). From the very beginning, Jesus
intended his message to sound forth not only to the people of Israel, but also
to the Gentiles who were living in darkness. Thus, Matthew's identification
of Jesus in Galilee along with the citation of Isaiah 9 foreshadow Jesus's later
commission for his disciples to preach the gospel to "all nations" (*panta ta
ethnē*). As Carson comments, "Matthew is not interested in the mere fact
that some prophecy was fulfilled in Galilee but in this particular prophecy:
from of old the Messiah was promised to 'Galilee of the Gentiles' (*Galilaia tōn
ehtnōn*), a foreshadowing of the commission to 'all nations' (*panta ta ethnē*,
28:19)."[1] Galilee becomes the launching pad for the universal mission given
to the disciples.[2]

We are also specifically told that Jesus directed his disciples to go to a
particular mountain. Although we cannot be certain regarding the precise
mountain (making it unimportant for today's reader), what is noteworthy
is the very mention of a mountain. That is, in Matthew's Gospel, the term
"mountain" is often associated with a place of teaching.[3]

- Seeing the crowds, he went up on the **mountain**, and when he sat
  down, his disciples came to him. And he opened his mouth and
  taught them, saying. . . . (5:1–2)

- And after he had dismissed the crowds, he went up on the **mountain**
  by himself to pray. (14:23)

- Jesus went on from there and walked beside the Sea of Galilee. And
  he went up on the **mountain** and sat down there. (15:29)

- And after six days Jesus took with him Peter and James, and John
  his brother, and led them up a **high mountain** by themselves. And
  he was transfigured before them. . . . And behold, there appeared to
  them Moses and Elijah. (17:1–3)

---

1. D. A. Carson, "Matthew" in EBC, vol. 9, rev. ed. (Grand Rapids: Zondervan, 2010), 145.
2. Grant R. Osborne, *Matthew*, ZECNT (Grand Rapids: Zondervan, 2010), 1077.
3. Bruner writes, "Ever since Sinai, mountains have been the classic loci of the Lord's great
   revelations. Now here in Galilee, the Lord gives the final revelation of his Gospel on a
   mountain" (Fredrick Dale Bruner, *Matthew: A Commentary*, vol. 2 [The Churchbook:
   Matthew 13–28], rev. and exp. [Grand Rapids: Eerdmans, 1990], 806).

- As he sat on the **Mount of Olives,** the disciples came to him privately, saying. . . . And Jesus answered them. . . . (24:3–4)

- And when they had sung a hymn, they went out to the **Mount of Olives.** Then Jesus said to them. . . . (26:30–31)

As seen in the examples above, Jesus is often portrayed as a teacher who is greater than Moses.[4] Consequently, Matthew again reminds the reader that the words that Jesus will soon convey to his disciples are of utmost importance. Just as God gave his commands to his people through Moses on Sinai, so also Jesus commissions his disciples on this mountain.

Verse 17 presents us with two different responses from the disciples when they saw Jesus: worship and doubt: "And when they saw him they worshiped him, but some doubted." There are at least three options as to precise identification of these two groups. (1) Those who worship and those who doubt are two separate groups from within the eleven disciples.[5] In this case, the phrase "but some" (*hoi de*) refers to the portion of the eleven who were not worshiping but instead were experiencing doubt. Although this may seem like the obvious reading based on the English translation, it is not conclusive. There are other cases in which the same phrase (*hoi de*) in Matthew can be (and in some cases *must* be) interpreted inclusively (i.e., the same group of people).[6] (2) Those who worship and those who doubt are the same group.[7] In this case, the verse could be translated "And when they saw him they worshiped him, but they [also] doubted." The verb translated "doubted" (*edistasan*) does not necessarily involve wholesale skepticism but could indicate hesitation.[8] (3)

---

4. See, e.g., R. T. France, *The Gospel of* Matthew, NICNT (Grand Rapids: Eerdmans, 2007), 157; Osborne, *Matthew*, 165, 1077; David L. Turner, *Matthew*, BECNT (Grand Rapids: Baker, 2008), 149, 688.

5. See France, *Matthew*, 1111; K. L. McKay, "The Use of *hoi de* in Matthew 28:17: A Response to K. Grayston," *JSNT* 24 (1985): 71–72; W. D. Davies and D. C. Allison, *Matthew*, ICC (Edinburgh: T&T Clark, 1997), 3:681–82.

6. See Donald A. Hagner, *Matthew 14–28*, WBC 33B (Dallas: Word, 1995), 884.

7. See Andreas J. Köstenberger and Peter T. O'Brien, *Salvation to the Ends of the Earth: A Biblical Theology of Mission* (Downers Grove, IL: InterVarsity, 2001), 102; Osborne, *Matthew*, 1077 (tentatively).

8. Cf. Matthew 14:31, the only other NT usage which occurs in the context of Peter walking on the water with Jesus but is distracted and begins to sink. Jesus's response is "Why did you doubt (*edistasas*)?" Peter was not struggling with intellectual skepticism but with staying focused on Jesus. France states, "It denotes not intellectual doubt so much as practical uncertainty, being in two minds" (France, *Matthew*, NICNT [Grand Rapids: Eerdmans, 2007], 1111) or "the disorientation produced by an unfamiliar and overwhelming situation" (*Matthew: Evangelist and Teacher* [Grand Rapids: Zondervan, 1989], 314 n. 83). Similarly, Hagner writes, "It is natural to believe that the eleven would have been in a state of hesitation and indecision. Too much had happened too fast for them to be able to assimilate it" (*Matthew 14–28*, 885).

Those who worship are the eleven disciples and those who doubt are another group.[9] The problem with this view is that Matthew does not mention another group in the context. Additionally, this position is built on the assumption that the same person cannot worship and doubt simultaneously.

Thus, option (3) is the least likely option. It is likely that either some or all of the disciples doubted (i.e., were hesitant, confused, or indecisive). They recognized Jesus, worshiped him as the risen Savior, but were still uncertain as to the full implications of the resurrection. The fact that some (or all) *worship* Jesus, should not be overlooked.[10] Just as the women who saw the risen Lord bowed in worship (v. 9), so also when the disciples meet him, they worship. According to Jewish theology, only God was to be worshiped. And not only do the disciples worship Jesus, but he receives this worship (cf. Rev. 22:8–9). The clear implication is that Jesus is God—a claim that is consistent with the rest of the New Testament and with Jesus's subsequent words to his disciples.

Matthew 28:18

Although verse 18 does not contain the command to "make disciples," and is therefore sometimes not considered a part of the commission proper, it should not be separated from what follows. Because of the disciples' fears, doubts, or hesitation, Jesus unequivocally declared, "All authority in heaven and on earth has been given to me." Before giving them their marching orders, which undoubtedly would have been overwhelming or perhaps seemed impossible, Jesus reminded them of his universal and sovereign rule over all his creation. Jesus not only has the power to forgive sins (9:6) but earlier he proclaimed, "All things have been handed over to me by my Father" (11:27).[11] Because his Father had given him all things and because of his now exalted status as the resurrected Savior, Jesus affirmed his status as the all-powerful Son of God.[12]

---

9. See Carson, "Matthew," 663–64; Leon Morris, *The Gospel according to Matthew* (Grand Rapids: Eerdmans, 1992), 745. Morris writes, "It can scarcely mean that the hesitators were among the worshipers; Matthew is saying that there were those who worshiped and there were those who hesitated."

10. Bruner explains: "For Matthew, worship means ultimacy (cf. 4:10). Worship means that Jesus really is God with us (1:23); worship means that Jesus is more than a Teacher (or, better, that he is the *supreme* Teacher), because he is the divine Lord and the Son of God" (*Matthew*, 2:808).

11. "Jesus' authority has been emphasized often, see in 4:23–24 and 9:35 (authority to heal all); 7:29 (authority of his words); 8:9 (authority to command); 8:29–32; 12:22; and 17:18 (authority over demons); 9:6, 8 (authority to forgive sins); 10:1 (passing his authority on the disciples); 13:41 (authority to judge); 21:23–27 (authority from God to perform his deeds)" (Osborne, *Matthew*, 1079).

12. Carson reminds us that Jesus possessed "all authority" before his resurrection: "[It is altogether wrong] to claim that the resurrection conferred on Jesus an authority incomparably greater than what he enjoyed before his crucifixion. . . . It is not Jesus' authority per se that

It is possible, if not likely, that Jesus is echoing Daniel 7:14: "And to him was given dominion and glory and a kingdom, that all peoples, nations, and languages should serve him; his dominion is an everlasting dominion, which shall not pass away, and his kingdom one that shall not be destroyed." O'Brien summarizes the significance of Jesus's echo of Daniel 7:14 and his claim to fulfill the role as the "Son of Man": "Jesus is portrayed as the exalted eschatological rule of the world's kingdoms (enthronement); by assuring the disciples of his continuing presence, Jesus affirms his covenant with them (covenant renewal); and, reminiscent of Old Testament commissioning narratives, Jesus issues to his followers his final charge (commissioning)."[13]

The divine passive ("has been given") clearly implies that God the Father is the one who has bestowed all authority to his Son. In answer to the question concerning the source of Jesus's power, Matthew Henry writes, "He did not assume it, or usurp it, but it was *given* him, he was legally entitled to it, and invested in it, by a grant from him who is the Fountain of all being, and consequently of all power."[14] This power and authority of the Son is a result of his exaltation and enthronement as the eschatological ruler and judge. The climax of Jesus's vindication is that he is granted divine authority.

The comprehensive nature of Jesus's authority is indicated by the word "all." And, in case there is any doubt as to what "all" actually includes, Jesus announces that it in fact comprises all the authority "in heaven and on earth." Jesus is claiming that all authority is his. All authority that exists can be found in only two realms: heaven and earth. Thus, he is the possessor of absolute authority over the entire universe. He possesses all authority in heaven, which indicates that he has power and dominion over all the angels (Eph. 1:20–21) and all authority on earth, since no human king or kingdom can thwart his plans. It is this all-encompassing authority which Jesus declares to his disciples that will propel them to take his message to the ends of the earth. Indeed, the all-encompassing nature of Jesus's rule is further affirmed by the subsequent uses of "all" in the Great Commission. Not only is Jesus given "all authority" (v. 18), but his followers are to go and make disciples of "all nations" (v. 19), teaching those new disciples to follow "all" that Jesus commanded them (v. 20) with the promise that Jesus will be with them "always" (literally, "all the days"; v. 20). Thus, "His promotion to universal authority serves as an eschatological marker inaugurating the beginning of his universal mission."[15]

It is important to note that Jesus's declaration regarding his universal authority precedes the command in the subsequent verse. The impetus for the

---

becomes more absolute. Rather, the spheres in which he now exercises absolute authority are enlarged to include all heaven and earth, i.e., the universe" ("Matthew," 665).

13. Köstenberger and O'Brien, *Salvation to the Ends of the Earth*, 102.
14. Matthew Henry, *Matthew Henry's Commentary on the Whole Bible* (Peabody, MA: Hendrickson, 1991), 5:361 (emphasis original).
15. Carson, "Matthew," 665.

disciples' mission and their commitment to see it through is not based on their own efforts but on the unmovable foundation of Jesus's authority. Or as Christopher Wright comments, "The identity and the authority of Jesus of Nazareth, crucified and risen, is the cosmic indicative on which the mission imperative stands authorized."[16]

Summary

At the request of Jesus, the disciples obediently travel to Galilee where they are confronted by the risen Savior. The response of the disciples is mixed: They worship, but at the same time some (or all) of them doubt. Knowing their hearts and minds, Jesus proclaims his universal authority that God the Father granted to his Son. It is the pronouncement of this authority that propels the disciples with confidence and assurance to accomplish the Great Commission.

REFLECTION QUESTIONS

1. Why does Jesus summon his disciples to a mountain?

2. Do you think it is possible to worship Jesus and doubt at the same time? Bruner comments, "*'Doubting worshipers'* are Jesus' material in mission . . . [which indicates] that we must not be perfectionistic about who can be used by Jesus for his missionary purposes."[17] Do you agree with this statement?

3. Can you identify the fourfold use of "all" in Matthew 28:16–20? What is the significance of this usage?

4. Did Jesus have authority before the resurrection? If so, how has his authority changed post-resurrection?

5. What fears do you have in taking the gospel to the nations? Does Jesus's authority give you comfort and encouragement to accomplish his mission?

---

16. Christopher J. H. Wright, *The Mission of God: Unlocking the Bible's Grand Narrative* (Downers Grove, IL: IVP Academic, 2006), 60.
17. Bruner, *Matthew*, 2:811.

What Is the Main Command of the Great Commission?

If Jesus's final words to his disciples in Matthew are accurately given the title "The Great Commission," then it is incumbent upon us to know precisely what is the heart of that commission. Unfortunately, most English Bible versions do not provide us with the clarity that is found in the original Greek. This is not so much a deficiency of the translations that we possess as it is the limitations that are often experienced when translating from one language into another. Consequently, in English it is difficult to accurately detect the central focus of Jesus's command. In Matthew 28:19–20 we read:

> **Go** therefore and **make disciples** of all nations, **baptizing** them in the name of the Father and of the Son and of the Holy Spirit, **teaching** them to observe all that I have commanded you.

Notice that there are four verbs or activities associated with Jesus's statement: (1) going, (2) making disciples, (3) baptizing, and (4) teaching. Which of these verbs is the main command and why?

The Main Command

Although there are two commands (imperatives) and two gerunds (participles) in the English translation above, the Greek has only one main verb, the imperative "make disciples" (*mathēteusate*). The other forms are participles, even though the first participle ("go") is translated as an imperative (see Question 16). Thus, the heart of the Great Commission is to make disciples. The three other verbs (going, baptizing, teaching) are all subordinate to this main idea. In particular, what is stressed is not the idea of "going" but disciple-making. Going is merely a means to an end.

The verb translated "make disciples" in Matthew 28:19 occurs only three other times in the New Testament.

- And he said to them, "Therefore every scribe who **has been trained** (*mathēteutheis*) for the kingdom of heaven is like a master of a house, who brings out of his treasure what is new and what is old." (Matt. 13:52)

- When it was evening, there came a rich man from Arimathea, named Joseph, who also **was a disciple** (*emathēteuthē*) of Jesus. (Matt. 27:57)

- When they had preached the gospel to that city and **had made many disciples** (*mathēteusantes*), they returned to Lystra and to Iconium and to Antioch. (Acts 14:21)

From these examples it is clear that the term conveys the idea of a person submitting to the teaching and training of another.[1] More technically, it means "to be [or cause one to be] a pupil, with the implication of being an adherent of the teacher."[2] Or, "to be a follower or a disciple of someone, in the sense of adhering to the teachings or instructions of a leader and in promoting the cause of such a leader."[3] Elsewhere Jesus said, "Take my yoke upon you, and learn from me, for I am gentle and lowly in heart, and you will find rest for your souls" (Matt. 11:29). Although the term "make disciples" is not used, the concept is certainly present. Jesus invites his followers to take his yoke and learn from him. Discipleship is a commitment to wholeheartedly learn from and follow someone.

Furthermore, according to Acts 14:21, the task of making disciples can be distinguished (though not completely separated) from the task of preaching the gospel or evangelism. Notice that the verb "make disciples" is placed after, and distinguished from, the verb "preach the gospel": "When they had **preached the gospel** (*euangelisamenoi*) to that city and **had made many disciples** (*mathēteusantes*). . . ." The first step involved initial evangelization and the following step involved discipleship. In other words, people who are evangelized and come to faith in Christ then need to be discipled. Thus, the verb *mathēteusate* ("make disciples") emphasizes the long-term commitment and not simply the initial commitment to follow Jesus.

---

1. Schnabel notes, "Disciples are people who hear, understand and practice Jesus' teaching." He continues, "Disciples are people who live in community, in fellowship with teachers and with other followers of Jesus" (Eckhard J. Schnabel, *Early Christian Mission*, vol. 1, *Jesus and the Twelve* [Downers Grove, IL: InterVarsity, 2004], 355).
2. BDAG, 609.
3. Louw and Nida, 470 (§ 36.31).

The Implications of the Command

One of the implications of Jesus's commission is that the task of the church is to make disciples and not merely to produce converts. We are after disciples, not decisions.[4] It is not sufficient to call people to repentance and faith and then leave those who respond positively to find their own way in the Christian life. They must be taught, encouraged, rebuked, helped, and nurtured. If possible, they must be brought into a community of believers where they can grow alongside others. They need to receive input from others and at the same time they need to be able to use their gifts to serve the body of Christ. As Osborne explains,

> It is critical to note that the command is not to evangelize but to perform the broader and deeper task of "discipling" the nations. Many denominations and mission groups misunderstand this and spend all their effort winning new converts rather than anchoring them in the Christian faith (in spite of the many studies that show that too few are truly converted in that initial decision). Jesus mandates that all mission activity emulate his pattern of discipling followers as exemplified in this gospel.[5]

The task before for us involves not only church planting but also church nurturing. Christopher Wright warns of the dangers of doing the former without doing the latter: "The bad result of separating evangelism from discipleship and prioritizing the first is shallowness, immaturity and vulnerability to false teaching, church growth without depth and rapid withering away."[6] Going and evangelizing are important, but they are not the goal. The task the church was called to perform is to make disciples—mature believers who have the desire and ability to make more disciples.

---

4. Michael Green states: "The apostles are not called to evoke decisions but to make disciples. And that is an altogether tougher assignment" (*The Message of Matthew*, The Bible Speaks Today [Leicester: InterVarsity, 2000], 322). Similarly Paul Borthwick comments: "Our goal is not simply to make converts or to solicit evangelistic decisions. Our goal is to work with people (and ourselves!) to produce wholehearted, integrated, obeying-all-things disciples of Jesus" (*Great Commission, Great Compassion* [Downers Grove, IL: InterVarsity, 2015], 35).

5. Grant R. Osborne, *Matthew*, ZECNT (Grand Rapids: Zondervan, 2010), 1080. We should also point out that evangelism is part of making disciples in the sense that new converts should taught and encouraged to tell others about Jesus (evangelism).

6. Christopher J. H. Wright, *The Mission of God's People: A Biblical Theology of the Church's Mission* (Grand Rapids: Zondervan, 2010), 285. We should note that there is also a danger of "going deep" and neglecting evangelism. Evangelism should be part of a new convert's learning to go deep.

Another implication of the Great Commission is that the task of the church involves an ecclesiological dimension. That is, the goal is not just individual converts but converts who gather into communities of disciples. Schnabel argues that "missionary work and church work must not be separated, since the very goal and purpose of missionary work is the creation of a community of disciples."[7] In order for a disciple of Jesus to obey all that Jesus commanded, it is necessary for that disciple to be associated with other fellow disciples. For instance, all of the "one another" commands of Jesus presuppose other disciples since the command involves a mutual or reciprocal relationship. O'Brien brings together the twin concepts of producing (1) disciples who (2) belong to a community of believers: "Proclaiming the gospel meant for Paul not simply an initial preaching or with it the reaping of converts; it included also a whole range of nurture and strengthening activities which led to the firm establishment of congregations."[8]

A final implication is that making disciples requires time and sacrifice. There is obviously a time commitment in going, a commitment that sometimes involves great sacrifice. Leaving the comforts of one's home and culture is often difficult. Learning another language and culture can be time-consuming and frustrating. Additionally, there is the time and effort it takes to teach "them to observe all that I have commanded you" (Matt. 28:20). And yet, there is great joy in serving our risen Savior when we realize the great privilege we have in proclaiming the greatest news ever and instructing others to worship the true and living God.

The Extent of the Command

Astonishingly, Jesus commanded his disciples to make disciples of "all the nations" (*panta ta ethnē*). The scope of disciple-making extends not only to individuals and various people groups, but to all the nations. This indeed is a grand and startling vision. It is no wonder that Jesus preceded this command with a declaration that he has been granted all authority in heaven and on earth. In fact, "therefore" (*oun*) specifically links the commission back to Jesus's sovereignty over all creation. As Osborne declares, "The Risen Lord's universal authority makes possible the universal mission."[9] It is because of his unrivaled authority that he can commission his disciples to embrace a nearly impossible charge.

---

7. Schnabel, *Early Christian Mission*, 356.
8. Peter T. O'Brien, *Gospel and Mission in the Writings of Paul: An Exegetical and Theological Analysis* (Grand Rapids: Baker, 1995), 43.
9. Osborne, *Matthew*, 1079.

Although some interpret "all the nations" to mean every nation except Israel (i.e., "all the Gentiles"),[10] this interpretation is not likely.[11] In Matthew 10:5–6, Jesus commands his disciples, "Go nowhere among the Gentiles (*ethnōn*) and enter no town of the Samaritans, but go rather to the lost sheep of the house of Israel." Because the "Gentiles" are juxtaposed to "the house of Israel," it is possible to argue that a similar use of *ethnos* is used in Matthew 28:19 that would also exclude Israel.[12] With this interpretation, Jesus instructs his disciples to turn from the early mission to Jews to focus exclusively on reaching the Gentiles.

The above interpretation, however, should be rejected for the following reasons. First, in at least three other texts, Matthew uses the term *ethnos* to denote all nations without any restrictions.[13]

- For **nation** will rise **against nation** (*ethnos epi ethnos*), and kingdom against kingdom, and there will be famines and earthquakes in various places. (Matt. 24:7)

- And this gospel of the kingdom will be proclaimed throughout the whole world as a testimony **to all nations** (*pasin tois ethnesin*), and then the end will come. (Matt. 24:14)

- Before him will be gathered **all the nations** (*panta ta ethnē*), and he will separate people one from another as a shepherd separates the sheep from the goats. (Matt. 25:32)[14]

Each of these texts is uttered in the context of the last judgment with "nations" clearly used inclusively of every nation, including Israel. Second, the all-inclusive nature of nations fits the all-inclusive nature of Jesus's authority mentioned in the previous verse. As Schnabel explains, "It is impossible to relate the authority of the risen Lord to the entire earth while excluding Israel

---

10. See D. Hare and D. Harrington, "Make Disciples of All the Nations," *CBQ* 37 (1975): 359–69. They maintain that Matthew's use of *ethnē* always refers to Gentiles (exclusive of Jews).
11. W. D. Davies and D. C. Allison, *Matthew*, ICC (Edinburgh: T&T Clark, 1997), 3:684; Donald A. Hagner, *Matthew 14–28*, WBC 33B (Dallas: Word, 1995), 887; and D. A. Carson, "Matthew," in EBC 9, rev. ed. (Grand Rapids: Zondervan, 2010), 666–67.
12. Though Keener rightly notes, "Those who prefer to translate 'Gentiles,' however . . ., are correct that Gentile people are where the emphasis lies, because this statement extends the commission in chapter 10, which was explicitly limited to Jews" (Craig Keener, *The Gospel of Matthew: A Socio-Rhetorical Commentary* [Grand Rapids: Eerdmans, 2009], 719).
13. See J. P. Meier, "Nations or Gentiles in Matthew 28:19?" *CBQ* 39 (1977): 94–102; R. T. France, *Matthew: Evangelist and Teacher* (Grand Rapids: Zondervan, 1989), 235–37.
14. See also Matthew 20:25 and 24:9 for the same (possible) meaning. On the contrary, the following verses use *ethnē* as a reference to non-Jews: Matthew 4:15; 6:32; 10:5, 18; 12:18; 20:19.

from the mission of his disciples."[15] Third, Matthew 10:23 makes little sense if Jesus did not envision a continued mission to Israel: "When they persecute you in one town, flee to the next, for truly, I say to you, you will not have gone through all the towns of Israel before the Son of Man comes." Fourth, because earlier Jesus specified the restrictive nature of his command to his disciples (i.e., not to go to the Gentiles but only to the lost sheep of Israel; Matt. 10:5–6), we would expect a similar qualification here not to go to the Jews. Keener adds that "the Gentile mission extends the Jewish mission—not replaces it; Jesus nowhere revokes the mission to Israel (10:6), but merely adds a new mission revoking a previous prohibition (10:5)."[16] Finally, if Jesus excluded the Jewish people from his command, the apostles and the early church failed to comprehend Jesus's intention since they did in fact continue to preach the good news among the Jews (cf. Rom. 1:16; 10:18; 1 Cor. 9:20). Even though Paul understood his mission as primarily reaching Gentiles, he indicated that the gospel was for the Jew first, which he demonstrated by visiting synagogues of the cities he visited (Rom. 1:16). Thus, there is no clear indication in Matthew (or elsewhere) that the mission to Israel would come to an end.[17]

Summary

At the very heart of the Great Commission is the imperative (command) "make disciples." Although the other verbs (going, baptizing, and teaching) are important, they are secondary in the sense that they are what is needed to be done in order to achieve the goal of making disciples. Several implications of this focus on disciple-making are (1) we are after disciples not merely converts; (2) we are to gather communities of disciples not merely isolated individuals; and (3) we must be willing to take the time and effort needed to produces mature disciples who can then multiply themselves by training new disciples. Finally, the command to make disciples extends to "all nations" (*panta ta ethnē*) or people groups (see the next question), which includes the Jewish people.

---

15. Schnabel, *Early Christian Mission*, 361. Davies and Allison argue, "Inclusion of the Jews harmonizes with the universalism of the rest of the passage" (*Matthew*, 3:684). Cf. also Luke 24:47 ("and that repentance and forgiveness of sins should be proclaimed in his name to all nations [*ta ethnē*], beginning from Jerusalem"), which includes the Jewish people.
16. Keener, *Matthew*, 719.
17. Davies and Allison conclude: "It is historically implausible that, in Matthew's time and place, there were no longer Christian missionaries to Jews" (*Matthew*, 3:684). Schnabel summarizes: "Jesus's commission to go to 'all nations' rescinds the restriction of missionary work to Israel (Mt 10:5) without excluding Israel (i.e., the Jewish people) from the mission of the disciples" (*Early Christian Mission*, 363).

REFLECTION QUESTIONS

1. Did you know that the main command in the Great Commission is to "make disciples"? If not, what was your understanding?

2. How do the other verbs (going, baptizing, and teaching) relate to the concept of making disciples?

3. Of the three implications mentioned related to the concept of disciple-making, which do you think is the most misunderstood by the church today?

4. How do Jesus's words in Matthew 28:18 relate to the need to make disciples of "all nations"?

5. Do you think Jesus's command to make disciples of all nations incudes the Jewish people? Why is that important?

What Is the Meaning of "All Nations"?

When we read the Bible and seek to understand its meaning, we always have to be cautious that we don't import a later concept into the meaning of the text. For example, when the Gospel of Matthew uses the term "church" (*ekklēsia*; 16:18; 18:17), it is tempting to read our understanding of church into the text. But such anachronistic interpretation must be avoided. We must always first ask the question, "What did the term mean at the time it was used?" Interestingly, when the now-famous Bible translator William Tyndale translated the term *ekklēsia*, he used the term "congregation." Unfortunately, the KJV and subsequent English versions opted not to adapt Tyndale's word choice and instead used "church." The reason that "congregation" (or "assembly") is a better choice is that it conveys the idea of people instead of a building (you can say, "Let's go to church" but you can't say, "Let's go to congregation"). So, when we read the term "church" in the New Testament, we must be careful to think of people and not a location.

Similarly, how do we understand the word "nation"? Because Matthew did not write his Gospel in English we must ask ourselves, "What did the word *ethnē* mean in the first century? This question is important if we are to understand and obey the Great Commission.

The Meaning of "All Nations" (*panta ta ethnē*)

Most modern New Testament scholars and missiologists agree that the term *ethnē* does not refer to modern nation-states in the way the term "nation" connotes today. That is, there is basic agreement that *ethnē* is better understood as referring to various "people groups." What exactly is a people group? Here is the well-known definition that resulted from the Lausanne Strategy Working Group (1982):

> [A people group] is a significantly large grouping of individuals who perceive themselves to have a common affinity

for one another because of their shared language, religion, ethnicity, residence, occupation, class or caste, situation, etc. or combinations of these. . . . [It is] the largest group within which the Gospel can spread as a church planting movement without encountering barriers of understanding or acceptance.[1]

Essentially, a "people group" is a group with its own identity in regards to language, location, religion, values, and worldview. John Piper has noted that the singular *ethnos* never refers to an individual but always refers to a "nation" or "people group."[2] The plural form, however, can refer to (1) Gentile individuals[3] or (2) or ethnic groups;[4] the context must decide the precise meaning. The term "all nations" (*panta ta ethnē*) occurs eighteen times, only one of which refers to Gentile individuals (Matt. 25:32). Here are several examples where the term clearly refers to people groups:[5]

- Is it not written, "My house shall be called a house of prayer for **all the nations** (*pasin tois ethnesin*)"? But you have made it a den of robbers. (Mark 11:17)

- They will fall by the edge of the sword and be led captive among **all nations** (*ta ethnē panta*), and Jerusalem will be trampled underfoot by the Gentiles, until the times of the Gentiles are fulfilled. (Luke 21:24)

- Now there were dwelling in Jerusalem Jews, devout men from **every nation** (*pantos ethnous*) under heaven. (Acts 2:5)

- . . . but in **every nation** (*panti ethnei*) anyone who fears him and does what is right is acceptable to him. (Acts 10:35)

1. Ralph Winter, "Unreached Peoples: Recent Developments in the Concept," *Mission Frontiers* (August/September, 1989): 12. See also C. Peter Wagner and Edward R. Dayton, "The People-Group Approach to World Evangelization," in *Unreached Peoples '81* (Elgin, IL: Cook, 1981), 23.
2. John Piper, *Let the Nations Be Glad*, 3rd ed. (Grand Rapids: Baker, 2110), 183–84. See Matthew 21:43; 24:7; Mark 13:8; Luke 7:5; 21:10; 23:2; Acts 2:5; 7:7; 8:9; 10:22, 35; 17:26; 24:2, 10, 17; 26:4; 28:19; John 11:48, 50–52; 18:35; 1 Peter 2:9; Revelation 5:9; 13:7; 14:6.
3. See Matthew 6:32; 10:5; 12:21; 20:25; Luke 2:32; 21:24; Acts 9:15; 13:46, 47; 15:7, 14, 23; 18:6; 21:11; 22:21; Romans 3:39; 9:24; 15:9–12, 16; 16:26; Galatians 2:9; 3:14; 2 Timothy 4:17; Revelation 14:18; 16:19; 19:15–20:8; 21:24.
4. See, e.g., Acts 13:19; Romans 4:17–18; Revelation 11:9.
5. Matthew 24:9, 14; 25:32; Mark 11:17; 13:10; Luke 12:29–30; 21:24; 24:47; Acts 2:5; 10:35; 14:16; 15:16–17; 17:26; Romans 1:5; Galatians 3:8; 2 Timothy 4:17; Revelation 12:5; 15:4.

- . . . that the remnant of mankind may seek the Lord, and **all the Gentiles** (*panta ta ethnē*) who are called by my name, says the Lord, who makes these things. (Acts 15:17)

- And he made from one man **every nation** (*pan ethnos*) of mankind to live on all the face of the earth, having determined allotted periods and the boundaries of their dwelling place. (Acts 17:26)

- And the Scripture, foreseeing that God would justify the Gentiles by faith, preached the gospel beforehand to Abraham, saying, "In you shall **all the nations** (*panta ta ethnē*) be blessed." (Gal. 3:8)

- She gave birth to a male child, one who is to rule **all the nations** (*panta ta ethnē*) with a rod of iron, but her child was caught up to God and to his throne. (Rev. 12:5)

- Who will not fear, O Lord, and glorify your name? For you alone are holy. **All nations** (*panta ta ethnē*) will come and worship you, for your righteous acts have been revealed. (Rev. 15:4)

After examining the evidence Piper concludes, "Therefore, in all likelihood, Jesus did not send his apostles out with a general mission to win as many individuals as they could but rather to reach all the peoples of the world and thus to gather the 'sons of God' which are scattered (John 11:52) and to call the 'ransomed from every tongue and tribe and people and nation' (Rev. 5:9), until redeemed persons from 'all the peoples praise him' (Rom. 15:11)."[6]

The Number of "All Nations" (*panta ta ethnē*)

Ralph Winter maintained there are about 24,000 people groups in the world.[7] The first edition of the *World Christian Encyclopedia* edited by David Barrett mentions 8,990 people groups but the second edition refers to 12,600.[8] Patrick Johnstone states, "All distinct ethno-linguistic groups with a sufficient distinctiveness within each nation for which church planting may be necessary [are] 12,017.[9] In specifying the number of unreached people groups, C. Peter

---

6. Piper, *Let the Nations Be Glad*, 210. This of course does not negate God's desire to see all people saved (1 Tim. 2:4; 2 Peter 3:9).
7. Ralph D. Winter, "Unreached Peoples: What, Where, and Why?" in Patrick Sookhdeo, ed., *New Frontiers in Mission* (Grand Rapids: Baker, 1987), 153.
8. David B. Barrett, ed., *World Christian Encyclopedia* (Nairobi: Oxford University Press, 1981), 110; and David B. Barrett, George T. Kurian, and Todd M. Johnson, eds., *World Christian Encyclopedia*, vol. 2 (New York: Oxford University Press, 2001), 16.
9. Patrick Johnstone, *Operation World* (Bromley, UK: STL Books and WEC Publications, 1987), 32.

Wagner writes, "For years many of us used the figure 16,750. . . . Some say the number may turn out to be 100,000 or more."[10]

How do we know our definition is correct?[11] In Romans 15:19 Paul writes, "from Jerusalem and all the way around to Illyricum I have fulfilled the ministry of the gospel of Christ." Surely Paul did not reach each and every people group according to our modern definitions. Piper concludes, "God probably did not intend for us to use a precise definition of people groups. That way we can never stop doing pioneer missionary work just because we conclude that all the groups with our definition have been reached."[12] And if God did intend a precise definition, why did he not provide us with one? Thus, it seems implausible that the completion of the Great Commission will occur when a single person from a single ethnolinguistic group responds to the gospel message. Yet, many treat the task in such mathematically measurable ways. Measuring faithfulness and engagement is important. Trying to assess precisely when the Great Commission may be fulfilled in relation to people group engagement has perhaps led to well-intended disparate answers to a question the Bible never asks of us.

The Significance of "All Nations" (*panta ta ethnē*)

If the completion of the Great Commission isn't tied directly to a determined number of people groups being engaged with the gospel, then why does the Bible speak of engagement and worshipers being gathered from "all nations" (*panta ta ethnē*)? One primary reason for taking the gospel to all nations seems apparent in the Scriptures—that it demonstrates God's supremacy over all of creation.

In the very first chapter of the Bible God is said to have created everything that exists, including man and woman being made in his own image (Gen. 1:25–26). Having authority over all creation, God stated his chief mission for his image bearers—to be fruitful and multiply to fill the earth, and to exercise dominion through viceregency (Gen. 1:28). Following man's rebellion, that fruitfulness began. However, instead of filling the earth with worshipers who were rightly related to God, the earth has become filled with the misdirected worship of image bearers whose relationship with God has been fractured through sin. The nations don't seem to emerge until the postdiluvian context. Humanity's rebellion comes to a head through their refusal to fill the earth

---

10. C. Peter Wagner, "On the Cutting Edge of Mission Strategy," in *Perspectives on the World Christian Movement*, 3rd ed., eds. Ralph D. Winter and Steven C. Hawthorne (Pasadena, CA: William Carey Library, 1999), 535.
11. Hoekema comments, "Into how many languages and dialects must the Bible, or parts of the Bible, be translated before that goal will have been reached? How many members of a nation must be evangelized before one can say that the gospel is a testimony to that nation? What, in fact, constitutes 'a nation'?" (139).
12. Piper, *Let the Nations Be Glad*, 212.

and subdue it as they were originally created to do. So in Genesis 11 God exercises his supremacy over them, confounding their language and spreading them throughout the earth. And thus, ethnolinguistic diversity is introduced in its seminal form.[13]

The ensuing diversity of nations, regardless of how we choose to define them, will not prove to be an insurmountable task for God. Our God is not a local deity with limited power like the gods he overcame in the Old Testament. What God created through the scattering of Genesis 11, he will gather in Revelation 5. Why? Because God is supreme over all creation.[14]

In addition to displaying God's supremacy over all creation, making disciples of "all nations" demonstrates God's glory.[15] God created humanity for a relationship with himself and that relationship is characterized by what we call worship. Yet again, our rebellion didn't change that fact that we were made to worship. Rather, sin misdirected our worship away from God, who alone is worthy. Thus, if God is to be worshipped by all people, then his gospel must be taken to all people because it alone transforms misdirected idolaters into awestruck worshipers. God's gathering of awestruck worshipers described in Revelation 5:9 highlights his supreme worth by noting that they come "from every tribe and language and people and nation." Gathering worshipers from one or some kinds of people would ascribe glory to God. Gathering worshipers from some of all kinds of people ascribes supreme, universal glory to him. He is worthy of the worship of all nations.

Summary

Though missiologists may not agree on how exactly to define mission strategy and number *ethnē*, there is agreement among evangelicals that God's mission is to gather worshipers from all of them. Various missions campaigns have arisen in recent times making too tight of a connection between the way we define and number the *ethnē* and missions strategy. While it is important to assess progress in the completion of the Great Commission, we mustn't import

---

13. The "Table of Nations" in Genesis 10 summarizes the outcome of God's intervention in Genesis 11.
14. See Piper, *Let the Nations Be Glad*, 221–24.
15. There is also debate as to the implications of reaching "nations" (i.e., "ethnic groups") with the message of the gospel. Some maintain that because the mission is to reach "ethnic groups," we must seek to preserve the ethnic identity of each individual group. Consequently, the most appropriate method of reaching such groups is via group conversion. Such an interpretation of Jesus's commission, however, goes beyond the evidence. The phrase after "make disciples of all nations" is "baptizing *them* (*autous*)." The use of the masculine pronoun (*autous*) indicates that the antecedent is not "nations" (we would expect the neuter form, *auta*) but is individual converts. So, although Jesus commands his disciples to reach "all the nations" (Jews and non-Jews), the pronoun "them" highlights the need for individuals to repent and believe in Christ (see Craig L. Blomberg, *Matthew*, NAC 22 [Nashville: B&H, 1992], 432).

extrabiblical understanding that may then give us an inaccurate measurement. People-group lists like those from the Joshua Project or the IMB's Global Research Department can be helpful when determining priorities in funding and personnel. Ultimately, however, if those lists somehow transform the task of missions into a formula to reach "all nations," we may find ourselves solving the equation only to learn that we were using the wrong formula.

REFLECTION QUESTIONS

1. How has your own interpretation of "all nations" affected your involvement in Great Commission ministry?

2. What problems might arise when mission organizations connect their strategy too rigidly to a single definition of "nation"?

3. What are some ways that the Bible assesses progress in the task of missions?

4. How might we utilize the various people group tools to guide our missions strategy in a healthy way?

5. How is the supremacy of God displayed by him receiving worship from "all nations"?

Should the Verb "Go/Going" Be Understood as a Command?

A s was discussed earlier (Question 14), the main command of the Great Commission is to "make disciples." How, then, should we understand the participle *poreuthentes*? Is it best translated "as you go" or as a command, "Go!"?[1] In other words, are we to understand the verse as stating that our disposition as we go about our daily routine should be to make disciples? Or, is this verse stating imperatively that believers are commanded to leave their homes and go to a foreign land for the express purpose of making disciples? The focus of this chapter will be on answering this important question.

The Evidence for "As You Go"

Some maintain that the aorist participle *poreuthentes* should be viewed as a temporal (adverbial) participle and should therefore be translated "as you go." Grammatically, this is certainly possible and should not be dismissed too quickly. Temporal participles are very common and are sometimes viewed as the default category if no other category fits. In his grammar, Wallace notes that when an aorist adverbial participle (e.g., *poreuthentes*) is related to an aorist main verb (e.g., *mathēteusate*), the participle will often communicate contemporaneous time to the action of the main verb.[2] Therefore, if *poreuthentes* is interpreted as a temporal participle, it could be rightly translated "when you go" or "as you go."

---

1. For a more exhaustive treatment of this question, see Benjamin L. Merkle, "Should the Great Commission Be Translated 'Go' or 'As You Go'?," *STR* 9, no. 2 (2018): 21–32.
2. Daniel B. Wallace, *Greek Grammar beyond the Basic: An Exegetical Syntax of the New Testament* (Grand Rapids: Eerdmans, 1996), 624. It should be noted that Wallace does not think that in Matthew 28:19 *poreuthentes* is a temporal participle.

What would be the implications of such an interpretation? After noting that the main command is to make disciples, one author notes, "Presupposed by this basic command is the fact that Christian believers are already to be deployed on the scene of their missionary labors."[3] In other words, there is no commission to go, only a commission to make disciples. The same author continues by claiming that "the point of the great commission is that wherever they are they are to be carrying it out—making disciples. . . . Make disciples in the particular nation among whom you dwell. You need not go somewhere else to operate on the great commission program!"[4] His paraphrase of the verse also clarifies his position: "As ye go, therefore, and wherever you may be . . . make disciples of all nations."[5]

More recently, Marshall and Payne have made a similar argument. After affirming that "we should be sending out missionaries to the ends of the earth and seeking to reach the whole world for Christ," they raise the question: "But is that really what Matthew 28 is calling upon us to do?"[6] Here is (at least in part) their answer:

> Traditionally (or at least for Carey), this has been read as a missionary mandate, a charter for sending out gospel workers to the world. . . . But the emphasis of the sentence is not on "going." In fact, the participle is probably better translated "when you go" or "as you go." The commission is not fundamentally about mission out there somewhere else in another country. *It's a commission that makes disciple-making the normal agenda and priority of every church and every Christian disciple.*[7]

In addition, although it stands alone as one among dozens of well-known and trusted English versions, the International Standard Version (ISV) translates the participle temporally: "Therefore, *as you go*, disciple people in all nations, baptizing them in the name of the Father, and the Son, and the Holy Spirit."[8]

Studying the Greek of Matthew 28:19 does not easily or quickly solve the issue as to how this verse should be understood. Some argue that the phrase is best understood as a temporal adverbial participle, and therefore communicates the idea of "as you go."

---

3. Robert D. Culver, "What Is the Church's Commission? Some Exegetical Issues In Matthew 28:16–20," *BSac* 125 (1968): 245.
4. Ibid., 252.
5. Ibid., 253.
6. Colin Marshall and Tony Payne, *The Trellis and The Vine* (Kingsford, Australia: Matthias Media, 2013), 11.
7. Ibid., 13.
8. Emphasis added. See also God's Word translation: "So wherever you go, make disciples of all nations."

The Evidence for "Go!"

Most New Testament scholars, however, disagree with the above interpretation and heavily favor taking the participle with an imperatival force.[9] In this case the participle is not interpreted as a temporal participle but a participle of attendant circumstance.[10] This type of participle is coordinate or parallel to the main verb (in Matt. 28:19 the imperative *mathēteusate*, "make disciples") and thus takes on the mood of that verb.[11] It is usually translated as a finite verb (e.g., an imperative) with "and" inserted between the participle and the main verb ("Go and make disciples"). Wallace lists five criteria that all occur in about 90 percent of the instances of attendant circumstance: (1) the tense of the participle is usually *aorist*; (2) the tense of the main verb is usually *aorist*; (3) the mood of the main verb is usually *imperative* or *indicative*; (4) the participle will *precede the main verb*; and (5) the participle occurs frequently in *historical narratives*.[12] Matthew 28:19 meets all five of these criteria. Although the participle and the main verb are translated as coordinate verbs, the participle is still grammatically subordinate, with emphasis falling on the main verb.

We will demonstrate this use of the participle from both the Septuagint (the Greek translation of the Old Testament) as well as from other texts in the Gospel of Matthew. First, there are several key texts in the Septuagint that demonstrate that the participle often functions imperatively.[13]

- Rebekah tells her son Jacob, "Let your curse be on me, my son; only obey my voice, and **go** (*poreutheis*), **bring** (*enegke*) them to me" (Gen. 27:13). Several items are worth noting here. First, this text closely resembles Matthew 28:19 as we have an aorist participle (*poreutheis*) followed by an aorist imperative (*enegke*). Second, in the Hebrew text, both of these verbs are imperatives. Third, it would not make sense to translate the participle temporally ("as you go, bring . . .") since it clearly bears an imperatival force ("go, bring . . ."), which is confirmed by the Hebrew original.

- Jacob instructs his son Joseph, "**Go** (*poreutheis*) now, **see** (*ide*) if it is well with your brothers and with the flock, and bring me word" (Gen.

---

9. Keener, *Matthew*, 718.
10. See Andreas J. Köstenberger, Benjamin L. Merkle, and Robert L. Plummer, *Going Deeper with New Testament Greek: An Intermediate Study of the Grammar and Syntax of the New Testament* (Nashville: B&H, 2016), 336–37; and Wallace, *Greek Grammar*, 640–45.
11. Morris correctly notes, "Where the participle is linked in this way with an imperative, it shares the imperatival force (cf. 2:8, 13; 11:4; 17:27)" (Leon Morris, *The Gospel according to Matthew* [Grand Rapids: Eerdmans, 1992], 746). See also Carson, "Matthew," 666.
12. Wallace, *Greek Grammar*, 642.
13. See Cleon Rogers, "The Great Commission," *BSac* 130 (1973): 260.

37:14). As with the previous example, the Hebrew has an imperative that the Septuagint renders as a participle.

- Pharaoh commands the people of Israel, "**Go** (*poreuthentes*) now and **work** (*ergazesthe*). No straw will be given you, but you must still deliver the same number of bricks" (Exod. 5:18).

- After the tenth plague (the death of the first born), Pharaoh orders Moses and Aaron, "**Take** (*analabontes*) your flocks and your herds . . . and **be gone** (*poreuesthe*)" (Exod. 12:32).

- The sons of the prophets say to Elisha concerning Elijah, "Please let them **go** (*poreuthentes*) and **seek** (*zētēstōsav*) your master" (2 Kings 2:16).[14]

The above texts are highly instructive because they confirm the use of the participle that functions imperatively.[15] Instead of using two coordinate imperatives, it was common to use a participle followed by an imperative. It was understood, however, that the participle mirrored the mood of the imperative, being taken as a command.

Other uses in Matthew's Gospel also confirm the attendant circumstance use of the participle. Not only does Matthew use this construction often; he uses the construction with the same verb (*poreuomai*) as an aorist participle, followed by an aorist imperative.

- King Herod urgently commands the wise men, "**Go** (*poreuthentes*) and **search** (*exetasate*) diligently for the child" (2:8). There is no doubt that Herod was not merely stating "as you go" or "when you go." Rather, he was forcefully commanding them to go and search for the child.

- Jesus states, "**Go** (*poreuthentes*) and **learn** (*mathete*) what this means" (9:13).

- Jesus told John's disciples, "**Go** (*poreuthentes*) and **tell** (*apangeilate*) John what you hear and see" (11:4).

- Jesus instructs Peter, "**go** (*poreutheis*) to the sea and **cast** (*bale*) a hook and take the first fish that comes up" (17:27).

---

14. The Hebrew form is a jussive with an imperatival force. See also 1 Maccabees 7:7 (πορευθεὶς ἰδέτω).

15. The use of the participle as attendant circumstance should not be confused with the imperatival participle. The former is somewhat common, is used in construction with a main verb, and is found mostly in historical narratives whereas the latter is very rare, is used in a construction that lacks a main verb, and is found most in Romans 12 and 1 Peter.

- The angel at the empty tomb tells the women, "Then **go** (*poreutheisai*) quickly and **tell** (*eipate*) his disciples that he has risen from the dead" (28:7).[16]

Again, the above texts demonstrate that the attendant circumstance was a common use of the participle in Matthew's Gospel (note that each text meets all five of Wallace's criteria).[17] In each case, it would not make much sense to translate the participle as "when/as you go" but instead the participle clearly functions as an imperative. Therefore, when we come to Matthew 28:19 ("Go [*poreuthentes*] therefore and make disciples [*mathēteusate*] of all nations"), it would be natural to take the verb "go/going" as an imperative.

This interpretation is also confirmed by English translations. Every major English version translates *poreuthentes* as an imperative.[18] Again, this does not mean that the participle is the main point. The main verb is "make disciples." And yet, simply because the participle is not the main verb it does not make it unimportant or dispensable. Instead, such participles are a necessary prerequisite to complete the main command. Rogers comments, "Without the action of the participle having taken place it would not be possible to carry out the command. The participle proposes the way for the fulfilling of the main verb and in this way also has the form of an imperative."[19] This function of the participle is especially obvious in the context of the Great Commission, which includes making disciples of *all nations*. Rogers continues, "Without the going, the making disciples is not possible, and especially when 'all nations' is the object."[20] Finally, arguing this same position, Wallace summarizes: "There

---

16. See also Matthew 2:13, 20; 5:24; 9:6; 11:4; 21:2 for uses of the participle of attendant circumstance in construction with imperatives. Interestingly, when Jesus meets the women a few verses later, they are instructed "go (*hypagete*) and tell (*apangeilate*) my brothers to go to Galilee" (Matt. 28:10). Notice here that two imperatives are used.

17. In the cases where the aorist indicates a temporal function, the present participle is used: Matthew 10:7 ("And proclaim as you go [*poreuomenoi*], saying, 'The kingdom of heaven is at hand'"); 11:7 ("As they went away [*poreuomenōn*], Jesus began to speak to the crowds concerning John"); 28:11 ("While they were going [*poreuomenōn*], behold, some of the guard went into the city").

18. The one noticeable exception is the International Standard Version (ISV): "Therefore, as you go, disciple people in all nations, baptizing them in the name of the Father, and the Son, and the Holy Spirit." Interestingly, the ISV does not consistently translate the participle in this way.

19. Rogers, "The Great Commission," 261.

20. Ibid., 262. Rogers concludes that this "construction indicates that 'going' is an integral part of making disciples and is to be translated as an imperative" (266). Also see Schnabel who writes, "The participle is implicitly imperatival; the Twelve can reach 'all nations' only if they leave Galilee (or Jerusalem) and go beyond the confines of Judea to other reasons and other cities" (*DJG*, 2nd ed., 607). Carson adds, "In a context that demands that this ministry extend to 'all nations,' it is difficult to believe that 'go' has no imperatival force" ("Matthew," 666).

is no good grammatical ground for giving the participle a mere temporal idea. To turn [*poreuthentes*] into an adverbial [temporal] participle is to turn the Great Commission into the Great Suggestion!"[21] The rationale for such a statement is that nearly all uses of an aorist participle with an aorist imperative in narrative literature involve an attendant circumstance. Furthermore, in Matthew's Gospel, every instance of the aorist participle of *poreuomai* preceding an aorist main verb is clearly attendant circumstance.[22]

The Implications of the Imperatival Force of *poreuthentes*

If we are correct that the participle *poreuthentes* should be interpreted (and translated) with an imperatival force, then how are we to obey the text? Does it mean that every Christian must leave their native land and live in a cross-cultural context? We will offer three implications that will help us better understand this text.

First, this understanding of the text mandates that the church must be *intentional* about reaching the nations. If the command is to go into all the nations and make disciples, then that would seem to require a plan to make sure the church is fulfilling Jesus's commission. Leon Morris notes, "From this fact [i.e., because 'go' is a participle and not an imperative] some have drawn the conclusion that Jesus did not command his followers to go; all that they were to do was make disciples of such people as they happened to encounter." He rightly adds, however, "Jesus was commanding his followers to go as well as to make disciples, though the emphasis falls on the making of disciples."[23] It is appropriate (and even mandatory) for the church to prioritize reaching all of the nations with the gospel of Jesus Christ in order to make disciples.

Second, there must be a willingness on the part of the church to invest its resources (time and money) to fulfill Jesus's commission. It would be tragic if Jesus's final commission to the church was ignored or minimalized. It is far too easy for churches to get consumed in extending their local kingdom while failing to extend the worldwide kingdom of God.

Third, there must be a willingness on the part of individuals and families to go. Nobody argues that every Christian must participate in fulfilling the Great Commission in the same way. Some cannot or should not go (if we are limiting the concept of "going" to cross-cultural missions). We wholeheartedly acknowledge that some participate through their giving and praying. And yet, there seem to be far too few who are willing to leave their family and friends behind in order to bring the good news to those who have never heard. Many in the early church understood the importance of Jesus's last

---

21. Wallace, *Greek Grammar*, 645.
22. In addition to the participle + imperative used as attendant circumstance in Matthew, also see the use of the participle + indicative (Matt. 21:6; 22:15; 25:16; 26:14–15; 27:66).
23. Morris, *Matthew*, 756.

marching orders. They were willing to leave all to obey their king. May we be willing to do the same to honor our King Jesus.

Summary

Although the participle *poreuthentes* is not the main verb (and thus not the main command) in the Great Commission, it carries an imperatival force ("Go!"). Consequently, the church is given a command to go to the nations in order to make disciples. Those who prefer to translate the text "As you go" misunderstand the original Greek and are thereby weakening the force of Jesus's commission, which requires the church to go.

REFLECTION QUESTIONS

1. What evidence is there for the "as you go" interpretation of Matthew 28:19?

2. What is the meaning of that interpretation? Do you find that interpretation compelling? Why or why not?

3. What evidence is there for the "Go!" interpretation of Matthew 28:19?

4. What is the meaning of that interpretation? Do you find that interpretation compelling? Why or why not?

5. Which of the three implications of viewing the participle *poreuthentes* with an imperatival force is the one you struggle with the most?

How Do Baptism and Teaching Relate to the Great Commission?

In previous questions we determined that the main command of the Great Commission is to "make disciples" and that the participle "going" (*poreuthentes*) should be interpreted with an imperatival force ("Go!"). The question still remains, however, as to the function of the two following participles "baptizing" and "teaching." How are these two verbs related to the main idea of making disciples?

The Function of "Baptizing" and "Teaching"

There is almost universal agreement that the participles "baptizing" (*baptizontes*) and "teaching" (*didaskontes*) are subordinate to the main idea of making disciples. But what is the precise relationship between these two participles and the main verb? In other words, how do "baptizing" and "teaching" relate to "make disciples"?

There are at least three possible answers to this question. First, some take the participles in a similar fashion as "go/going" and interpret them as participles of *attendant circumstance*. In this case, the participles likewise take on an imperatival force: "Go therefore and make disciples . . . *baptize* them . . . and *teach* them."[1] Second, some interpret the participles as communicating the *means* by which we make disciples. In other words, a disciple is one who is baptized and one who is taught to live according to all the commands of Jesus.[2] Wallace explains: "The means by which the disciples were to make

---

1. See Donald A. Hagner, *Matthew 14–28*, WBC 33B (Dallas: Word, 1995), 886; *and* Grant R. Osborne, *Matthew*, ZECNT (Grand Rapids: Zondervan, 2010), 1080.
2. See Andreas J. Köstenberger, Benjamin L. Merkle, and Robert L. Plummer, *Going Deeper with New Testament Greek: An Intermediate Study of the Grammar and Syntax of the New Testament* (Nashville: B&H, 2016), 436 n. 3; and Daniel B. Wallace, *Greek Grammar beyond the Basic: An Exegetical Syntax of the New Testament* (Grand Rapids: Eerdmans, 1996), 645.

disciples was to baptize and then to teach."[3] Third, others maintain that the participle does not express the means of making disciples but the characteristic *mode* (or *manner*) of making disciples.[4] Carson writes, "Baptizing and teaching are not the *means* of making disciples, but they characterize it."[5]

So which of the above views is the best? Interestingly, there is probably some validity to all of them, though the last two are most likely. The first view is the weakest because it is not common for attendant circumstance participles to follow the main verb or be in the present tense.[6] And yet, based on the context, it is evident that the participles carry an implicit imperatival force (though weaker than the previous participle translated as "Go!"). If the disciples were to make other disciples, it would certainly necessitate that they baptize and teach others. Nevertheless, because the participles follow the main verb, the principal force is not imperatival (thus they should not be translated as imperatives).[7]

The other two options (*means* or *mode/manner*) are to be preferred. But are baptism and teaching the means by which disciples are made or the mode of making disciples? Despite the insistence of some, there does not appear to be any major significant difference between the two positions.[8] It seems that those who argue for mode are fearful of a mechanical view of disciple-making that merely involves baptizing and teaching people without a prior faith commitment. Although their concern is valid, we must remember that the various grammatical categories are somewhat artificial, since native speakers/writers were not conscious of such categories but instinctively knew how the terms function in a particular context. In fact, although Robertson labels the verbs as modal (manner) participles, he claims, "it is not always clear where manner shades off into means."[9] What is clear is that proper disciple-making must

---

3. Wallace, *Greek Grammar*, 645.
4. See D. A. Carson, "Matthew," in EBC 9, rev. ed. (Grand Rapids: Zondervan, 2010), 668; Andreas J. Köstenberger and Peter T. O'Brien, *Salvation to the Ends of the Earth: A Biblical Theology of Mission* (Downers Grove, IL: InterVarsity, 2001), 104–5; Eckhard J. Schnabel, *Early Christian Mission*, vol. 1, *Jesus and the Twelve* (Downers Grove, IL: InterVarsity, 2004), 357; and A. T. Robertson, *A Grammar of the Greek New Testament in the Light of Historical Research*, 4th ed. (Nashville: Broadman, 1934), 1128.
5. Carson, "Matthew," 668.
6. Wallace, *Greek Grammar*, 645.
7. See NJB ("baptise them in the name of the Father and of the Son and of the Holy Spirit, and teach them to observe all the commands I gave you") and NIrV ("Baptize them in the name of the Father and of the Son and of the Holy Spirit. Teach them to obey everything I have commanded you").
8. Carson overstates his case when he claims, "The syntax of the Greek participles for 'baptizing' and 'teaching' forbids the conclusion that baptizing and teaching are to be construed solely as the means of making disciples" ("Matthew," 667). It is not the Greek syntax, but the greater context, that suggests repentance and faith are also necessary.
9. Robertson, *Greek Grammar*, 1128.

include baptism and teaching. Carson rightly notes, "The NT can scarcely conceive of a disciple who is not baptized or is not instructed."[10]

The Meaning of "Baptizing"

The first characteristic of a disciple involves the act of baptism. The implication, then, is that Jesus expects his disciples to baptize new converts. Many commentators note that this is the first mention of baptism in Matthew's Gospel since chapter 3 where we read of the baptism of John and Jesus's acceptance of John's baptism. Although we have no record of Jesus calling for his disciples to receive baptism, it should probably be assumed based on the testimony of the early church. For example, when Peter preached to the multitudes on the Day of Pentecost, they asked him, "Brothers, what shall we do?" (Acts 2:37). Peter's immediate response was, "Repent and be baptized every one of you in the name of Jesus Christ for the forgiveness of your sins, and you will receive the gift of the Holy Spirit" (Acts 2:38). Morris writes, "We have no knowledge of a time when the church was without baptism or unsure of baptism. It is difficult to explain this apart from the definite command of Jesus."[11]

Baptism is the initiatory rite whereby those who give a credible profession of faith in Jesus Christ are immersed or dipped into water. According to Paul, it is a sign or symbol of a believer's union with Christ in his death, burial, and resurrection (see Rom. 6:3–4; Col. 2:11–12).

Jesus gave his disciples the command to baptize new converts (Matt. 28:19) but Paul gives the theology of baptism: it is a picture of the believer's death to sin and his new life in Christ.[12]

Baptism not only signifies our union with Christ; it is also a sign of our unity with other believers. Paul teaches that there is "one Lord, one faith, one baptism" (Eph. 4:5). He also states, "For in one Spirit we were all baptized into one body—Jews or Greeks, slaves or free—and all were made to drink of one Spirit" (1 Cor. 12:13). These verses emphasize the participation of all believers in baptism, demonstrating the importance of this rite. The unity of believers is signified by their one baptism. Baptism is shared in common by all those who are united to Christ by faith (Gal. 3:27).

Baptism is the visible initiation into the Christian community. After publicly confessing their sins and believing in Jesus as Lord and Savior, new converts were immediately baptized. In the early church, baptism normally occurred on the same day as conversion.[13] There was not a long time of

---

10. Carson, "Matthew," 668.
11. Leon Morris, *The Gospel according to Matthew* (Grand Rapids: Eerdmans, 1992), 747.
12. See Daniel Akin, "The Meaning of Baptism," in *Restoring Integrity in Baptist Churches*, eds. Thomas White, Jason G. Duesing, and Malcom B. Yarnell III (Grand Rapids: Kregel, 2008), 63–80.
13. See Robert H. Stein, "Baptism in Luke-Acts," in *Believers Baptism: Sign of the New Covenant in Christ*, eds. Thomas R. Schreiner and Shawn D. Wright (Nashville: B&H, 2006), 33–66.

teaching and testing beforehand. If baptism is a symbol of our death and resurrection with Christ and our entrance into the body of Christ, it makes sense that baptism should be done as close to conversion as possible. Thus, in the early church, teaching followed baptism.

The singular "name" with the Trinitarian formula (Father, Son, Holy Spirit) suggests an early understanding of the Trinity.[14] France states, "The fact that the three divine persons are spoken of as having a single 'name' is a significant pointer toward the Trinitarian doctrine of three persons in one God."[15] We also note that this baptism is "into" (*eis*) the name of the Trinity. Carson notes that the preposition *eis* ("into") "strongly suggests a coming-into-relationship-with or a coming-under-the-lordship of."[16]

Although we should be careful not to read too much into the order of the verbs, there does seem to be an intentional ordering: (1) go, (2) make disciples, (3) baptize, and (4) teach. As Schnabel writes, "It surely is significant that baptism is mentioned after the winning of disciples: it is people who have been converted to faith in Jesus Christ who are baptized (not vice versa, baptized people being made into disciples by the teaching of the church)."[17]

The Meaning of "Teaching"

The second characteristic of a disciple involves being taught to obey all of Jesus's teachings. Note that it is the teachings of Jesus, and not the Torah, that are to be obeyed. This is yet another example of Jesus claiming superiority to the OT Law and to Moses himself. Throughout his Gospel, Matthew has been emphasizing Jesus as a teacher (Matt. 4:23; 5:2; 7:29; 9:35; 11:1; 13:34; 21:23; 26:55) who delivers five sermons (chs. 5–7; 10; 13; 18; 23–25). The disciples are now given the task of teaching. Bruner remarks, "This is the first time that Jesus ever applies the verb 'teaching' to the work of the *disciples*."[18] Up to this

---

14. Though cf. Acts 2:38; 8:16; 10:48; 19:5; 22:16; Romans 6:3; Galatians 3:27 which lack the Trinitarian formula. Köstenberger and O'Brien state, "It appears . . . that the early church felt no contradiction between Jesus' command to baptize in the name of the Father, the Son and the Holy Spirit, and its practice of baptizing in the name of Jesus, since the latter implied the former" (*Salvation to the Ends of the Earth*, 105). R. T. France adds: "The reader of Matthew will probably remember that when Jesus himself was baptized, God, the Holy Spirit, and God's Son were all involved (3:16–17). They will also remember that Jesus has been introduced as the one who will baptize with the Holy Spirit (3:11)" (*The Gospel of Matthew* [Grand Rapids: Eerdmans, 2007], 1117 n. 41).

15. France, *Gospel of Matthew*, 1118. Blomberg declares, "Jesus has already spoken of God as his Father (Matt 11:27; 24:36), of himself as Son (11:27; 16:27; 24:36), and of blasphemy against God's work in himself as against the Spirit (12:28). . . . That Jesus should gather together into summary form his own references . . . in his final charge to the disciples seems quite natural" (Craig L. Blomberg, *Matthew*, NAC 22 [Nashville: B&H, 1992], 432).

16. Carson, "Matthew," 668.

17. Schnabel, *Early Christian Mission*, 357.

18. Fredrick Dale Bruner, *Matthew: A Commentary*, vol. 2 (The Churchbook: Matthew 13–28), rev. and exp. (Grand Rapids: Eerdmans, 1990), 824 (emphasis original).

point Jesus had done all the teaching. Specifically, they are to teach converts to "observe" (*tērein*) all the things that Jesus had commanded them.[19] Thus, we see that Jesus's commission has a distinctively ethical dimension. Although Christianity is not based on the OT law, it does have a moral code that its adherents are expected to follow.

The disciples are also commanded to teach "all that I have commanded you," which recalls all the teaching of Jesus in Matthew's Gospel. Earlier Jesus stated, "Do not think that I have come to abolish the Law or the Prophets; I have not come to abolish them but to fulfill them. . . . Therefore whoever relaxes one of the least of these commandments and teaches others to do the same will be called least in the kingdom of heaven, but whoever does them and teaches them will be called great in the kingdom of heaven" (Matt. 5:17–19). He later claimed, "Everyone then who hears these words of mine and does them will be like a wise man who built his house on the rock" (Matt. 7:24). The expectation is that the disciples of Jesus will not only know what Jesus taught, but that they will live according to that teaching.[20] This includes not some, but *all* of Jesus's teaching. As Morris explains, "Jesus is not suggesting that his followers should make a selection from his teachings as it pleases them and neglect the rest. Since the teaching of Jesus is a unified whole, disciples are to observe *all* that this means."[21]

We should again emphasize that obeying the commands of Jesus are the result of being his disciple. In other words, apart from a prior faith-commitment to Jesus, there is neither the desire or ability to keep Jesus's commands. As Bruner clarifies, "Therefore, *keeping Jesus' commands* may be understood as an obedience that flows out of a prior believing *worship of Jesus' person*." Consequently, "The main way we worship Jesus' person is by keeping his commands."[22] Thus, a disciple is one who observes or obeys Jesus's teaching.

Summary

Though not the main verbs of the Great Commission, "baptizing" and "teaching" should not be marginalized. These verbs express the *means* or, better, the characteristic *mode* of disciple-making. Baptism represents the initiatory rite whereby those who have expressed faith in Christ are immersed into water as a symbol of their union with Christ and initiation into the Christian community. In addition, disciples were to be taught all of Jesus's teachings. The goal, however, is never just to know the teachings but to live according to them.

---

19. Earlier, Matthew used the verb "observe" (*tēreō*) in 19:17 for keeping the Ten Commandments and in 23:3 for keeping the Torah.
20. Based on Jesus's words in Matthew 28, Köstenberger and O'Brien warn, "The present charge makes clear that mission entails the nurturing of converts into the full obedience of faith, not merely the proclamation of the gospel" (*Salvation to the Ends of the Earth*, 105).
21. Morris, *Matthew*, 749.
22. Bruner, *Matthew*, 2:826.

REFLECTION QUESTIONS

1. How do the participles "baptizing" and "teaching" relate to the main verb ("make disciples")?

2. What is the significance of baptism? Is it necessary for salvation?

3. When do you think a convert should be baptized? Why?

4. How long do you think it takes to teach a new disciple all the teachings of Jesus?

5. How well do you know the teachings of Jesus? How well can you detect false teaching?

What Is a Summary of Jesus's Commands for His Disciples?

Jesus commissioned his followers to make disciples by teaching obedience to everything he commanded. Yet, John finishes his Gospel account by noting that if everything Jesus did or taught were written, all the books in the world could not contain them (John 21:25). How then are we supposed to teach obedience with so much content from which to draw?

Missionary George Patterson was asked that question by a group of semi-literate pastors that he mentored in Honduras decades ago. Together, they set out to study the four Gospel accounts, writing down more than forty things that Jesus explicitly commanded. Remarkably they found that they could categorize most of Jesus's imperative commands into what has become known by many as "The Basic Commands."[1] Next, they studied through the rest of the New Testament and found that those basic commands were reiterated and often applied or expanded upon in the Epistles. They also noted that the Acts 2 account of the birth of the church displays that all of the basic commands seemed to be prioritized (see Acts 2:36–47). What exactly are the "Basic Commands of Jesus"?

The Basic Commands of Jesus[2]

In this section each command will be listed, followed by a sample Scripture reference where Jesus communicated it, a New Testament story that demonstrates it, a reference to how it featured in the birth of the church, and

---

1. George Patterson and Richard Scoggins, *Church Multiplication Guide: The Miracle of Church Reproduction* (Pasadena, CA: William Carey Library, 2002), 22.
2. See http://noplaceleft.net/wp-content/uploads/2016/03/3fe2a5_e3fcf1252871418ca19a1d-3e41d0fa90.pdf for a downloadable pdf guide with an expanded version of the commands and stories.

finally other verses that provide similar commands that come from Jesus.[3] Keep in mind that there are a plethora of other references that serve to give a fuller understanding of what it means to teach obedience to Jesus.

1. Repent, Believe the Gospel, and Receive the Holy Spirit

The Command: "The time is fulfilled, and the kingdom of God is at hand; repent and believe in the gospel" (Mark 1:15); "And when he had said this, he breathed on them and said to them, 'Receive the Holy Spirit'" (John 20:22).

A Story: The Sinful Woman Trusts Jesus and Turns from Her Sin (Luke 7:36–50).

In the Church: "Now when they heard this they were cut to the heart, and said to Peter and the rest of the apostles, 'Brothers, what shall we do?' And Peter said to them, 'Repent and be baptized every one of you in the name of Jesus Christ for the forgiveness of your sins, and you will receive the gift of the Holy Spirit. For the promise is for you and for your children and for all who are far off, everyone whom the Lord our God calls to himself'" (Acts 2:37–39).

Other Commands: repent (Matt. 4:17); follow me (Matt. 4:19); rejoice when you are persecuted for following Jesus (Matt. 5:12); repent from sin by cutting off the temptation (Matt. 5:29–30); choose the narrow way that leads to life (Matt. 7:13–14); take my yoke upon you (obey Jesus's teaching) (Matt. 11:29); deny yourself, take up your cross and follow Jesus (Luke 9:23); repent from sin and turn to Jesus for salvation (Luke 18:9–14); be born again (John 3:7; Luke 15:11–32); receive God's power (Luke 24:49).

2. Be Baptized

The Command: "Go therefore and make disciples of all nations, baptizing them in the name of the Father and of the Son and of the Holy Spirit" (Matt. 28:19).

---

3. See http://paul-timothy.net/pages/jesus/docs/300_commands_of_jesus.html for a complete list of more than three hundred commands from the Gospels.

A Story: Philip and an Ethiopian Official Display the Importance of Baptism (Acts 8:26–39).

In the Church: "And with many other words he bore witness and continued to exhort them, saying, 'Save yourselves from this crooked generation.' So those who received his word were baptized, and there were added that day about three thousand souls" (Acts 2:40–41).

3. Love God above All, and Love Others above Yourself

The Command: "And he said to him, 'You shall love the Lord your God with all your heart and with all your soul and with all your mind. This is the great and first commandment. And a second is like it: You shall love your neighbor as yourself'" (Matt. 22:37–39).

A Story: The Parable of the Good Samaritan (Luke 10:25–37).

In the Church: "And they devoted themselves to the apostles' teaching and the fellowship, to the breaking of bread and the prayers. And awe came upon every soul, and many wonders and signs were being done through the apostles. And all who believed were together and had all things in common. And they were selling their possessions and belongings and distributing the proceeds to all, as any had need. And day by day, attending the temple together and breaking bread in their homes, they received their food with glad and generous hearts, praising God and having favor with all the people. And the Lord added to their number day by day those who were being saved" (Acts 2:42–47).

Other Commands: let your light shine by good deeds (Matt. 5:16); do not be angry with your brother (Matt. 5:21–22); do not insult others (Matt. 5:22); be reconciled with the one you offended (Matt. 5:24–25); do not covet a married woman (Matt. 5:27–28); don't say more than "yes" or "no" when testifying (Matt. 5:37); do not retaliate against evil persons (Matt. 5:38–39); sacrifice beyond what others demand you give (Matt. 5:38–42); love your enemies (Matt. 5:44); be perfect as God is perfect (Matt. 5:48); seek God's Kingdom (Matt. 6:33); do not judge (Matt. 7:1–3); do unto others as you would have them do unto you (Matt. 7:12);

fear God, not man (Matt. 10:26, 28); do not blaspheme God's name (Matt. 12:31); honor your parents (Matt. 15:4); go to reconcile with those who wrong you (Matt. 18:15); forgive those who wrong you (Matt. 18:21–22); stay married (Matt. 19:6; 5:31–32); never seek to rule over other believers (Matt. 20:26–28); be a people producing fruit (Matt. 21:4); show hospitality to those in need (Luke 14:12–14); love the Lord with all your heart, mind, and soul (Matt. 22:37–38); worship God alone (Matt. 6:9); love your neighbor (Matt. 22:39); if you love Jesus, keep his commandments (John 14:15); love one another (John 13:34).

4. Celebrate the Lord's Supper and Worship God

The Command: "And he took bread, and when he had given thanks, he broke it and gave it to them, saying, 'This is my body, which is given for you. Do this in remembrance of me.' And likewise, the cup after they had eaten, saying, 'This cup that is poured out for you is the new covenant in my blood'" (Luke 22:19–20).

A Story: Jesus's Last Supper (Luke 22:7–20).

In the Church: "And they devoted themselves to . . . the breaking of bread. . . . And day by day, attending the temple together and breaking bread in their homes, they received their food with glad and generous hearts, praising God" (Acts 2:42, 46).

Other Commands: break bread and drink the cup in remembrance (Matt. 26:26–28; Mark 14:22–24; Luke 22:19).

5. Pray at All Times for All Things

The Command: "Pray then like this: 'Our Father in heaven, hallowed be your name. Your kingdom come, your will be done, on earth as it is in heaven. Give us this day our daily bread, and forgive us our debts, as we also have forgiven our debtors. And lead us not into temptation, but deliver us from evil'" (Matt. 6:9–13).

A Story: The Parable of the Persistent Widow (Luke 18:1–8).

In the Church: "And they devoted themselves to . . . the prayers. And awe came upon every soul, and many wonders and signs were being done through the apostles" (Acts 2:42–43).

Other Commands: pray for those who persecute you (Matt. 5:44); do not pray to be seen by others (Matt. 6:5–6); do not pray repetitious prayers (Matt. 5:7–8); be persistent in prayer—ask, seek, and knock (Matt. 7:7–8); pray God sends co-laborers to spread good news (Matt. 9:38); watch and pray (Matt. 26:41).

6. Give Generously of Time, Talent, and Treasure

The Command: "[G]ive, and it will be given to you. Good measure, pressed down, shaken together, running over, will be put into your lap. For with the measure you use it will be measured back to you" (Luke 6:38).

A Story: Generosity in the Early Church Exemplified by Barnabas (Acts 4:32–37).

In the Church: "And they devoted themselves to . . . the fellowship. . . . And all who believed were together and had all things in common. And they were selling their possessions and belongings and distributing the proceeds to all, as any had need. . . . [T]hey received their food with glad and generous hearts, praising God and having favor with all the people" (Acts 2:42, 44–47).

Other Commands: give in secret and not where others can see (Matt. 6:1–4); do not lay up treasures on earth (Matt. 6:19–20); beware of covetousness (Luke 12:15); give to Caesar what belongs to Caesar (Matt. 22:19–21); give to God what belongs to God (Matt. 22:19–21); be good stewards (Matt. 25:29; cf. Matt. 13:12); be wise with money (Luke 16:1–16).

7. Make Disciples by Teaching Others to Obey Jesus

The Command: "Go therefore and make disciples of all nations, baptizing them in the name of the Father and of the Son and of the Holy Spirit, teaching them to observe all that I have commanded you" (Matt. 28:19–20).

A Story: Samaritan Woman at the Well Tells Others and Brings Her Town to Jesus (John 4:4–42).

In the Church: "And they devoted themselves to the apostles' teaching . . . having favor with all the people. And the Lord added to their number day by day those who were being saved" (Acts 2:42, 47).

Other Commands: teach God's law (Matt. 5:17–18); do not cast pearls before skeptics (Matt. 7:6); beware of false prophets (Matt. 7:15); be wise as serpents (Matt. 10:16); beware of the Pharisees (Matt. 15:6; 16:6; 23:23); despise not little children (Matt. 18:10); make the name of God known (John 17:6); await Jesus's return and do not be fooled (Matt. 24:4–6, 23–27); strive to understand Jesus's teachings (Matt. 13:12); feed Jesus's sheep (John 21:15–16); baptize Jesus's disciples (Matt. 28:19); teach the nations to obey all that Jesus commanded (Matt. 28:19); make disciples of all nations (Matt. 28:20).

"Teaching" versus "Teaching Obedience"

Much of what people call discipleship actually falls short of Jesus's example in that it emphasizes acquisition of knowledge separated from application. A curriculum-based approach to discipleship has inherent limitations unless it is paired with mentoring. The score card for success we choose will influence how we approach disciple-making. If we believe that a disciple is one who knows what Jesus taught, then we will focus on the transference of copious amounts of information. However, if we believe that a disciple is someone who *does* what Jesus taught, then we will focus on teaching in such a manner as to cultivate a response of obedience as the primary indicator of understanding. The difference is teaching versus teaching to obey. This means that how we teach, the process, is as important as what we teach.

Jesus seemed to approach his disciples in such a way as to communicate this emphasis on application and obedience. From the outset, he cast a vision for reproduction, "Follow me, and I will make you fishers of men" (Matt. 4:19). Unlike other rabbis of his day, Jesus was inviting his disciples into a life where the world was their classroom and their relationship with him would be the canvas that made lessons visible. Their love for Jesus simply could not be separated from their obedience to Jesus. He told them, "If you love me, you will keep my commandments" (John 14:15). The disciples were to reproduce both their love for Jesus and their obedience to him. If our approach to disciple-making fails to produce both, then we need to work at keeping these two complementary goals together by building them into our strategies.

"Legalism" versus "Faith-fueled Obedience"

Whenever the topic of obedience arises, there is always a chance that legalism is a potential outcome. Legalism is the antithesis of gospel fruit, and thus should be avoided at all cost. Is it possible to teach obedience in such a way that legalism is avoided and the gospel cherished? Paul seemed to think so as he wrote the introduction to his epistle to the Romans, highlighting his desire "*to bring about the obedience of faith*" (Rom. 1:5). Paul is describing a faith-fueled obedience to Jesus throughout that letter, whereby grace is the power behind and enabler of obedience. Thus, it makes sense that Paul bookends his letter to the Romans by reiterating that faith-fueled obedience is indeed his aim in ministry (16:26).[4]

All true obedience is done in the power of grace, not our own strength. Obedience then is the fruit, not the root of our relationship with God. Romans 10:16 speaks of obeying the gospel, as does 2 Thessalonians 1:8 and 1 Peter 4:17. N. T. Wright notes, "The gospel issues a command, an imperial summons; the appropriate response is obedience."[5] Spurgeon concludes that gospel-glorifying obedience is always to be the goal in our teaching:

> We preach the obedience of faith. Faith is the fountain, the foundation, and the fosterer of obedience. Men obey not God till they believe him. We preach faith in order that men may be brought to obedience. To disbelieve is to disobey. . . . Obedience is the grand object of the work of grace in the hearts of those who are chosen and called: they are to become obedient children, conformed to the image of the Elder Brother, with whom the Father is well pleased.[6]

Summary

Making disciples of Jesus necessarily entails teaching not only the content, but obedience to all that Jesus commanded. An obedience-based approach to disciple-making does not have to produce a legalistic approach to following Jesus. Rather, when Jesus's foundational command to "repent and believe the good news" is obeyed, the indwelling Holy Spirit of God begins the transformation process as believers are conformed to the image of Christ. If we are to obey the Great Commission, we must know what Jesus commanded and teach it in such a way that our hearers are converted and conformed to his

---

4. Because the phrase "obedience of faith" is found in the introduction and conclusion to Paul's epistle to the Romans, it forms a literary "inclusio," highlighting that all of the material between the two form the basis of how it will be accomplished.

5. N. T. Wright, "The Letter to the Romans," in *New Interpreter's Bible*, vol. 10, ed. Leander E. Keck (Nashville: Abingdon, 2002), 420.

6. Charles Haddon Spurgeon, from the sermon "The Obedience of Faith," delivered August 21, 1890, at the Metropolitan Tabernacle, Newington.

will for their lives. Understanding the "Basic Commands of Jesus" provides a simple and reproducible framework to begin that process.

REFLECTION QUESTIONS

1. How might an emphasis on teaching rather than teaching obedience affect a believer's development as a disciple of Jesus?

2. What are some of the inherent dangers of an obedience-based approach to disciple-making, and how might you avoid them?

3. Are there any other commands of Jesus beyond those featured in this chapter that you would consider to be essential for a new believer?

4. What are some ways that mentoring might help you in teaching obedience to Jesus?

5. How would you explain the relationship between faith and obedience to a person who is considering following Jesus?

What Is the Meaning of "I Am with You Always, to the End of the Age"?

Jesus concludes the Great Commission with the promise of his abiding presence: "And behold, I am with you always, to the end of the age" (Matt. 28:20). Certainly the disciples needed this assurance, since earlier we are told that when they saw the resurrected Jesus "some doubted" (v. 17). But precisely what does Jesus mean by this statement? Is there any Old Testament precedence to which Jesus is alluding? If Jesus is now in heaven, how is he also with his disciples? In other words, in what way is Jesus presently with his people?

The Old Testament Background

Jesus's promise to be with his disciples is similar to promises God made to those he commissioned in the Old Testament:[1]

- [To Jacob God says,] Behold, **I am with you** and will keep you wherever you go, and will bring you back to this land. For I will not leave you until I have done what I have promised you. (Gen. 28:15)

- And the LORD appeared to [Isaac] the same night and said, "I am the God of Abraham your father. Fear not, for **I am with you** and will bless you and multiply your offspring for my servant Abraham's sake." (Gen. 26:24)

---

1. France notes, "In OT commissioning scenes the assurance of God's presence was to empower his often inadequate servants to fulfill the task he had called them to. . . . So here it is to the commissioned disciples as they set about their daunting task that the divine presence is promised, without which they cannot be expected to succeed" (R. T. France, *The Gospel of Matthew*, NICNT [Grand Rapids: Eerdmans, 2007], 1119).

- He said [to Moses], "But **I will be with you**, and this shall be the sign for you, that I have sent you: when you have brought the people out of Egypt, you shall serve God on this mountain." (Exod. 3:12; see also 4:12)

- After the death of Moses the servant of the LORD, the LORD said to Joshua the son of Nun, Moses's assistant. . . . "Be strong and courageous. Do not be frightened, and do not be dismayed, for **the LORD your God is with you** wherever you go." (Josh. 1:1, 9; see also 1:5)

- And the angel of the LORD appeared to [Gideon] and said to him, "**The LORD is with you**, O mighty man of valor. . . . **I will be with you**, and you shall strike the Midianites as one man." (Judg. 6:12, 16)

- But the LORD said to [Jeremiah], . . . "Do not be afraid of them, for **I am with you** to deliver you, declares the LORD." (Jer. 1:7–8)

- Then Haggai, the messenger of the LORD, spoke to the people with the LORD's message, "**I am with you**, declares the LORD." (Hag. 1:13; see also Deut. 20:4; 31:6; Isa. 41:10; 43:5)

Thus, Jesus's words are not merely a statement that he will be thinking about his disciples, or even that he will be present with them. Rather, his words reflect the promises of Yahweh's abiding in the midst of his people, to be with them and cause them to succeed. In essence, Jesus is proclaiming his divine status by claiming to do something that was unique to Yahweh.[2]

The New Testament Significance

The concluding words of the Great Commission begin with "And behold (*idou*)" (Matt. 28:20).[3] This is the final time (of sixty-two occurrences) the term *idou* ("behold") is used in Matthew's Gospel. Here, this term is used for "emphasis on the . . . importance of something."[4] Matthew Henry comments, "This exceeding great and precious promise is ushered in with a *behold*, to strengthen their faith, and engage their observation of it."[5] Bruner similarly

---

2. Donald A. Hagner writes, "Where Yahweh was formerly with his people, Jesus is now with his people, the church" (*Matthew 14–28*, WBC 33B [Dallas: Word, 1995], 888).
3. Other English translations render the Greek term *idou* as "lo" (KJV, NKJV, RSV, NASB), "surely" (NIV), "remember" (NRSV, NET, CSB), and "look" (NJB).
4. BDAG 468.
5. Matthew Henry, *Matthew Henry's Commentary on the Whole Bible* (Peabody, MA: Hendrickson, 1991), 5:363.

writes, "The final 'look' of a look-filled Gospel directs disciples not to one more command but to one final, definitive assurance."[6]

Jesus's abiding presence is not something that will only come to fruition in the future but is a present reality. He does not say, "I *will be* with you" but "I *am* (*eimi*) with you." His presence is not something his disciples must hope for in the future but something they can always count on. The emphatic position of "I" (*egō*) further encourages the disciples that Jesus himself will walk with them, encourage them, and strengthen them for the task ahead.[7] Specifically, his assurance/promise is to be "with them." As was noted earlier, the promise that God is with his people is a common theme in the Old Testament. Here, Jesus promises that which only deity can promise.[8] Therefore, if God himself is with his disciples, why should they fear or trust in anything else to accomplish their commission? As Bruner summarizes, "Jesus' divine 'with' means not only protection and defense, though it is also mercifully these, but it especially means 'I will *enable your Great Commission obedience!'*—give you courage to move out, wisdom in discipling, effectiveness in encouraging baptism, and creativity in teaching."[9] In Matthew 1:23 Jesus was introduced with the name "Immanuel" which means "God with us." Now, at the end of the Gospel, Jesus stresses that he will continue to be with his people.

Jesus promises to be with his disciples "always" (literally, "all the days").[10] The risen Messiah promises to be present with his disciples every day until the consummation of the ages. Again, Bruner reminds us of the significance of this statement: "Jesus' 'all the days' means that it is not just 'most days' or 'good days,' or days disciples feel spiritually fit, or feel they have prayed enough, but on *all* days Jesus is present with them, much more faithful to them that they are to him. In modern English we could translate this phrase to read, 'And look! I myself am right there with you *every single day of your life*, even if you don't realize it.'"[11] It is not just the end that is in view, but every day until we reach the consummation.

---

6. Fredrick Dale Bruner, *Matthew: A Commentary*, vol. 2 (The Churchbook: Matthew 13–28), rev. and exp. (Grand Rapids: Eerdmans, 1990), 828.
7. Greek: ἐγὼ μεθ' ὑμῶν εἰμι (*egō meth' hymōn eimi*).
8. Bruner maintains, "The divinity of Jesus is as strongly attested in our Gospel's final verses as it is in the opening verses of John's Prologue" (*Matthew*, 2:830).
9. Ibid., 829. Henry states, "It was an unlikely thing that they should unhinge national constitutions in religion, and turn the stream of so long a usage; that they should *establish* a doctrine contrary to the genius of the age and persuade people to become the disciples of a *crucified* Jesus; but lo, *I am with you*, and therefore you shall *gain your point*" (*Matthew*, 5:363, emphasis original).
10. Moule renders the phrase "the whole of every day" (C. F. D. Moule, *An Idiom-Book of New Testament Greek*, 2nd ed. [Cambridge: Cambridge University Press, 1959], 34).
11. Bruner, *Matthew*, 2:830.

Finally, Jesus's promise will continue "to the end of the age,"[12] a reference to the consummation of the kingdom of God and the end of history. Bruner draws out an important implication of Jesus's words: "If Jesus' presence is ours right up into (*heōs*) Jesus' return, the Last Judgment, and the absolute end of the aeon's history, then we can endure the great tribulation in which we now live, and we can bring mission into the world amid all the tests of the end (Matt 24:13–14)."[13] As the disciples carry on the mission of Jesus, they are assured that he will not leave or forsake them, but will continue to be with them. The actions commanded in the Great Commission are empowered by the two encompassing assurances given by Jesus: (1) because all authority has been given to him and (2) because he will be with his disciples every day until the consummation, they will have success in making disciples of all the nations.[14] "The Jesus who commands difficult obedience is at the same time the ever-graceful divine presence."[15] Matthew's Gospel, then, ends not with the ascension but with a reference to Jesus's abiding presence with his disciples.

The Nature of Jesus's Abiding Presence

But exactly how is Jesus with his disciples every day until the end? Simply put, he is with his disciples through the presence of the Holy Spirit. Three factors make this point evident. First, although Jesus is God and is all-knowing and all-seeing, his physical body is with the Father in heaven (Eph. 1:20; Col. 3:1; Heb. 1:3; 10:12; 12:2; 1 Peter 3:22). Therefore, he is not physically with his disciples today but is spiritually present through the Holy Spirit. Second, the Holy Spirit is also called the "the Spirit of Jesus" (Acts 16:7), "the Spirit of Christ" (Rom. 8:9; 1 Peter 1:11), "the Spirit of Jesus Christ" (Phil. 1:19), and "the Spirit of his Son" (Gal. 4:6). Therefore, to have the Spirit is to have Jesus. The Spirit of Jesus dwells in the hearts of believers and empowers them. Third, in John's Gospel, Jesus himself indicated that he would be leaving his disciples but would continue to be present with them through the ministry of the Holy Spirit.

- And I will ask the Father, and he will give you **another Helper**, to be with you forever, even **the Spirit of truth**, whom the world cannot receive, because it neither sees him nor knows him. You know him, for he dwells with you and will be in you. (John 14:16–17)

---

12. For other uses of this phrase in Matthew's Gospel, see 13:39, 40, 49; 24:3 (cf. Heb. 9:26). Hagner explains that "to the end of the age" "refers to the end of the present age through the parousia of the Son of Man and the experience of the final judgment of the wicked and reward of the righteous" (*Matthew 14–28*, 889).
13. Bruner, *Matthew*, 2:832.
14. "The Great Commission is thus framed by the omnipotence (v. 18) and omnipresence (v. 20b) of Christ" (Grant R. Osborne, *Matthew*, ZECNT [Grand Rapids: Zondervan, 2010], 1082).
15. W. D. Davies and D. C. Allison, *Matthew*, ICC (Edinburgh: T&T Clark, 1997), 3:689.

- These things I have spoken to you while I am still with you. But **the Helper, the Holy Spirit**, whom the Father will send in my name, he will teach you all things and bring to your remembrance all that I have said to you. (John 14:25–26)

- Nevertheless, I tell you the truth: it is to your advantage that I go away, for if I do not go away, **the Helper** will not come to you. But if I go, I will send him to you. (John 16:7)

It is clear then that Jesus is present with his disciples and he is with them through the indwelling of the Holy Spirit.

Summary

Just as Yahweh commissioned his servants and gave them the promise that he would be with them, resulting in the success of their mission, so also Jesus's commission included the assurance that he would be with his disciples. The abiding presence of Jesus means that he will be with them every day ("always") until the final consummation ("to the end of the age"). The means by which Jesus is present with his disciples is through the indwelling presence of the Spirit.

REFLECTION QUESTIONS

1. What Old Testament parallel(s) is/are Jesus alluding to when he says, "I am with you always"?

2. In what way does Jesus's statement demonstrate his divinity?

3. Why were these words extremely important for the disciples to hear?

4. How is Jesus now present with his disciples?

5. How does Jesus's promise of his continued presence encourage you?

Biblical-Theological Questions about the Great Commission

Questions Related to the Various Versions of the Great Commission

What Is the Contribution of Mark's Version of the Great Commission?

Each of the four Gospels and Acts has a version of the Great Commission that is different than what is recorded in the Gospel of Matthew.

- And Jesus came and said to them, "All authority in heaven and on earth has been given to me. Go therefore and make disciples of all nations, baptizing them in the name of the Father and of the Son and of the Holy Spirit, teaching them to observe all that I have commanded you. And behold, I am with you always, to the end of the age." (Matt. 28:18–20)

- And [Jesus] said to them, "Go into all the world and proclaim the gospel to the whole creation. Whoever believes and is baptized will be saved, but whoever does not believe will be condemned. And these signs will accompany those who believe: in my name they will cast out demons; they will speak in new tongues; they will pick up serpents with their hands; and if they drink any deadly poison, it will not hurt them; they will lay their hands on the sick, and they will recover." (Mark 16:15–18)

- [Jesus] said to them, "Thus it is written, that the Christ should suffer and on the third day rise from the dead, and that repentance and forgiveness of sins should be proclaimed in his name to all nations, beginning from Jerusalem. You are witnesses of these things. And behold, I am sending the promise of my Father upon you. But stay in the city until you are clothed with power from on high." (Luke 24:46–49)

- Jesus said to them again, "Peace be with you. As the Father has sent me, even so I am sending you." (John 20:21)

- But you will receive power when the Holy Spirit has come upon you, and you will be my witnesses in Jerusalem and in all Judea and Samaria, and to the end of the earth. (Acts 1:8)

This question and the subsequent questions in this section will compare and contrast Matthew's version of the Great Commission with these similar statements found in the other Gospels and Acts, highlighting the unique contribution of each.

The Legitimacy of the Commission

Before we consider the location and the language of Mark's version of the Great Commission, we need to address the issue of the text's legitimacy. In other words, Mark's version is found in a passage of Scripture that is viewed by most scholars *not* to have been penned by Mark and is therefore textually disputed. For example, James Edwards states, "It is virtually certain that [Mark] 16:9–20 is a later addition and not the original ending of the Gospel of Mark."[1] Even in most English Bible versions it is set off by double brackets with a note such as the one found in the ESV: "Some of the earliest manuscripts do not include 16:9–20." Thus, Mark's version of the Great Commission is questionable since there is significant (but not conclusive) evidence that his version is not original (i.e., that it was not written by Mark).

Because we don't possess the original manuscripts of the New Testament authors, we are dependent upon copies. Providentially, today we possess nearly six thousand Greek New Testament manuscripts. Consequently, we can be certain that we have the text of the original author. Sometimes, however, we are not certain which reading is correct if there happens to be a difference among the various manuscripts. Textual criticism, then, is the science and art of determining which textual variant is correct when there are different readings between the manuscripts. There are two main factors that are considered: (1) external evidence and (2) internal evidence.

The external evidence is mixed. Although the longer ending of Mark (16:9–20) is found in most manuscripts, it is excluded from the two oldest Greek uncials (א and B), the Old Latin codex Bobiensis, the Sinaitic Syrian manuscript, nearly one hundred Armenian manuscripts, the two oldest Georgian manuscripts, and from both Clement of Alexandria and Origen. Garland notes, "It does not appear in any Greek manuscripts before the fifth century, but Irenaeus, who lived in the second century, knows it."[2]

The internal evidence, however, strongly favors the omission of Mark 16:9–20 for three main reasons. (1) *Vocabulary:* there are fifteen words used

---

1. James R. Edwards, *The Gospel according to Mark*, PNTC (Grand Rapids: Eerdmans, 2002), 497.
2. David E. Garland, *A Theology of Mark's Gospel* (Grand Rapids: Zondervan, 2015), 538.

in the longer ending of Mark that do not appear elsewhere in Mark and other words that are used with a difference sense. (2) *Style:* (a) the connection between verse 8 and verse 9 is awkward and abrupt (verse 8 mentions women, but verse 9 begins with a masculine singular participle); (b) Mary Magdalene is mentioned in verse 9 as though she had not been already introduced (cf. 15:40, 47; 16:1); and (c) the women who were commissioned with Mary Magdalene to tell the disciples about Jesus's resurrection in verse 7 are not mentioned in the longer ending. (3) *Context:* "the content of vv. 9–20 appears to be a summary of postresurrection appearances from the other gospels."[3] Some examples include: (a) Jesus's appearance to Mary Magdalene alone (vv. 9–11, based on John 20:11–18); (b) that Mary Magdalene had been possessed by seven demons (v. 9, based on Luke 8:2); (c) the hesitancy of the disciples to believe Mary's report (v. 11, based on Luke 24:11); (d) the appearance to two disciples on a journey (vv. 12–13, based on Luke 24:13–35); and (e) the ascension of Jesus (v. 19, based on Luke 24:51 and/or Acts 1:9).

If, as we are suggesting, Mark's Gospel ended at verse 8, then his Gospel ended as follows: "And they [Mary Magdalene, Mary the mother of James, and Salome] went out and fled from the tomb, for trembling and astonishment had seized them, and they said nothing to anyone, for they were afraid." Because the other Gospels end with post-resurrection appearances, and (perhaps) because it was viewed as unnatural to end the Gospel with a reference to the women's fear, an alternate ending was created to alleviate these tensions.

Metzger's *Textual Commentary* summarizes the data: "On the basis of good external evidence and strong internal considerations it appears that the earliest ascertainable form of the Gospel of Mark ended with 16:8."[4] The committee added, "At the same time, however, out of deference to the evident antiquity of the longer ending and its importance in the textual tradition of the Gospel, the Committee decided to include verses 9–20 as part of the text, but to enclose them within double brackets in order to indicate that they are the work of an author other than the evangelist."[5] Mark Strauss states that although "the external evidence is divided, the internal evidence is overwhelmingly against the long ending."[6]

---

3. David E. Garland, "Mark," in EBC, vol. 9 (Grand Rapids: Zondervan, 2010), 988. See also Mark L. Strauss, *Mark*, ZECNT (Grand Rapids: Zondervan, 2014), 728.
4. Bruce M. Metzger, ed., *A Textual Commentary on the Greek New Testament*, 2nd ed. (Stuttgart: United Bible Societies, 1994), 105.
5. Ibid., 105–6.
6. Strauss, *Mark*, 728. For a detailed discussion of the textual issues related to the longer ending of Mark, see Robert H. Gundry, *Mark: A Commentary on His Apology for the Cross* (Grand Rapids: Eerdmans, 1993), 1009–21.

Based on his rejection of the longer ending of Mark, Schnabel declares, "The Gospel of Mark does not record an explicit missionary commission."[7] Instead of explaining the content of Mark 16:15, he merely states that Mark left several indications throughout his Gospel that encourage his readers to affirm Jesus's desire for a Gentile mission. Specifically, he highlights Mark 13:10 and 14:9. Regarding Mark 13:10 ("And the gospel must first be proclaimed to all nations"), Schnabel comments, "In the time before the end, the good news that Jesus had preached will be preached to all nations (i.e., to Gentiles)."[8] He further notes that Mark 14:9 ("And truly, I say to you, wherever the gospel is proclaimed in the whole world, what she has done will be told in memory of her") "announces a universal ministry of Jesus' followers, whose message of the good news will include a reference to Jesus' anointing by a woman before the crucifixion."[9]

Is the message of Mark 16:15 true? Although Schnabel does not affirm the authenticity of Mark 16:15 he admits, "This text, although not part of the original Gospel of Mark, is based on elements from Mt 28:16–20 and possibly the theme of the book of Acts, presented in an abbreviated and summarized version."[10]

The Location of the Commission

The variations of the Great Commission found in the four Gospels are probably not different versions of the same utterance but are based on four different accounts given at different times. They all took place during the forty days between Jesus's resurrection and ascension and occurred at various locations or settings. Matthew specifies that Jesus declared the words in the mountains of Galilee (28:16). In Mark's version, the commission occurs after Jesus appeared to Mary Magdalene (16:9) and to two people who were walking in the countryside (16:12). Jesus then appears to the eleven who were reclining at a meal (16:14) and commissions them to "Go into all the world and proclaim the gospel to the whole creation" (16:15).

The Language of the Commission

We will now proceed with the assumption that Mark's version of the Great Commission is a later addition, but that it reflects the essence of the teaching found in the New Testament, especially the Great Commission in Matthew 28. For example, in both Mark and Matthew, the opening word of the commission proper is "go" (*poreuthentes*).[11] The main verb, however, is different.

---

7. Eckhard J. Schnabel, *Early Christian Mission*, vol. 1, *Jesus and the Twelve* (Downers Grove, IL: InterVarsity, 2004), 376.

8. Ibid.

9. Ibid.

10. Ibid., 378.

11. Interestingly, Matthew uses the participle *poreuthentes* six other times, whereas it is only found here in Mark (16:15).

Whereas in Matthew, Jesus commands his followers to "make disciples," in Mark Jesus instructs them to "preach" (*kēruxate*) the gospel. The location of where the disciples are to go is also similar. The call to preach the gospel "to the whole creation" (or better, "to every creature") recalls Matthew's version of the Great Commission to make disciples of "all nations" (28:19–20) as well Jesus's instruction in Acts 1:8 to be witnesses "to the ends of the earth."

Furthermore, the close connection between faith and baptism found in Mark 16:16 is also found in Acts 2:38 ("And Peter said to them, 'Repent and be baptized every one of you in the name of Jesus Christ for the forgiveness of your sins, and you will receive the gift of the Holy Spirit'"). Likewise, the resulting condemnation for those who refuse to believe is a theme found in John 3:18 ("Whoever believes in him is not condemned, but whoever does not believe is condemned already, because he has not believed in the name of the only Son of God"; see also John 3:36).

The miraculous signs that will accompany God's messengers (Mark 16:17) are somewhat parallel to the language found in John 14:12 ("Truly, truly, I say to you, whoever believes in me will also do the works that I do; and greater works than these will he do, because I am going to the Father") and Acts 5:12 ("Now many signs and wonders were regularly done among the people by the hands of the apostles"). In particular, the confirmatory signs of casting out demons and speaking in tongues are found in Acts (see 16:18 where Paul casts our a demon from a girl in Philippi and 2:4; 10:46; and 19:6 where new believers speak in tongues).

Mark 16:18 mentions the handling of snakes and the drinking of deadly poison without consequence. Perhaps this is based on Luke 10:19 where Jesus gives the promise of protection over snakes and scorpions ("Behold, I have given you authority to tread on serpents and scorpions, and over all the power of the enemy, and nothing shall hurt you"). Such a promise appears to come to fruition when Paul was bit by a snake on the island of Malta without being harmed (Acts 28:3–6). Finally, verse 18 mentions healing through the laying on of hands, which can be found in Acts 9:12, 17, and 28:8.

Summary

We are convinced that the longer ending of Mark (16:9–20) is not original but was a later addition to the text which was created to conform Mark to the pattern of the other Gospels. The Markan version of the Great Commission then draws from those Gospels (and Acts) and so it mostly echoes truths found elsewhere. Plummer gives us helpful advice in how to treat the material found in the longer ending of Mark: "while the commission in Mark 16:15 is correct theologically in that it corresponds to Scriptures like Matthew 28:19, we would do well not to quote later additions of Scripture as if they have scriptural authority."[12]

REFLECTION QUESTIONS

1. In what ways is Mark 16:15 similar to Matthew 28:19–20? In what ways is it different?

2. Do you think the longer ending of Mark (16:9–20) was originally written by Mark? What are the arguments for and against its inclusion?

3. If the longer ending of Mark is not original, do you think it should be included in modern English versions?

4. Nearly all the statements made in Mark 16:15–18 are found in the other Gospels and Acts. Do you think these parallels suggest literary dependence?

5. What other verses in Mark demonstrate Mark's understanding of the Great Commission?

---

12. Robert L. Plummer, "The Great Commission in the New Testament," *SBJT* 9, no. 4 (2005): 8.

What Is the Contribution of Luke's Version of the Great Commission?

As demonstrated in the last question, each of the Gospels contains a unique version of the Great Commission (although Mark's version is textually disputed). Luke's account, which apparently took place on the evening of the day of Jesus's resurrection,[1] occurs after Jesus appears to the two disciples walking from Jerusalem to Emmaus (24:13–15). After the two quickly return to Jerusalem to share what they experienced with the eleven disciples, Jesus comes to them and declares:

> This is what is written: The Messiah will suffer and rise from the dead on the third day, and repentance for the forgiveness of sins will be preached in his name to all nations, beginning at Jerusalem. You are witnesses of these things. I am going to send you what my Father has promised; but stay in the city until you have been clothed with power from on high. (Luke 24:46–49, NIV)

It is important to remember that the commission accounts in the various Gospels record *different* accounts of Jesus's words to his disciples, though they all contain the same basic commission to reach the nations with the gospel.[2] Matthew's account occurs in Galilee whereas Luke's account takes place near Jerusalem. Marshall highlights some of the similarities of Luke with Matthew and John: "Luke shares with Mt. the commission to go to the nations and the

---

1. Eckhard J. Schnabel, *Early Christian Mission*, vol. 1, *Jesus and the Twelve* (Downers Grove, IL: InterVarsity, 2004), 368; and Darrell L. Bock, *Luke (Volume 2: 9:51–24:53)* (Grand Rapids: Baker, 1996), 1928.
2. Bock writes, "These are distinct accounts of distinct events" (*Luke*, 1928).

promise of divine power. He shares with Jn. the promise of the Spirit and the reference to forgiveness of sins."[3]

The Fulfillment of OT Promises

Luke's version of the Great Commission begins with Jesus linking his suffering, resurrection, and subsequent preaching of repentance to the nations as fulfillment of Old Testament prophecy. The phrase "it is written" (*gegraptai*) is often used in the Gospels to designate the fulfillment of what was written in the Old Testament. But where is this written in the Old Testament that the "the Christ should suffer and on the third day rise from the dead" and that "repentance for the forgiveness of sins should be proclaimed in his name to all nations" (Luke 24:46–47)? It appears that Jesus is not quoting a particular passage from the Old Testament but is summarizing the particular themes scattered over its pages. As Green explains, "The point of Jesus' words is not that such-and-such a verse has now come true, but that the truth to which all of the Scriptures point has now been realized!"[4] And yet, it is helpful to note some key verses related to these topics that Jesus might have been referencing.

Suffering Messiah	**Psalm 22**	"My God, my God, why have you forsaken me? Why are you so far from saving me, from the words of my groaning? . . . But I am a worm and not a man, scorned by mankind and despised by the people. All who see me mock me; they make mouths at me; they wag their heads" (vv. 1, 6–7).
	Psalm 31	"Into your hand I commit my spirit. . . . For I hear the whispering of many—terror on every side!—as they scheme together against me, as they plot to take my life" (vv. 5, 13).
	Isaiah 53	"He was oppressed, and he was afflicted, yet he opened not his mouth; like a lamb that is led to the slaughter, and like a sheep that before its shearers is silent, so he opened not his mouth. By oppression and judgment he was taken away; and as for his generation, who considered that he was cut off out of the land of the living, stricken for the transgression of my people?" (vv. 7–8; cited in Acts 8:32–33).

---

3. I. Howard Marshall, *The Gospel of Luke*, NIGTC (Grand Rapids: Eerdmans, 1978), 903.
4. Joel B. Green, *The Gospel of Luke*, NICNT (Grand Rapids: Eerdmans, 1997), 857.

Resurrected Messiah	**Psalm 16:10**	"For you will not abandon my soul to Sheol, or let your holy one see corruption" (cited in Acts 2:27; 13:35).
	Psalm 110:1	"The LORD says to my Lord: 'Sit at my right hand, until I make your enemies your footstool'" (cited in Acts 2:34).
	Hosea 6:2	"After two days he will revive us; on the third day he will raise us up, that we may live before him."
Proclaimed Messiah	**Isaiah 42:6**	"I am the LORD; I have called you in righteousness; I will take you by the hand and keep you; I will give you as a covenant for the people, a light for the nations."
	Isaiah 49:6	"[The LORD] says: 'It is too light a thing that you should be my servant to raise up the tribes of Jacob and to bring back the preserved of Israel; I will make you as a light for the nations, that my salvation may reach to the end of the earth.'"

Jesus's contemporaries expected a Messiah who would come and deliver his people. But Jesus also emphasizes that it was part of God's sovereign plan that the Messiah would suffer, be resurrected, and then be proclaimed throughout the world. Bock summarizes: "The key point of this passage is that everything from suffering to universal proclamation was predicted in the Scriptures."[5]

The Commission

Although it is (rightly) argued that the essence of Jesus's commission in Matthew and Luke are the same, there are some notable differences. Oftentimes these differences highlight a distinct emphasis in each particular Gospel. For example, whereas the Great Commission in Matthew appears as a command or imperative ("make disciples"), in Luke it is given in the form of a prediction ("will be preached").[6] The written promise or, better, prediction is that the gospel will be proclaimed to all the nations. Jesus speaks with certainty

---

5. Bock, *Luke*, 1941.
6. It should be noted that the Greek text does not include a future tense verb but contains a series of three parallel infinitives: παθεῖν (*pathein*), ἀναστῆναι (*anastēnai*), and κηρυχθῆναι (*kēruxthēnai*). Thus, the text could be translated: "Thus it is written, the Christ is *to suffer* and *to rise* from the dead on the third day, and repentance for the forgiveness of sins is *to be preached* in his name to all nations" (Luke 24:46–47). Since the infinitives indicate predictions based on the Old Testament, however, they function similar to future tense verbs.

to his disciples that the ultimate success of the commission is not in doubt or jeopardy. Just as the myriad of other predictions have been fulfilled according God's sovereign plan, so also this prediction will someday come to fruition. God has declared that it will happen and so the result is certain—despite the failure of many Christians to joyfully comply with and participate in the task of the Great Commission. A lackadaisical or disobedient attitude toward participating in God's plan of redemption cannot stop the divine progress of the gospel. And yet, the certainty of victory to spread the gospel to all the nations should give us confidence and propel us to participate in the task. In addition, God will hold us accountable for our willingness to obey his commands when Jesus returns to finally and fully establish his kingdom.

Specifically, "repentance for the forgiveness of sins" is what will be proclaimed to the nations. Bock explicates the meaning of repentance: "People must change their minds about God and the way to him, especially their thinking about sin, their inability to overcome sin on their own, Christ's essential role in forgiveness, and the importance of depending on him for spiritual direction. . . . People must also change their minds about who they are and how they can approach God. Repentance involves turning to and embracing God in faith."[7] In addition, this repentance is "in his name." This phrase refers to Yahweh's authority which has been given to Jesus who is the mediator of God's promises (1 Tim. 2:5).

To All Nations

The message of repentance for the forgiveness of sins is to be preached "to all nations." Consistent with Luke's emphasis on the poor, outcasts, and outsiders, the universal message of hope is available to anyone from any nation or people group (cf. Luke 2:32; Acts 13:47). The commission is also portrayed in geographical terms: the disciples are to begin in Jerusalem.[8] We also know that in Luke's second volume the disciples are to continue their mission to Judea, Samaria, and finally to the ends of the earth (Acts 1:8). Thus, the gospel is to first permeate the Jewish regions but then quickly spread to Gentile

---

Furthermore, since *kēruxthēnai* ("to be preached") represents a portion of the prediction not yet fulfilled (when uttered by Jesus), the infinitive also carries an imperative force.

7. Bock, *Luke*, 1940.
8. See the following Old Testament passages: "For out of Zion shall go forth the law, and the word of the LORD from Jerusalem" (Isa. 2:3); "Blow a trumpet in Zion; sound an alarm on my holy mountain! Let all the inhabitants of the land tremble, for the day of the Lord is coming. . . . And it shall come to pass that everyone who calls on the name of the LORD shall be saved. For in Mount Zion and in Jerusalem there shall be those who escape, as the LORD has said, and among the survivors shall be those whom the LORD calls" (Joel 2:1, 32); "and many nations shall come, and say: 'Come, let us go up to the mountain of the LORD, to the house of the God of Jacob, that he may teach us his ways and that we may walk in his paths.' For out of Zion shall go forth the law, and the word of the LORD from Jerusalem" (Mic. 4:2).

territory. Köstenberger and O'Brien note, "The holy city, with its unparalleled position in salvation history, is not only the focus of opposition to and rejection of Jesus, and the place where he suffers, dies (Luke 9:51; 13:33; 18:31), rises again and appears (24:1–11, 36–49). It is also the all-important starting point for the gospel mission to Israel and then to the nations."[9]

And yet, the disciples were not to remain in Jerusalem waiting for the nations to flow in, but they were to be faithful witnesses who take the gospel to the nations. This appears to be a distinctive transition from the Old Testament model. As Schnabel explains, "Whereas the Jews expected the nations to come from the 'outside' to Jerusalem as the center of the world, Jesus tell his disciples that they will begin in Jerusalem and then move out to the nations."[10] This orientation denotes a change from a centripetal to a centrifugal model.[11]

The apostle Paul understood Jesus's commission and seems to follow the model of going from Jerusalem to the nations (or from the Jewish nation to the Gentiles). In Romans 1:17 he states that the gospel contains the power of God that leads to salvation for everyone who believes "to the Jew first and also to the Greek." Regarding his mission, Paul writes how the gospel spread geographically (and thus ethnically): "from Jerusalem and all the way around to Illyricum I have fulfilled the ministry of the gospel of Christ" (Rom. 15:19). Paul followed the same pattern that Jesus outlined by preaching the gospel to the Jews first and then to Gentiles.

Disciples as Witnesses

The disciples, who were eyewitnesses of the resurrection, were to proclaim the truth of what they saw and experienced firsthand.[12] Thus, the apostles had a unique eyewitness role (cf. Isa. 43:10; 44:8). "For Luke," clarifies Schnabel, "'witnesses' are the early Christian preachers who proclaim the message of Jesus Christ authentically and without distorting it—both the 'external events' linked with the life, death, and resurrection of Jesus of Nazareth, and the 'internal significance' of Jesus the Messiah and the procurement of salvation for people."[13] Just as the disciples were earlier sent out by Jesus to proclaim his message to all of Israel, now they are commissioned to announce the message to all the world.[14]

---

9. Andreas J. Köstenberger and Peter T. O'Brien, *Salvation to the Ends of the Earth: A Biblical Theology of Mission* (Downers Grove, IL: InterVarsity, 2001), 126.
10. Schnabel, *Early Christian Mission*, 370.
11. See Green, *Luke*, 857.
12. See Acts 1:8, 22; 2:32; 3:15; 5:32; 10:39, 41; 13:31; 22:15, 20; 26:16.
13. Schnabel, *Early Christian Mission*, 369.
14. Stein comments, "The earlier mission of the Twelve (Luke 9:1–6) and the seventy (10:1–12) were a proleptic foretaste of the future mission of Jesus' witnesses after the resurrection" (Robert H. Stein, *Luke*, NAC [Nashville: B&H, 1992], 621).

But does this mean that the role of being a witness to the truth of the resurrection is limited to the original disciples? Nolland helpfully notes, "Luke 24 makes it clear that the role of the Apostles, though central, is in no way meant to exclude or excuse the wider disciple community from the witnessing task."[15] What the apostles began is to be continued by those who give their allegiance to Jesus and can testify to the salvation they have received through faith.

Based on what we find in Acts, the resurrection of Jesus was the central focus of the apostles' message.[16] The speeches/sermons in Acts are examples of how the disciples served as witnesses of Jesus's life, death, and resurrection. In Luke's Gospel account the apostles were commissioned and appointed to preach the good news to the nations, but it is only after they receive the Spirit in the book of Acts that the mission really begins.

Empowerment from the Spirit

In the final portion of the Lukan commission, Jesus announces, "I am going to send you what my Father has promised; but stay in the city until you have been clothed with power from on high" (Luke 24:49, NIV). As is clear from the Farewell Discourse in John 14–17, the Spirit is what the Father promised and is the one who will clothe the disciples with power. The success of the spread of the gospel to the nations is not dependent on the efforts of humanity, even the apostles. They are told to wait in Jerusalem until they "are clothed with power from on high." The Old Testament prophesied how God would pour out his Spirit as part of the new covenant.[17] The empowerment from the Spirit was clearly displayed in Jesus's own ministry (Luke 4:14; 5:17). Garland notes, "The same Holy Spirit that overshadowed Mary (Luke 1:35) and empowered Jesus will clothe them to fulfill their commission."[18] The coming of the Spirit demonstrates the inauguration of the blessings of God's kingdom promised in the Old Testament. Specifically, the endowment of the Spirit is to empower the apostles to proclaim the good news about Jesus. In Acts, Luke continues the theme of the Spirit-empowered spread of the gospel through different regions.[19]

Summary

Luke's version of the Great Commission has both similarities and differences to Matthew's version. Not only were the Messiah's suffering, death, and resurrection foretold in the Old Testament, but the proclamation of this

---

15. John Nolland, *Luke 18:35–24:53*, WBC 35C (Dallas: Word, 1993), 1220.
16. See Acts 2:23–24, 32; 3:15; 4:2, 10, 33; 5:30; 10:41; 13:30–37; 17:3, 18, 31.
17. See Isaiah 32:15; 44:3; Ezekiel 39:29; Joel 2:28–29.
18. David E. Garland, *Luke*, ZECNT (Grand Rapids: Zondervan, 2011), 969.
19. See Acts 1:8; 2:4, 17–18; 4:8, 31; 5:32; 6:10; 8:29, 39; 10:19, 44; 11:12; 13:2–4.

good news was also predicted. In particular, the message will spread from Jerusalem to all the nations. In order for this to occur, the disciples, as faithful witnesses, must wait for the empowerment which comes from the indwelling power of the Holy Spirit. This commission, then, is passed on to all disciples of Jesus who are charged to finish the task begun by the apostles.

REFLECTION QUESTIONS

1. How is Luke's version of the Great Commission different than Matthew's version?

2. How do we know these are not merely variations of the same commission?

3. Can you point to Old Testament texts that speak of the Messiah's suffering and resurrection?

4. The Lukan commission centers on the proclamation of "repentance for the forgiveness of sins" (NIV). Can you explain what is meant by "repentance"?

5. Luke highlights that the gospel is to be taken (1) to the nations (2) by faithful witnesses (3) who rely on the Holy Spirit. Which of these do you struggle with? That is, are you weakest in (1) willingness to serve on a foreign field, (2) evangelism, or (3) trusting in the Spirit and not your own gifts?

What Is the Contribution of John's Version of the Great Commission?

When reading the Gospel of John it becomes obvious that John's intent was to present material that was lacking in the other Gospel accounts. Thus, it should not surprise us that his version of the Great Commission is somewhat unique. John records Jesus's words in Jerusalem on the day of the resurrection as the disciples met secretly. Schnabel calls this the "least detailed" commission but, from a theological point of view, the "most striking."[1]

> "Peace be with you. As the Father has sent me, even so I am sending you." And when he had said this, he breathed on them and said to them, "Receive the Holy Spirit. If you forgive the sins of any, they are forgiven them; if you withhold forgiveness from any, it is withheld." (John 20:21–23)

In this postresurrection appearance, Jesus first announces "peace be with you" to his disciples who were meeting behind closed doors because they feared the Jews (John 20:19). He then shows the disciples both his hands and side (John 20:20). For a second time, Jesus declares "peace." Although a standard Jewish greeting (i.e., "peace" or *shalom*), the unique context of Jesus's words suggest that this pronouncement is loaded with theological significance.[2] In his farewell discourse, Jesus declared to his disciples, "Peace I leave with you; my peace I give to you. Not as the world gives do I give to you. Let not your hearts be troubled, neither let them be afraid" (John 14:27). Through

---

1. Eckhard J. Schnabel, *Early Christian Mission*, vol. 1, *Jesus and the Twelve* (Downers Grove, IL: InterVarsity, 2004), 378.
2. Beasley-Murray states, "Never had that 'common word' been so filled with meaning as when Jesus uttered it on Easter evening" (*John*, WBC 36 (Waco, TX: Word, 1987), 378).

his death and resurrection, Jesus satisfied the wrath of God and now offers true peace to his followers. On that evening, "Christ's use of the term 'peace' is less a greeting and more a pronouncement of blessing, a declaration that the peace of God—the eschatological peace promised in the OT—has now been made accessible through Jesus Christ."[3] Indeed, it was the wounds of Jesus from the cross that brought peace. As Isaiah 53:5 states, "the punishment that brought us peace was on him, and by his wounds we are healed" (NIV). Consequently, the blessing and favor of God can rest upon those who believe in Jesus.[4]

The Divine Paradigm

Before Jesus announces to his disciples that he is in fact "sending" them, he first offers a parallel with his own mission: "As the Father has sent me, even so. . . ." (John 20:21). That is, Jesus's command to his disciples is couched in language that mirrors his own mission: Just as the Father sent Jesus into the world to redeem it, so also Jesus is sending his disciples into the world with the message of redemption and the forgiveness of sins. Earlier in John's Gospel we read: "For God did not send his Son into the world to condemn the world, but in order that the world might be saved through him" (John 3:17).[5] Jesus was sent by God on a mission to accomplish the salvation of his people. Jesus now passes the torch to the disciples who will continue to do the mission that he began.[6] Carson explains: "Jesus was sent by his Father into the world (3:17) by means of the incarnation (1:14) with the end of saving the world (1:29); now that Jesus' disciples no longer belong to the world (15:19), they must also be sent back into the world (20:21) in order to bear witness, along with the Paraclete (15:26–27)."[7] In what ways are the disciples to emulate Jesus's ministry? Köstenberger explains: "Jesus' followers are to embody the qualities characteristic of their Lord during his earthly mission. As Jesus did his Father's will, they have to do *Jesus'* will. As Jesus did the Father's works, they have to do *Jesus'* works. As Jesus spoke the words of his Father, they have

---

3. Edward W. Klink, *John*, ZECNT (Grand Rapids: Zondervan, 2016), 859.
4. Schnabel writes, "The peace that Jesus gives is an important foundation for the mission of the disciples, a mission that demonstrates and confirms the reliability of life with Jesus Christ in the midst of political uncertainty, social insecurity and personal vulnerabilities. The message of the disciples is about peace: about the restoration of peace with God through Jesus' death on the cross, about the atonement and forgiveness of sins, about the reconciliation of rebellious humankind with God" (*Early Christian Mission*, 379).
5. There are more than forty passages where Jesus declares that he was sent by the Father in the Gospel of John: 4:34; 5:23–24; 30; 36–38; 6:29, 38–39, 44, 57; 7:16, 18, 28–29, 33; 8:16, 18, 26, 29, 42; 9:4; 10:36; 11:42; 17:3, 8, 18, 21, 23, 25; 12:44–45, 49; 13:16, 20, 24; 15:21; 16:5.
6. We must note that Jesus did not fail in his mission or leave his mission incomplete. He accomplished all that the Father intended. Rather, the message of Jesus's finished work must continue to be proclaimed throughout the world.
7. D. A. Carson, *The Gospel according to John*, PNTC (Grand Rapids: Eerdmans, 1991), 648.

to speak *Jesus'* words. Their relationship to their sender, Jesus, is to reflect Jesus' relationship with *his* sender."[8]

The disciples are not commissioned to begin a new work. Rather, they are commissioned to carry on the work that their Lord had been doing (Acts 1:1–8). Thus, the mission of the disciples is nothing other than the mission of the exalted Jesus. The church does not replace Jesus or supplement the function of Jesus. The church does, however, extend the message of Jesus to the nations.

The Sending of the Disciples

John 20:21 contains Jesus's commission to the disciples, "As the Father has sent me, even so I am sending you."[9] What Jesus prayed for earlier in his high priestly prayer was now proclaimed to the disciples. Earlier Jesus declared: "As you sent me into the world, so I have sent them into the world" (John 17:18). Although the geographic scope of the disciples' mission is not explicitly stated in John 20:21, the context of John (specifically 17:18) makes it clear that the "world" is in view. Schnabel rightly notes that "world" in the context of John's Gospel refers to "all human beings who are distant from and antagonistic toward God."[10] Although the nations are not specifically referenced in the commission or in Jesus's earlier prayer, being sent to the "world" includes both Jews and Gentiles.

Up to this point it was not altogether obvious from the Old Testament or from Jesus's teaching that the disciples would be sent to other nations. Indeed, the Old Testament often describe the nations *coming* to Israel as opposed to Israel being *sent* to the nations.[11]

---

8. Andreas J. Köstenberger and Peter T. O'Brien, *Salvation to the Ends of the Earth: A Biblical Theology of Mission* (Downers Grove, IL: InterVarsity, 2001), 222. Carson adds, "In so far as Jesus was entirely obedient to and dependent upon his Father, who sealed and sanctified him and poured out the Spirit upon him without limit (1:32; 3:34; 4:34; 5:19; 6:27; 10:36; 17:4), so far also does he constitute the definitive model for his disciples: they have become children of God (1:12–13; 3:3, 5; 20:17), the Spirit has been promised to them (chs. 14–16) and will soon be imparted to them (*cf.* notes on v. 22), they have been sanctified by Christ and will be sanctified by God's word (17:17) as they grow in unqualified obedience to and dependence upon their Lord" (*John*, 648–49).
9. Many have noted that the Greek contains two different words for "sent" (*apostellō* and *pempō*). It is likely that these two verbs are used interchangeably here and the shift is merely stylistic (so most commentators).
10. Schnabel, *Early Christian Mission*, 380.
11. Scobie writes, "First, the ingathering of the nations *is an eschatological event*. . . . Secondly, the ingathering of the nations *is not the work of Israel*. Frequently it is the nations themselves who will take the initiative. In a number of significant passages it is God who gathers the nations. . . . Thirdly, these prophetic passages all envisage *the nations coming to Israel, not Israel going to the nations*. The recurring verb is 'come': "They will *come* to you . . .'" (Micah 7:12), "nations shall *come* . . ." (Isa. 60:3), etc. This movement from the periphery to the center has been appropriately labeled 'centripetal'" (Charles Scobie, "Israel and the Nations: An Essay in Biblical Theology," *TynBul* 43, no. 2 [1992]: 291–92).

But now the flow has changed. Instead of the nations coming to Israel, the church is to go to them. Goheen rightly notes this transition: "This is a great turning point in redemptive history. . . . The change from a centripetal to a centrifugal movement, indeed the transformation of the very form of God's people, can be explained only on the basis of these words of Jesus."[12]

The Receiving of the Holy Spirit

Similar to Luke's account, John mentions the Spirit in the context of the disciple's commission: "And when he had said this, he breathed on them and said to them, 'Receive the Holy Spirit'" (John 20:22).[13] It is the Spirit who empowers the disciples to successfully engage in the task of world evangelization. The Spirit guarantees the effectiveness of the disciples' task of taking the gospel to a hostile world (John 15:25–26; 16:8–11).

But precisely what is John referring to when he says that Jesus breathed on the disciples and said, "Receive the Spirit"? There are at least three main interpretations of this passage: (1) John's version of Pentecost; (2) a partial reception of the Spirit; and (3) a proleptic reception of the Spirit. The first view states that John is recasting the events that originally happened at Pentecost into his own narrative. That is, the apostles received the promised new covenant endowment of the Spirit.[14] It is doubtful, however, that John would take the liberty to reinterpret such a historical event. Further, it is unlikely he would contradict his own statements earlier in his Gospel where Jesus states that the Spirit would only be given subsequent to his glorification which included his return to the Father.[15]

The second view affirms a partial impartation of Holy Spirit but still allows some significance to what took place on Pentecost. As such, some insist that the disciples received the *gift* of the Spirit in John 20:22 and only the *empowerment* of the Spirit at Pentecost in Acts 2. Others, such as Calvin, Westcott, and Bruce, maintain that Jesus *sprinkled* the disciples (with the Spirit) but did not *saturate* them. Whitacre likewise affirms a two-step giving of the Spirit. He asserts that the events at Pentecost are distinct from the events in John 20. The breathing of the Spirit by Jesus, although it is climatic in John's Gospel, does not bring about the results promised earlier in the Gospel. Consequently,

---

12. Michael W. Goheen, *A Light to the Nations: The Missional Church and the Biblical Story* (Grand Rapids: Baker, 2011), 115. Kaiser, however, argues that Israel's mission in the OT also had centrifugal impetus that was by and large, left incomplete (Walter C. Kaiser, *Mission in the Old Testament: Israel as a Light to the Nations*, 2nd ed. [Grand Rapids: Baker, 2012]).

13. The Greek word for "breathed" (*emphysaō*) is used only here in the NT but is used ten times in the Septuagint. Most notably are the uses in Genesis 2:7 where God breathes life into Adam after forming him from the dust, and Ezekiel 37:9 where the Spirit of the Lord breathes life into those slain.

14. See, e.g., George R. Beasley-Murray, *John*, WBC 36 (Waco, TX: Word, 1987), 381–82.

15. See John 7:39; 14:12, 16–18, 25–26; 16:12–15.

the giving of the Spirit "is a complex and not a simple, one-time event" since John's account only describes a "preliminary stage" of ministry preparation for the disciples.[16] He explains: "The Spirit is now unleashed into the world in a new way and begins to bring about new life where he finds faith. The disciples enter into a new phase in their life with God, but it is not yet the time of their active witness, as it will be from Pentecost on. Thus, it would seem John is describing the conception of the church, and Luke (in Acts), the birth."[17]

The third view interprets Jesus's words as referring to a future promise. The strength of this view is that it seeks to harmonize Jesus's earlier words in John's Gospel which indicate that the Spirit will not come until Jesus has departed to the Father.

> Now this he said about the Spirit, whom those who believed in him were to receive, for as yet the Spirit had not been given, because Jesus was not yet glorified. (John 7:39)

> Nevertheless, I tell you the truth: it is to your advantage that I go away, for if I do not go away, the Helper will not come to you. But if I go, I will send him to you. (John 16:7)

In addition, it should be noted that the Greek text says, "he breathed" and not "he breathed *on them*." Consequently, Carson states that this reference should "be regarded as a symbolic promise of the gift of the Spirit later to be given (*i.e.* at Pentecost)."[18] He rightly notes that all positions would affirm the symbolic nature of Jesus's action. The difference is whether the symbolic act refers to something that immediately took place or to something that would soon take place. There are examples of similar statements made by Jesus in John's Gospel that refer to a future fulfillment. For example, in John 17:5 Jesus says, "And now, Father, glorify me in your own presence with the glory that I had with you before the world existed" (cf. John 13:31). The fulfillment of this verse took place at a later time (i.e., at his resurrection, ascension, and exaltation), not when Jesus spoke the words.

Another reason why the first view is often rejected (along with some versions of the second view) relates to the behavior of the disciples. If the apostles received the Spirit in a new covenant sense, then why did their immediate actions not demonstrate such a transformation enabled by the indwelling of the Spirit? They were still fearful, as they met in secrecy with doors locked (John 20:26). Thomas did not believe in Jesus until he saw Jesus (John 15:26–27). The disciples returned to Galilee to their old employment (John 21:1–3). That

16. Rodney A. Whitacre, *John*, IVPNTCS (Downers Grove, IL: IVP Academic, 1999), 482.
17. Ibid.
18. Carson, *John*, 651.

is, they returned to being fishers of fish instead of fishers of men. Carson maintains that all this is "a far cry from the power, joy, exuberant witness, courageous preaching and delight in suffering displayed by the early Christians after Pentecost in Acts."[19] He adds that if the events are understood as the Johannine Pentecost, the results are "desperately disappointing" and the promises in John 14–16 are "vastly inflated."[20] Whatever the interpretation, the point in John 20:21 is that the empowerment of the Holy Spirit is needed to accomplish the mission entrusted to the disciples. Mounce is correct when he notes: "A special infilling of the Holy Spirit is still the primary requirement for effective ministry."[21]

The commission ends with a word regarding the forgiveness of sins: "If you forgive the sins of any, they are forgiven them; if you withhold forgiveness from any, it is withheld" (John 20:23). Mark 2:7 makes it clear that only God can forgive sins. Thus, the meaning is that forgiveness is given when the gospel message is accepted and it is withheld when it is rejected. Beasley-Murray writes, "Disciples proclaim forgiveness of sins and so entry into the saving sovereignty of God through the redemption of Christ, and judgment on those who reject the revelation and redemption of Christ."[22]

Summary

Jesus's commission to his disciples in John's Gospel occurs on the evening of the resurrection. After twice announcing peace to them, he states, "As the Father has sent me, even so I am sending you" (John 20:21). Just as the missionary God takes the initiative in sending his only Son, so also Jesus now sends his disciples into the world. Those who embrace the gospel message receive the forgiveness of sins but those who reject the message are judged.

REFLECTION QUESTIONS

1. When Jesus twice announces "peace" to his disciples (John 20:19, 21), do you think this is simply a common greeting or is it something more?

2. In what ways is the mission given to the disciples similar to Jesus's own mission?

3. What is your reaction to the following statement? "If God is to be properly described as missionary, then appropriate Christian worship of God can

---

19. Ibid., 653.
20. Ibid.
21. Robert H. Mounce, "John," EBC 10, rev. ed. (Grand Rapids: Zondervan, 2007), 649.
22. Beasley-Murray, *John*, 384.

only be done by a missionary church. The lack of missions in so many of our churches is not to be explained by poor strategies or programs but by poor worship."[23]

4. Which view of the phrase "Receive the Holy Spirit" do you think is best? What is the link between the commission given by Jesus and the Holy Spirit?

5. What do you think is meant when Jesus says, "If you forgive the sins of any, they are forgiven them; if you withhold forgiveness from any, it is withheld" (John 20:23)?

---

23. Klink, *John*, 867.

What Is the Contribution of Acts' Version of the Great Commission?

Although we have already discussed the version of the Great Commission in the Gospel of Luke (see Question 22), we thought it would also be beneficial to give attention to Jesus's commission to his disciples found in the beginning of Acts. The first part of this two-volume work (the Gospel of Luke) presents "all that Jesus began to do and teach, until the day when he was taken up" (Acts 1:1–2). The second part of Luke's work (The Acts of the Apostles) begins just prior to Jesus's ascension and "recounts the continuing work of Jesus through his witnesses empowered by the Holy Spirit."[1] He instructed his disciples to wait in Jerusalem for the promise of the Holy Spirit. During that time, the disciples ask Jesus whether he would restore the kingdom to Israel when the Spirit is given (Acts 1:6).

Jesus does not directly answer the disciples' misguided question but instead responds by stating, "It is not for you to know times or seasons that the Father has fixed by his own authority" (Acts 1:7). Although there is much debate regarding the appropriateness of the disciples' question, at a minimum we can state that they were misguided in their desire to know the times or dates regarding the consummation of the kingdom, supposing that the kingdom would come immediately. Beale writes that "verse 7 is a response to their wrong assumption that it was proper for them to know the precise time (cf. 1 Thess. 5:1–11) about when the kingdom would be restored to Israel;

---

1. Andreas J. Köstenberger and Peter T. O'Brien, *Salvation to the Ends of the Earth: A Biblical Theology of Mission* (Downers Grove, IL: InterVarsity, 2001), 128. Stott writes, "Jesus' ministry on earth, exercised personally and publicly, was followed by his ministry from heaven, exercised through his Holy Spirit by his apostles" (John R. W. Stott, *The Message of Acts*, BST [Leicester: InterVarsity, 1990], 32).

such knowledge is reserved for the Father alone."[2] Regardless of one's view of the appropriateness of the disciples' question, it is clear that Jesus corrects them by focusing not on the *time* of restoration but on the *task* of restoration. Jesus depoliticizes and redirects the question with the call to a worldwide mission. Thus, Jesus follows up his divine *correction* with a divine *commission*.

> But you will receive power when the Holy Spirit has come
> upon you, and you will be my witnesses in Jerusalem and in
> all Judea and Samaria, and to the end of the earth. (Acts 1:8)

This statement constitutes Jesus's second postresurrection commission (recorded by Luke) which also serves as the narrative structure of the book of Acts. As Jesus's final and conclusive words before his ascension, this verse is certainly programmatic for the disciples. There are many conceptual and verbal parallels with the earlier commission recorded in Luke 24:46–49: (1) the coming of the promise/Holy Spirit upon the disciples ("I am sending the promise of my Father upon you" [Luke 24:49]; "But you will receive power when the Holy Spirit has come upon you" [Acts 1:8]); (2) the designation of the disciples as "witnesses" ("You are witnesses of these things" [Luke 24:48]; "you will be my witnesses" [Acts 1:8]); and (3) reference to the extent of their witness ("to all nations, beginning from Jerusalem" [Luke 24:47]; "in Jerusalem and in all Judea and Samaria, and to the end of the earth" [Acts 1:8]). In sum, "The disciples were to be the true, 'restored' Israel, fulfilling its mission to be a 'light for the Gentiles' so that God's salvation might reach 'to the ends of the earth.'"[3]

Power: Empowerment from the Holy Spirit

Earlier Jesus ordered his disciples not to depart from Jerusalem (Acts 1:4). The reason for delaying their mission to reach the nations is clarified by Jesus: They need the emboldening power of the Holy Spirit.[4] Jesus states, "But you will receive power when the Holy Spirit has come upon you" (Acts 1:8). The clear implication is that without this indwelling and strengthening

---

2. G. K. Beale, *A New Testament Biblical Theology: The Unfolding of the Old Testament in the New* (Grand Rapids: Baker, 2011), 139. According to Longenecker, Jesus's answer stresses that "the disciples were to revise their thinking about the divine program, leave to God the matters that are his concern, and take up the things entrusted to them" (Richard N. Longenecker, "Acts," EBC, rev. ed. [Grand Rapids: Zondervan, 2007], 718). Bruce maintains, "The question in v. 6 appears to have been the last flicker of their former burning expectation for an imminent political theocracy with themselves as its chief executives" (F. F. Bruce, *Commentary on the Book of the Acts* [Grand Rapids: Eerdmans, 1984], 38).

3. John B. Polhill, *Acts*, NAC 26 (Nashville: Broadman, 1992), 85.

4. The Holy Spirit is "the promise of the Father" (Luke 24:49; Acts 1:4; 2:38) who is sent by the resurrected Lord (Luke 24:49). Thus, Jesus continues his divine mission by means of the Spirit as the Spirit works through the ongoing mission of the disciples.

new-covenant power of the Holy Spirit, the disciples would be ineffective in accomplishing their task. The earlier track record of the disciples confirms this conclusion. When Jesus was arrested in the garden of Gethsemane, they all fled. Peter later denied Jesus three times. The two disciples on the road to Emmaus felt defeated and discouraged. Even after the resurrection many of the disciples returned home to their previous employment.

But after the events of Pentecost in Acts 2 the disciples seem to be almost completely transformed. Peter preached with incredible faith and persuasion on that day so that three thousand were saved. Later, both Peter and John were willing to be arrested and beaten for the sake of the gospel of Jesus. Paul was repeatedly harassed, beaten, and imprisoned for his faith in Jesus the Messiah. Throughout the book of Acts, the Spirit empowers the disciples of Jesus to speak boldly by testifying to God's work through his Son Jesus Christ. In the end, it is the power of the Holy Spirit that causes effectiveness in our missionary endeavors. Schnabel writes, "It is not their organizational or rhetorical gifts that explain the growth of the church, but the presence of God himself and of the risen Jesus Christ in their life and ministry."[5]

People: Jesus's Witnesses

The next clause of Jesus's concluding commission is both a prediction and a command:[6] "and you will be my witnesses." It is a prediction because, like the previous (parallel) verb that uses the future tense ("you will receive"), this verb is also a declaration of what the sovereign Lord indicates will happen. At the same time, it also hits the hearer (and reader) as a command that needs to be heeded. Specifically, Jesus's disciples are to be his *witnesses*. A witness "is someone who helps establish facts objectively through verifiable observation."[7] The apostles were instrumental in confirming the life, death, resurrection, and ascension of the Lord Jesus Christ. They are witnesses who confirm and establish the facts for others. The truths of the Christian faith are not affirmed by "blind faith." Rather, they are established by the eyewitness testimony of the apostles. Indeed, earlier in Acts we read of the qualifications for Judas's replacement: "So one of the men who have accompanied us during all the time that the Lord Jesus went in and out among us, beginning from the baptism of John until the day when he was taken up from us—one of these men must become with us a witness to his resurrection" (Acts 1:21–22). The prominence of the concept of "witness" in Acts is demonstrated by fact that various forms of the term appear almost forty times.[8]

---

5. Eckhard J. Schnabel, *Acts*, ZECNT (Grand Rapids: Zondervan, 2012), 87.
6. Polhill, *Acts*, 85.
7. Darrell L. Bock, *Acts*, BECNT (Grand Rapids: Baker, 2007), 64.
8. See, e.g., Acts 2:32; 3:15; 5:32; 10:39; 13:31; 22:15.

Schnabel helpfully summarizes the role of the apostles as witnesses:

> The Twelve are witnesses to Jesus's resurrection (Luke 24:48; Acts 1:8, 21–22; 2:32; 3:15; 4:2, 10, 33; 5:32) and to Jesus's deeds more generally (Acts 10:39). Having been called and commissioned by Jesus, they are Jesus's authorized ambassadors, witnesses to his life, death, and resurrection, and expounders of his significance for Israel and for the Gentiles.
>
> The Twelve are authoritative teachers who expound Scripture and who explain the life, death, and resurrection/exaltation of Jesus to Israel and to Gentiles (2:42, 44–47; 4:2, 30–31; 5:21–22, 28, 42). Their main activity is the ministry of God's Word (6:2, 4). They explain the good news about Jesus to unbelievers (4:2, 17; 5:20, 25) and teach the Christian community (2:42; 5:42). As Luke describes the growth of the church as the growth of God's Word (6:7; 12:24; 19:20), the ministry of the apostles is indispensable for the church and her growth.[9]

Program: To the Ends of the Earth

The location in which Jesus's followers are to be his witnesses is also stated: "in Jerusalem and in all Judea and Samaria, and to the end of the earth."[10] Three stages of expansion are evident from this text: (1) Jerusalem, (2) Judea and Samaria, and (3) the end of the earth. Jerusalem is the center of the mission and the starting point of their missionary work.[11] Judea refers to the southern region of Israel, but here probably includes the region of Galilee.[12] Samaria is the region between Judea and Galilee and historically was populated with Jews who had intermarried with foreigners and were thus not considered Israelites. The phrase "end of the earth" refers to "the farthest reaches of the inhabited world known at the time."[13] This reference alludes to Isaiah 49:6, which declares, "I will make you as a light for the nations, that my salvation may reach to the end of the earth."[14] What God declares for his Servant to accomplish in Isaiah, Jesus instructs his disciples to do.

To be obedient to Jesus's charge, the gospel is to go to all nations or to the end of the earth. That is, the message of the good news of Jesus Christ is to

---

9. Schnabel, *Acts*, 87.
10. The Greek of Acts 1:8 literally reads: "to the end [singular: *eschatou*] of the earth" which is reflected in the ESV, though not in most English translations.
11. Polhill notes, "The story of Jesus led *to* Jerusalem; the story of the church led *from* Jerusalem" (*Acts*, 86).
12. Schnabel, *Early Christian Mission*, 372. Schnabel notes that "when Luke wrote Acts, Galilee was no longer a separate political entity as it was during Jesus' ministry, but integrated into the Roman province of Judea" (*Acts*, 78; see also Polhill, *Acts*, 86).
13. Schnabel, *Acts*, 79; idem, *Early Christian Mission*, 372.
14. For other allusions to Isaiah 49:6, see Luke 2:32; 24:46–47; and Acts 13:47.

cross all *geographic* and thus also all *ethnic* barriers. [15] There is *no place* and *no people* that should be excluded.

Summary

Jesus's final words before his ascension reiterate the charge to take the gospel to the nations. The disciples were to wait in Jerusalem until the Holy Spirit empowered them to accomplish this God-sized task. Specifically, they were to be faithful witnesses of the things that they heard and saw and to proclaim that message boldly to all. But they were also called to bring the message of the resurrected Messiah strategically to both those who lived near them and to those who were on the other side of the world. Regarding the meaning of the phrase "to the end of the earth," Schnabel writes that it "describes the geographical scope of the missionary assignment of the disciples: they will have fulfilled their commission only when they have penetrated the borders of the earth. The mission of the disciples is world mission. Jesus directs his disciples to initiate an international and universal mission that begins in Jerusalem, reaches the surrounding regions of Judea (including Galilee) and Samaria, and then extends as far as the border regions of the earth."[16]

REFLECTION QUESTIONS

1. Why was the question the disciples asked in Acts 1:6 misguided?

2. In what ways does the Spirit empower believers to be faithful witnesses?

3. Can you describe the transformation that the disciples experienced after the event of Pentecost?

4. In what ways were the apostles unique witnesses of Jesus? What does it mean for us to be faithful witnesses?

5. What is meant by "to the end of the earth"? What are some obstacles to accomplishing this task?

---

15. Bock comments that *the end of the earth* "is geographic and ethnic in scope, inclusive of all people and locales" (*Acts*, 65).
16. Schnabel, *Early Christian Mission*, 375–76.

Questions Related to Biblical Theology and the Great Commission

How Does the Great Commission Relate to God's Creation Order in Genesis?

Though most evangelicals now believe, at least in theory, that the Great Commission is binding upon all Christ-followers, few understand that the mission to "make disciples of all nations" is actually grounded in God's original "Creation Order."[1] This chapter will argue that the concept of disciple-making is grounded in the gospel's redeeming *and sanctifying* work to reconcile God's fallen image-bearers to himself and to make them new through empowering the reordering of their worship. In addition, the mandate to these redeemed image-bearers to make disciples of all nations is the means by which God is accomplishing his original purpose of filling the earth with worshipers who are rightly related to him and live for his glory.

What Is a "Disciple"?

The term *disciple* (*mathētēs*) first appeared in the ancient Greek writings of Herodotus, predating the New Testament era by five centuries, carrying the connotation of *learner*. Michael Wilkins suggests that the term eventually garnered the idea of making a devoted commitment to following a teacher

---

1. The concept of "Creation Order" is not primarily a reference to the chronological ordering of events as they occurred in Genesis 1 and 2. Rather, the emphasis in this concept is upon the intended function and purpose that underlies God's original design. "Creation Order" assumes that God created all things to function in such a way as to bring glory to himself, and that the disordering of creation is both the result of man's sin and the subsequent cause of any chaos that exists. Ultimately the work of Christ is reconciling all things to God (2 Cor. 5:19a) to bring about a reordering and restoration of all things to fulfill God's original purposes (Rev. 21:5–6). See Mark D. Liederbach, *The Convergent Church: Missional Worshipers in an Emerging Culture* (Grand Rapids: Kregel, 2009), 119–32.

and his teachings and was referenced by both Plato and Socrates.[2] When Jesus comes along in first-century Palestine, the concept of discipleship is already present and understood in the culture. Jesus flipped the concept, however, by becoming the teacher who sought out disciples rather than taking the traditional approach of having qualified candidates apply to study under the teacher. This shift is significant because Jesus was not merely inviting his disciples to study his teachings, but to become relationally and spiritually attached to his very life. The ensuing commitment made by those disciples that remained until the ascension was one that the risen Jesus would use to continue the invitation up to our very day.

What about before Jesus's incarnation, or before Socrates, Plato, and Herodotus? Was the concept of discipleship present then? Maybe not in the same sense, though there are many examples of apprenticeship in the Old Testament such as Elijah and Elisha or Moses and Joshua. Is it possible that something of a discipling relationship existed between God and Adam? If we take Jesus's reinterpretation of the term and apply it to the first man and his relationship with God, we do find some similarities. For example, Adam walked with God, received instruction and learned from God, was blessed by God, and even bore the image of God before all creation. And it is to this final distinctive we will now turn in our quest to understand how disciple-making may indeed be rooted into God's Creation Order.

Imago Dei

Genesis 1 and 2 provide the backdrop for God's relationship with humanity and with the rest of creation. It is here that we find creation as God intended. The aforementioned concept of Creation Order is not merely a reference to the chronological ordering of events as documented in these first few chapters of the Bible. Rather, the concept is intended to convey how things within God's creation relate to him as Creator and to the rest of his creation in a regulative or dispositional sense. Chronology is merely one way to bring about order.

At the culmination of God's creative order we find him making man *imago dei*, or in his own image (1:26a). John H. Walton lends insight to this term noting, "Throughout the ancient Near East, an image was believed to contain the essence of that which it represented. That essence equipped the image to carry out its function."[3] And the function that humanity was intended to carry out is explicitly stated in 1:26b–28:

---

2. Michael Wilkins, *Following the Master: A Biblical Theology of Discipleship* (Grand Rapids: Zondervan, 1992), 73–75.

3. John H. Walton, "Genesis," in *Zondervan Illustrated Bible Backgrounds Commentary*, vol. 1 (Grand Rapids: Zondervan, 2009), 20.

Then God said, "Let us make man in our image, after our likeness. And let them *have dominion over* the fish of the sea and over the birds of the heavens and over the livestock and over all the earth and over every creeping thing that creeps on the earth." So God created man in his own image, in the image of God he created him; male and female he created them. And God blessed them. And God said to them, "Be fruitful and multiply and *fill the earth and subdue it, and have dominion* over the fish of the sea and over the birds of the heavens and over every living thing that moves on the earth." (emphasis added)

John Sailhamer notes that the author of the Pentateuch subtly contrasts the creation of the man and the woman with his previous creative work.[4] Instead of "Let there be . . ." as earlier creative acts noted, the text reads, "Let us make . . ." In addition, earlier creatures were made "according to their own kind" but the man and woman are made "after our (Triune God) likeness," emphasizing that we are more like God than like other creatures. Yet, another distinction is that only the man and woman are given dominion, or vice-regency, over all creation. All of this uniqueness is embedded in the *imago dei*. Again, Walton adds that among ancient Near Eastern peoples, "[I]n an image, it was not physical likeness that was important, but a more abstract idealized representation of identity relating to the office/role and the value connected to the image."[5] So our identity as God's image-bearers carries functional purpose related to the task he has made us for, namely bringing him glory through being fruitful, multiplying, and thereby having dominion over the rest of creation.

While the idea of a "cultural mandate" that is often tied to these verses has been skewed taking on a negative destructive connotation, nothing could be further from the truth.[6] The inherent harmony that existed and is conveyed repeatedly in Genesis 1 was not threatened by man's dominion, but rather accentuated. Following each day of creation God looked at his work and declared it to be "good." What standard was God using in his assessment of creation? "Good" does not exist abstractly apart from God. Rather, God's pronouncement that his work was "good" conveys that creation was rightly

---

4. John H. Sailhamer, *The Pentateuch as Narrative: A Biblical-Theological Commentary* (Grand Rapids: Zondervan, 1992), 94–96.
5. Walton, "Genesis," 21.
6. For a better understanding of the positive tone of this term, see Andy Crouch, *Culture Making: Recovering Our Creative Calling* (Downers Grove, IL: InterVarsity, 2008). Crouch notes, "Culture is, first of all, the name for our relentless, restless human effort to take the world as it's given to us and make something else" (23). Thus, culture can be either good or bad contingent upon the heart behind the vice-regent.

related to himself and thus existing as a display of his glory. And, after creating man and woman in his image to have dominion and compound his ordered purposes, God declares all that he has made to be "very good." Why?

God's image-bearers, like a clean, unbroken mirror, were rightly related to God and thus reflect God's goodness and glory by ruling over all that he had made. The relational "likeness" between God and humanity and the harmony in that relationship served to build up, not abuse and destroy, the rest of created order. Keep in mind that at this time, there was no sacred/secular dichotomy. Every task was sacred. All of life was an unbroken act of worship and obedience giving glory to the One whose image the man and woman bore. As long as God's image-bearers were rightly related to God, everything that God made would function harmoniously fulfilling his creative purposes. So what went wrong?

Imago Dei Fractured

The very identity of the man and the woman was inseparably grounded in their relationship with God. Bearing the image of God, they were made to be worshipers. Worship was not something they did as some dichotomized activity. It was who they were; and that identity permeated the motive and method behind everything they did. As long as their relationship with God was intact, their lives, and therefore their worship, were rightly ordered.

The biblical narrative documents in Genesis 3 exactly what went wrong in Adam and Eve's relationship with God and how the subsequent brokenness spread through the entirety of the creation they were made to steward. In Genesis 3:1 the reader is introduced to a Serpent who is "more crafty" than the other animals God had made. Scholars note that the word "crafty" carries the connotation of *wisdom* that has been twisted.[7] This is crucial because the Serpent had been a part of God's good creation, but at some point had taken the wisdom he had been imbued with and twisted it inward on himself by questioning the good character of God.[8]

Being cast down from the heavens, this angelic being brings his twisted wisdom into the realm of the vice-regency of the man and woman and tempts them to question God's good word and thereby his good character. God had issued a single prohibitive command to his image bearers in 2:17 forbidding them to eat from the Tree of Knowledge of Good and Evil.[9] This was, however,

---

7. D. A. Carson, *The God Who Is There: Finding Your Place in God's Story* (Grand Rapids: Baker, 2010), 30–31.

8. It is beyond the scope of this chapter to explain the varying theories related to the concept of theodicy—the problem of evil and its origin. For our purposes here we will limit our study to examining the point at which evil affected humanity and subsequently the earth they were made to rule over.

9. Carson suggests that infinite God is able to know of the possibilities of evil without being a cause or participant by virtue of his omniscience. However, as finite creatures humans

in the context of radical generosity offering them unlimited opportunities for obedience in the form of every other plant (2:16). As the woman, *and* the man who "was there with her" (3:6), weighed the crafty proposal that was before them, they too questioned God's good word and his good character. It was damaged but not destroyed. Their relationship to the God whose image they bore was shattered—but *NOT erased.*

The image of God that constituted the essence of the man and woman was fractured in that encounter, though not altogether erased. Being made as worshipers, they could not cease to worship—but they could change the focus of their worship, which is exactly what they did. Paul speaks of this in Romans 1:21–25, which culminates in a summary of the terrible exchange: "they exchanged the truth about God for a lie and worshiped and served the creature rather than the Creator." Note that Paul emphasizes that they did not cease being worshipers, but shifted the object of their worship from the Creator God to the creation that they were made to have dominion over. The irony is that the man and the woman, and we their progeny, choose to submit ourselves in worship to those things that we were created to rule over!

The brokenness of sin manifests itself in the form of misdirected worship. Awestruck worshipers became brazen idolaters and ceased to accurately image forth God's goodness in the world. So the brokenness that began in mankind naturally extends to the entirety of the realm which we were made to steward (see Gen. 3:14–19). Expanding on this thought, Noel Due states,

> The curse that follows the entrance of sin into the Garden, in its several different elements, reveals dislocation at every level. The rest found in God's nearer presence; the communion of intimate fellowship with him and with one another; the harmony of the created order; and both the joy of procreation and the ability to rejoice in other elements of the mandate are all affected. The mandate the primal couple had been given now becomes the arena for the curse. The key functions of multiplying and filling, keeping and tilling, ruling and subduing are all accompanied by pain, suffering, hard labour, and ultimately physical death and decay.[10]

As the offspring of fractured image bearers, all of humanity is cursed with a bent toward misdirecting our worship away from God and toward creation

---

are incapable of knowing apart from experience and participation. This does *not* mean that the man and woman were set up by God destined to fall into sin. God's instruction, or discipling of Adam, was intended to warn him that there are things that were beyond his knowledge that needed to stay that way (see *The God Who Is There,* 32).

10. Noel Due, *Created for Worship: From Genesis to Revelation to You* (Scotland: Mentor Imprint, 2005), 48.

and ultimately ourselves (Rom. 5:12). The next time someone asks, "If God is so good, then why . . . ?", the only answer is, "It is my fault. And if you'd be honest about your own brokenness you would admit that it is your fault too." We are not just victims of circumstance. We are sinners by nature and by choice. And we cannot fix ourselves.

Imago Dei Redeemed

While the taste of the forbidden fruit was still on their lips, Adam and Eve were already beginning to be cognizant of the unraveling of Creation Order, for they had been "naked and were not ashamed" (Gen. 2:25). Now seven verses later, they are trying to cover their nakedness because of shame. Genesis 3:7 portrays the couple "sew[ing] fig leaves together" and making themselves loincloths. This was no crafting project, but rather a misguided and unsuccessful attempt to undo what they now knew to be sinful misdirected worship. Yet, their efforts were futile, for fig leaves once removed from the tree wither and die. In order to cover their nakedness they would have to return and repeat this process again and again. This is why we believe that this sewing project is the first instance of manmade vain religion. Interestingly there is another passage of Scripture that speaks about fig leaves that may lend some insight. In Matthew 21 Jesus sees a fig tree that is green and leafy from a distance, but upon his approach he finds no figs so he curses it (Matt. 21:19). Why did Jesus curse the fig tree? Because it gave the appearance of fruitfulness but had no fruit. Manmade religion displays guilt of the same infraction. For all of our acts of religious devotion, we cannot produce the righteousness that God demands of us and we cannot reconcile ourselves to Him. They, and we too, simply cannot fix our own brokenness. But God can—and he did!

You do not have to go much further in Genesis 3 to see that God would have willingly made costly provision to redeem his image-bearers. Rather than condemn and destroy, our merciful God pursued the man and woman in their brokenness. The question, "Where are you?" is not intended to convey that God was not privy to their rebellion or location. God's word is intended to bring clarity to the now spiritually blind and disoriented couple. They had just rejected God's word and now he would graciously speak again. His words would issue forth judgment and mercy, consequence and hope. Because the image-bearers had been given authority over all creation, the curse for their sin would extend it as far. Michael D. Williams expounds, "The creature meant to be God's image bearers, his covenant mediator within creation, has declared war against God. Alienation takes the place of covenant intimacy. Hostility, rather than obedient servanthood, now characterizes man's relationship to God."[11]

---

11. Michael D. Williams, *Far as the Curse Is Found: The Covenant Story of Redemption* (Philipsburg, NJ: P&R, 2005), 67.

Yet, in the midst of this pervasive and devastating string of consequences, God makes a promise that theologians commonly call the *protoevangelion*, or the "first good news." Genesis 3:15 reads, "I will put enmity between you and the woman, and between your offspring and her offspring; he shall bruise your head, and you shall bruise his heel." In these condemning words to the Serpent, God would offer hope of a future Rescuer who would in John's interpretation, "destroy the works of the devil" (1 John 3:8b). In the Septuagint, "the seed" of the woman" is singular and conveys that one man would accomplish this task of fixing the brokenness of creation by crushing the Serpent and his offspring.[12] Perhaps this is one reason why the Bible portrays a preoccupation with genealogies—because God's people were to look for the identity of this promised Rescuer.[13]

Consider how Matthew begins his Gospel: "The book of the genealogy of Jesus Christ, the son of David, the son of Abraham" (Matt. 1:1). Matthew is declaring to those who have been waiting, "Here he is! Here is that Rescuer that was promised long ago!" Luke's Gospel concludes by affirming that the Rescuer had to suffer in order to set things right (Luke 24:26). It would take "the image of the invisible God," the very Son of God by whom all things were created, to bring about the reconciliation of all things to himself through the shedding of his own blood (Col. 1:15–24).

Noel Due states, "Where the first Adam failed and brought the tyranny of false worship to the race, the obedient worship of the second Adam would lead a new humanity to the liberating glory of the worship for which it was created."[14] The second Adam would replace the ever-wilting insufficient fig

---

12. "It has also been argued that, on the basis of the Septuagint translation of Genesis 3.15, Jews were already reading the 'seed' of Eve as referring to a singular person who would 'crush' the serpent: This evidence has to do with the pronoun one uses with the word *seed*. In Hebrew, *zera'* is masculine, so one would use the masculine pronoun 'he' (*hû'*) whether one wanted to speak of one descendant or all of them. But in Greek the word for 'seed' (*sperma*) is neuter, so if one wants to use the word to refer to all the descendants, one follows it with the neuter personal pronoun 'it' (*auto*). In contrast, if one wants to use the word 'seed' to refer to a single descendant, one uses a masculine or feminine pronoun: 'he' (*autos*) or 'she' (*autē*). In this passage, the Septuagint uses the masculine pronoun *autos*, indicating that 'seed' refers to a single male descendant of Eve" (quoted from http://hermeneutics.stackexchange.com/questions/9315/what-is-the-historical-basis-for-viewing-genesis-315-as-the-protoevangelium). See also Donald Fairbarn, *Life in the Trinity: An Introduction to Theology with the Help of the Church Fathers* (Downers Grove, IL: InterVarsity, 2009), 122 n. 10.
13. Stephen G. Dempster notes that, "A key purpose of genealogies in some contexts is to show a divine purpose that moves history to a specific goal." He goes on to say that, "the rest of the story (after Genesis 3) recounts the restoration of the relationship (between God and humanity) through the twin themes of geography (dominion) and genealogy (dynasty)." Thus, the hope represented in the Bible's genealogies is directly tied to the fulfillment of the promise that they would exercise dominion over all creation (*Dominion and Dynasty: A Theology of the Hebrew Bible* [Downers Grove, IL: InterVarsity, 2003], 47–49).
14. Due, *Created for Worship*, 20.

leaves of our vain self-help religion with his all-sufficient atoning sacrifice. In so doing he would redeem all that was lost in the fall, enabling those who come by faith to be immediately reconciled to God and progressively made new through the process of sanctification—which also comes by faith in his gospel. Is it not interesting that it was by the rebellious rejection of God's word that misdirected worship entered the world and it is by humble submission to God's word by faith that reconciliation and rightly ordered worship is once again made possible? Graeme Goldsworthy summarizes,

> *Original sin* involved the suppression of the truth of God in nature and conscience, and also the rebellion against every supernatural word from God. Ever since the original sin of Adam and Eve, all of mankind has been involved in sin and is characterized by sin. The saving acts of God involve a new supernatural revelation from God given progressively throughout the whole history of redemption. . . . As Adam refused every supernatural word of God through which human existence and the world could be truly understood, so the children of Adam are born rebels who suppress the truth of God within them, and reject the supernatural world from without. Only God's grace in the saving work of Christ can restore the proper relationship between God and man, and thus cause us to accept the truth.[15]

It is to this reordering of worship by faith in the gospel of Jesus Christ that we now turn.

Imago Dei Restored

Having been redeemed by faith in God's gospel promise, believers are at once reconciled to an inviolable relationship with their Creator based upon trust in his goodness established through the person and work of Jesus Christ. This reconciliation of relationship is the necessary first step in the ongoing application of the gospel in the life of a believer. Paul seems to have Creation Order in mind in Romans 5:19, "For as by the one man's disobedience the many were made sinners, so by the one man's obedience the many *will be made* (*katastathēsontai* is also translated as 'will be appointed') righteous." In Romans 4:5 Paul refers to believers as being "*counted* righteous" (*logizetai* is also translated as "reckoned") because of their faith in Christ. Both of these terms speak of a restoration by God's own work of something that was lost in the fall—the former in the future tense and the latter in the past tense. Being

---

15. Graeme Goldsworthy, *According to Plan: The Unfolding Revelation of God in the Bible* (Downers Grove, IL: IVP Academic, 1991), 59–60.

counted righteous takes place in our once and for all justification and being made righteous takes place through progressive sanctification.[16]

This restoration goes beyond a return to Adam and Eve's Edenic state as is seen by Paul's statement in 1 Corinthians 15:49, "Just as we have borne the image of the man of dust, we shall also bear the image of the man of heaven." G. K. Beale underscores this stating, "people, formerly conformed to the world's image (Romans 1:18–32), begin to be transformed into God's image (Romans 8:28–30; 12:2; 2 Cor. 3:18, 4:4) . . . . This process of transformation into the divine image will be completed at the end of history, when Christians will be resurrected and fully reflect God's image in Christ (1 Cor. 15:45–54; Phil 3:20–21)."[17] In our being reconciled to God through faith we are set on a course of conformity to the image of Christ (see also 1 John 3:2).

Making Disciples to Fulfill Jesus's Last Command

The central imperative in the classic Great Commission (Matt. 28:18–20) is *mathēteusate*, usually translated as "make disciples." It has been noted that the other verbs found in that text, *poreuthentes* ("going"), *baptizontes* ("baptizing"), and *didaskontes autous tērein* ("teaching them to observe") are all participles outlining how one is to make disciples of all nations.[18] However, as Leon Morris asserts, "From this fact some have drawn the conclusion that Jesus did not command his followers to go; all they were to do was make disciples of such people as they happened to encounter. But where a participle is linked in this way with an imperative, it shares in the imperatival force" (see Question 16).[19]

The reason this is crucial is that the earth is filled with idolatrous worshippers who bear the fractured image of the first man and woman.[20] Fundamentally disciples are made by intentionally going *to all nations* (*panta ethnē*, which here carries the connotation of race or ethnic groups outside of Judaism), proclaiming the gospel and baptizing those who repent and believe, and then teaching them to obey Jesus through the enabling power of the indwelling Holy Spirit. Jesus's emphasis stands in stark contrast to how

---

16. For a fuller explanation of sanctification, see William D. Barrick, "Sanctification: The Work of the Holy Spirit and Scripture," *The Master's Seminary Journal* 21, no. 2 (2010): 179–91.

17. G. K. Beale. *We Become What We Worship: A Biblical Theology of Worship* (Downers Grove, IL: InterVarsity, 2008), 282.

18. D. A. Carson notes, "While it remains true to say that the main imperative force rests with 'make disciples,' not with 'go,' in a context that demands that this ministry extend to 'all nations,' it is difficult to believe that 'go' has no imperatival force" ("*Matthew*," EBC, vol. 9, rev. ed. [Grand Rapids: Zondervan, 2010], 666).

19. Leon Morris, *The Gospel according to Matthew*, PNTC (Grand Rapids: Eerdmans, 1992), 746.

20. Michael D. Williams notes, "An idol is anything in creation that man turns to in worship rather than God. Idolatry is not merely one sin among many, but the epitome of all sin, the disobedience that denies God his rightful place over his creation and our lives" (*Far as the Curse Is Found*, 66).

most churches approach disciple-making as a class or curriculum in which believers participate. Christians have inadvertently substituted "discipleship" (a noun) for "disciple-making" (a verb). This seemingly subtle change has produced a passive, rather than active approach to fulfilling Christ's last command. If Jesus's last words were not enough to convince us of his purposes of gathering worshipers for himself from among all nations, perhaps if we saw these final words as a restatement of God's first words to the man and woman in Genesis 1:28 we would understand the pervasiveness of his intentions.

Making Disciples to Fulfill God's First Command

Returning to the first chapter of Genesis, it is important to note the content of God's first recorded words to the man and woman together. Genesis 1:28 was referenced earlier with emphasis placed upon the image-bearer's role in stewarding creation through exercising dominion. However, such dominion would not be possible for the two alone to accomplish. This is why the text contains the imperative, "*Be fruitful and multiply and fill the earth and subdue it, and have dominion*" (emphasis added). In other words, the means by which dominion would be exercised would be through the intentional multiplication and dispersion of image-bearers throughout the earth. God's plan for humanity has always been that we spread his image throughout all creation and exercise our vice-regency as worshippers that are rightly related to Him. By now it should be apparent that Jesus's last command to "make disciples" is beautifully similar to this first command recorded in Scripture. The intent behind both is that God's image-bearers multiply and fill the earth with rightly ordered worship, which in effect accentuates the wholeness that God established in Creation Order.[21] Such wholeness is impossible when humanity's worship is misdirected away from God and toward any created thing, including ourselves.

Summary

Jesus's command to make disciples explains how God's original purposes will ultimately be fulfilled in a broken world. When we are reconciled to God through faith in Christ, our worship begins to be reordered through the Spirit-empowered process of sanctification—which comes by *learning obedience* to God's word (Matt. 28:20). As we are conformed to the image of Christ, we too are to be fruitful and multiply—not merely through physical procreation, but rather through spiritual multiplication. Disciple-making is grounded in Creation Order and is ultimately how God's original purposes will be fulfilled. John Piper puts it so very well, "Missions exists because worship doesn't. Worship is ultimate, not missions, because God is ultimate, not man. When this age is over, and countless millions of the redeemed fall on

---

21. שָׁלוֹם, transliterated *shalom*, communicates all things working rightly together.

their faces before the throne of God, missions will be no more. It is a temporary necessity. But worship abides forever."[22] God's purposes will be fulfilled as John portrays in the new song being sung to the Lamb in Revelation 5:9–10, "Worthy are you to take the scroll and to open its seals, for you were slain, and by your blood you ransomed people for God from every tribe and language and people and nation, and you have made them a kingdom and priests to our God, and they shall reign on the earth." The blood-bought image-bearers from all nations fill the earth with their worship to Christ and exercise dominion to bring about flourishing as God intended in the beginning. The only thing that stands between this moment and that one is the command to make disciples and the promise that God will honor our efforts and grant success.

REFLECTION QUESTIONS

1. In what ways might the thought that you were made for the Great Commission affect the ways you approach your everyday life?

2. How might the idea that discipleship is the reordering of worship around the gospel of Jesus change our approach to missions strategy?

3. How would you explain to someone that God's first recorded command and Jesus's last command are related?

4. What is at stake if we build our rationale for the Great Commission solely from New Testament passages?

5. How might the trajectory of God's mission in the restoration bring encouragement to Christians living on mission?

---

22. John Piper, *Let the Nations Be Glad: The Supremacy of God in Missions*, 3rd ed. (Grand Rapids: Baker, 1210), 15.

How Does the Old Testament Relate to the Great Commission?

The Great Commission found in Matthew 28:19–20 should not have been a complete surprise to the disciples. After all, God has been working his plan of redemption since Adam and Eve fell into sin and he promised that a seed of the woman would crush the head of the serpent (Gen. 3:15). In addition, God promised Abraham that he would bless him and make him the father of many nations (Gen. 12:3). Therefore, it is not surprising when Jesus commands his followers to take the good news to all the nations.

Everyone is accountable to God since he is the sovereign creator who made the heavens and the earth (Gen. 1:1; cf. Ps. 33:8–9, 14–15).[1] In Genesis 3–11 the stage is set for the *need* of the Great Commission. Following Adam's disobedience to God's command (Gen. 3), Genesis records mankind's sin ranging from Cain killing his brother (4:8) to arrogant defiance of God's clear command to fill the earth (11:4; cf. 1:28). Man's heart is thoroughly evil (6:5; 8:21), and as Mark Rooker reminds us, "Because God is holy He cannot wink at sin."[2] Genesis 3–11 clearly demonstrates that humanity does not worship God in a manner befitting his holiness. We will sketch an answer to our question by looking at several key texts: Genesis 12:1–3; Exodus 34:6–7; Isaiah 42:6–7; 49:6; Amos 1:2–2:16; and the book of Psalms. We will divide these texts into the Law, the Prophets, and the Writings.[3]

---

1. See Robin Routledge, *Old Testament Theology: A Thematic Approach* (Downers Grove, IL: IVP Academic, 2008), 318.
2. Mark F. Rooker, "The Genesis Flood," *SBJT* 5, no. 3 (2001): 68.
3. On the various ways to view the Old Testament canon, see Eugene H. Merrill, Mark F. Rooker, and Michael A. Grisanti, *The World and the Word: An Introduction to the Old Testament* (Nashville: B&H Academic, 2011), 102–7.

The Law

Genesis 12 reveals the solution to the problem of mankind's wickedness found in Genesis 3–11.[4] Kenneth Mathews explains, "As the two parts of an hourglass are joined by a slender neck, the role of this one man [Abram] connects the universal setting of chaps. 1–11 and the worldwide vista of the promissory call."[5] Genesis 12:1–3 reads,

> Now the LORD said to Abram, "Go from your country and your kindred and your father's house to the land that I will show you. And I will make of you a great nation, and I will bless you and make your name great, so that you will be a blessing. I will bless those who bless you, and him who dishonors you I will curse, and in you all the families of the earth shall be blessed."

In light of the nature of sin, it is an act of divine grace that God calls Abram to be an instrument of divine blessing to "all the families of the earth." The blessing of the nations is "the reversal of sin's curse and the restoration of creation's fullness."[6] This blessing for the nations is referenced even in later parts of the Old Testament.[7] For example, Isaiah 19:24–25 states, "In that day Israel will be the third with Egypt and Assyria, a blessing in the midst of the earth, whom the LORD of hosts has blessed, saying, 'Blessed be Egypt my people, and Assyria the work of my hands, and Israel my inheritance.'" This will be accomplished by Jesus, the son of Abraham (Matt. 1:1) when the nations follow him (Matt. 28:19). As Richard Bauckham puts it, "The gospel is that in Jesus Christ the curse has been set aside and God's creative purpose for the blessing of his creation is established beyond any possibility of reversal."[8]

---

4. John H. Sailhamer writes about Genesis 12 and its place in the narrative: "It is a new beginning insofar as it is a return to God's original plan of blessing (cf. 1:28)" ("Genesis," *EBC: Genesis–Leviticus*, rev. ed., eds. Tremper Longman III and David E. Garland [Grand Rapids: Zondervan, 2008], 151). Cf. similar connections of Genesis 12 with the preceding biblical chapters in Gordon J. Wenham, *Genesis 1–15*, WBC 1 (Waco, TX: Word, 1987), 275, 281–82; and James Hamilton, "The Seed of the Woman and the Blessing of Abraham," *TynBul* 58, no. 2 (2007): 254 n. 2.
5. Kenneth A. Mathews, *Genesis 11:27–50:26*, NAC 1B (Nashville: B&H, 2005), 105.
6. Michael W. Goheen, *A Light to the Nations: The Missional Church and the Biblical Story* (Grand Rapids: Baker Academic, 2011), 31.
7. Richard Bauckham specifically mentions Psalm 72:17; Isaiah 19:24–25; Jeremiah 4:2; and Zechariah 8:13 (*Bible and Mission: Christian Witness in a Postmodern World*, Easneye Lectures, Frumentius Lectures [Grand Rapids: Baker Academic, 2003], 30).
8. Ibid., 36.

All nations can experience God's mercy.[9] For example, Exodus 34:6–7 states, "The LORD passed before him and proclaimed, 'The LORD, the LORD, a God merciful and gracious, slow to anger, and abounding in steadfast love and faithfulness, keeping steadfast love for thousands, forgiving iniquity and transgression and sin, but who will by no means clear the guilty, visiting the iniquity of the fathers on the children and the children's children, to the third and the fourth generation.'" But as is clear from other Old Testament passages, God's amazing mercy and just judgment are not directed to Israel alone.[10] Indeed, the description of God mentioned in Exodus 34 is referenced in other biblical contexts—several contexts that include the nations.[11] For example, God's mercy and justice are referenced in regard to the city of Nineveh in both Jonah 4:2 and Nahum 1:3, respectively.

The Prophets[12]

The prophets proclaimed both judgment and the offer of salvation for the nations. The prophet Amos, for example, proclaimed that all nations are accountable to God.[13] Amos preached judgment oracles against Damascus, Gaza, Tyre, Edom, Ammon, Moab, along with Judah and Israel (1:2–2:16). Gary Smith explains the purpose of this section: "Because the Israelites accepted the application of these theological principles to their enemies, Amos was able to use the logic of these concepts when he addressed Israel's [own] violence. . . . Amos's sermon came to the shocking conclusion that Israel was no better than the heathen."[14] Amos's sermon to Israel was, in part, effective because of the established fact of God's judgment against the nations. Still, there is hope for the nations who receive God's light.

The inclusion of the nations into the people of God is an eschatological promise throughout the Bible. Here we will only look at two examples, both from Isaiah. Isaiah 42:6–7 states, "I am the LORD; I have called you in righteousness; I will take you by the hand and keep you; I will give you as a

---

9. See the discussion and biblical references in Christopher J. H. Wright, *The Mission of God: Unlocking the Bible's Grand Narrative* (Downers Grove, IL: IVP Academic, 2006), 457–58, 460–62.

10. See the discussion on both mercy and judgment in Douglas K. Stuart, *Exodus*, NAC 2 (Nashville: B&H, 2006), 715–17.

11. John I. Durham helpfully lists passages that refer back to Exodus 34. They are Numbers 14:18; Nehemiah 9:17; Psalms 86:15; 103:8; 145:8; Joel 2:13; Jonah 4:2; Nahum 1:3 (*Exodus*, WBC 3 [Waco, TX: Word, 1987], 453–54).

12. The book of Jonah is often discussed in regard to missions. See the helpful comments in Köstenberger and O'Brien, *Salvation to the Ends of the Earth*, 44–45.

13. See also Isaiah 13–23; Jeremiah 46–51; Ezekiel 25–32; and Zephaniah 2:1–3:5. Paul R. House mentions these references along with "Yahweh's sovereignty over every inch of the earth" (*Old Testament Theology* [Downers Grove, IL: InterVarsity, 1998], 283).

14. Gary V. Smith, *The Prophets as Preachers: An Introduction to the Hebrew Prophets* (Nashville: B&H, 1994), 56, 58.

covenant for the people, a light for the nations, to open the eyes that are blind, to bring out the prisoners from the dungeon, from the prison those who sit in darkness." What role does Israel play in this passage and in the rest of the Old Testament in relation to reaching the nations? Was Israel to be a holy people, and, therefore, bear witness to the nations by their lifestyle ("centripetal missions")?[15] Or was Israel to "go" to the nations and share God's message ("centrifugal missions")?[16] Or both?[17] These questions are not easily answered, but as answered earlier, the testimony of the Old Testament points to a centripetal type of motion. Nevertheless, the light for the nations (42:6) is given "to open the eyes that are blind, to bring out the prisoners from the dungeon, from the prison those who sit in darkness" (42:7). Gary Smith explains that "these phrases [are] metaphors of God's deliverance of people from the prison of spiritual darkness (blindness) and ignorance (9:2; 42:19–20; 43:8; 44:18–19)."[18] Ultimately, this light is Jesus himself.

Isaiah 49:6, which is alluded to in Acts 1:8, is another similar text: "[H]e says: 'It is too light a thing that you should be my servant to raise up the tribes of Jacob and to bring back the preserved of Israel; I will make you as a light for the nations, that my salvation may reach to the end of the earth.'"[19] Elsewhere in Isaiah, the "ends of the earth" is in reference to "coastlands" and "farthest corners" (41:5, 9). It also relates to God as Creator, redeemer of Israel and worthy of praise (40:28; 42:10; 43:6; 48:20). The role of Isaiah 49:6 as quoted in Acts 13:47 also supports the idea that Isaiah 49:6 is a missional text in the Old Testament itself. Howard Marshall explains that the Isaiah citation in Acts "serves to motivate and legitimize the mission to the Gentiles as part of God's plan foretold in Scripture."[20]

The Writings
The Psalms are central in regards to a concern for the nations. Here are a few samples from the Psalms:

---

15. This position is argued in Wright, *The Mission of God*, 501–5.
16. This position is argued in Walter C. Kaiser Jr., *Mission in the Old Testament: Israel as a Light to the Nations*, 2nd ed. (Grand Rapids: Baker Academic, 2012). Wright mentions Kaiser and explains their positions further: "Kaiser addresses many of the same texts we have surveyed in this book, and at a fundamental level we are in agreement on the strong missional message of the Old Testament. I am not yet convinced, however, of his interpretation of these texts as implying a missionary mandate that ought to have resulted in Israel engaging in centrifugal missions to the nations" (*The Mission of God*, 502 n. 2).
17. Both positions are argued in Routledge, *Old Testament Theology*, 326–28.
18. Gary V. Smith, *Isaiah 40–66*, NAC 15B (Nashville: B&H, 2009), 169.
19. Smith prefers to translate the verse in such a way as to bring out the point that the servant himself "is not just a means of getting God's salvation to the ends of the earth (45:20–24); somehow he himself will be God's salvation" (*Isaiah 40–66*, 349).
20. I. Howard Marshall, "Acts," in *Commentary on the New Testament Use of the Old Testament*, eds. G. K. Beale and D. A. Carson (Grand Rapids: Baker Academic 2007), 588.

- All the ends of the earth shall remember and turn to the LORD, and all the families of the nations shall worship before you. (22:27)

- Be still, and know that I am God. I will be exalted among the nations, I will be exalted in the earth! (46:10)

- May God be gracious to us and bless us and make his face to shine upon us, that your way may be known on earth, your saving power among all nations. (67:1–2)

- Declare his glory among the nations, his marvelous works among all the peoples! . . . Say among the nations, "The LORD reigns!" (96:3, 10a)

- Praise the LORD, all nations! Extol him, all peoples! (117:1)

- Let everything that has breath praise the LORD! Praise the LORD! (150:6)

These psalms either refer to God's glory among the nations or declare his glory among the nations. As Mark Futato powerfully asserts, "The Lord's glory is so great that it must transcend the boundaries of Israel and encompass the nations (see Ps. 108:5)."[21] Psalm 67 is a prayer for God to bless Israel so that the nations would know God and then praise him.[22] This psalm can also be read alongside Psalm 66 (e.g., 66:1, "Shout for joy to God, all the earth"). In the Psalms there is a deep dependence upon God even for the accomplishing of missions. John Piper helpfully summarizes Psalm 117 and the Great Commission: "Missions is telling the nations to praise God and then giving them evidences that this is good to do and showing them how God has made a way for sinners to do it because of the blood and righteousness of Jesus Christ. . . . We explain who he is and what he is like and how he has worked in history and spoken to us in the Bible and in his Son."[23] Praying and singing the Psalms can be an encouragement toward living out this mission.[24]

---

21. Mark D. Futato, *Interpreting the Psalms: An Exegetical Handbook*, ed. David M. Howard Jr., Handbooks for Old Testament Exegesis (Grand Rapids: Kregel Academic, 2007), 114.
22. Allan M. Harman, *Commentary on the Psalms*, Mentor (Fearn, Ross-shire: Christian Focus, 1998), 237; Marvin E. Tate, *Psalms 51–100*, WBC 20 (Dallas: Word, 1990), 155, 159.
23. John Piper, "Psalm 117: Everlasting Truth for the Joy of All Peoples," in *The Psalms: Language for All Seasons of the Soul*, eds. Andrew J. Schmutzer and David M. Howard Jr. (Chicago: Moody, 2013), 258. Psalm 117 is also quoted in Romans 15:11—a text that shows the connection between the Old Testament, Christ, and the place of the Gentiles.
24. So Ray Van Neste states, "The psalms were central to the life of the early church as they—following Jesus—preached, prayed, and sang them. Surely the church today ought to follow this same pattern" ("Ancient Songs and Apostolic Preaching: How the New Testament Laid

Summary

The scope of God's authority over the world in the Old Testament helps to illuminate Jesus's words: "All authority in heaven and on earth has been given to me" (Matt. 28:18). God's plan and promises concerning the nations form the basis of the Great Commission in the New Testament. This is especially seen with Abraham in Genesis 12—reaching back to Genesis 1–11 and forward throughout the rest of the Bible. We have seen the mercy of God from Exodus, the means of salvation in Isaiah, and the need for God's presence in the Psalms—to name a few. Several themes from Matthew 28 reach back to themes developed in the Old Testament. Certainly more could be said on how the Old Testament relates to the Great Commission. This survey has shown that it was God's intention from the beginning to bless the nations. Jesus's commission to the disciples, then, represents the beginning of the final stage in bringing such promises to fruition.

REFLECTION QUESTIONS

1. How does the storyline of the Old Testament help to answer the question of the Great Commission in the Old Testament? What other themes relate to missions?

2. How does the sinfulness of humanity relate to the need for the Great Commission?

3. What role does Abraham play in God's plan for the nations? What does it mean to be "blessed"?

4. The salvation of the nations was God's plan in the Old Testament. How is this an encouragement for the church today?

5. How might we sing and pray the Psalms to prepare us for missions? How does God's offer of mercy compel us to serve the nations?

Claim to the Psalms," in *Forgotten Songs: Reclaiming the Psalms for Christian Worship*, eds. C. Richard Wells and Ray Van Neste [Nashville: B&H Academic, 2012], 50).

How Do the Major Themes in Matthew Relate to the Great Commission?

The message and theology in the Great Commission are found throughout Matthew's Gospel. In other words, Matthew 28:16–20 includes the *culmination* of what has gone before in Matthew's Gospel. Gundry calls the Great Commission "a compendium of important Matthean themes."[1] Throughout Matthew, Jesus receives worship, has authority, and his mission includes both Jews and Gentiles.[2] Jesus also commands obedience and discipleship and his presence enables accomplishment of the mission. We will look at each of these thematic elements below.

---

1. Robert H. Gundry, *Matthew: A Commentary on His Handbook for a Mixed Church under Persecution*, 2nd ed. (Grand Rapids: Eerdmans, 1994), 593. He notes that various themes include "Jesus as the greater Moses, the deity of Jesus, the authority of his commands, the trinitarian associations of baptism, the danger of doubt among disciples, the teaching ministry of disciples, discipleship as keeping Jesus's law, the presence of Jesus with his disciples, and the directing of Christian hope to the consummation. Paramount among these themes, however, is the mission to all the nations."
2. See also W. D. Davies and Dale C. Allison, *The Gospel according to Saint Matthew*, ICC (Edinburgh: T&T Clark, 1997), 3:687; R. T. France, *The Gospel of Matthew*, NICNT (Grand Rapids: Eerdmans, 2007), 1107–8; Donald A. Hagner, *Matthew 14–28*, WBC 33B (Dallas: Word, 1995), 881; Craig S. Keener, *The Gospel of Matthew: A Socio-Rhetorical Commentary* (Grand Rapids: Eerdmans, 2009), 713; Frederick Dale Bruner, *Matthew*, vol. 2 [*The Churchbook Matthew 13–28*], rev. and exp. (Grand Rapids: Eerdmans, 1990), 806; David L. Turner, *Matthew*, BECNT (Grand Rapids: Baker, 2008), 691; and Craig L. Blomberg, *Matthew*, NAC 22 (Nashville: B&H, 1992), 429. Blomberg lists the following themes: "(1) the move from particularism to universalism in the preaching of the gospel of the kingdom; (2) discipleship and the establishment of the church; (3) Jesus's commands as ultimately incumbent on Christians; and (4) the abiding presence of Jesus as teacher, as divine Son of God, and the risen and sovereign Lord of the universe."

The Worship of Jesus

Jesus gave the Great Commission in the context of receiving worship (Matt. 28:17; cf. 28:9). Matthew records very early in his Gospel that "wise men from the east" (2:1) traveled to worship Jesus after his birth. They announce, "Where is he who has been born king of the Jews? For we saw his star when it rose and have come to worship him" (2:2). After they found the child, "they fell down and worshiped him" (2:11). King Herod pretended to want to worship him (2:8). After his miraculous walking on the water and his authority over the wind, the disciples worshiped Jesus exclaiming, "Truly you are the Son of God" (14:33). Even children offer praise to Jesus as he was in the temple (21:15; cf. the crowds in 21:9). In this context, there is an emphasis on the location of worship being in the "temple" (21:12 [2x], 14, 15). The temple in the Old Testament was clearly associated with the worship of God (e.g., 1 Kings 8). The Great Commission implies the divinity of Christ. If it is true that Jesus possesses full authority, calls for worldwide allegiance, bears the divine name, and is the very presence of God, then the worship of Jesus is a logical result. Richard Bauckham reminds us that worship "is accorded to God especially as sole Creator of all things and as sole Ruler of all things," and that we worship Jesus "as response to his inclusion in the unique divine identity."[3] Worshipping God compels us to go to the nations so that they too may worship the risen, living Savior.

The Authority of Jesus

The authority of Jesus is also a theme that runs through Matthew's Gospel. At his birth, Jesus already possessed kingly authority since he was "the son of David" (1:1). The chief priests and scribes informed Herod that, according to Micah 5:2, the Messiah would be born in Bethlehem and from that city "shall come a ruler who will shepherd" Israel (2:6). Jesus has authority to heal all (4:23–24; 9:35), authority to command others (8:9), authority over demonic spirits (8:29–32; 12:22; 17:18), authority to forgive sins (9:5–8), authority to send out disciples with power over unclean spirits and power to heal (10:1), and authority to judge (13:41).[4] Jesus taught with authority even as he spoke of matters concerning the Old Testament law and commands (7:28–29). He boldly announced, "All things have been handed over to me by my Father" (11:27). Jesus himself possesses "the keys" of the kingdom, since he alone can rightly be the one who gives authority to the church (16:19). Jesus also claims that he will sit on the throne "in the new world" (19:28; cf. 20:20–23; 25:31).[5] The religious leaders questioned Jesus's authority as tensions continued to

---

3. Richard Bauckham, *God Crucified: Monotheism and Christology in the New Testament* (Grand Rapids: Eerdmans, 1998), 34–35.

4. Grant R. Osborne, *Matthew*, ZECNT (Grand Rapids: Zondervan, 2010), 1079.

5. The word here for "new world" (*palingenesia*) means "the renewal of creation during the Messiah's eschatological reign" (Charles L. Quarles, *Matthew*, EGGNT [Nashville: B&H Academic, 2017], 229).

escalate leading up to crucifixion (21:23–27). These descriptions about the authority of Jesus end with Jesus saying that "all authority in heaven and on earth has been given to me" (28:18). Jesus had authority both before and after his resurrection, though something happened from a salvation-historical perspective with the resurrection: Jesus is exalted and reigns as the end-time king of the world.

The Mission of Jesus

Matthew concludes his Gospel with Jesus's words to make disciples of all nations (28:19). There are several places in Matthew's Gospel that prepare the reader for this command, even with Matthew 10:5–6 limiting the ministry of the Twelve to "the lost sheep of the house of Israel." Jesus ministered to Gentiles throughout his ministry. Gentiles would have heard Jesus's preaching of repentance (4:12–17).[6] Jesus healed a centurion's servant and said about the centurion: "Truly, I tell you, with no one in Israel have I found such faith" (8:10). He healed two demon-possessed men from the country of the Gadarenes (8:28–34). He also healed a Canaanite woman's daughter after seeing her faith (15:21–28). The inclusion of the Gentiles into God's plan is found throughout Matthew's Gospel: Gentile women mentioned in the genealogy (1:3–5), the wise men from the east (2:1–12), the citation of Isaiah 9:1–2 that references "Galilee of the Gentiles" (4:15–16), and the testimony of the centurion who declares, "Truly this was the Son of God!" (27:54).

So when we come to the command to make disciples of all the nations in Matthew 28:19, Donald Hagner comments, "Now we finally arrive at the full inclusion of the Gentiles in the history of salvation (cf. Dan 7:14), something hinted at in the Gospel from the very beginning and throughout (cf. the allusion to Abraham in 1:1 but also the magi in 2:1–12, the centurion in 8:5–13, and the Canaanite woman's daughter in 15:21–28)."[7] Jesus and the nations will be considered more below in Question 27.

The Commands of Jesus

Christians obey and follow Jesus because he is Lord over all things (Acts 10:36). The teaching of Jesus is well-known in Matthew with five major blocks of instruction (Matt. 5–7; 10; 13; 18; 24–25). Jesus teaches that everyone who obeys him is like a wise man, but everyone who disobeys him is like a foolish man (7:24–27). Key to Jesus's commands are the great commandments: love God and love neighbor (22:37–40). He commands love of enemies (5:44), and

---

6. Cf. Craig L. Blomberg, "Matthew," in *Commentary on the New Testament Use of the Old Testament*, eds. G. K. Beale and D. A. Carson (Grand Rapids: Baker Academic, 2007), 18–19.
7. Hagner, *Matthew 14–28*, 887. Cf. D. A. Carson, "Matthew," in EBC, rev. ed., vol. 9 (Matthew–Mark) (Grand Rapids: Zondervan, 2010), 667.

"whatever you wish that others would do to you, do also to them" (7:12). His teaching also should be read in light of Old Testament law (e.g., 19:16–22).

We are taught to follow Jesus in several places in Matthew (e.g., 8:18–22). In fact, Hagner comments, "The word for 'disciple' (*mathētēs*) occurs far more often in Matthew (73 times) than in the other Synoptic Gospels, and the verb 'to make disciples/be discipled' (*mathēteuō*) is found only in Matthew among the four Gospels (13:52; 27:57; 28:19). This underlines the importance of discipleship for Matthew."[8] The commands of Jesus include more than only specific terms. As Ben Cooper explains, "Important metaphors of commitment . . . include fruit-bearing, laying up treasure in heaven, entering by a narrow gate and so forth."[9] Again, we see that the Great Commission concludes with themes that have already been taken up throughout Matthew's Gospel. All Christians are called to follow Jesus in obedience, not a select group within Christianity.[10]

The Presence of Jesus

The book of Matthew ends like it began, with the presence of Jesus. That is, the very one who is called Immanuel (1:23) declares that he will always be with his people (28:20).[11] R. T. France writes, "In context this assurance is focused not on the personal comfort of the individual disciple but on the successful completion of the mission entrusted to the community as a whole."[12] France helpfully clarifies how Jesus's presence functions in Matthew 28 and elsewhere. It is true that Jesus's presence is a personal encouragement. Nonetheless, his presence is purposeful. In Matthew 1:23 his presence signifies the coming of the Davidic kingdom and the salvation of his people (see 1:20 and Isa. 7:1–9:7).[13] The promise of Jesus's presence later in Matthew's Gospel also relates to accomplishing a task (18:20). He says that he will be right there in the middle of his assembled church to help in addressing sin (18:15) and other church matters (18:19). Thus, Jesus is with his disciples so that they can make other disciples (28:19–20). Davies and Allison provide the context of the promised presence of God:

---

8. D. A. Hagner, "Matthew," in *New Dictionary of Biblical Theology*, eds. T. Desmond Alexander and Brian S. Rosner (Downers Grove, IL: InterVarsity, 2000), 266.

9. Ben Cooper, *Incorporated Servanthood: Commitment and Discipleship in the Gospel of Matthew*, LNTS 490 (London: Bloomsbury T&T Clark, 2013), 11 (cf. p. 4).

10. Michael J. Wilkins writes, "Today many incorrectly use the title 'disciple' to refer to a person who is more committed than other Christians or to those involved in special 'discipleship programs.' But we can see from Jesus's commission that all Christians are disciples" (*Matthew*, NIVAC [Grand Rapids: Zondervan, 2004], 956).

11. Carson, "Matthew," 662.

12. France, *Gospel of Matthew*, 1119.

13. On the broader context of Isaiah 7:14, see Blomberg, *Matthew*, 60.

> Mt 28.16–20, like 1 Chr 22.1–16 and Jer 1.1–10, deliberately
> borrows from the traditions about Moses. Readers are to
> exercise their scripturally informed imaginations and set
> the end of Jesus beside the end of Moses. Just as Moses, at
> the close of his life, commissioned Joshua both to go into
> the land peopled by foreign nations and to observe all the
> commandments in the law, and then further promised his
> successor *God's abiding presence*, so similarly Jesus: at the
> end of his earthly ministry he told his disciples to go into
> all the world and to teach the observance of all the com-
> mandments of the new Moses, and then further *promised
> his assisting presence.*[14]

The Old Testament and New Testament show God's presence to be with his people for specific reasons. Davies and Allison point out to the reader of Matthew's Gospel how the Great Commission would have sounded to the original audience steeped in the Old Testament Scriptures. God's presence was an encouragement and enablement for Israel's life and mission; so it is with Immanuel—God with us.

Summary

The Great Commission includes the culmination of what has gone before in Matthew's Gospel. Matthew mentions thematic elements several times before concluding with the Great Commission itself. The Great Commission was not an appendix tacked onto the end of the book, but it is deliberately connected with the rest of the First Gospel. Therefore, the Gospel of Matthew in general, and not just the ending, has a missional purpose. Worship prepares us to go and make disciples of all the nations. Jesus's authority demands it, his example modeled it, and his abiding presence enables it.

REFLECTION QUESTIONS

1. Can you list examples of Jesus being worshiped in Matthew's Gospel? How does that relate to Jesus's deity?

2. How does Jesus demonstrate his authority in Matthew's Gospel? Does his authority change after the resurrection?

3. In what ways was Jesus's mission different than ours? How is it the same?

---

14. Davies and Allison, *Matthew*, 3:680.

4. How is Jesus's presence with us today?

5. Can you think of other ways the Great Commission might relate to the rest of Matthew's Gospel?

How Does Jesus's Life and Mission Relate to the Great Commission?

In the previous question, we looked at the Great Commission in Matthew's Gospel. This question will broaden the scope to include all four Gospels. Jesus's life and mission was focused on bringing the kingdom of God into reality. Mark summarizes Jesus's message: "The time is fulfilled, and the kingdom of God is at hand; repent and believe in the gospel" (Mark 1:15; see also Matt. 4:17, 23; Luke 4:43). The appropriate response to the arrival of the King and the increasing nearness of his kingdom was to repent and believe in the good news he announced. The Great Commission carries out the will of the true King by expanding his kingdom through the proclamation of the good news and by the subsequent discipleship of his followers. In this chapter, we will look at Jesus's proclamation of his mission, his concern for the nations, his miracles, and his crucifixion and death—all part of the coming of the kingdom of God.

Jesus's Mission Proclaimed

When Jesus returned to his hometown of Nazareth, he entered the synagogue and read out loud the scroll of Isaiah. Luke records that he specifically read Isaiah 61:1–2: "The Spirit of the Lord is upon me, because he has anointed me to proclaim good news to the poor. He has sent me to proclaim liberty to the captives and recovering of sight to the blind, to set at liberty those who are oppressed, to proclaim the year of the Lord's favor" (Luke 4:18–19). Luke 4:14–30 is regularly seen as "programmatic" to Jesus's mission.[1] But why is

---

1. E.g., I. Howard Marshall, *The Gospel of Luke: A Commentary on the Greek Text*, NIGTC (Grand Rapids: Eerdmans, 1978), 177–78; John Nolland, *Luke 1–9:20*, WBC 35A (Dallas: Word, 1989), 195. Darrell L. Bock calls it "a representative sample of Jesus' ministry, a paradigm for his ministry" (*Luke 1:1–9:50*, BECNT [Grand Rapids: Baker, 1994], 394).

this specific passage so important in understanding Jesus's work? Joel Green lists five reasons why it is of "central importance for the narrative as a whole": (1) Luke 4:16–30 is a "concrete representation" of the summary in 4:14–15; (2) Luke places this event at the beginning of Jesus's public ministry; (3) this is the only recorded sermon inside a synagogue, even though Luke records other synagogue visits; (4) the passage explains and connects the ministry of the Spirit with Jesus in relation to his mission; and (5) other summaries refer back to this section (see Luke 7:21–22; Acts 10:38).[2]

Jesus came to preach specifically to certain groups of people: the poor, captives, blind, and oppressed. These groups refer not only to the economically poor, but also metaphorically to those who are humble and who recognize their need for God.[3] In his Gospel, Luke mentions both the literal poor (e.g., Luke 21:3) and those who are humble (6:20).[4] Likewise, the blind are both given sight (e.g., 7:22) but people are also described as "those who sit in darkness and in the shadow of death" (1:79). Jesus summarized his mission: "Those who are well have no need of a physician, but those who are sick. I came not to call the righteous, but sinners" (Mark 2:17).

Specifically, Jesus's message centered on the arrival of the kingdom of God.[5] The phrases "kingdom of God" and "kingdom of heaven" are found in sixty-three separate kingdom sayings of Jesus (eighty-five if parallel statements are included).[6] Interestingly, neither Jesus nor the Gospel writers explain these terms, demonstrating that the concept was not new but was based on the Old Testament. When Jesus began preaching he stated, "The time is fulfilled," which suggests that such a time was anticipated by the Jewish people. Goppelt writes, "When Jesus announced the coming of the kingdom he was not introducing a new term. He proclaimed not that there was a kingdom of God, but that it was now coming."[7] In the Old Testament, God is frequently

---

2. Joel B. Green, *The Gospel of Luke*, NICNT (Grand Rapids: Eerdmans, 1997), 207.
3. See comments and references in Robert H. Stein, *Luke*, NAC 24 (Nashville: Broadman, 1992), 156.
4. Cf. ibid., 200.
5. The kingdom of God was Jesus's central message. For example, Stein comments, "The central theme of the teaching of Jesus is the coming of the kingdom of God" (Robert H. Stein, *The Method and Message of Jesus's Teaching*, rev. ed. [Louisville: Westminster John Knox: 1994], 60). See also Thomas R. Schreiner, *New Testament Theology: Magnifying God in Christ* (Grand Rapids: Baker, 2008), 45, 79.
6. See Stein, *Method and Message*, 60. "Kingdom of God" is found fifty-three times (five instances in Matthew, fourteen in Mark, thirty-two in Luke, and two in John). "Kingdom of heaven" or more literally "kingdom of the heavens" is found thirty-two times—all in Matthew. It should be noted that these references do not include statements that only refer to the "kingdom" with no qualifying phrase.
7. Leonhard Goppelt, *Theology of the New Testament*, ed. Jürgen Roloff, trans. John E. Alsup (Grand Rapids: Eerdmans, 1981), 1:45.

referred to as the King of Israel and all the world.[8] And yet, there was also the expectation that God will one day rule over all people in an unprecedented manner.[9] Ladd explains: "While God is King over all the earth, he is in a special way the King of his people, Israel. God's rule is therefore something realized in Israel's history. However, it is only partially and imperfectly realized. Therefore, the prophets look forward to a day when God's rule will be fully experienced, not by Israel alone but by all the world."[10] Additionally, the Old Testament states that God the king has a "kingdom" (see, e.g., Pss. 22:27–28; 103:19) and that the fullness of God's kingdom would one day be established (Dan. 2:44). Thus, when Jesus came preaching that the kingdom of God had come, his Jewish audience knew that he was referring to the complete rule of God over Israel and all the nations.

The kingdom of God refers not so much to a physical realm as to the reign of God.[11] Jesus himself said, "My kingdom is not of this world. If my kingdom were of this world, my servants would have been fighting, that I might not be delivered over to the Jews. But my kingdom is not from the world" (John 18:36). Therefore, in the Gospels the kingdom refers to the final, decisive exercising of God's sovereign reign. This reign was inaugurated in Jesus's ministry and will be consummated upon his return.

Jesus often used parables to teach about the kingdom of God. In fact, this theme is the most common theme of Jesus's parables, with several different features of the kingdom being highlighted.[12] First, Jesus taught that the kingdom of God was a present reality.[13] Through various parables, Jesus taught

---

8. King of Israel (Exod. 15:18; Num. 23:21; Deut. 33:5; Isa. 43:15). King of all the world (2 Kings 19:15; Pss. 29:10; 47:2; 96:10; 97:1; 99:1–4; 145:11; Isa. 6:5; Jer. 46:18).

9. See Isaiah 24:23; 33:22; 52:7; Zephaniah 3:15; Zechariah 14:9.

10. George Eldon Ladd, *The Presence of the Future: The Eschatology of Biblical Realism* (Grand Rapids: Eerdmans, 1974), 46.

11. For example, Bavinck states, "The kingdom of God in the teaching of Jesus is not a political reality but a religious-ethical dominion" (Herman Bavinck, *The Last Things: Hope for This World and the Next*, ed. John Bolt, trans. John Vriend [Grand Rapids: Baker, 1996], 99). Bright defines the kingdom of God as "the rule of God over his people, and particularly the vindication of that rule and people at the end of history" (John H. Bright, *The Kingdom of God: The Biblical Concept and Its Meaning for the Church* [Nashville: Abingdon-Cokesbury, 1953], 18). See also Ladd, *Presence of the Future*, 122–48.

12. Blomberg writes, "The central theme uniting all of the lessons of the parables is the kingdom of God. It is both present and future. It includes both a reign and a realm. It involves both personal transformation and social reform. It is not to be equated either with Israel or the church, but is the dynamic power of God's personal revelation of himself in creating a human community of those who serve Jesus in every area of their lives" (Craig L. Blomberg, *Interpreting the Parables* [Downers Grove, IL: InterVarsity, 1990], 326).

13. See, e.g., the parables of the Wedding Feast and Fasting (Mark 2:18–20), the Wineskins (Mark 2:22), the Strong Man (Matt. 12:28–29), the Mustard Seed (Matt. 13:31–32), the Leaven (Matt. 13:33), the Weather Signs (Luke 12:54–56), the Great Supper (Luke 14:16–24), and the Wedding Banquet (Matt. 22:1–4).

that the kingdom, although it might seem small and insignificant now (like a mustard seed or a little bit of yeast), will one day become something amazing. Second, Jesus taught that the kingdom of God should be pursued and entered, no matter the cost.[14] He emphasized the sacrifice one should make in order to enter the kingdom, which is compared to a valuable treasure and a pearl of great price. The kingdom is so valuable, it is worth selling everything to obtain it. Elsewhere Jesus's followers, who are compared to a dishonest manager and unsharing bridesmaids, must do whatever it takes to be ready for the future. Third, Jesus taught that those who have entered the kingdom by faith will live transformed lives.[15] Someone who is part of the kingdom, who has truly received the Word, will produce the necessary fruit. Fourth, Jesus taught that the God of the kingdom is gracious.[16] Because God is gracious and gives his people more than they deserve, no one should begrudge God his generosity. If he chooses to bless those who have squandered much of their lives, those who have lived "righteously" for most of their lives should rejoice that others have experienced the grace of God. Fifth, Jesus taught that those who fail to enter God's kingdom will experience God's judgment and wrath.[17]

Jesus taught that the kingdom of God/heaven is both a present reality and a future hope.[18] That is, when Jesus (the King) came to earth he ushered in the kingdom. This kingdom, however, will not be fully experienced until every knee bows and every tongue confesses Jesus as the King (Phil. 2:9–11).

Jesus's Concern for the Nations

We have already discussed the nations in Matthew's Gospel (Questions 15 and 26). The remaining three Gospels also provide insight into how Jesus's mission relates to the nations. We will simply highlight some ways the Gospels mention the nations in a way that connects to making disciples of all nations. Mark's Gospel shows Jesus ministering to Gentiles. There are summary statements where Jesus healed Gentiles from the surrounding regions (Mark 3:7–12; 6:53–56). These places would have included Gentiles among

---

14. See, e.g., the parables of the Treasure (Matt. 13:44), the Pearl of Great Price (Matt. 13:45–46), the Tower and War (Luke 14:28–32); the Dishonest Manager (Luke 16:1–9), and the Ten Bridesmaids (Matt. 25:1–13).

15. See, e.g., the parables of the Sower (Matt. 13:3–8; Mark 4:3–8) and the Rich Fool (Luke 12:16–21).

16. See, e.g., the parables of the Prodigal Son (Luke 15:11–32) and the Workers in the Vineyard (Matt. 20:1–16).

17. See, e.g., the parables of the Great Net (Matt. 13:47–50), the Wheat and the Tares (Matt. 13:24–30), the Sheep and the Goats (Matt. 25:31–46), and the Rich Man and Lazarus (Luke 16:19–31).

18. Present reality (Matt. 11:11; 12:28; Mark 1:15; 9:1; Luke 11:2; 17:20–21). Future hope (Matt. 6:9–10; 7:21; 8:11–12; Mark 14:25). See G. R. Beasley-Murray, *Jesus and the Kingdom of God* (Grand Rapids: Eerdmans, 1986).

the population.[19] Not only are specific cities mentioned but also different types of places in general: villages, cities, countryside, market-places (6:56). Places like the "marketplaces" (*agora*) would have been areas with a mixture of people doing daily activities.[20]

Luke's Gospel includes an introduction to Jesus's birth and early years, and already there are hints of Jesus's life and mission regarding the nations. For instance, Simeon, who had been led by the Holy Spirit, spoke of Jesus as a child who would be "a light for revelation to the Gentiles, and for glory to your people Israel" (Luke 2:32). Jesus brought his salvation to both Israel and the nations. This fact is not for informational purposes only, but so that we too can rejoice. As Darrell Bock reminds us, "In sum, Simeon is a picture of redemption's joy in that he senses the significance of who Jesus is and rests in that knowledge."[21] Luke's Gospel regularly emphasizes the joy Christ brings to people (1:44, 47; 2:10; 6:23; 10:20; 19:6, 37; 24:41, 52). For instance, at Jesus's birth, an angel of the Lord declared to the shepherds, "Fear not, for behold, I bring you good news of great joy that will be for all the people" (2:10).

In John's Gospel, the nations are referred to as the "world." John 3:16–17 states, "For God so loved the world, that he gave his only Son, that whoever believes in him should not perish but have eternal life. For God did not send his Son into the world to condemn the world, but in order that the world might be saved through him." D. A. Carson notes, "Even so, God's love is to be admired not because the world is so big and includes so many people, but because the world is so bad: that is the customary connotation of *kosmos* ('world')."[22] The Gospels show the purpose of Jesus's mission to the nations. The kingdom of God invades every part of the earth, bringing the joy of salvation and love to a sinful world. This is the proclamation of what has occurred in making disciples of all nations.

Jesus's Miracles

Miracles are a common thread in all four Gospels. Assuming the authenticity of miracles,[23] why would the Gospel writers record them in the first

---

19. R. T. France, *The Gospel of Mark: A Commentary on the Greek Text* (Grand Rapids: Eerdmans, 2002), 154. I. Howard Marshall speaks of some of the miracles in Mark to show that "these stories take place outside Judea and Galilee in territory inhabited overwhelmingly by non-Jews, and they give the impression that the coming of Jesus was not solely for the benefit of the Jews" (*New Testament Theology: Many Witnesses, One Gospel* [Downers Grove, IL: IVP Academic, 2004], 65).
20. Moisés Silva, ed., *New International Dictionary of New Testament Theology and Exegesis* (Grand Rapids: Zondervan, 2014), 1:139–40.
21. Bock, *Luke 1:1–9:50*, 245.
22. D. A. Carson, *The Gospel according to John*, PNTC (Grand Rapids: Eerdmans, 1991), 205.
23. Craig L. Blomberg writes, "If the resurrection of Jesus really happened, then none of the Gospel miracles is in principle incredible" (*The Historical Reliability of the Gospels*, 2nd ed. [Downers Grove, IL: IVP Academic, 2007], 150).

place? They served different functions depending on the context. I. Howard Marshall interprets Jesus giving sight to a blind man (Mark 10:46–52) as "a visible paradigm of discipleship."[24] This is indeed one of the reasons for this miracle because Mark explains that the man "recovered his sight and followed him on the way" (Mark 10:52).[25] Other responses of people healed by Jesus include proclamation (Mark 5:20; Luke 8:39), service (Luke 4:39), glorifying God (Luke 13:13), and belief (John 4:53; cf. 9:38).

Jesus also healed people to demonstrate his authority. Authority is a continual theme in the life of Jesus including the Great Commission. Jesus performed a miracle in front of skeptical scribes in Mark 2:1–12 (see also Matt. 9:1–8; Luke 5:17–26). Before he healed the paralytic, he said to the scribes, "that you may know that the Son of Man has authority on earth to forgive sins" (2:10). James Brooks explains, "Ironically, the scribes evidently thought it was easier to affirm the forgiveness of sins than to heal because the former could not be verified and the latter could."[26] There is clearly more going on in Mark 2 than *only* healing.[27] Jesus performed miracles to encourage faith. For example, John interprets Jesus's "signs" by saying that "these are written so that you may believe that Jesus is the Christ, the Son of God, and that by believing you may have life in his name" (John 20:31).[28] Jesus also performed miracles in order to manifest God's presence on earth. Luke, in the book of Acts, shows this when he records Peter's sermon. Peter refers to Jesus as "healing all who were oppressed by the devil, for God was with him" (Acts 10:38). In other words, Jesus could heal because of God's presence.

The Great Commission calls for a response from the nations. The miracles of Jesus provide several illustrations of people responding to him. Matthew 28:16–20 makes a number of claims about Jesus: he is worshipped, the supreme ruler of the world, calls for a worldwide following, commands complete obedience, and is ever present. The miracles of Jesus—including his resurrection right before the Great Commission—are additional proof for these claims.

Jesus's Death

Since the Great Commission includes the nations following Jesus as the exalted king, John's Gospel helps us to see the link with Jesus's crucifixion.

---

24. Marshall, *New Testament Theology*, 71.
25. The Gospel writers do not always record what the response was by the one healed, which shows the importance of when the writers do include the response. See Luke 17:11–19 for Jesus's own view of responding to him.
26. James A. Brooks, *Mark*, NAC 23 (Nashville: Broadman, 1991), 59.
27. Cf. Darrell Bock, *Mark*, NCBC (New York: University of Cambridge, 2015), 140–41.
28. There is no need here to distinguish between John's view and Jesus's purpose since Jesus explicitly says as much in John 9:35.

Jesus says in John 12:32, "And I, when I am lifted up from the earth, will draw all people to myself." The language of "lifted up" refers to Jesus's death (12:33).[29] Christ himself is sovereign in the act of bringing people to himself. The drawing of "all people" refers to both Jews and Gentiles "without distinction, and every type of person rather than everyone without exception."[30] The extent of people benefiting from Jesus's sacrifice is again highlighted in John's Gospel: "He did not say this of his own accord, but being high priest that year he prophesied that Jesus would die for the nation, and not for the nation only, but also to gather into one the children of God who are scattered abroad. So from that day on they made plans to put him to death" (11:51–53). John writes elsewhere, outside the Gospels, of Jesus's death: "Worthy are you to take the scroll and to open its seals, for you were slain, and by your blood you ransomed people for God from every tribe and language and people and nation, and you have made them a kingdom and priests to our God, and they shall reign on the earth" (Rev. 5:9–10). While the church "makes disciples" of Jesus, John shows that it is Jesus who "draws," "gathers," and "ransoms" people in the world. Jesus's presence with us makes this mission of drawing all people effective.

Summary

The kingdom of God is open for all people to enter by faith and repentance. With God's kingdom comes his salvation for the nations. There is an urgency since the King has come. We have looked at some important elements in the life and mission of Jesus, including his ministry to the nations, his miracles, and his crucifixion. The church's mission is a continuation of his mission. The commitment to follow Jesus comes with an exceeding joy and love to a sinful world. Jesus's life and mission calls for a response from every part of the world. Jesus himself is active, even in his presence with us, in bringing about the accomplishment of the Great Commission.

REFLECTION QUESTIONS

1. What are the central aspects to Jesus's life and mission?

2. How does Jesus's teaching on the kingdom relate to the church's mission?

---

29. Thomas R. Schreiner calls the "lifted up" language a "suggestive allusion" to Isaiah 52:13 (*Magnifying God in Christ: A Summary of New Testament Theology* [Grand Rapids: Baker Academic, 2010], 75).
30. Murray J. Harris, *John*, EGGNT, eds. Andreas Köstenberger and Robert W. Yarbrough (Nashville: B&H Academic, 2015), 234.

3. What is the relationship between Jesus's mission and the church's mission?

4. Why did Jesus perform miracles?

5. What did Jesus's crucifixion accomplish in the salvation of the nations?

How Does the Great Commission Relate to Jesus's Second Coming?

In the Great Commission Jesus commands his followers to make disciples of all the nations (Matt. 28:19). Earlier in Matthew 24, Jesus declared, "And this gospel of the kingdom will be proclaimed throughout the whole world as a testimony to all nations, and then the end will come" (v. 14). Based on this statement, some theologians, missionaries, and churchgoers are convinced that Jesus will not return again until the gospel is preached to every known people group.[1] That is, the second coming of Jesus cannot occur until the last people group has been reached. Conversely, when the last people group is reached, the end will come.

In addition, Peter states, "The Lord is not slow to fulfill his promise as some count slowness, but is patient toward you, not wishing that any should perish, but that all should reach repentance. . . . [Therefore] what sort of people ought you to be in lives of holiness and godliness, waiting for and hastening the coming of the day of God" (2 Peter 3:9, 11–12). In the context, Peter is clearly referring to the return of Christ and how some were mocking Christians because of Jesus's delay. Peter reminds his readers that the delay of Jesus's return is a sign of God's grace because it gives people time to repent. In light of this reality, Peter's readers are urged to live holy and godly lives as they wait for *and hasten* the second coming. The NIV states it more directly: "as you look forward to the day of God and *speed its coming*" (emphasis added).

---

1. Matthew 24:14 has been used as a rallying cry to focus on targeting unreached people groups and rapidly reproducing churches (church planting movements). Massey writes, "Interpreting this passage as the task of missions today has been a driving force for missions among some denominations since the nineteenth century" (John D. Massey, "Wrinkling Time in the Missionary Task: A Theological Review of Church Planting Movements Methodology," *Southwestern Journal of Theology* 55.1 [2012]: 104). See also Matthew Bennett, "Finishing the Task? A Cautionary Analysis of Missionary Language," *STR* 9, no. 2 (2018): 33–53.

Does our faithful mission activity speed up the timetable of God's plan for the world, including the return of his Son? Must all the people groups hear (and believe) the message of the kingdom before Jesus can return? How should our eschatology related to our missiology? This chapter will seek to address these questions, focusing our attention primarily on Matthew 24:14.

The Context of Matthew 24:14

Although it has been often said, the statement "Context is king" needs to be repeated. In Matthew 24:14 Jesus states, "And this gospel of the kingdom will be proclaimed throughout the whole world as a testimony to all nations, and then the end will come." In the context, Jesus is delivering what is now known as the Olivet Discourse, where he teaches about the destruction of the temple and his return in reply to the disciples' question. Responding to Jesus's prophecy that the temple would soon be destroyed, the disciples ask Jesus, "Tell us, when will these things be, and what will be the sign of your coming and of the end of the age?" (Matt. 24:3). Although some interpreters insist that Jesus ignores the first part of the disciples' question (regarding the temple) and only answers the second part (regarding the second coming), such a response is unlikely. Carson notes, "It is very difficult to imagine that a Christian reader of any of the Synoptics at any period during the first one hundred years of the existence of these documents would fail to see a refer- ence to the destruction of Jerusalem."[2] He continues, "How could the disciples think Jesus was *not* answering their question but describing a *second* destruc- tion of the city, unless Jesus explicitly disavowed their understanding?"[3]

Thus, most scholars affirm that Jesus not only addresses the question re- garding his second coming, but also declares truth regarding the temple's de- struction.[4] As such, we must be open to the possibility (if not probability) that Jesus's statement in Matthew 24:14 relates primarily (or at least initially) to the destruction of the temple in A.D. 70. Indeed, the previous eight items men- tioned in Matthew 24:4–13 are preliminary events that do not yet indicate that the end is near. Blomberg notes, "All nine of these preliminary events in fact occurred before A.D. 70, though most if not all have recurred many times since then as well."[5] He continues by stating that the fulfillment of Matthew 24:4–14 "demonstrates that everything necessary for Christ's return was accomplished within the first generation of Christianity, so that every subsequent generation has been able to believe that Jesus could come back in their times. It should

---

2. D. A. Carson, "Matthew," in EBC, rev. ed., vol. 9 (Matthew–Mark) (Grand Rapids: Zondervan, 2010), 552.
3. Ibid., 556.
4. See D. A. Carson, "Matthew," in EBC, rev. ed., vol. 9 (Matthew–Mark) (Grand Rapids: Zondervan, 2010), 551–57; Robert H. Stein, *Mark*, BECNT (Grand Rapids: Baker, 2008), 586–92; and David L. Turner, *Matthew*, BECNT (Grand Rapids: Baker, 2008), 575.
5. Craig L. Blomberg, *Matthew*, NAC 22 (Nashville: B&H, 1992), 356.

lead us to reject all views that claim to know for sure that Christ is returning in a given year, decade, or century on the basis of some unique event that has never previously occurred in Christian history."[6] Thus, the context affirms that Jesus may be referring to the temple's destruction rather than the second coming (though the latter event may be in view as well).

The Exegesis of Matthew 24:14

So what precisely does Jesus mean when he states that the gospel will be heralded "throughout the whole world" before the end comes? Again, we must avoid reading our situation back into the text and let the original context drive the meaning. The phrase "the whole world" (*holē tē oikoumenē*) refers to the "the entire inhabited earth."[7] The same phrase refers to the extent of the famine in Acts 11:28 and the extent of Artemis worship in Acts 19:27. In Colossians 1:6 Paul speaks of the gospel "bearing fruit and growing all over the world (*panti tō kosmō*)" (NIV) and in Romans 16:26 it already "has been made known to all nations (*panta ta ethnē*)" (cf. Rom. 10:18). In Romans 15:18–24 Paul can speak of the regions he ministered to (Jerusalem to Illyricum) being fully evangelized as he declares, "I have fully proclaimed the gospel of Christ" (Rom. 15:19).[8] "Thus, in most instances, even when a broad meaning is evident, [the inhabited world, *hē oikoumenē*] indicates first and foremost 'the world of the heathen Graeco-Roman Empire threatened by the powers of darkness.'"[9] The point is that the gospel will be heralded far beyond Judea.

Therefore, it is possible that this portion of Matthew 24:14 relates to the destruction of the temple and that the gospel was considered proclaimed to the inhabited world at the time of A.D. 70.[10] France offers us this warning:

> The phrase "all the nations" has also been pressed into a program to bring the gospel to every known nation and tribe in the modern world (including those unknown to the Eurasian world of Jesus' day) so as to hasten the *parousia*. But that is to take this text quite out of context. In particular, this passage does not speak of worldwide evangelism as the cause of the "end," but as a necessary preliminary.[11]

---

6. Ibid., 357.
7. BDAG 699; Louw and Nida, 10 (1.39).
8. See also Luke 4:5 and 21:26.
9. NIDNTTE 478, quoting M. Paeslack.
10. Bruner maintains, "The 'whole world' (*oikoumenē*) to first-century readers was the Roman Empire" (Frederick Dale Bruner, *Matthew*, vol. 2 [*The Churchbook Matthew 13–28*], rev. and exp. [Grand Rapids: Eerdmans, 1990], 493).
11. R. T. France, *The Gospel of Matthew*, NICNT (Grand Rapids: Eerdmans, 2007), 908–9. Osborne offers a similar interpretation: "This does not mean that all the nations will be

What Jesus predicted is certain to come to pass. It is possible, however, that this prophecy was already fulfilled (at least in part) by the time the temple was destroyed as the message of Jesus spread across the Roman Empire during the latter half of the first century.[12]

But let's assume for the sake of the argument that this verse is linked at least in some way to Jesus's second coming and has yet to be fulfilled. Could this verse be used to propel the notion that once all the nations (*ethnē*) receive the gospel, the end will come? Part of the problem relates to the intentional ambiguity often found in prophecy. What does it mean for the gospel to be "proclaimed" to the entire world?[13] Does it include the conversion of those who hear the preaching of the word? If so, how many must be converted? And how are we to understand the meaning of "nations" (*ethnesin*)? Does it refer to every individual "people group" as defined by modern missiologists? If so, whose definition of "people group" are we to use? (see Question 15). And how do we know if our definition is correct? And what about those people groups that might not be reached now but were reached in the past? The problem is that it is impossible for us to know exactly how this verse will be fulfilled in history. In Romans 15:19 Paul writes, "from Jerusalem and all the way around to Illyricum I have fulfilled the ministry of the gospel of Christ." Surely Paul did not reach each and every people group according to our modern definitions. Consequently, our understanding of people groups may be different than what is mentioned in Matthew 24:14. Could Jesus come back now? Or must the gospel first be preached to more unreached people groups? Based on this verse alone Jesus could come back at any time since we cannot know for certain exactly how this verse will be fulfilled. This ambiguity is intentional since we have also been told that no one knows when Jesus will return (Mark 13:32). If we knew precisely what was meant by this verse, we could then calculate when the end would come.

Some may object to this view, stating that such ambiguity only gives rise to doubt and uncertainty. But the seemingly contradictory emphasis on the

---

converted before the end can come but rather that the universal proclamation will continue until the end" (Grant R. Osborne, *Matthew*, ZECNT [Grand Rapids: Zondervan, 2010], 877).

12. Not only is there debate regarding the precise meaning of how and when the gospel will be preached to all the world but there is also debate as to the meaning of "the end" in Matthew 24:14. For example, France maintains that "the end" does not refer to the end of the world, but to the end of the temple (*Matthew*, 909). France interprets Matthew 24:4–35 as all referring to the destruction of the temple and vv. 36–51 as referring to the second coming. Others note that while the first part is referring to the destruction of the temple (i.e., the gospel message proclaimed to the world prior to A.D. 70), the end is interpreted as the end of history and the final judgment (so Osborne, *Matthew*, 877; Morris, *Matthew*, 602; Craig S. Keener, *The Gospel of Matthew: A Socio-Rhetorical Commentary* [Grand Rapids: Eerdmans, 2009], 572).

13. See Benjamin L. Merkle, "Could Jesus Return At Any Moment? Rethinking the Imminence of the Second Coming," *Trinity Journal* 26 (2005): 279–92.

imminence and the delay of the second coming was designed to make it impossible for us to know the exact time of Jesus's return. Ladd explains, "This is where the Gospels leave us: anticipating an imminent event and yet unable to date its coming. Logically this may appear contradictory, but it is a tension with an ethical purpose—to make date-setting impossible and therefore to demand constant readiness."[14] Yes, we strive to understand the signs of the times, but we must also admit that the precise fulfillment of many verses of Scripture is ambiguous to us. This ambiguity is God's design so that we will always be ready for Jesus's return.

The Implications of Matthew 24:14

There are several implications from our study of Matthew 24:14. First, Jesus could return at any moment. Although it is true that certain events will transpire before the second coming (the gospel preached to the nations, the great tribulation, the coming of the Antichrist), the fulfillment of such prophecies are often given in veiled language so that we do not know the time of Christ's return.

Second, the church must constantly be prepared for Jesus's return (Matt. 24:42–44; 25:13; 1 Thess. 5:1–2, 6; 2 Peter 3:10; Rev. 16:15). If Jesus could *not* return at any moment, then these verses referenced would lose their impact. If certain events have yet to be fulfilled, might the church become lackadaisical knowing that Jesus's return is not imminent? Bruner expresses a similar concern: "I fear, however, that this *geographical* reading ('since the whole world has not yet been fully evangelized, the Lord will not yet come') will lame Jesus' single most emphatic teaching in the last half of his sermon—his repeated calls to alertness because of his *any-time* Coming."[15] Additionally, it is important that the Church awaits the return of Christ without getting fixated on the signs that will precede his coming. Bruner adds,

> Nor should Christians at any time await the appearance of anyone or anything else *except Jesus Christ himself*—not even a remarkable Antichrist . . . or a conversion of the Jews or anything else except Jesus Christ himself. This Christ-centered expectation is at the heart of the NT witness, and no other teaching, however well meant, should be allowed to eclipse him. Jesus' mission word would *not* have been heard by Matthew's readers then, and it should not be heard by his readers today, either as a relaxant ("he can't come yet because world mission isn't done yet") or as a stimulant ("we'd better

---

14. George Eldon Ladd, *The Presence of the Future* (Grand Rapids: Eerdmans, 1974), 328.

15. Bruner, *Matthew*, 2:493.

do mission fast so he can come soon," as though our actions determined God's), but rather as *good news*.[16]

Third, our mission strategy should not prioritize speed over quality.[17] In an effort to fulfill Matthew 24:14, some have prioritized the rapid advance of the gospel (at virtually any cost) in an effort to hasten the return of Christ. As Massey explains, "The belief that finishing the task within a given time frame (hastening the coming of the Lord) places the value of speed at the core of the missiological enterprise, short-circuiting key aspects of the missionary task for the sake of rapid reproduction."[18] Jesus's statement in Matthew 24 and the Great Commission itself should not cause us to short-circuit our mission strategy in an effort to hasten Jesus's return. Christopher Wright warns, "We should not treat the Great Commission as a ticking clock, just waiting for the last people group to 'hear' the gospel before the Lord is, as it were, permitted to return."[19] According to 2 Peter 3:11–12, the reality that might accelerate the return of Christ is the godly behavior of believers.[20]

Summary

Although Matthew 24:14 is often used as evidence that Jesus will not return again until the gospel is preached to every known people group, such an interpretation it not without its difficulties. It is possible that Jesus's statement that the gospel of the kingdom must be proclaimed throughout the whole world was fulfilled in the first century before the temple was destroyed. But even if that is not the case, we can have no certainty that our understanding of nations or "people groups" is precisely what Jesus had in mind. Consequently, we must admit that Jesus could return at any moment and be prepared for his coming, while we continue to develop mature and ministering disciples among the nations.

---

16. Ibid., 2:494.
17. Though we believe that it is possible to have both speed and quality.
18. Massey, "Wrinkling Time in the Missionary Task," 105.
19. See Christopher J. H. Wright, *The Mission of God's People: A Biblical Theology of the Church's Mission* (Grand Rapids: Zondervan, 2010), 285. He later adds, "The Great Commission is not a timetable for the end of the world" (ibid.). Schnabel likewise writes, "It is safe to conclude that the timing of Jesus' second coming does not depend upon the missionary activity of the church or upon the obedience of Christians to the missionary commission" (*Early Christian Missions*, 367).
20. See Richard J. Bauckham, *Jude, 2 Peter,* WBC 50 (Waco, TX: Word, 1983), 325; Thomas R. Schreiner, *1, 2 Peter, Jude,* NAC 37 (Nashville: B&H, 2003), 390; Gene L. Green, *Jude & 2 Peter,* BECNT (Grand Rapids: Baker, 2008), 334; and Douglas J. Moo, *2 Peter, Jude,* NIVAC (Grand Rapids: Zondervan, 1996), 198.

REFLECTION QUESTIONS

1. Do you think the events mentioned in Matthew 24:4–13 relate to the destruction of the temple, the second coming, or both? How will your interpretation impact your mission?

2. What does "the whole world" mean? Is it possible that this verse is already fulfilled?

3. Do you think Jesus could return at any moment? Why or why not?

4. Must every people group be reached before Jesus can return?

5. What are some of the dangers of embracing a mission strategy that puts the rapid reproduction of churches as its highest priority?

How Does the Book of Acts Relate to the Great Commission?

There are several ways that Acts relates to the Great Commission and so only a few can be considered in addition to what has already been discussed above (see Question 23). The focus will be on (1) the work of the Father, Son, and Spirit, (2) opposition to the fulfillment of the mission, and (3) baptism and teaching. It is fitting that baptism and teaching are considered in Acts because of their key role in Matthew 28:19–20. Acts is thoroughly missions-driven, and so only a few cursory discussions can be attempted.

God's Work in Missions

There is a need for prayerful dependence upon God the Father for missions because God is sovereign in bringing about salvation. God is the one commanding repentance (Acts 17:30) even as Paul preached to the people (17:22–34). God is sovereignly speaking as his servants proclaim the gospel throughout the world. The Son is also sovereign in salvation. Stephen Walton explores the characterization of Jesus in Acts and concludes, "Jesus is now present in heaven, at God's right side, but in such a way that he can continue to be active on earth in the *missio dei*, guiding his people and drawing others into the body of Jesus-believers."[1] To provide just one example, when Jesus sent Ananias to Saul (Paul), he told him, "Go, for he is a chosen instrument of mine to carry my name before the Gentiles and kings and the children of Israel. For I will show him how much he must suffer for the sake of my name" (9:15–16). Jesus emphasizes his own

---

1. Steve Walton, "Jesus, Present and/or Absent? The Presence and Presentation of Jesus as a Character in the Book of Acts," in *Characters and Characterization in Luke-Acts*, eds. Frank E. Dicken and Julia A. Snyder, LNTS 548 (London: Bloomsbury T&T Clark, 2016), 140.

role in sending Paul on his mission by using the terminology of "chosen instrument."[2] Jesus is clearly active in orchestrating salvation for Jews and Gentiles since Paul was, according to Jesus, an instrument "of mine" and carried "my name."

The Holy Spirit enables witnesses of Jesus to speak with boldness. In Acts 4 Peter and John are arrested (4:3) and threatened (4:18, 21) for their witness. They went and met with others and "when they had prayed, the place in which they were gathered together was shaken, and they were all filled with the Holy Spirit and continued to speak the word of God with boldness" (Acts 4:31). The Holy Spirit's ministry through people in Acts includes both the act of speaking (the gospel)[3] and bold speech (despite opposition). Acts 4:31 parallels the filling of the Spirit with speaking.[4] There is a similar idea in the Old Testament when Micah states, "But as for me, I am filled with power, with the Spirit of the LORD, and with justice and might, to declare to Jacob his transgression and to Israel his sin" (Mic. 3:8). While Luke may not have had Micah specifically in mind when writing Acts 4, there is a similarity between Micah and the apostles in Acts.[5] When the prophets spoke of judgment, as in the case of Micah, it was for the purpose of turning the people from their evil ways and back to God (2 Kings 17:13; cf. Acts 3:26). Both Old Testament and New Testament messengers spoke by the Spirit in the midst of opposition.[6]

Speaking with boldness in a context like Acts 4 means to speak with courage or confidence.[7] Boldness is confident trust in God's word as spoken in the midst of opposition. Whenever the world is set against the gospel, the temptation can be to doubt, be silent, or become angry. With boldness from the Spirit, Christians can overcome these temptations. Calvin encourages the church today regarding boldness from the Spirit as "a perpetual

---

2. For a discussion on "instrument/vessel" (*skeuos*), see Craig S. Keener, *Acts: An Exegetical Commentary* (Grand Rapids: Baker, 2013), 2:1655–57.

3. See also Huber L. Drumwright, "The Holy Spirit in the Book of Acts," *SwJT* 17 (1974): 8.

4. Keener writes, "The primary effect of being filled with the Spirit, though, is speaking God's message boldly, fitting the primary activity of the Spirit in Acts (see esp. 1:8; 2:17–18)" (*Acts*, 2:1175). See also Darrell L. Bock, *Acts*, BECNT (Grand Rapids: Baker, 2007), 210.

5. Barker and Bailey demonstrate the connection of the OT to the NT when they write, "All true prophets were the Lord's Spirit-filled messengers (see 2 Pet 1:20–21). Such empowerment is related to the Spirit's enablement for the New Testament gospel mission as well (Acts 1:8)" (Kenneth L. Barker and Waylon Bailey, *Micah, Nahum, Habakkuk, Zephaniah*, NAC 20 [Nashville: Broadman, 1999], 78).

6. Cf. Bruce K. Waltke, *A Commentary on Micah* (Grand Rapids: Eerdmans, 2007), 175.

7. See BDAG, "παρρησία," 781–82 (see also the verb form παρρησιάζομαι in 18:26 and 19:8).

profit of prayer, which is also set before us for an example."[8] Boldness is a "divine gift."[9]

Opposition to the Great Commission

Acts shows people obeying the Great Commission despite opposition to it. In addition to the arrest and threats in Acts 4, opposition includes murder (7:54–60), persecutions (8:1–3), prison (16:23–24), criticism (11:2–3; 28:22), spiritual warfare (16:16–18), beatings (16:22–23; 21:32), and mob tactics (17:5; 19:29). Despite this list of challenges, the book of Acts still ends by referencing Paul teaching "with all boldness" (the same term from Acts 4:31) and "without hindrance" (*akōlytōs*; 28:31).[10] Richard Longenecker comments, "Since the final word of Acts is the crisp adverb *akōlytōs* ["without hindrance"], we may say with reasonable confidence that it was Luke's desire to close his two-volume work on this victorious note, namely, that the apostolic proclamation of the kingdom of God and the Lord Jesus Christ, despite all difficulties and misunderstandings, had moved forward throughout the Jewish homeland and into the Roman Empire 'without hindrance.'"[11] Challenges to the Great Commission may vary by time and place, but the Spirit's power can enable every Christian's witness to the ends of the earth.

Baptism and Teaching in Acts

Acts shows how missions includes the work of baptism and teaching. Water baptism is consistently referenced throughout Acts:

- Peter commands repentance and baptism (2:38).

- Philip preaches; men and women are baptized (8:12–13).

- Philip disciples an Ethiopian and then baptizes him (8:35–36, 38).

- Ananias commands and baptizes Saul—later called Paul (9:18; 22:16).

---

8. John Calvin, *Commentary upon the Acts of the Apostles*, trans. Christopher Fetherstone, ed. Henry Beveridge (Grand Rapids: Baker, 1999), 189. Ephesians 6:18–20 calls Christians to this example: "Praying at all times in the Spirit, with all prayer and supplication. To that end keep alert with all perseverance, making supplication for all the saints, and also for me, that words may be given to me in opening my mouth boldly to proclaim the mystery of the gospel, for which I am an ambassador in chains, that I may declare it boldly, as I ought to speak."

9. Stanley B. Marrow, S.J., "*Parrhēsia* and the New Testament," *CBQ* 44, no. 1 (1982): 443.

10. See BDAG, "ἀκωλύτως," 40.

11. Richard N. Longenecker, "Acts," EBC rev. ed., ed. Tremper Longman III and David E. Garland (Grand Rapids: Zondervan, 2007), 1101; cf. David G. Peterson, *The Acts of the Apostles* (Grand Rapids: Eerdmans, 2009), 723; Richard I. Pervo, *Acts*, Hermeneia (Minneapolis: Fortress, 2009), 687.

- Peter (again) commands people to be baptized (10:44–48).

- Lydia, a woman from Thyatira, is baptized along with her household (16:14–15).

- A prison guard in Philippi is baptized along with his household (16:32–33).

- Crispus, the ruler of a synagogue in Corinth, is baptized along with his household; other Corinthians are baptized (18:8).

- Disciples in Ephesus are baptized in the name of the Lord Jesus (19:5).

There are several common traits that are found in the above passages regarding baptism. First, there is often a command to be baptized. Second, there are both individuals and entire households being baptized.[12] Third, in each instance mentioned above, the message is delivered *before* baptism.[13] Fourth, the regularity of baptisms in Acts shows that Jesus expects the baptism of new converts. Robert Stein argues that even when baptism is not explicitly mentioned in the New Testament, it can be assumed when conversion is mentioned.[14] In addition to the assumption that new believers are baptized, there is the opportunity to ask new believers about their family members so that they too can come to know Christ.

The book of Acts regularly refers to preaching and teaching. For example, Acts records the first sermon by chapter 2 and ends with Paul teaching in Rome in 28:31.[15] Luke explains the missionary travels of Paul and Barnabas: "When they had preached the gospel to that city and had made many disciples, they returned to Lystra and to Iconium and to Antioch, strengthening the souls of the disciples, encouraging them to continue in the faith, and saying that

---

12. Cf. Bock, *Acts*, 338. Even in the case of the individual, baptism incorporates the person into a local body of believers (cf. 1 Cor. 12:13).
13. This has implications for how to interpret "households" being baptized (cf. Acts 16:32 with 16:33).
14. His full thesis is: "In the New Testament, conversion involves five integrally related components or aspects, all of which took place at the same time, usually on the same day. These five components are repentance, faith, and confession by the individual, regeneration, or the giving of the Holy Spirit by God, and baptism by representatives of the Christian community" (Robert H. Stein, "Baptism and Becoming a Christian in the New Testament," *SBJT* 2, no.1 [1998]: 6).
15. David A. deSilva helpfully categorizes the speeches in Acts: "[E]vangelistic sermons in Acts 2, 3, 13 and 17; speeches in a council's deliberations in Acts 15; a farewell speech in Acts 20; defense speeches in Acts 22, 24 and 26" (*An Introduction to the New Testament: Contexts, Methods & Ministry Formation* [Downers Grove, IL: InterVarsity, 2004], 351). One could then add the references to teaching in general (such as "the apostle's teaching" in 2:42).

through many tribulations we must enter the kingdom of God. And when they had appointed elders for them in every church, with prayer and fasting they committed them to the Lord in whom they had believed" (14:21–23). There are several principles for missions in this passage.[16] Great Commission work includes extended teaching and equipping the local church with spiritual leadership. Teaching toward the goal of spiritual maturity involves an emphasis on a person's *commitment* (14:22). Detwiler writes, "It is not enough to rejoice in the decision people make to trust in Christ; older disciples must do all they can to help new disciples along in this commitment (and they should seek ongoing help for themselves as well)."[17]

Summary

The work of God the Father, Son, and Holy Spirit in Acts encourages disciple-makers to fulfill the Great Commission. Consequently, Christians can engage in courageous speech in the middle of opposition to the gospel. Finally, baptism and teaching referenced in Matthew 28 are given concrete expression in the book of Acts. Those who affirm Jesus as the Messiah are baptized and taught to obey Jesus's commands.

REFLECTION QUESTIONS

1. How does God's sovereignty in missions encourage you in the work of missions? How can you depend more on the Holy Spirit as you obey and follow Jesus?

2. What challenges do you face personally or socially that tempt you not to continue on mission? How does the book of Acts strengthen you to face these obstacles?

3. Should baptism be practiced as it was in Acts? Why or why not?

4. How does investing extended time in teaching and making disciples balance with the need for reaching other people groups with the gospel?

5. What are some other principles for missions in the book of Acts that were not mentioned in this chapter?

---

16. David F. Detwiler, "Paul's Approach to the Great Commission in Acts 14:21–23," *BSac* 152 (1995): 33–41.
17. Ibid., 41.

How Do Paul's Epistles Relate to the Great Commission?

Although it is largely recognized that Paul's epistles do not explicitly identify the Great Commission as a motive in the early church's missionary endeavors,[1] the lack of explicit reference to the Great Commission does not constitute a lack of continuity between Jesus's command and Paul's ministry and message.[2] While there may not be a literary dependence between the epistles of Paul and the Gospel of Matthew, there is continuity between the goal of the Great Commission ("make disciples") and the means of accomplishing it ("going," "baptizing," and "teaching"). This chapter will seek to evaluate the ministry and message of the apostle Paul according to his letters in light of the Great Commission.

The Goal of the Great Commission

As we have seen (see Question 14), the goal of the Great Commission is to "make disciples of all nations" (Matt. 28:19). A disciple is one who has been trained not only to understand the message of the kingdom of God, but also to teach it to others (Matt. 13:52; 27:57). Making disciples includes going to those who have not heard ("go"), forming believers into the body of Christ ("baptizing them"), and instructing them in the faith ("teaching them"). This picture of discipleship reflects the ministry and message of the apostle Paul as seen in his letters.

---

1. See Robert L. Plummer, *Paul's Understanding of the Church's Mission: Did the Apostle Paul Expect the Early Christian Communities to Evangelize?* (Milton Keynes, UK: Paternoster, 2006), 7 n. 12.
2. This chapter is an abbreviated summary of "The Great Commission according to Paul" by Benjamin L. Merkle and Michael Guyer, *The Journal: Mid-America Baptist Theological Seminary* 1 (2014): 51–66.

Paul's Ministry

In Romans 15:14–21 Paul provides a summary of his ministry. After approximately twenty-five years of ministry, Paul claims, "from Jerusalem and all the way around to Illyricum I have fulfilled the ministry of the gospel of Christ" (v. 19), to the degree that he no longer had any room to work in those areas (v. 23). Having fulfilled the gospel in those regions, Paul communicates his desire for future ministry: "I make it my ambition to preach the gospel, not where Christ has already been named, lest I build on someone else's foundation" (v. 20). Paul's desire was to preach the gospel in Spain in the same way that he had "fulfilled the gospel" from Jerusalem to Illyricum.

Paul's ministry certainly included initial evangelism in these new areas, but this was not the totality of Paul's ministry. Paul also aimed at strengthening believers and establishing local churches. While Paul did not stay to pastor the churches he planted, the goal of his ministry was not merely the planting of these churches but also the watering of them. In this way Paul's ministry demonstrates continuity with Jesus's command to "make disciples of all the nations" by not only aiming at bringing people into relationship with Christ but to establish local churches in which believers were able to grow into mature disciples.

Paul's Message

In a summary statement of the goal of his preaching, Paul states, "Him we proclaim, warning everyone and teaching everyone with all wisdom that we may present everyone mature in Christ" (Col. 1:28). Paul views his primary task as the proclamation of the gospel. The goal of his proclamation is "to make the word of God fully known" (Col. 1:25). In Romans, Paul saw the fulfilling of the gospel in terms of the establishment of Christian communities in which further ministry would continue. In Colossians, Paul explains the fulfilling of the word of God in terms of establishing the Colossian church as a body of mature disciples.

In Ephesians 4:11–16 Paul lays out the task of both the leaders and the members within the local church. In verses 11–12 Paul describes the various leaders of the church (apostles, prophets, evangelists, and pastor-teachers) as gifts given for the building up of the body. The preaching of the gospel and the teaching of believers was all towards one goal—maturity in Christ: "to mature manhood, to the measure of the stature of the fullness of Christ" (v. 13). Maturity, much like a "disciple" in the Gospel of Matthew, is defined in relation to Christ. Mature disciples are those who have come to know Christ, progressively become more like Christ, and will finally and fully attain the fullness of Christ in the age to come. According to Paul, mature disciples are made and grow in and through the ministry of the local church.

The Means of Fulfilling the Great Commission

Going

As stated earlier (see Question 16), the participle *poreuthentes* ("going") functions as an imperative. Thus, it is best translated, "Go, therefore, and make disciples of all nations." The act of "going" was certainly not optional since the command was to make disciples of *all the nations*, a pattern Paul established in his ministry.

Going and Paul's Ministry

The scope of Paul's ministry reflects the scope of the Great Commission— "all the nations." Paul's understanding of his mission to all the nations is evident in the course he took in his missionary travels. In fact, the book of Acts demonstrates Paul's commitment to "go" to all the nations. Paul's ministry extended to Damascus, Arabia, Jerusalem, Syria, Cilicia, Antioch, Southern Galatia, Pamphylia, Macedonia, Achaia, Ephesus, Illyricum, Judea, Rome, Spain, and Crete. Paul's ministry in these places was to both Jews and Gentiles. Paul's mission reflected the universal mission outlined in the Great Commission. In his own words, Paul states, "I have become all things to all people, that by all means I might save some" (1 Cor. 9:22). But what motivated Paul to go to all the nations becoming all things to all people? He notes, "I do it all for the sake of the gospel, that I may share with them in its blessings" (1 Cor. 9:23). For Paul the message of the gospel determined the extent to which he must go and to which the church must go in order to fulfill the Great Commission.

Going and Paul's Message

In Paul's message, the focus is not so much on the "going" of the messenger but on the "going" of the message. The message of the gospel is presented as a dynamic force in Paul's letters.[3] The gospel, Paul reminds the Corinthians, did not originate with them, nor are they the only ones whom it has reached (1 Cor. 14:36). Furthermore, the gospel is depicted as *arriving* in Thessalonica: "our gospel came to you not only in word, but also in power and in the Holy Spirit and with full conviction" (1 Thess. 1:5). In addition, the gospel is said to have "come" to the Colossians and is "growing" and "bearing fruit" both among the Colossians and "in the whole world" (Col. 1:5–7). Paul's ministry is bound up with the advance of the gospel. In all of these passages Paul's missionary activity is stated in terms of the activity of the gospel. For Paul, the necessity of the advance of the gospel determined the "going" of his missionary activity.

---

3. See ibid., 55.

Just as the gospel was active through the work of the apostle Paul, it was also active through the church. In 1 Thessalonians 1:8 Paul states that the word of the Lord "has sounded forth from you not only in Macedonia and Achaia, but your faith in God has gone forth everywhere, so that we need not say anything." Most likely, this refers to the Thessalonians' evangelistic proclamation. Plummer notes, "As the 'word of the Lord' has progressed effectively through the apostle Paul, now it was advancing through the Thessalonian church (1 Thess. 1:8; 2:13–14; 2 Thess. 3:1)."[4] The message of the gospel, according to Paul, seems to ensure the "going" of the church to the nations.

Another key text in Paul's epistles is Romans 10:13–15. Paul begins by stating, "everyone who calls on the name of the Lord will be saved" (v. 13). This serves as the climax of the chain in verses 14–15. Paul explains the logic of salvation using four rhetorical questions, concluding with its foundational element. People cannot call upon the Lord without believing, they cannot believe without hearing, they cannot hear without someone preaching, and no one will preach unless they are sent. In summary, Paul argues that salvation is not possible apart from the preaching of the gospel. Hearing the gospel, as was the case with Israel, does not ensure that one will believe the gospel (v. 16). Believing the gospel "entails whole-hearted commitment to God."[5] The entire process, though, hangs on the sending of someone to preach.

Baptizing

In Matthew's account of the Great Commission, "baptism" indicates entrance into the new community of believers and submission to the Lordship of Christ. This baptism is to be done "into the name of the Father, Son, and Holy Spirit" (Matt. 28:19). The preposition "into" (*eis*) has the idea of identification. Carson argues that it "strongly suggests a coming-into-relationship-with or a coming-under-the-Lordship-of."[6] Since the participle "baptizing" indicates the means or mode of "making disciples," it is clear that the act of baptism is for those who have willingly identified themselves as followers of Christ.

Baptizing and Paul's Ministry

Paul's letters include very little information about his practice of baptizing new believers. In fact, 1 Corinthians 1:13–17 is the only explicit text that deals with Paul's practice of baptism in his ministry. In the Corinthian church, Paul was attempting to downplay the significance of those who perform the baptism because they had elevated various leaders to such a degree that it was causing division in the church. Paul's concern is that this division was taking away their focus from what was most important—the message of the cross.

---

4. Ibid., 62.
5. Thomas R. Schreiner, *Romans*, BECNT (Grand Rapids: Baker, 1998), 570.
6. D. A. Carson, "Matthew," in EBC 9, rev. ed. (Grand Rapids: Zondervan, 2010), 587.

Lest the Corinthian believers start claiming to have been "baptized in the name of Paul," he puts baptism in its proper place (v. 13). Schreiner states, "Baptism was important to Paul. It must be understood, however, in light of the gospel, so that the gospel (and not baptism) receives priority."[7]

This does not downplay the significance of baptism, but rather contributes to what Paul envisioned as the goal of his ministry—the preaching of the gospel and the establishing of local churches in which believers could grow into mature disciples. In fact, Paul states, "For Christ did not send me to baptize but to preach the gospel" (1 Cor. 1:17). Paul's practice of ministry demonstrates that he did not see baptism as effecting salvation. Such was the work of the gospel, "the word of the cross." Paul's approach to baptism also reflects his commitment to the local church and its leaders. While Paul only baptized a few new believers in Corinth (Crispus, Gaius, and the household of Stephanus), some of these new believers became leaders in the church and were, it would seem, charged with baptizing the others (cf. 1 Cor. 16:15).[8]

Baptizing and Paul's Message
In the New Testament, including Paul's letters, baptism is associated with conversion. Paul often places greater emphasis in his letters on conversion itself than on the act of baptism. Furthermore, it is not often clear whether Paul's references to baptism always include the idea of water baptism (see Rom. 6:3–4; 1 Cor. 12:13; Gal. 3:27; Eph. 4:5; Col. 2:11–12). It seems best to say that even when "water" baptism is not directly referenced, it serves as an outward marker of the inward realities experienced in conversion.[9] For Paul, the imagery and act of baptism is used to express the believers' conversion and their inclusion into the body of Christ.

Baptism signifies the believer's conversion through union with Christ. For Paul baptism is a symbol of the believer's union with Christ in his death, burial, and resurrection (Rom. 6:3–4; Col. 2:11–12). In both Romans and Colossians, Paul's emphasis is that the believers' union with Christ has broken the power of sin and freed them to live new lives in Christ (Rom. 6:4; Col. 2:23; 3:1). "Jesus gave his disciples the command to baptize new converts (Matt. 28:19), and here Paul gives us the theology of baptism: it is a picture of the believer's death to sin and his new life in Christ."[10]

---

7. Schreiner, *Paul: Apostle of God's Glory in Christ* (Downers Grove, IL: InterVarsity, 2001), 377.
8. See Eckhard Schnabel, *Paul the Missionary: Realities, Strategies, and Methods* (Downers Grove, IL: InterVarsity, 2008), 231.
9. See Schreiner, *Paul*, 376; Robert H. Stein, "Baptism in Luke-Acts," in *Believers Baptism: Sign of the New Covenant in Christ*, eds. Thomas R. Schreiner and Shawn D. Wright (Nashville: B&H, 2006), 33–66.
10. Benjamin L. Merkle, "Paul's Ecclesiology," in *Paul's Missionary Methods: In His Time and Ours*, eds. Robert L. Plummer and John Mark Terry (Downers Grove, IL: InterVarsity, 2012), 62.

Baptism also signified the believer's inclusion into the body of Christ, including his reception of the Spirit. In 1 Corinthians 12:13 Paul states, "For in one Spirit we were all baptized into one body." In this context, Paul is dealing with the identity of the body of Christ, in particular, "how the many of them, diverse as they are, are in fact one body."[11] The key aspect to the believers' identity and unity is their common reception of the Holy Spirit. This takes places at conversion, in which the believer is immersed in the Spirit. Paul uses the metaphor of baptism to express this point, but does not explicitly refer to water baptism. Water baptism follows after Spirit baptism, which takes place at conversion, and serves as a sign of the believer's union with Christ and unity in the body of Christ (see also Ephesians 4:5, where baptism serves as a ground for unity in the church).

A person is not saved by baptism, but those who believe the gospel are to be baptized. Those who are baptized make up the local church, and it is the local church that Paul sees as the context for making mature disciples. Thus, baptism, according to Paul, is integral to making disciples in the context of the local church as it seeks to carry out the Great Commission.

Teaching

The final participial phrase characterizing the means of fulfilling the Great Commission in Matthew 28:19–20 is "teaching them to observe all that I have commanded you." Teaching emphasizes the importance of the ongoing process of discipleship. Disciples are not only brought in through baptism, but they are built up through teaching and instruction. This instruction is also not merely transferring information, but it is instruction with a view toward obedience—"teaching them *to obey* all that I have commanded you" (emphasis added). Finally, this aspect of making disciples ensures the ongoing work of the Great Commission. Teaching new believers "everything" that Jesus commanded would most certainly include teaching them the Great Commission itself.

Teaching and Paul's Ministry

Paul saw his ministry, at least in part, as a teaching ministry. This does not negate the primacy of evangelism for Paul. It demonstrates, however, that Paul's ministry did not stop with the initial gospel proclamation. Rather Paul's ministry aimed to establish believers as mature disciples within the context of the local church. This requires both preaching the gospel and teaching those who believe it. In Colossians 1:28 Paul demonstrates that the means by which he accomplishes his goal of making mature disciples is through "teaching" and "warning." Much like Jesus's instruction to the disciples (Matt. 28:20; "teaching them *everything* that I have commanded you"), Paul's view

---

11. Gordon D. Fee, *God's Empowering Presence* (Peabody, MA: Hendrickson, 1994), 178.

of teaching is comprehensive as demonstrated by his emphatic repetition of "all"—"teaching *everyone* and admonishing *everyone* with *all* wisdom, that we may present *everyone* mature in Christ" (Col. 1:28, emphasis added).

The importance of teaching or ongoing discipleship is clearly seen in Paul's ministry through visiting churches, writing letters, and sending co-workers.[12] First, Paul's practice of revisiting churches is a key characteristic of his ministry, and can be summed in one word: "strengthening" (Acts 14:22; 15:41; 18:22). The pattern of Paul's ministry indicates that this strengthening took place through teaching or instructing from God's Word (cf. Acts 18:11; 20:18–20, 27, 31; 28:11). Paul's letters also express his desire to visit and revisit churches for the sake of their being established in the faith (cf. Rom. 1:11; 1 Cor. 16:5–9; 2 Cor. 1:15–16; 1 Thess. 2:17–20). Second, Paul not only revisited the churches he established, but he wrote letters to further strengthen them in their faith. "Paul's letter writing, then, demonstrates his concern for the on-going growth of the churches he planted. His goal was not merely to plant churches and let them loose, regardless of the consequences. Rather, Paul wisely maintained a healthy on-going relationship with his churches so that the work of the gospel continued to flourish."[13] Third, Paul also frequently sent coworkers (such as Timothy and Titus) to churches he had established in order to strengthen them in their faith.

Teaching and Paul's Message

Paul's letters demonstrate the importance of teaching in the life of the church. This is true for everyone within the church, not just its leaders. Teaching is the general responsibility of every member of the church. In Colossians Paul makes it clear that the church is to carry out the same type of ministry he did while among them: "Let the word of Christ dwell in you richly, teaching and admonishing one another in all wisdom, singing psalms and hymns and spiritual songs, with thankfulness in your hearts to God" (Col. 3:16). This teaching ministry is not defined in individualistic terms but rather in corporate terms, putting emphasis on those characteristics that foster community. Paul's command to let the "word of Christ dwell in you richly" should be understood in light of the corporate worship of the church. The expression of the indwelling message about Christ should be seen in the mutual "teaching" and "admonishing" among members of the church (see also Rom. 15:14; Eph. 4:15; 2 Thess. 3:15). Paul sees the means of "making disciples" through "teaching" believers to obey God's Word as being carried out the context of the local church by the members of the local church.

---

12. See Benjamin L. Merkle, "The Need for Theological Education in Missions: Lessons Learned from the Church's Greatest Missionary," *SBJT* 9, no. 4 (2005): 50–61.

13. Ibid., 55.

Teaching is also a distinctive responsibility of the leaders of the local church. Without dismissing the responsibility of all believers to "teach" one another, Paul's letters emphasize the role of the leaders of the local church in carrying out the ministry of teaching. An overseer must be "able to teach" (1 Tim. 3:2) and "must hold firm to the trustworthy word as taught, so that he may be able to give instruction in sound doctrine and also to rebuke those who contradict it" (Titus 1:9). Elders are those who "labor in preaching and teaching" (1 Tim. 5:17). Elsewhere, Paul encourages Timothy to "preach the word; be ready in season and out of season; reprove, rebuke, and exhort, with complete patience and teaching" (2 Tim. 4:2). The responsibility of leaders was for equipping and building up the church (cf. Eph. 4:12–16; 1 Tim. 3:15). Paul urges Timothy to pass on the gospel that has been entrusted to him: "[W]hat you have heard from me in the presence of many witnesses entrust to faithful men who will be able to teach others also" (2 Tim. 2:2). The teaching responsibility of the church ensures more than the health of the church, it also advances the mission of the church by multiplying disciples.

Summary

Although there is no evidence of a literary connection between Matthew's Gospel and Paul's letters, there is continuity between the two. Paul's ministry goals and instruction in his letters reveal that he emphasized the need to make disciples by means of going, baptizing, and teaching.

REFLECTION QUESTIONS

1. Why do you think that Paul never directly quotes or references the Great Commission?

2. In what ways does Paul's ministry and message demonstrate the importance of making disciples?

3. In what ways does Paul's ministry and message demonstrate the importance of "going"?

4. In what ways does Paul's ministry and message demonstrate the importance of baptizing new converts?

5. In what ways does Paul's ministry and message demonstrate the importance of teaching Jesus's commands?

How Do the General Epistles Relate to the Great Commission?

The General Epistles contain at least three types of references about the Great Commission. First, there are direct statements referring to carrying out the mission. Second, some letters assume obedience to the Great Commission and are written to members who have been suffering for the gospel. In other words, the church was already bearing witness while the authors were writing the General Epistles. Third, certain truths about God imply a call to action in order to align with God's global purpose.

Direct Statements Involving the Great Commission

One of the clearest examples of the Great Commission in the General Epistles is found in 3 John 5–8: "Beloved, it is a faithful thing you do in all your efforts for these brothers, strangers as they are, who testified to your love before the church. You will do well to send them on their journey in a manner worthy of God. For they have gone out for the sake of the name, accepting nothing from the Gentiles. Therefore we ought to support people like these, that we may be fellow workers for the truth." John's third letter opens with the tight connection between love and truth (v. 1). The author ("the Elder") commends Gaius for specifically loving a group of "brothers" who travelled as preachers of the gospel. Gaius demonstrated love by taking care of their physical needs (vv. 5–6). John also encouraged continued support of these missionaries (vv. 6–8). Truth was spread by the unified work of the missionaries and those who supported them.

In these few verses there are several principles for Christians who support Great Commission work. Christians can be assured that God is pleased when the church takes care of one another, including providing for those who actively are involved in missions. John writes that it is a "faithful thing" that Gaius was doing (v. 5; cf. "you will do well" in v. 6). We can support those who we do not necessarily know personally, for the preachers were practically strangers to Gaius (v. 5). This would be analogous to supporting a mission board that we know is doctrinally faithful, but where we do not know the individual missionaries. Mission work has implicit travel costs, and so it is often helpful for someone to invest financially in travelling teachers and evangelists. This is to be done in a manner "worthy of God" (v. 6).[1]

Missionary support is therefore a spiritual matter where supporters like Gaius focus on what is worthy of what God expects. Supporters are essential since missionaries often make financial sacrifices for the sake of their calling. Their motivation was to serve Christ and not money.[2] In the case of 3 John, the traveling preachers were "accepting nothing from the Gentiles" (v. 7). This contrasts with ones like the Cynics who "generally were recognizable by their appearance: barefoot, long hair and beard, a ragged and dirty cloak, a walking staff, and a carrying bag that doubled as a begging bowl."[3] I. Howard Marshall explains, "To take payment for the gospel would be to nullify the offer of free grace. At the same time it would have reduced the missionaries to the level of the various popular philosophers and religious preachers who sought payment for their services."[4] Since missionaries often forego certain financial advantages, there is necessity laid upon the church members to support them (vv. 7–8). Missionaries and missionary supporters work side-by-side in the spreading of the truth.

The manner of sharing the gospel comes into view when turning to 1 Peter. A godly life accompanies the believer's witness, and Peter gives the specific case of wives' submission (3:1). One of the reasons for this type of conduct is the "winning" of the unbelieving spouse to the faith. The language of "won" is the same as that used five times in 1 Corinthians 9:19–22 where Paul clearly speaks of salvation. Like Peter, Paul speaks of conduct in relation to spreading the gospel (1 Cor. 9:23). The gospel that the husbands would have already heard can now be persuasive "without a word" via their wives'

---

1. For different views of the phrase "worthy of God," see Karen H. Jobes, *1, 2, & 3 John*, ZECNT (Grand Rapids: Zondervan, 2014), 303. Cf. Philippians 1:27; Colossians 1:10; 1 Thessalonians 2:12.

2. D. Edmond Hiebert writes, "They were not individuals engaged in private business pursuits, but men who had initiated their journey to further the cause of 'the Name.'. . . . That name was the inspiration for the life and outreach of the church and provided the highest motive for cooperation by believers in its dissemination" ("An Exposition of 3 John 5–10. Studies in 3 John Part 2," *BSac* 144 [1987]: 199).

3. P. R. Eddy, "Cynics and Cynicism," in *DJG*, 2nd ed., eds. Joel B. Green, Jeannine K. Brown, and Nicholas Perrin (Downers Grove, IL: IVP Academic, 2013), 163; cf. Adolf Deissmann, *Light from the Ancient East: The New Testament Illustrated by Recently Discovered Texts of the Graeco-Roman World*, trans. Lionel R. M. Strachan (New York: Harper & Brothers, 1922), 109. See Deissmann for the famous example of a Syrian slave begging on behalf of a Syrian goddess.

4. I. Howard Marshall, *The Epistles of John*, NICNT (Grand Rapids: Eerdmans, 1978), 87.

"respectful and pure conduct" (1 Peter 3:2). Wayne Grudem explains the relationship between sharing the gospel and a Christian wife's lifestyle:

> Peter does not exactly say that Christian wives should never talk about the gospel message to their unbelieving husbands (indeed, it is hard to imagine that the Christian wives among Peter's readers would never have explained to their husbands what it meant to become a Christian), but he does say that the means God will use to win their husbands generally will not be the wives' words but their behavior. This knowledge should increase prayer both for grace to live rightly and for God's silent working in the husband's heart.[5]

The way we share the faith is significant. Peter writes, "But even if you should suffer for righteousness' sake, you will be blessed. Have no fear of them, nor be troubled, but in your hearts honor Christ the Lord as holy, always being prepared to make a defense to anyone who asks you for a reason for the hope that is in you; yet do it with gentleness and respect, having a good conscience" (1 Peter 3:14–16a). The Christian faith is shared with a firm conviction of the divinity of Christ. Jesus as both Lord and holy is highlighted in the context of suffering (3:14).[6] Not being afraid but having a proper perspective of Christ "is precisely the kind of spiritual backbone that Peter is trying to build into his readers."[7] Suffering can lead others to ask about a Christian's hope. The Great Commission often implies preparation for these future opportunities (3:15). And when these opportunities arise, the defense of the faith ought to be delivered "with gentleness and respect, having a good conscience" (3:15–16). The respect (or "fear") very likely refers to the Christian's fear of God (cf. 2:17; Isa. 8:12–13).[8] Still, our posture before God has implications for how we treat our neighbor.[9] Our firm convictions in our hearts can be shared with non-Christians with humility. A harsh presentation of God's grace for sinners would be counterproductive in winning people to Christ.

---

5. Wayne Grudem, "Wives Like Sarah, and the Husbands Who Honor Them: 1 Peter 3:1–7," *Recovering Biblical Manhood and Womanhood: A Response to Evangelical Feminism*, eds. John Piper and Wayne Grudem (Wheaton: Crossway, 2006), 202.
6. 1 Peter 3:15 could be translated either as "sanctify Christ as Lord" or "sanctify the Lord, namely, Christ" (see Isa. 8:12–13). See also Paul J. Achtemeier, *1 Peter*, Hermeneia (Minneapolis: Fortress, 1996), 232; Greg W. Forbes, *1 Peter*, EGGNT (Nashville: B&H, 2014), 115; and Mark Dubis, *1 Peter: A Handbook on the Greek Text* (Waco, TX: Baylor University Press, 2010), 110.
7. D. A. Carson, "1 Peter," in *Commentary on the New Testament Use of the Old Testament*, eds. G. K. Beale and D. A. Carson (Grand Rapids: Baker, 2007), 1038.
8. See Dubis, *1 Peter*, 112.
9. So J. Ramsey Michaels, *1 Peter*, WBC 49 (Waco, TX: Word, 1988), 189.

The Great Commission Assumed

The original recipients of Hebrews and 1 Peter were suffering because they followed Christ. Köstenberger and O'Brien write, "For it is *assumed* that believers in Christ have confessed their faith to the outside world and that they are identified with their Christian profession whether their witness in a given instance entails specific verbal testimony or various forms of the witness of a godly life. Similar to Peter in his first epistle, the author of Hebrews upholds Christ as believers' ultimate example in suffering."[10] For example, the author of Hebrews sought to remind his listeners of their previous commitment to Christ where they suffered. He exhorted them, "But recall the former days when, after you were enlightened, you endured a hard struggle with sufferings, sometimes being publicly exposed to reproach and affliction, and sometimes being partners with those so treated. For you had compassion on those in prison, and you joyfully accepted the plundering of your property, since you knew that you yourselves had a better possession and an abiding one" (Heb. 10:32–34).[11] The author reminds his audience of how they used to bear witness to the watching world and suffered because of their identification with Christ. Likewise, 1 Peter 4:14 and 16 says, "If you are insulted for the name of Christ, you are blessed, because the Spirit of glory and of God rests upon you . . . yet if anyone suffers as a Christian, let him not be ashamed, but let him glorify God in that name." The context of suffering was "for the name of Christ" and "as a Christian." Peter was shepherding the church because of the consequences of their witness. In many places, obedience to the Great Commission comes with the threat of suffering. Hebrews and 1 Peter are encouraging letters for the discipleship of believers in hostile places.

Knowledge of God That Leads to Action

The Christology in John's first letter implies the church's mission. Jesus Christ is described as "the propitiation for our sins, and not for ours only but also for the sins of the whole world" (1 John 2:2). Similarly, the Son is called "Savior of the world" (4:14). These descriptions emphasize the extent of God's salvation, giving confidence to missionaries who will call individuals across the world to believe. Christology leads to the church's mission. One reason the church shares the life of Jesus with the world is because "the world is passing away" (2:17) and "the whole world lies in the power of the evil one" (5:19). Karen Jobes clarifies, "But 'world' in John's writings is often used to refer not to the planet or all its inhabitants, but to the system of fallen human culture, with its values, morals, and ethics as a whole."[12] God's love is active in the midst of this sinfulness of the world (4:9).

---

10. Andreas Köstenberger and Peter O'Brien, *Salvation to the Ends of the Earth* (Downers Grove, IL: InterVarsity, 2001), 237 (emphasis added).
11. For examples of the taking of property because of being Christian, see William L. Lane, *Hebrews 9–13*, WBC 47B (Dallas: Word, 1991), 300.
12. Jobes, *1, 2, & 3 John*, 80.

Second Peter reveals God's heart for the world. Peter writes, "The Lord is not slow to fulfill his promise as some count slowness, but is patient toward you, not wishing that any should perish, but that all should reach repentance" (2 Peter 3:9).[13] This statement is found in the context of God's judgment and coming kingdom (3:1–10). The call to repentance is elsewhere connected to God's kingdom (e.g., Matt. 11:20–24; Mark 1:15). As in 1 John, the extent of God's salvation is highlighted with "all" people. The knowledge of God leads Christians into action. Meditating on what God desires for all people can change our desires to become more in line with his.

Summary

The Great Commission in the General Epistles can be viewed from several different angles. In 3 John and 1 Peter there are explicit statements about the church's participation in mission. The church also can find encouragement when difficulties arise in obedience to the Great Commission. There are clear implications that arise out of the theology of the General Epistles such as Christology and anthropology. These perspectives naturally flow from the place of the letters in redemptive history. In other words, after Jesus ascended, it is natural that the Great Commission would be assumed and implied in several statements within the later New Testament letters.

REFLECTION QUESTIONS

1. How does 3 John relate to the support of missionaries?

2. How does 1 Peter 3:1–2 relate marriage to the church's mission?

3. How does an understanding of Christ define how you view missions?

4. How does an understanding of God's love for the world lead you to action?

5. What other passages in the General Epistles teach us about the Great Commission?

---

13. Thomas Duke helpfully explains, "In verse 9, as throughout chapter 3, Peter is primarily concerned with eschatology, not soteriology, seeking to confirm in the minds of his readers the certainty of Christ's Parousia [coming] for the purpose of motivating them to holy living. Nonetheless, it is possible to pull from verse 9 some insights into the mechanics of salvation. Thus, God in fact wants all people to be saved" ("An Exegetical Analysis of 2 Peter 3:9," *Faith & Mission* 16, no. 3 [1999]: 11).

PART 5

Practical-Missiological Questions about the Great Commission

How Does the Bible Display the Gospel to Advance the Great Commission?

If the Great Commission were just a few texts within the larger storyline of Scripture, it could be relegated to one priority among many. However, if God's great redemptive mission centering on the gospel is the backdrop for the entire storyline, then it must be our top priority. Christopher Wright draws attention to this in his book, *Mission of God*, where he argues for a missional hermeneutic of the Bible.[1] Wright walks through the grand metanarrative of the Bible, noting four primary plot movements and the centrality of mission to each. He approaches creation, fall, redemption, and restoration, looking through the lens that God is on mission and that we, his people, play an important part of the fulfillment of that mission. Mission was behind God's good creation of all things, and man's rebellion was an attempt to redirect that mission. Yet, God would not allow his purposes to be thwarted and promised to send a Rescuer to provide for the redemption of all that was broken in the fall, thereby securing the future restoration of all things to God and his purposes. Thus, the gospel of Jesus Christ lay at the heart of God's rescue mission. When we embrace the gospel through repentance and faith, we find our part in the story as disciples of Jesus living on mission with him.

What is the gospel? There is perhaps no more crucial question facing the church in the twenty-first century. As postmodern thought continues to spread and many are questioning whether there is such a thing as truth, the Bible stands as an unchanging and infallible source of all things pertaining to life and godliness. The Bible is true truth. And the Bible not only contains the gospel, but at its very foundation is the redemptive message of God—which is the best news ever communicated. While many have been guilty of rejecting

---

1. Christopher Wright, *Mission of God: Unlocking the Bible's Grand Narrative* (Downers Grove, IL: Intervarsity, 2006).

or at least reducing the gospel message, we must be committed to putting forth the gospel message with an unyielding submission to the inerrancy, infallibility, and sufficiency of the Bible.

The lack of biblical literacy both outside and inside the church has often led to a faulty approach to the Bible whereby the stories contained within are understood as being disjointed and sometimes unrelated. We must combat that faulty approach by recognizing that all sixty-six books and 1,189 chapters of Scripture have one underlying, foundational purpose: to communicate that God Almighty is on a mission to rescue humanity from its fallen and idolatrous condition. This fact has massive implications for the way the church has traditionally evangelized in contemporary culture. Whereas churches have become accustomed to presenting the gospel as a list of propositions derived from various verses of the Bible, the Scripture itself is redemptive in its very nature. We should labor to communicate the whole message so that its parts can be properly understood in light of the whole. This chapter is meant to help the reader communicate that timelessly relevant message of the gospel of Jesus Christ. The following is a summary of how the gospel and mission of God is displayed throughout the grand metanarrative of the Bible.[2]

Creation: God's Purpose to Fill the Earth with Worshipers

How did it all begin? The "true story of the whole world"[3] doesn't begin with creation; it begins with God. It may seem unnecessary to state it, but nothing could be more important to confront our man-centered thinking. "In the beginning, God" (Gen. 1:1). There was never a time when he wasn't. He has always existed and always will. He alone has no beginning and end. The Psalmist affirms, "Before the mountains were brought forth, or ever you had formed the earth and the world, from everlasting to everlasting you are God" (Ps. 90:2). He alone is God. All-powerful. All-knowing. Full of love and grace and truth. And purpose. God did not create because he needed anything. He has eternally existed in perfect love and community as Father, Son, and Holy Spirit—the Triune Godhead. So why then did God create?

God created the heavens and the earth, all that there is, out of the overflow of his perfection. And because he is perfect, everything that he created was made perfectly. He made all things to work together perfectly from the tiniest of atoms to the grandest of galaxies. He always made the unity of creation to

---

2. See www.viewthestory.com for more resources that display the evangelistic and missional understanding of the grand narrative of Scripture. The author of this chapter (George Robinson) consulted with SpreadTruth Ministries on the development of some of those resources and this chapter follows the same basic outline.

3. This is the phrase that Craig Bartholomew and Michael Goheen use to designate the storyline of the Bible in their book, *The Drama of Scripture: Finding Our Place in the Biblical Story*, 2nd ed. (Grand Rapids: Baker Academic, 2014).

teem with diversity. From colors to plants to the birds, fish and animals—everything was made to reflect his goodness and glory.

Everything God made reflected his goodness and glory, but the crown jewel of his creation was mankind. The man and woman were made uniquely in God's image and likeness (Gen. 1:26–27). At the very least that uniqueness means that we relate to God differently than everything else. While "the heavens declare the glory of God" (Ps. 19:1), we as his image-bearers relate to him as worshipers expressed through our obedience. We were made for this kind of relationship with God. And the harmony of our relationship with God originally was shared with all of creation. The earth was meant to be filled with worshipers living in right relationship to him, to one another, and to all that was entrusted to their care. That's why God blessed the man and the woman and commissioned them to "be fruitful and multiply and fill the earth . . . and subdue it" (Gen. 1:28). And then God declared his creation to be "very good" (Gen. 1:31).

- *How did it all begin? Tell the story of creation and God's purpose to fill the earth with worshipers emphasizing God, creation, and harmony.*

Fall: God's Character Questioned and Man's Worship Misdirected

It doesn't take very long to discover that the world we live in certainly isn't characterized by uninterrupted harmony. Creation hasn't come completely unraveled, but brokenness is evident at every turn. This is not how things were meant to be. If God created everything "very good," then what went wrong?

Genesis 3 documents the part of the story we call "the fall." God created the man and woman as worshipers to live in harmonious relationship with himself and with all of creation. He gave them freedom to make decisions and govern the earth with one rule: not to eat fruit from a specific tree. In the middle of their garden home, God placed one forbidden tree among the multitude of others to which they had unlimited access. That forbidden tree was given to test, or prove, mankind's trust of God. One day, God's enemy, a fallen angel named Satan, wanted to overthrow God so he took the form of a serpent and lied to Adam and Eve. He deceived them into thinking that God was not good and did not have their best interest in mind. They ate the fruit, deciding that they, not God, would determine right and wrong. Unfortunately, they failed the test and disobeyed God. And we would have as well—"for all have sinned and fall short of the glory of God" (Rom. 3:23).

The consequences of their (and our) actions are devastating! Because of their distrust of God, that relationship was fractured leaving them and us incapable of fulfilling our original purpose. The effects of their rebellion has affected all of creation, distorting things from God's original, perfect design. Eventually Adam and Eve, along with their descendants, were fruitful and multiplied and filled the earth. They didn't cease to be worshipers. In fact, we cannot not worship! So the earth has been filled with misdirected worship resulting in the unraveling of harmony into brokenness. And tragically, we can't fix it or ourselves. We are in a place of desperate need—a need that can only be met through God's intervention.

- *What went wrong? Tell the story of the fall and how we have all disobeyed God, questioning his character, the consequence of which is the fracturing of our relationship with him and with all of his created order, misdirecting our worship from the Creator to the creation—and ultimately to ourselves. And because we can't fix ourselves, we are in desperate need.*

Rescue/Redemption: God's Character Vindicated and Man's Worship Redirected

Because God is committed to his glory and his purposes can't be thwarted, in love he made a promise to our rebellious forebears that he would indeed intervene and send a Rescuer.[4] In some respects, the rest of the Old Testament is a long, detailed answer to the question that all of humanity faces—is there any hope? Over the centuries, God prepared the way to keep his promise and to send the Rescuer into the world (Gen. 3:15). Exact details of his birth, life, and death are recorded in the Bible long before he came.

So who is this Rescuer? The promised Savior was God Himself. God became human in the person of Jesus Christ almost two thousand years ago (John 1:14; also Matt. 1:23), fulfilling his original promise in the garden, and all of the subsequent promises in the Old Testament. Jesus's birth was miraculous and his life was unique. He enjoyed fellowship with God the Father and perfectly obeyed without sin. He truly fulfilled God's purpose for creating, showing us what we were made for. But Jesus was more than just our example to follow. He ultimately laid his life down, dying an agonizing death on a Roman cross, willingly, obediently, and sufficiently paying for the sins of all mankind. And all of this was to fulfill God's original plan.

Jesus's substitutionary death was the greatest display of worship and obedience that there ever has or ever will be. He kept all of God's promises offering mercy and hope to every rebel that would trust God's good character by putting their trust in Jesus. The perfectly innocent died to rescue the hopelessly guilty from brokenness, making God's original purpose for us attainable by faith. The Bible says, "For Christ also suffered once for sins, the righteous for the unrighteous, that he might bring us to God" (1 Peter 3:18). All of this is possible because death could not overcome Jesus. Three days after laying down his life, he was raised from the dead, emerged from the tomb, fulfilling his earthly mission to reconcile us to God as promised. And forty days later, Jesus ascended to heaven, where he reigns as the rightful King.

---

4. See, e.g., Genesis 3:15; 12:3; 49:8–12; Isa. 7:14; 9:6; 53:1–12; 62:1–3.

- *Is there any hope? Tell the story of God's rescue summarized in his promise made and kept through the person and work of Jesus Christ. Through repentance and faith in Jesus's perfect, sinless life, and vicarious, substitutionary death, we can be reconciled to God, redirecting our worship and obedience, and fulfill his original purpose.*

Restoration: God's Mission Fulfilled and the New Creation Filled with Worshipers

The story of God's rescue is good news! But that's not the end of the story for us or for God's creation. What does the future hold? For all those who trust in Jesus alone, God has also promised he will make all things new. That begins now as we grow in our trust and obedience. But one day he will restore all of his creation and that new heaven and earth will be completely free of sin and brokenness—a place of perfect relationship with God, others, and all he has created. Everything will be restored to the way it was meant to be. The new earth will once again be the perfect home God intended for his creation. God's original purpose will flourish, as those who trust him will grow in our grand purpose of worship and loving obedience. The earth will be filled with rightly ordered worship as it was originally created to be.

The most wonderful part of this new world is that we will be with God forever, experiencing complete joy with him. We will be restored to a perfect relationship with the One who created, loved, and died for us. The Bible says, "Behold, the dwelling place of God is with man. He will dwell with them, and they will be his people, and God himself will be with them as their God. He will wipe away every tear from their eyes, and death shall be no more, neither shall there be mourning, nor crying, nor pain anymore, for the former things have passed away" (Rev. 21:3–4).

- *What will the future hold? Tell the story of God's restoration, making all things new, fulfilling his original purpose in creating. Emphasize that for those who repent of their distrust and rebellion toward God, trusting Jesus alone, they will be reconciled to God and will live out his purpose for their lives in eternal and joyful worship and obedience.*

Summary

If the gospel is the true story of God's redemptive plan (and it is!), then we in the church must become master storytellers heralding this good news both near and far. In this chapter you will find a summary of the four key points of the Bible's grand narrative: creation, fall, rescue, and restoration. This biblical storyline provides the answer to four universal worldview questions making it transculturally relevant. This approach is not only helpful in evangelism, it also provides a fantastic tool in making disciples whose lives are built upon the Bible. Communicating this story and the transformative power therein is what the Great Commission is all about.

REFLECTION QUESTIONS

1. In what ways does communicating the gospel in the context of the grand metanarrative provide the framework for disciple-making?

2. What is at stake if we communicate the gospel without the biblical narrative framework?

3. How might this approach to evangelism be transculturally relevant? What role do the worldview questions play in accomplishing that relevance?

4. Which parts of the story have you been most prone to overlook or to skip when sharing the gospel?

5. Why do you think it is important to tie the gospel back to God's original purpose in creation?

What Is the Responsibility of Each Christian to the Great Commission?

William Carey, the "Father of Modern Missions," set out in 1792 to answer the very question posed by this chapter, resulting in the publication of an essay entitled *An Enquiry into the Obligations of Christians to Use Means for the Conversion of the Heathens*.[1] Carey was convinced, in spite of opposition from some of his hyper-Calvinist friends, that the Great Commission was binding on all Christians of all times. The essay provided a theological rationale for individual Christians to do their part in spreading the gospel to the ends of the earth.

While most Christians would not necessarily argue theologically that the Great Commission does not apply today, a host of other excuses have become prevalent. The notion that one must have a special calling from God to get involved in evangelism and disciple-making coupled with the professionalization of ministry seem to be appeasing the consciences of many. That Jesus's words from Matthew 28:18–20 still apply today should be apparent (see Question 2). That they apply to all Christ-followers in the same way may be more difficult to prove. While not every Christian needs to get a passport, pack their bags, move to a foreign land, learn the language and culture, evangelize the masses, and start indigenous churches, all should be disciple-makers committed to the task of spreading the fame of Jesus's name. Charles Spurgeon is reported as saying, "Every Christian is either a missionary or an imposter."[2] Wrongly understood, these words can send us on a guilt trip. Rightly understood, they can motivate us to find our place in God's mission.

---

1. William Carey, *An Enquiry into the Obligations to Use Means for the Conversion of the Heathens* (Dallas: Criswell Publication, 1988).
2. C. H. Spurgeon, *The Metropolitan Tabernacle Pulpit*, vol. 54 (Pasadena, TX: Pilgrim Publications, 1978), 476.

The following material is a simple and straightforward application of Jesus's final words to individual Christians to help us live on mission with God.

Trusting Jesus's Power

It is no coincidence that the classic Great Commission text that Carey built his argument on is preceded by an acknowledgement that there may have been some hesitation even among the first disciples. "And when they saw him they worshiped him, but some doubted" (Matt. 28:17). Some doubted? The resurrected Christ was standing before them visibly and he was speaking audibly. Thomas had already probed Jesus's wounds to alleviate his doubt (John 20:24–29). Peter had already eaten fish with him on a beach and taken a walk to be restored from his doubt (John 21:15–19). Why, then, does Matthew record that here, immediately prior to Jesus's ascension to the Father, that some doubted?

Scholars debate whether the doubting was among the Eleven or the broader crowd who gathered on that day.[3] Perhaps their doubt was similar to what many Christians experience when they wrestle with the implications of the good news of the gospel juxtaposed against the brokenness of the world. Such is not doubt in whether Jesus is who he says he is. Rather, it is hesitation related to the implications of that reality for our everyday living.[4] It takes faith to believe. It also takes ongoing faith to trust that Jesus's power to save extends beyond we who have already repented and put our faith in him. Bruner reminds us, "The good news of the Great Commission is that Jesus addresses and uses exactly such worshiping-doubting disciples."[5]

All Authority Everywhere

It seems that Jesus noticed the hesitation in the crowd on that day and he addressed it head on by proclaiming his universal authority. He did so because, "they will win their war with doubt simply by obeying his mission command."[6] Christian responsibility to the Great Commission begins with a humble acceptance that our success is not contingent upon the measure of our doubting faith, nor upon our ability to persuade. There is no place we can go and no person we can bear witness to that is not already under the comprehensive authority of the risen Christ. We must rest in his authority and then act upon it.

---

3. See Question 13; also see Michael J. Wilkins, "Matthew" in *The NIV Application Commentary* (Grand Rapids: Zondervan, 2004), 948–49 for a detailed list of various interpretations. See also Frederick Dale Bruner, *Matthew*, vol. 2 (*The Churchbook Matthew 13–28*), rev. and exp. (Grand Rapids: Eerdmans, 1990), 809–11.
4. Wilkins, "Matthew," 948–49.
5. Bruner, *Matthew*, 2:810.
6. Ibid.

Acting on Jesus's Plan

Trusting that Jesus has all authority everywhere is one thing from the comfort of our churches, and it is quite another in a pioneer mission setting. After acknowledging that Jesus possesses all authority, Christians must also acknowledge that he has a plan for each of us. Plans are meant to be acted upon. A house plan on paper is one thing. A completed house is quite another. The difference between the two involves a lot of activity that is guided by the plan itself. What is Jesus's plan, and what does it require of Christians?

Going to Your Neighbors and the Nations

Jesus's plan for Christians is laid out in the classic Great Commission passage—namely, to make disciples. Making disciples is not a stationary task that occurs in the static environment of a classroom. Many Christians view discipleship as something that the truly dedicated receive. Discipleship is more than the introspective subject of spiritual formation. The Great Commission has an intentional external focus that demands going.

But to whom do we go? The answer to that question is rather simple. Start where you are and within the relationships and circles of influence that you already have. But, do not limit your disciple-making to your existing relationships. Had the Eleven perceived Jesus's commission to be limited in that way, the gospel would have never traveled beyond the region of Galilee. Jesus's plan involved our going both to our neighbors and to the nations.

In our contemporary globalizing context, neighbor and nations may be closer than you might think. The nations (think *ēthne*, not geopolitical entities) are on the move. So much so that there is an emerging focus on diaspora missions.[7] Christians have unprecedented opportunities to welcome the nations who have moved near to us. Whether one of the hundreds of thousands of international students studying in universities, refugees that are being resettled, or immigrants who have made your town their new home, you have a responsibility to welcome them and to share the love and hope of Jesus with them.

Regardless of whether the nations are geographically near or far, Jesus's plan is that the gospel is to be proclaimed to all of them. The goal in our going to neighbors and nations is making disciples not just of more people, but of more peoples.

Bearing Witness to the Gospel

The first step in making disciples of either our neighbors or the nations is learning how to bear witness to the gospel. Unfortunately, when evangelism is mentioned to many Christians, the doubting or hesitancy begins. Yet, Jesus made clear from the outset of his call to discipleship that those who

---

7. See Enoch Wan, *Diaspora Missiology: Theory, Methodology and Practice* (Portland, OR: Institute of Diaspora Studies, 2011).

follow him would also become "fishers of men" (Matt. 4:19). Bearing witness is rooted in our very identity as Christians. This is why every Christ follower should know how to tell their own story of how they came to repent and believe the good news. But our personal testimony is not in itself the gospel. Rather it is the affirmation of the gospel's effect on our life. It is simply telling others of our own experience in coming to faith in Jesus through the gospel.

In addition to sharing our own story or testimony, Christians should understand how to communicate the truths of the gospel in a simple and reproducible way. Paul reminded the Christians in Corinth what the core gospel message was, saying, "For I delivered to you as of first importance what I also received: that Christ died for our sins in accordance with the Scriptures, that he was buried, that he was raised on the third day in accordance with the Scriptures" (1 Cor. 15:3–4). The righteous life, substitutionary death and burial, and vicarious bodily resurrection of Jesus is the good news. Yet, that good news has as its backdrop all of the history of the Old Testament. Paul references this twice in the text saying, "in accordance with the Scriptures." Christians should be able to give the gospel core against the backdrop of all God's gospel promises—which trace all the way back to Genesis 3:15 in what theologians call the *protoevangelion*, or first mention of the gospel. Missionaries often have to give the back story in order to make sense of why a Jewish man dying on a cross two thousand years ago has any relevance to a person on the other side of the globe. As a result, it has become fairly common for missionaries to share the gospel in a "Creation to Christ" manner. Even in post-Christian societies where a biblical worldview is a thing of the past, Christians should be prepared to share the good news in like manner.[8]

Baptizing Those Who Repent and Believe

If there was any doubt that Christians bearing witness to the gospel is tied to our identity, Jesus commanded us to be baptized which serves that very purpose. Believer's baptism is the first step of obedience for the person who has responded to the gospel through repentance and faith. Baptism is a public display of our identification with Christ in his death, burial, and resurrection. Baptism doesn't save us, but it does tell those who witness it that we have been saved. Thus, our bearing witness to the gospel begins with our baptism, but should continue on through our verbal proclamation to our neighbors and the nations.

Christians who are bearing witness to the gospel should be prepared to disciple those who respond in repentance and faith. Discipleship begins as we

---

8. See Question 32 for how one might do this. In that chapter, www.thestoryfilm.com is referenced as a resource that approaches the gospel in this manner. The five-minute film is available in more than twenty languages, to help you as you go to your neighbors and the nations. There is also a JesusFilm app that we highly commend.

share the gospel, but continues as we baptize those who repent and believe, thereby giving them the opportunity to begin bearing witness to their circles of influence.[9]

Teaching Obedience to All Jesus's Commands

Evangelism is fundamentally teaching an unbeliever the gospel and urging them to obey through repentance and faith. Thus, every Christian is empowered and commanded to teach obedience to Jesus. This goes beyond the mere transference of lessons and concepts. Teaching is incomplete until the disciple is obediently applying what they have learned. Christians should be familiar with the commands of Christ, applying them in their own life, and be prepared to teach others to obey through relational disciple-making.[10]

Jesus taught far more than the gospel proper. In more than three hundred commands in the four Gospels, Jesus taught the implications of the good news. Therein the Christian will find the commands to pray and give toward the expansion of the gospel. Jesus told his disciples to, "pray earnestly to the Lord of the harvest to send out laborers into his harvest" (Matt. 9:38). Just a few verses later they become the answer to their own prayer as they are sent out by Jesus. Prayer for missions leads to deeper participation in missions. Sacrificial giving is also foundational to the Great Commission. Jesus exemplified this in his own incarnation and he encouraged it in his disciples (Luke 14:33). It is the responsibility of every Christian to pray and give sacrificially toward missions and to teach that same obedience to others. In addition to going, praying, and giving as Great Commission obedience, Christians should be welcoming the nations through gospel-centered hospitality, and they should be mobilizing other believers onto mission. These five areas comprise what some have called "5 Habits of a World Christian."[11]

Making Reproducing Disciples

Christians should begin bearing witness to the gospel and making disciples right where they are among their neighbors. But how does that local witness get to the nations? Earlier we noted that not all Christians must necessarily move to another country in their Great Commission obedience, though more should than currently are doing so. The Great Commission will not ultimately be fulfilled through the obedience of a few talented missionaries and evangelists. Contrary to what some may believe, that's not how Christianity spread in the first century either. Church historian Michael Green argues that it was the simple obedience of ordinary Christians to

---

9. For a fuller discussion on who has the authority to baptize new believers, see Question 34.
10. For a fuller explanation of how to teach obedience to all of Christ's commands, see Question 18.
11. For a fuller explanation of the "5 Habits of a World Christian," see Question 37.

share their faith and make disciples everywhere they went that lay behind the rapid expansion of Christianity in the early church.[12] And those disciples were taught to obey, which entailed bearing witness and making disciples of others. The rapid expansion of the church in those early days occurred because ordinary Christians made reproducing disciples. If we are to obey the Great Commission, then that will be our focus as well—to make reproducing disciples of our neighbors and among the nations.

Resting in Jesus's Presence until the End

Perhaps the restlessness that so many Christians experience in their own personal spiritual formation is rooted in their refusal to join God on his mission. Great Commission obedience involves going to make reproducing disciples of Jesus. But it also involves resting in Jesus's presence. Jesus promised his enduring and comforting presence to those who join him on this great mission. His promised presence is enduring because there are so many who have yet to hear the good news and respond in repentance and faith. And, his promised presence is comforting because we hesitant doubters need to be reminded often that our success is not contingent upon our own authority or abilities. Christians who are actively going and making disciples, baptizing, and teaching obedience to all Jesus commanded do so in his power and authority and resting in his presence—until the nations worship.

Summary

William Carey's efforts corrected a misunderstanding of the Great Commission that inadvertently removed all responsibility for missions from Christian individuals and local churches. Carey's *Enquiry* argued that the Great Commission is still binding today and that all Christians should leverage their lives toward obedience that takes the gospel to the ends of the earth. Even though few evangelicals would rebut Carey's argument today, proportionately few are leveraging their lives for what they claim to be true. Ultimately we are responsible for reaching our neighbors and the nations with the gospel. Christ gives us his authority, plan, and presence along with this responsibility. All that remains is for us to make disciples both near and far, baptizing them and teaching them to obey him.

---

12. Michael Green, *Evangelism in the Early Church*, rev. ed. (Grand Rapids: Eerdmans, 2003), 3–4.

REFLECTION QUESTIONS

1. How does your life reflect the responsibility that Christ has entrusted to you with his Great Commission?

2. What is at stake when we add stipulations to who can participate in Great Commission activities?

3. What is at stake when we live as if the responsibility for making disciples of all nations belongs to a limited group of people within the church?

4. How would you communicate this responsibility to others in your local church?

5. How might the shirking of responsibility hinder an individual's personal spiritual growth?

What Is the Responsibility of the Local Church to the Great Commission?

In Acts 1:8 Jesus explicitly tied the birth of the church to mission saying, "But you will receive power when the Holy Spirit has come upon you, and you will be my witnesses in Jerusalem and in all Judea and Samaria, and to the ends of the earth." The church came into existence for the purpose of mission. The mission was defined by God. And the church was designed by God for his mission. Jurgen Moltmann says, "It is not the church that has a mission of salvation to fulfill in the world; it is the mission of the Son and the Spirit through the Father that includes the church."[1] If the church was designed by God for mission, what is the responsibility of the local church to the Great Commission?

Equip All Believers as Obedient Disciples

The local church was uniquely designed by God for mission through its role in equipping all believers as obedient disciples. Unfortunately, many churches (if not most) have lost sight of this mission and are subsequently focused on maintenance at best or worse yet, mere survival. The scorecard for success in local church ministry needs to be changed. Rather than trying to fill seats for a worship service, churches would do well to emphasize equipping its membership as obedient disciples of Jesus.

The leadership God has given to the church is to serve the end of every member ministering. Paul speaks to this explicitly, saying, "He [God] gave the apostles, the prophets, the evangelists, the shepherds and teachers, to equip the saints for the work of ministry, for building up the body of Christ" (Eph. 4:11–12). It should be noted that three of the five types of leaders God has

---

1. Jurgen Moltmann, *The Church in the Power of the Spirit: A Contribution to Messianic Ecclesiology* (London: SCM Press, 1977), 64.

given to the local church serve to equip it for externally focused ministry.[2] Churches should be equipping its membership to be active participants in the mission of God by cultivating both personal spiritual formation and externally focused evangelism and disciple-making.

Empower All Believers as Reproducing Disciple-Makers

In order to empower all believers as disciple-makers, pastor/elders must understand that they are to be the lead reproducing disciple-makers in the church. This means that success for the pastor is not determined by his church's seating capacity, but rather by its sending capacity.[3] This may mean that he spend less time in sermon preparation and more developing other leaders so that the disciple-making impact is more pronounced. Sermons and Sunday services are not bad or wrong, but they are also not the underlying purpose of the church. If local churches are going to be missional, then their leaders must make developing and empowering all members as disciple-makers a top priority.

How should local church pastors go about cultivating an *ethos* of disciple-making that permeates the entire church? It begins with his own example. If the membership of a church doesn't view their pastor as the lead disciple-maker, but rather as a preacher or chaplain of sorts, then their focus will likely be consumeristic and reflexive rather than outward focused. He can't lead by example if he is not with the people under his leadership. The clergy/laity divide has become increasingly problematic as it tends to perpetuate spiritual immaturity.

The local church that is Great Commission focused will likely be the one whose leadership understands the value of "withness." Calendars should be organized around people, not just events. Disciple-making doesn't mean adding more meetings to a leader's calendar. It entails adding more people to the events that are already on his calendar. For example, a disciple-making pastor doesn't do sermon preparation alone, but instead identifies a few individuals to share that time with understanding that his investment in them will have a much greater impact than his own sermon ever could.

A disciple-making pastor does not delegate evangelism and missions out to someone else in order to get it off of his list of responsibilities. Instead,

---

2. Apostles, prophets, and evangelists are externally oriented, while pastor/teachers tend to be focused within the church. See Alan Hirsch, *5Q: Reactivating the Original Intelligence and Capacity of the Body of Christ* (Los Angeles: 100Movements, 2017).

3. The original quote, "The mark of a great church is its sending capacity, not its seating capacity" is attributed to a pastor named Mike Strachura; however, no original reference could be found. More recently (in 2015), "Sending Capacity, Not Seating Capacity: Why a Church Gains the Most When It Sends Its Best" by J. D. Greear and Mike McDaniel was published as an Exponential Resources ebook (https://exponential.org/resource-ebooks/sending-capacity).

he brings others along with him, delegating aspects for the purpose of developing others through the investment. Missionaries coined the acronym MAWL (Model, Assist, Watch, Leave) in order to capture how leaders reproduce.[4] First, the leader must model what he desires to replicate allowing the mentees to observe and learn from his example. Next, he assists in doing the task with his mentee taking the time to communicate expectations and field questions. Then, he delegates the task to his mentee and watches, providing helpful feedback. Finally, the Great Commission leader entrusts the task to his mentee and leaves so that they can further develop on their own. This kind of informal mentoring and intentional disciple-making pours fuel on the fire of Great Commission focus in the local church. The local church leadership has the responsibility to lead by example and through "withness" in evangelism, disciple-making, and missions, thereby empowering all believers toward Great Commission obedience.

Entrust All Believers with All Aspects of Disciple-Making

Local churches were designed by God for the purpose of being on mission with him. Entire churches, not just pastors, should be involved in all aspects of disciple-making. When pastors withhold certain aspects of Great Commission obedience from their flock, they are failing at their primary role to equip the church for the work of the ministry.

Central to the identity of all Christ followers is that we are believer-priests. The doctrine of the priesthood of all believers described in 1 Peter 2:5–9 has twofold implications. First, it entails that all believers have direct access to God because Christ alone is our mediator. Second, the doctrine empowers all believers to live and serve as ministers in the church and in the world. Most Christians understand and appreciate the first aspect, while neglecting the second. The doctrine of the priesthood of all believers has been neglected by pastor and parishioner alike. Pastors like to feel needed and appreciated so they often do things for church members rather than equip them to do it on their own. And church members often enjoy being served by a pastor, since after all "He's paid to do that!" The end result of this dual temptation is that the Great Commission effectiveness of the church is minimized. But is the local church really responsible for entrusting *all believers* with *all aspects* of disciple-making and ministry?

Entrusting all believers with all aspects of disciple-making and ministry has wide-reaching implications. Who can evangelize? Who can baptize? Who can teach? Who can reproduce? These are all legitimate questions that happen to be highly controversial in most church circles. We will address them one by one.

---

4. This acronym is originally attributed to a missionary named Curtis Sergeant. For more information on the MAWL process see http://noplaceleft.net/mawl/.

Who can evangelize? In short, all Christians can and should evangelize. Evangelism isn't some spiritual gift given only to the strange extroverts in your church. While the Bible doesn't speak of the gift of evangelism, Paul does include "the evangelist" in Ephesians 4. The evangelist isn't necessarily some Billy Graham type of preacher who appeals to the masses. Nor is he necessarily the person brought in to speak in revival services. Paul makes it plain that the evangelist's role is to "equip the saints for the work of the ministry" (Eph. 4:12). Therefore, God has gifted certain people to help churches grow in their evangelistic effectiveness as a whole—not do it for them. By equipping all church members to share their faith, the church multiplies its Great Commission potential.

Every believer can and should share their faith—even if they've just trusted in Christ. That new believer may not have much of a testimony yet, but they can help someone take the step they just took, the step of repentance and faith. Children who are believers can and should evangelize. Evangelism doesn't have an age or maturity requirement. Introverts can and should evangelize. The gospel isn't carried forth because of an individual's personality type. The Holy Spirit loves to empower the weak so that Jesus gets all of the glory. The aged can and should evangelize. Sharing one's faith is not something you retire from or get promoted out of. The bottom line is this: All Christians can and should evangelize. Which means that all churches should entrust all Christians with that task and equip them for it.

Who can baptize? In short, all Christians can and should baptize those they have led to faith in Jesus.[5] Though this is controversial, it really need not be. To the pastor who believes that ordination is required of a person who baptizes new believers, are you going to tell your church to obey one part of the Great Commission (make disciples), while keeping them from obeying another (baptizing them in the name of the Father, Son, and Holy Spirit)? Most pastors encourage their congregations to evangelize. Few pastors invite their congregation

---

5. Interestingly, when churches commission missionaries to go live out the Great Commission in other countries, they expect those missionaries to baptize new believers. Why would we not commission all of our membership in like manner? When a church is present, baptism should certainly be done under the authority of the local church—but not necessarily "inside" the church building or administered by paid leaders! Missionaries who baptize new believers in areas where this is no local church are in effect forming the nucleus of a future church. It is problematic to ask the missionary to wait until there is a local church or until there is "critical mass" to baptize. Such restrictions seem to communicate that the authority for the church is man, rather than Christ. One proponent of this understanding is Wayne Grudem, who advocates that any mature believer can baptize new converts (see Wayne Grudem, *Systematic Theology* [Grand Rapids: Zondervan, 1994], 983–84). One example of someone who disagrees with this understanding is Kevin DeYoung (see https://www. thegospelcoalition.org/blogs/kevin-deyoung/who-can-baptize). DeYoung argues that theologically, Christ rules his church through undershepherds who have been examined and tasked with eldership.

to baptize those they see come to faith. Perhaps by entrusting baptism to all believers, churches will find that their Great Commission fervor increases.

Who can teach? All Christians who evangelize do, in effect, teach the gospel. Does that mean that not all Christians should evangelize? Certainly not! While the authors of this book hold to a complementarian understanding of gender roles within local church leadership, we need to be careful that we don't inadvertently teach disobedience to one commandment in order to encourage disobedience to another. Paul did instruct Timothy saying, "I do not permit a woman to teach or to exercise authority over a man; rather, she is to remain quiet" (1 Tim. 2:12). The context for this prohibition seems to be that the women teaching in Ephesus were neglecting their families and possibly even avoiding having children because of their participation.[6] Regardless of the reason for his prohibition in that text, in Titus 2:3–4 Paul exhorts older women to teach the younger. In short, though there is no biblical support for women in the position of a pastor/elder, there is plenty of support for their focused teaching ministry through evangelism and disciple-making, both of which are central to Great Commission obedience. Thus, churches have a responsibility to equip, empower, and entrust teaching obedience to Christ's commands to *all* of their members.

Who can reproduce? Dawson Trotman once preached a message that was made into a book entitled "Born to Reproduce," wherein he reminded Christians that inherent to their identity in Christ was their call to be disciple-makers.[7] The irony is that Christians would need to be reminded of something that is so fundamental to the clear teaching of Jesus. When Jesus called the disciples to follow him in the beginning of his public ministry, he cast a vision that their following would make them "fishers of men" (Matt. 4:19). Throughout his interaction with the disciples, Jesus modeled, assisted, and watched them reproducing what they had been taught. Then his last words served as a reminder that Christ's kingdom would grow as the disciples were faithful to make more disciples. This was the very purpose of the church that the Spirit birthed after Jesus ascended to the Father (Acts 1:8). And the first church "devoted themselves to the apostles' teaching. . . . And the Lord added to their number day by day" (Acts 2:42, 47). The church grew because the leaders were entrusting all believers with all aspects of disciple-making. Stephen, a deacon, preached a stunning prophetic message in Acts 7. Philip, another deacon, was preaching itinerantly and baptized the Ethiopian eunuch in Acts 8. Churches equipped, empowered, and entrusted their membership with the task of making reproducing disciples. We would do well today to follow their example.

---

6. Eckhard J. Schnabel, *Early Christian Mission*, vol. 2: *Paul and the Early Church* (Downers Grove, IL: InterVarsity, 2004), 1416.
7. Dawson E. Trotman, *Born to Reproduce* (Colorado Springs: NavPress, 1981).

Summary

In summary, the Great Commission was not just entrusted to individuals, but to local churches. Local churches serve a vital role in fulfilling the Great Commission because local churches equip the saints for the work of the ministry. In this chapter we have emphasized that local churches must equip all believers as obedient disciples, empower all believers as reproducing disciple-makers, and entrust all believers with all aspects of disciple-making. Making reproducing, obedient disciples of Jesus among all nations is the mission of the church. Thus, as believer-priests, all members of the church should be equipped, empowered, and entrusted to devote their lives and labors toward that end.

REFLECTION QUESTIONS

1. In what ways have you been equipped, empowered, and entrusted with Great Commission obedience through your local church?

2. Would a new member of your church readily feel equipped, empowered, and entrusted for Great Commission obedience?

3. What are some the risks associated with entrusting Great Commission obedience to someone too soon?

4. What are the risks of withholding it for any length of time?

5. Which aspects of equipping for Great Commission obedience are most lacking in your local church? Which are most prevalent?

Does the Great Commission Involve Social Action?

There may not be a more contentious and potentially divisive question in this entire book. In Question 4 we addressed the relationship between the Great Commission and the Great Commandment. The former centers on our making reproducing disciples of our neighbors and the nations. That aspect of mission is foundational to the latter because unless a person repents and places their faith in Jesus becoming his disciple, they can't love God or neighbor as they ought.

Authors Kevin DeYoung and Greg Gilbert frame the conversation in a helpful way in their book, *What Is the Mission of the Church?* They note that much of the controversy regarding the relationship between the Great Commission and social ministries centers upon advocates of both sides misunderstanding or even misrepresenting the other with regard to how they define "the gospel."

> Sometimes it (the New Testament) looks at the good news of Christianity with a wide-angle lens, calling "gospel" all the great blessings that God intends to shower on his people, starting with forgiveness but cascading from there all the way to a renewed and remade creation. . . . Other times, though, the New Testament looks at the good news of Christianity with a very narrow focus—with a zoom lens, if you will—and is quite happy to call "gospel" the singular blessing of forgiveness of sins and restored relationship with God through the sacrificial death of Jesus.[1]

---

1. Kevin DeYoung and Greg Gilbert, *What Is the Mission of the Church? Making Sense of Social Justice, Shalom, and the Great Commission* (Wheaton, IL: Crossway, 2011), 94.

They go on to argue that both understandings of the gospel are true, and thus, have implication for the mission of the church. They refer to the former as "the gospel of the kingdom" and the latter as "the gospel of the cross," being careful to insist that there are *not* two gospels. Acknowledging that the Bible speaks of the one gospel with both narrow and wide-angle implications is helpful. They conclude, "the gospel of the cross is the fountainhead of the gospel of the kingdom."[2] In other words, Christians can feed the hungry, clothe the naked, set free the captives, and transform their communities, but unless the gospel of the cross is foundational and explicit, they are not truly motivated by the love of God. Conversely, Christians can preach, translate Bibles, hand out tracts, and start new churches, but unless their message produces the fruit of genuine love for God and neighbor, their message is misunderstood and hollow.

Social Action in Jesus's Ministry

It is interesting that Jesus's public ministry begins with his reading from the scroll of Isaiah where God's "Suffering Servant" brings about a convergence of word and deed. The passage reads, "The Spirit of the Lord is upon me, because he has anointed me to proclaim good news to the poor. He has sent me to proclaim liberty to the captives and recovering of sight to the blind, to set at liberty those who are oppressed, to proclaim the year of the Lord's favor" (Luke 4:18–19; cf. Isa. 61:1–2). Jesus identifies his audience as the poor, the captives, the blind, and the oppressed. Certainly Jesus is concerned with social justice. Note, however, his ministry with each of those has proclamation as its foundation. He's proclaiming good news to the poor. He's proclaiming liberty to the captives and recovery of sight to the blind. And he's proclaiming the year of the Lord's favor to all. He speaks, then he acts. Both his word and deed are reflective of his identity.

Social Action in the Apostles' Ministry

No sooner had the Spirit come and the church been established in Jerusalem that we see the apostles, Peter and John, faced with our dilemma. Acts 3 documents their interaction with a lame beggar at the temple who asked for money. Their response? They offered him healing in the name of Jesus and then turned, entered the temple, and proclaimed the gospel of the cross to everyone gathered in Solomon's Portico. One would be hard-pressed to find an example of the apostles doing social justice ministry without an accompanying proclamation of the explicit gospel message. In fact in his Gospel, John highlights the "signs" of Jesus as confirmation of the saving identity of Jesus. In other words, John refuses to let his readers think

---

2. Ibid., 108.

that Jesus would meet physical needs without calling them to believe that Jesus is God's Rescuer, come to reconcile the repentant to God.[3]

Some who are reading this chapter may be thinking, "Well what about James 1:27?" That passage reads, "Religion that is pure and undefiled before God the Father is this: to visit orphans and widows in their affliction, and to keep oneself unstained from the world." Agreed! Authentic faith does move us to action. James isn't saying that one earns the Father's approval by caring for orphans and widows. He says that the person who already has saving faith will produce compassionate fruit. And exegetically, he was probably referring to needs that existed inside the churches.[4] Thus, saving faith cares and acts. Saving faith always results in both a genuine concern for the hurting and needy, and actions that reflect that concern.

Works, without Faith, Are Dead

You may have thought the subheading preceding this sentence is a typo. It is not. James does go on in his epistle to say, "faith apart from works is dead" (James 2:26). Our gospel mustn't have a hole in it, as some have claimed.[5] If we have received the gospel of the cross, we have inherited the gospel of the kingdom. We must proclaim the former and embody the latter.

DeYoung and Gilbert are once again helpful, "Ultimately, if the church does not preach Christ and him crucified, if the church does not plant, nurture and establish more churches, if the church does not teach the nations to obey Christ, no one else and nothing else will. And yet, many others *will* meet physical needs."[6] Many people will do good deeds reflective of the image of God (albeit fractured!) within them, and apart from repentance and faith, they will perish. Tragic! Yet, just as tragic is the thought that those of us who have repented and placed our faith in Jesus, being reconciled to God, would do good works for hurting and broken people that leave them in their sin and separated from God. Those kinds of works, without faith, are dead.

GC2: Great Commission and Great Commandment

Paul Borthwick writes of a convergence of Great Commission and Great Commandment in the life of a Christian that he calls "Complete Sensory Evangelism." Perhaps his penetrating questions for self-examination will prove helpful as you cultivate a life of "GC2" obedience. Borthwick prompts,

---

3. Jesus's identity as savior runs throughout John's Gospel. See, e.g., John 1:1, 14; 6:35, 51; 8:12, 42; 10:27–30; 14:6; 17:5; 18:5.
4. Douglas J. Moo, *The Letter of James*, PCNT (Grand Rapids: Eerdmans, 2000), 96–97.
5. Richard Stearns, *The Hole in Our Gospel: What Does God Expect of Us? The Answer That Changed My Life and Might Just Change the World* (Nashville: Nelson, 2009).
6. DeYoung and Gilbert, *What Is the Mission of the Church?*, 238 (emphasis original).

- To people's hearing (1 Cor. 15:3–4): Am I prepared to give a loving and well-thought audible explanation of the hope that I have in Christ?

- To people's taste (Matt. 5:13): Am I a "salty" Christian, a flavor-enhancer who improves the quality of life of those around me?

- To people's sight (Matt. 5:14–16): Am I a light-of-the world person who dispels the darkness? Am I conspicuously Christian? Do people see my good works and get pointed to Jesus?

- To people's touch (Matt. 25:31–46): Am I the touch of Christ to needy people around me?

- To people's sense of smell (2 Cor. 2:14–16): Is there a fragrance of the love and life of Jesus Christ in my life that lingers—inviting people to think about eternal realities?[7]

Summary

The gospel of Jesus Christ is a message to be proclaimed that yields a life that is being restored. The gospel of the cross is foundational to not only the Great Commission, but also to the Great Commandment activities of loving one's neighbor. Social justice should absolutely be a concern for Christ followers. But we must remember that the temporal works of the gospel of the kingdom flow out of the eternal work of the gospel of the cross. In this chapter, we have sought to encourage social justice ministries that flow from the central call for all believers to make disciples of Jesus. We honor Christ best when we bear witness through both our words and deeds.

REFLECTION QUESTIONS

1. Why do you think many Christians find it easier to engage in social justice ministries than to proclaim the message of repentance and faith?

2. What are some ways that you have seen the tension between ministries focused on the word and ministries focused on deeds?

3. How might you grow in your faithfulness to both proclaim the word and live out works that display your hope in the gospel?

---

7. Paul Borthwick, *Great Commission, Great Compassion: Following Jesus and Loving the World* (Downers Grove, IL: InterVarsity, 2015), 189.

4. Are there any social justice needs that you feel particularly called to address?

5. In doing social justice, how will you keep the gospel of the cross and making disciples central to your strategy?

What Are Some Helpful Prayer Resources?

Every Christian should aspire to leverage their life toward obedience to the Great Commission. But what would that look like? God has gifted each person uniquely. And the diversity within the church should be an asset towards fulfillment of the church's mission.

Ralph Winter and Steve Hawthorne's edited volume, *Perspectives on the World Christian Movement*,[1] introduces the concept of being a "world Christian." This term describes a person who cultivates five fundamental "habits" in their life, each of which are in service to our fulfilling the Great Commission. This chapter and the next will introduce and briefly unpack those five habits providing helpful resources for the reader to employ in their pursuit of becoming a "world Christian."[2] Because prayer is foundational to our participation in God's mission, this entire chapter will be focused on Great Commission praying. Missionary Samuel Zwemer once said, "The history of missions is the history of answered prayer."[3]

A World Christian Prays Great Commission Prayers

Great Commission activity that lacks Great Commission praying, no matter how well-meaning, is futile—or worse still, prideful. The mission that we are called into as Christians belongs to God. And he alone has the power to fulfill that mission. And yet graciously he invites us to join him. One way that every Christian can and should join God is through fervent, focused, and

---

1. Ralph Winter and Steve Hawthorne, *Perspectives on the World Christian Movement: A Reader*, 4th ed. (Pasadena, CA: William Carey Library, 2009).
2. An even briefer summary can be found at http://www.perspectivesglobal.org/world-christian-habits.
3. Though references to this quote are ubiquitous and always attributed to Zwemer, no original source document could be found.

specific intercession. Dick Eastman agrees: "In no other way can the believer become as fully involved with God's work, especially the work of world evangelism, as in intercessory prayer."[4] It seems obvious, then, that we should pray. But *what* should we pray in regard to the Great Commission?

Pray for More Laborers

Consider the way Jesus tethered mission back to the Father through prayer: "Then he said to his disciples, 'The harvest is plentiful, but the laborers are few; therefore pray earnestly to the Lord of the harvest to send out laborers into his harvest'" (Matt. 9:37–38; Luke 10:2). A Great Commission Christian prays for laborers. Jesus came into the world to make the fulfillment of God's mission possible. And yet in his divine sovereignty he chooses to use us as laborers to bring in the harvest that his death, burial, and resurrection would yield. Interestingly, those Jesus implored to pray for laborers became laborers just a few verses later as they were sent out two by two. Perhaps there is a "laborer" problem in missions today because there is a prayer problem. When we align our heart with God's, we often get swept deeper into his mission.

As a practical step, some missionaries have begun setting an alarm to go off at either 9:38 or 10:02 to remind them to stop and pray for God to raise up more laborers to engage the harvest. What if everyone who calls themselves followers of Jesus stopped daily to pray that the Lord of the harvest would send out more laborers? At the very least doing so would unite our heart to God's with regard to getting the gospel out. Those who pray for missions often find themselves doing missions.

Pray That Laborers Minister in the Power of the Holy Spirit, Motivated by the Glory and Worth of Christ

All authority everywhere has been given by the Father to Jesus. And Jesus told his followers to wait until they had received the Holy Spirit before continuing the mission beginning in Jerusalem and expanding to the ends of the earth. So, it seems evident that we should pray for ourselves and for other laborers to be motivated by Christ's glory and empowered by God's Spirit. John Stott makes this connection stating, "Here lies the supreme missionary motivation. It is neither obedience to the Great Commission, nor compassion for the lost, nor excitement over the gospel, but zeal (even 'jealousy') for the honour of Christ's name . . . no incentive is stronger than the longing that Christ should be given the honour that is due His Name."[5] The magnitude of the mission could easily overwhelm laborers who are not tied to these truths. We should pray toward the end that missionaries work with the power and glory of God central to their lives.

---

4. Jason Mandryk, ed., *Operation World*, 7th ed. (Colorado Springs: Biblica, 2010), 301.
5. John Stott, *The Incomparable Christ* (Downers Grove, IL: InterVarsity, 2001), 163.

As a practical step, many missionaries distribute prayer cards or have e-mail distribution lists that can serve as a prompt for general or specific prayer matters. In addition, some mission organizations have missionary birthday lists that are intended to mobilize prayer for various missionaries every day of the year. If the old adage, "Out of sight, out of mind" is true, then world Christians are not content with missionaries being out of sight. Keep in mind however that many missionaries are serving in high security locations, which means that nothing printed may exist to prompt prayer for them. Though it is always better to intercede with specifics, having a list of restricted access countries and praying generally for laborers serving in those areas is better than not praying for them at all.

Pray for Our Neighbors and the Nations to See Their Need for the Gospel
It seems self-evident that Christians should know their neighbors and be proactive in sharing the gospel where we live. The author of this chapter has even mapped out his neighborhood noting names, details, and even specific prayer requests in an effort to live as a beacon of hope at home. But what about those faraway lands and peoples that have never heard the gospel? What of those places and peoples that are underserved? Two commendable resources have been instrumental in educating and mobilizing specific Great Commission praying. The first is *Operation World*, which was compiled for two main purposes: to inform prayer and to mobilize for ministry.[6] Best-selling author and former president of the International Mission Board David Platt, says, "Outside of the Bible, no book has had a greater practical impact on my personal prayer life."[7] The layout of *Operation World* is conducive to praying through nation-states with detailed descriptions of geography, culture, statistics, status updates, and even prayer requests unique to each. There is also a children's version of this resource entitled *Window on the World* that features full-color pictures of the people and places, and stories that highlight what children's lives are like there.[8]

While *Operation World* is organized by country and needs to be updated since its last publication in 2010,[9] Joshua Project is an online dynamic resource meant to catalyze prayer specific to each ethnolinguistic people group that remains unreached or underserved.[10] The site possesses a wealth of information on the least reached ethnic people groups. It also has tools, like the

---

6. Mandryk, *Operation World*, xxv.
7. Ibid. This quote is found in the unnumbered endorsements section.
8. Daphne Spraggett and Jill Johnstone, *Window on the World: When We Pray God Works* (Downers Grove, IL: InterVarsity, 2007).
9. It should be noted that Operation World also has an online version that provides additional resources to promote Great Commission praying.
10. See https://joshuaproject.net.

"People Group of the Day," that help bring the task of praying through those peoples into reach.

A world Christian is one that prays specifically for their neighbors and the nations. The resources mentioned above will help you do that in a strategic manner. As a practical step, you could download the Joshua Project app or sign up for the Operation World daily prayer e-mail. Doing so will begin to align your heart and prayers with the Father's heart and mission.

Pray against the Enemy Who Desires to Thwart God's Mission

God is on mission. Satan, the rebel, is on a counter-mission. Granted, the enemy of God will not prevail. But, he has veiled the gospel to those who are perishing apart from Christ. Paul explains, "the god of this world has blinded the minds of the unbelievers, to keep them from seeing the light of the gospel of the glory of Christ, who is the image of God. For what we proclaim is not ourselves, but Jesus Christ as Lord, with ourselves as your servants for Jesus' sake. For God, who said, 'Let light shine out of darkness,' has shone in our hearts to give the light of the knowledge of the glory of God in the face of Jesus Christ" (2 Cor. 4:4–6). With this in mind, Great Commission Christians should pray against the enemy and for those who have been blinded to see the light of Christ, and then repent and follow him by faith.

Intercession for the lost is an act of spiritual warfare. Peter had this in mind when he wrote, "Be sober-minded; be watchful. Your adversary the devil prowls around like a roaring lion, seeking someone to devour" (1 Peter 5:8). John Piper explains, "Life is war. That's not all it is. But it is always that. Our weakness in prayer is owing largely to our neglect of this truth. Prayer is primarily a wartime walkie-talkie for the mission of the church as it advances against the powers of darkness and unbelief."[11] A world Christian wields the weapon of prayer, not only as a defensive cover, but as our primary means of offensive missional advance.

A practical step might be to read a book that equips you for spiritual warfare that often accompanies Great Commission advance. A resource by Jerry Rankin and Ed Stetzer makes specific application of our role in spiritual warfare related to God's mission, *Spiritual Warfare and Missions: The Battle for God's Glory among the Nations.*[12] The authors note that among Satan's strategies are to "keep nations closed to the gospel," "keep people groups hidden from our awareness," "convince Christians that missions is

---

11. John Piper, *Let the Nations Be Glad*, 3rd ed. (Grand Rapids: Baker Academic, 2010), 65.
12. Jerry Rankin and Ed Stetzer, *Spiritual Warfare and Missions: The Battle for God's Glory* (Nashville: B&H Publishing, 2010). For a Bible study focused on how to wage spiritual warfare, see Chuck Lawless, *Putting on the Armor: Equipped and Deployed for Spiritual Warfare* (Nashville: Lifeway Press, 2007).

optional," and "distort the call of God." Missionaries and church members alike can be sidelined when we fall for Satan's strategies. But when we are aware and praying against them, God's mission advances both through us and other laborers.

Pray for Those Who Are Being Persecuted

World Christians understand that life is war, and thus laborers on the front lines will come under attack. The New Testament is replete with both examples of persecution and exhortation to pray for and stand with the persecuted. Jesus taught, "Blessed are those who are persecuted for righteousness' sake, for theirs is the kingdom of heaven" (Matt. 5:10). And, "Love your enemies and pray for those who persecute you" (Matt. 5:44). The author of Hebrews even exhorted his readers to remember how they once identified with others who were persecuted and to endure it once more as a display of the authenticity of their faith (Heb. 10:32–39; 13:3).

One resource that helps world Christians to identify with and pray for the persecuted is *Voice of the Martyrs*. This organization researches, lobbies, and mobilizes prayer support for Christians that are being persecuted around the globe. Their mission statement explains: "Voice of the Martyrs serves persecuted Christians through practical and spiritual assistance and leading other members of the Body of Christ into fellowship with them."[13] The site contains stories of individual Christians who are currently suffering for their faith, as well as countries and regions of the world where persecution is prevalent. As the Great Commission advances, opposition will be strong. It is paramount that world Christians pray for the persecuted and stand with them. And, we also should pray for the persecutors that they would be saved.

A World Christian Prays Scripture over Missionaries

David Platt gave a message in 2016 where he highlighted "16 Ways to Pray for Missionaries," using Acts 13–14 as a guide. Below are the primary points from that message:[14]

1. *Pray that they would be confident in God's Word* (Acts 13:4–5). Missionaries are sent not just to learn culture or do humanitarian relief but to confidently proclaim the Word of God.

2. *Pray that they would be filled with God's Spirit* (Acts 13:6–9). Believers already have the Holy Spirit in them, but at times the

---

13. See www.persecution.com.
14. See https://www.imb.org/2016/11/08/16-ways-to-pray-for-missionaries.

Spirit fills someone in a special way to enable him or her to proclaim God's Word.

3. *Pray for their victory in spiritual warfare* (Acts 13:10–12). When our brothers and sisters take the gospel into the nations, they are going into a war. The devil is dead set on destroying souls and diverting mission.

4. *Pray for their success in gospel witness* (Acts 13:12). Pray that many would come to know Christ in all walks of life from the faithful witness of our missionaries.

5. *Pray for peace with other believers* (Acts 13:13). Satan attacks from all angles, both inside and outside. Pray for peace within families, in marriages, with children, and with companions and ministry partners.

6. *Pray for favor with unbelievers* (Acts 13:14–15). Nonbelievers are blind to the gospel, and many are violently opposed to its message. Pray that missionaries would find favorable opportunities to share the gospel with them.

7. *Pray that the gospel will be clear through them* (Acts 13:16–47). Although cross-cultural communication is difficult, pray that missionaries, by grace, would clearly communicate the character of God, the sinfulness of man, the sufficiency of Christ, the necessity of faith, and the urgency of eternity.

8. *Pray that God will open hearts around them* (Acts 13:48). God alone draws people to himself. Pray that he will open hearts and minds to believe and be drawn to eternal life with Christ.

9. *Pray for their joy in the midst of suffering* (Acts 14:1–2). Missionaries often face various forms and levels of suffering in their work. Pray that they would experience the joy of intimacy with Christ in the midst of it.

10. *Pray for their kindness in the midst of slander* (Acts 14:1–2). Though missionaries face suffering and difficulty, pray that the character of Christ and the power of his Spirit would enable them to respond with grace.

11. *Pray for supernatural power to accompany them* (Acts 14:3). Pray that missionaries would speak the Word with boldness and that supernatural power would accompany its proclamation.

12. *Pray for Christlike humility to characterize them* (Acts 14:4–18). Pray that missionaries would overcome the temptation to be prideful in their work by the power of the Spirit.

13. *Pray for their patience* (Acts 14:8–18). Missionaries face ups and downs and wins and losses in their work. Pray that they might respond with longsuffering.

14. *Pray for their perseverance* (Acts 14:19–20). Pray for missionaries to persevere through setback after setback, beatdown after beatdown, and struggle after struggle.

15. *Pray that God would use them to make disciples* (Acts 14:21–23). Pray that missionaries would see fruit in their ministries as they seek to make disciples among the nations.

16. *Pray that God would use them to multiply churches* (Acts 14:24–28). Pray for the multiplication of churches filled with people who know the Word led by pastors who teach the Word.

Summary

A world Christian is one who prays in dependence upon God for the fulfillment of his mission around the world. In this chapter we have introduced several ways that you can pray for missions and resources that may help you toward those ends. We should establish regular rhythms in our lives where we are praying for more laborers, praying for the lost, praying against the enemy, and praying for those who are serving and suffering for Jesus. Establishing these focused times of prayer is the first and most crucial way that every Christian can be involved in the Great Commission.

REFLECTION QUESTIONS

1. Which of the rhythms of prayer from this chapter will you commit to implement in your own life?

2. Do you know any cross-cultural missionaries personally? If so, how have you focused your prayers for them? If not, how might you get to know one?

3. Do you know of anyone that has endured spiritual warfare or persecution? If so, what can you learn from their experience that will equip you to be more effective in praying as a world Christian? If not, make sure to visit www.persecution.com and learn more about people who have counted the cost of following Jesus.

4. Why do you think Jesus emphasized praying for more laborers for the harvest? What needs to change in your life in order for you to be an answer to that prayer?

5. How might praying Scripture over missionaries and mission work bring your own heart into alignment with God's will?

What Are Some Helpful Mobilization Resources?

In the last chapter, you were challenged to make Great Commission praying a regular rhythm of your life. Praying is foundational to cultivating the "5 Habits of a World Christian." In this chapter we will unpack the other four habits together as they are each related to mobilization. If you're praying for the completion of the Great Commission, then you should grow in your desire to send laborers, welcome the nations here, go to the nations where they are, and mobilize others to join you in this journey of faith and obedience.

A World Christian Sends Great Commission Workers

In the Gospel according to John, Jesus framed the Great Commission in terms of sending and being sent. There he said, "As the Father has sent me, even so I am sending you" (John 20:21). All followers of Jesus should be living as "sent ones," but there is a special sense in which cross-cultural missionaries should be sent out by their local church. There are several ways in which local churches and world Christians together send out laborers into God's harvest. The following are ways that you and your church can and should be helping to send out Great Commission laborers.

Confirming the Call

The concept of a specific "call" to missions is often shrouded with mystery. Is calling merely a matter of feeling led to go somewhere or do something? Are only some called to cross-cultural ministry or is everyone called to be involved in some way? Because calling can be such a confusing thing, it is important that local churches be prepared to help steward the callings of their members. Though an individual member of a local church may sense that they are being called to missions, others in that local church should be able to confirm his or her calling by virtue of witnessing evidences. If there is no evidence in a person's life that they are doing here and now what they feel called to do in some other place at some other time, then leadership in the church should encourage present-tense obedience that can serve as both preparation for and confirmation of a future calling.

Preparation and Commissioning

A local church is filled with opportunities to serve and grow in spiritual maturity. Some areas of service are better suited for preparation toward a call to missions than others. When this author was sensing his initial call to missions he met with a pastor who gave him valuable feedback and opened an opportunity to begin serving the church through cross-cultural ministry in his own community. That season of ministry was formative and helped bring confirmation of his calling as well as preparation for serving overseas. After a season of serving locally in an observable way with built in accountability, the church was prepared to commission and send him with the full support of the congregation.

Partnering Financially

Unless they will be bivocational, missionaries who are being sent out from their local church need the financial backing of their friends, family, and congregation. Most mission-sending organizations require that their personnel raise their own funds from their network of relationships in order to finance their role. Financial partnership can also serve as a powerful confirmation of one's calling. Again, there was a season when this author needed to raise funds while working with a global mission organization, and the financial backing of his church, family, and friends not only made that ministry possible, it also served to confirm his calling.

Pastoral Care and Support

One of the great challenges with being sent out from a local church to serve as a cross-cultural missionary is that distance lessens the vital spiritual connection and the hands-on care that often accompanies it. A crucial element in sending out missionaries is providing emotional support, spiritual accountability, and even sacrificial pastoral care when necessary. Because many missionaries being sent cross-culturally will be working in locations where there is no church to be a part of, the potential for spiritual dryness is high. Everything in their new land is different—culture shock is inevitable. Establishing patterns of regular check-ups with a pastor or friend back in one's sending church can serve to prolong tenure and increase effectiveness.

Partnering to Accomplish the Mission

Once a member of a local church is sent as a cross-cultural missionary, a partnership is formed. Communication is a necessity with clear expectations and shared goals. One missionary serving in a distant land with the support of an entire church can accomplish a great deal when the sender and the sent one are working in unison.

A World Christian Welcomes the Nations in Great Commission Obedience

Another habit of a world Christian, and one that is often overlooked by individuals and churches alike, is that of welcoming internationals into our lives. People from other countries and cultures move to the West for many reasons. Some come for work, some as students, and others as refugees. The USA is now home to the third largest number of unreached peoples.[1] Regardless of what brings internationals into our communities, world Christians must be prepared and intentional in welcoming the stranger (Lev. 19:33–34).

- *International students:* In 2016 international students studying in the US numbered over one million. The top three countries of origin are all home to some of the least reached people on earth—China, India, and Saudi Arabia.[2] Seventy-five percent of those students will never enter an American home and 80 percent will never enter an American church while living in the USA.[3]

- *Refugees:* Since Congress passed the Refugee Act of 1980, more than three million refugees have resettled, making the USA their new home. Among the current top countries of origin are Syria, Burma, Iraq, and Somalia—each of which is a restricted access context for missionaries.[4]

- *Immigrants and migrants:* The USA is home to more than 43 million immigrants. Add to that number their children born here and the size of that population segment doubles accounting for over a quarter of the total population for the country.[5] The leading countries of origin are India and China—the two most populous unreached countries on the planet.[6]

---

1. http://www.jdpayne.org/2015/09/reaching-unreached-peoples-in-north-america.
2. https://www.iie.org/opendoors.
3. http://www.isionline.org/GetInvolved.aspx.
4. http://www.pewresearch.org/fact-tank/2017/01/30/key-facts-about-refugees-to-the-u-s.
5. https://www.migrationpolicy.org/article/frequently-requested-statistics-immigrants-and-immigration-united-states#Numbers.
6. http://www.operationworld.org/hidden/unreached-peoples.

Some resources that can help you prepare to "welcome the stranger in your midst" include:[7]

- *World Relief:* "Working in partnership with the local church, World Relief is committed to helping refugees and immigrants from all countries resettle and rebuild their lives."[8]

- *International Students Inc.:* "ISI works closely with international student advisers and other college and university officials to help students. We offer friendship to any student, regardless of race, nationality, or religious preference. ISI staff and volunteers are working on 677 campuses across the country to orient and acquaint international students to their new home and cultural experience."[9]

- *"Welcoming the Nations":* This provides action plans and practical ideas on ways to reach out and minister to international students.[10]

A World Christian Is Willing to Go in Great Commission Obedience

A world Christian is not only willing to pray, send, and welcome, but also to go! While it may seem obvious that going is foundational to fulfillment of the Great Commission, sadly most Christians never give it much thought. Several excuses emerge when it comes to going:[11]

- *I'm not called to go* (I'm called to stay and support missions from here). While it is true that not every Christian is called to live overseas on mission, most who remain here are neither supporting those going nor living missionally here. If you're genuinely called to stay and support from here, do it with all of your heart. And make sure you're welcoming the strangers referenced in the previous section.

- *There are plenty of people here that need to hear about Jesus.* It is very true that many in the USA still need to hear about Jesus. As mentioned earlier, the USA is home to the third largest number of unreached peoples in the world. Yet, the vast proportion of Christians remaining here are not welcoming of the stranger, much less sharing

---

7. See Paul Borthwick, *Great Commission, Great Compassion* (Downers Grove, IL: InterVarsity, 2015), which features an entire chapter that is extremely helpful in practical ways to welcome the strangers in your midst.
8. https://www.worldrelief.org/about.
9. http://www.isionline.org.
10. https://welcomingthenations.com/resources/action-plans.
11. For a more detailed list of excuses and responses see http://www.thetravelingteam.org/articles/most-common-excuses.

the gospel with those UPGs and internationals. A quick look at the "Status of Global Evangelization" map puts things into perspective on how Great Commission Christians need to be deployed.[12]

- *My family is my primary ministry.* Living on mission with God isn't neglecting your family's spiritual health. It is actually a means for increasing it. Though living cross-culturally has many challenges, families living on mission together also have numerous opportunities to grow closer to God and one another. So if this is your excuse, make sure that you're not making your family into an idol and calling it ministry.

- *I could never live in a place that is dangerous or unclean.* A fallacy has been spread through churches in the USA that says, "The safest place to be is the center of God's will." Ironically, that phrase is usually interpreted conversely as, "The center of God's will is safe." When we read the Bible we quickly find that the center of God's will is often not safe at all. Consider Abraham, David, Peter, Paul, and most importantly, Jesus! Living in the center of God's will was costly for each of them. But it was worth it! And if God calls us out of comfort and into "risk," we can be assured that he will meet us there. Being in the center of God's will is not always safe, but it is always perfect (Rom. 12:2).

- *I'm not gifted or skilled enough to go.* The needs that exist on the mission field necessitate people with all kinds of giftings and skills, just like in the local church. Regardless of how God has uniquely gifted you, he can and will use you to minister to the nations. And skills can be cultivated through training and practice. Therefore, the most important characteristic of a person called to cross-cultural ministry is availability and a willingness to learn

Below is a selection of major missions organizations and their areas of specialization:[13]

- *Africa Inland Mission:* church planting, outreach and evangelism, medical care, logistics

- *Christar:* community transformation through education, medical care, entrepreneurship and creation care

---

12. https://www.imb.org/research-maps.
13. For a more complete list of mission agencies and the opportunity to receive personal guidance in seeing where you may fit in going, see http://www.thetravelingteam.org/agencies.

- *Cru (formerly Campus Crusade for Christ):* evangelistic campus ministries as students or teachers

- *Ethnos360 (formerly New Tribes Mission):* evangelism and church planting among UPGs

- *International Mission Board:* a denominational agency (SBC) that focuses on church planting among UPGs and in diaspora settings

- *Pioneers:* church planting among UPGs

- *Teach Beyond:* mobilizing teachers and administrators to serve through education in cross-cultural settings around the world

- *TWR (formerly TransWorld Radio):* global media outreach

- *WorldVenture:* a holistic approach that leverages social inroads for reaching UPGs, the unchurched, and the unwanted

- *Wycliffe Bible Translators:* translation of the Bible into the languages of the world

World Christians Leverage Their Life to Mobilize Great Commission Workers

Finally, world Christians not only focus on praying Great Commission prayers, sending Great Commission laborers, welcoming the nations that live among them, and going on mission themselves. World Christians look to leverage their life by challenging others to get involved as well. If the world is to be reached with the gospel, it is going to take more laborers. Many more! So multiply what you know and are living and bring others along with you on this great journey.[14]

Summary

As the Father has sent Jesus, so Jesus is sending you. A world Christian is one who prays like Jesus prayed, sends like Jesus sent, welcomes like Jesus welcomed, goes like Jesus went, and mobilizes others to join in the mission just like Jesus mobilized. These "5 Habits of a World Christian," if cultivated, will change your life and the lives of all who know you . . . and many who don't.

---

14. Because The Traveling Team is focused on mobilization, they have created their own summary and applications for the 5 Habits. See http://www.thetravelingteam.org/articles/every-christian-a-world-christian.

REFLECTION QUESTIONS

1. How faithful have you been to pray regularly and specifically for missionaries and the fulfillment of the Great Commission? What resources have helped you in that discipline?

2. Have you or your local church had the privilege of sending missionaries out for short- or long-term cross-cultural service? If so, in what ways did you encourage, train, and support them? If not, what priorities need to change in order for you or your church to send?

3. What other ethnolinguistic people groups are living around you or your local church? What are you doing to reach them with the gospel? What are some creative ways you could show hospitality to them?

4. Do you think that every Christian should go on mission? Why or why not? What are the advantages/disadvantages of going with the help of a mission agency?

5. What are you and your church doing to mobilize Christ followers to leverage their lives for the Great Commission? How might you utilize these "5 Habits of a World Christian" to aid in your mobilization efforts?

How Should the Great Commission Influence Our Mission Strategy?

In two millennia the church has made amazing progress in getting the gospel out, yet the Great Commission remains unfulfilled. In fact, population growth in areas where UPGs call home is trending higher. Though the gospel has gone to the ends of the earth geographically, it has yet to penetrate all peoples ethnolinguistically. What is the status of the Great Commission? It is incomplete, and the task is growing bigger rather than smaller. Yet, Jesus promised that there would come a day when worshipers "from every nation, from all tribes and peoples and languages" would be gathered (Rev. 7:9–10). The difference between the way things are and the way things should be is the realm of strategy. So how should the Great Commission task influence our missions strategy?

Is There a Biblical Strategy?

Missiologists would agree that the Bible does indeed provide us with guidance regarding strategy for fulfilling the Great Commission. But guidance does not necessarily mean that there is a single strategy that is the "biblical" one. Some missionaries look to the book of Acts or the ministry of Paul and try to do what they see therein. Others prefer to see the narrative portions of Scripture as containing principles, but not an actual strategy. How one approaches with regards to this missiological question depends very much upon how they approach hermeneutics.

Some believe that the narratives were intended solely to describe what the apostles did, and are not intended to prescribe what we are to do in contemporary missions. There are dangers on both sides of the "descriptive vs. prescriptive" debate. For those who view Acts, for example, as descriptive only, by what criteria do you decide what to apply in your life from reading such passages? And for those who view Acts as prescriptive, what do you do when the events aren't repeatable? Ultimately we should all agree that, "All Scripture is breathed out by God and profitable for teaching, for reproof, for correction, and for training in righteousness, that the man of God may be complete, equipped for every good work" (2 Tim. 3:16–17). This verse means that all Scripture matters for life and for mission. Most missionaries won't be shaking vipers off of their hands, drinking poison, or practicing "shadow healings," but we will be intentionally engaging lostness with the gospel with the desire to make reproducing disciples who obey Jesus. And we will gather them together, forming churches. After all, that seems to be the core missionary task as modeled by both Jesus and Paul.

What Is the Core Missionary Task?

Missionaries with the International Mission Board have collaborated in their research and practice, determining that the core missionary task has six components as follows:[1]

1. ***Entry:*** Identify, locate, understand, and engage those who are far from God.

2. ***Evangelism:*** Because there is no salvation apart from explicit faith in Jesus Christ, we must communicate the gospel in biblically faithful and culturally understandable ways.

3. ***Discipleship:*** The Great Commission says that we must "teach them to obey" all that Jesus commanded so that they grow in faith, knowledge, character, obedience, and that they reproduce that in others.

4. ***Healthy Church Formation:*** Disciples gathering to worship and obey should be formed into churches where both discipleship and reproduction continues both inside and outside of the church.

5. ***Leadership Training:*** As disciples mature they should be equipped and released as leaders according to their gifting and skill, so that churches continue to multiply and more who are far from God are reached.

---

1. A fuller description is available at https://www.imb.org/topic-term/six-components-missionary-task. For an example of a mission strategy that is built around these core tasks, see the "Four Fields of Kingdom Growth" manual by Nathan and Kari Shank, http://noplaceleft.net/four-fields.

6. *Partnership and Exit:* Missionaries should work themselves out of their job through raising up local indigenous leaders who are committed to the completion of the Great Commission.

Though Jesus didn't technically plant churches, we can see these tasks in Luke 8–11. Paul's first missionary journey in Acts 13–14 makes these core missionary tasks even clearer (see Appendix for a chart that displays how Paul's journey reflects Jesus's strategy). If the Great Commission is to be fulfilled in our lifetime, it is going to take the mobilization of all who follow Christ and a laser focus on these core missionary tasks. A ministry of addition will not even keep up with the population growth among those people groups that are least reached. We need to multiply laborers who have a Great Commission vision and equip them with simple, reproducible training and tools.

One volunteer network that is committed to just that is called "No Place Left." Their website reads:

> NO PLACE LEFT is a voluntary network of individuals and existing churches devoted to co-laboring in God's Harvest through prayer, evangelism, intentional and reproducing disciple-making, gathering new believers into new or existing churches and equipping leaders for exponential engagement until there's no people or ethnic group, city or population segment lacking access to the gospel of Jesus Christ.[2]

The network gets its name from Paul's declaration in Romans 15:23 that the gospel had been "fully proclaimed from Jerusalem all the way around to Illyricum." He could say that precisely because the core missionary task had been kept foundational as churches multiplied generationally. The No Place Left network is not tied to any denomination or mission agency, but instead mobilizes its volunteer army of practitioners and trainers to spread simple, reproducible training and tools related to the "Four Fields of Kingdom Growth" training manual.[3]

Missiologists have been emphasizing a return to a biblical strategy in an effort to fulfill the Great Commission for over a century now. Roland Allen, when observing the early twentieth-century mission strategies, authored a watershed book entitled, *Missionary Methods: St. Paul's or Ours?* Allen argued that what missionaries were doing in his day hardly reflected what Paul did in his, and that the success of Paul's missionary journeys were not the result of some special set of circumstances. Rather, Paul's approach to missions strategy should be replicated regardless of time or location, and such is possible when we stick

---

2. http://noplaceleft.net.
3. http://noplaceleft.net/four-fields.

to simple, reproducible, biblical approaches. It took decades for Allen's exhortation to be taken seriously as he was initially thought to be naïve.

Eventually other missiologists started to return to strategies that were shaped more by Scripture than by sociology, more by a desire to fulfill the Great Commission than to maintain the status quo. Though not without its critics, Donald McGavran highlighted the need for "people movements," whereby the gospel would quickly spread through a population segment without significant barriers to receptivity.[4] Ralph Winter helped refocus strategy by identifying "hidden peoples" and emphasizing UPGs.[5] David Garrison documented "church planting movements" and identified common characteristics of them.[6] Each of them contributed to our understanding of the remaining task and ways that God is working to fulfill it. Like Allen though, none of them were without their critics.[7]

Regardless of your position related to any of the aforementioned missiologists and their nuanced strategies, one thing seems to tie them together with the apostle Paul—a commitment to entering barren fields, evangelizing those far from God, making disciples who obey Jesus and reproduce, gathering them into churches that reproduce, developing indigenous leaders that reproduce, and exiting those fields with a partnership that will help ensure health and growth—the core missionary task! But how should we assess our own lives and the work of our local churches toward those ends? That leads us to what we call "The Acts 1:8 Local Church Mission Strategy."

Developing an Acts 1:8 Local Church Missions Strategy

In the Acts iteration of the Great Commission, Jesus lays out a vision for the geographical advance of the mission that he started. Some scholars even believe that Acts 1:8 serves as a sort of "Table of Contents" for the unfolding

---

4. Donald McGavran, *The Bridges of God: A Study in the Strategy of Missions* (London: World Dominion Press, 1955); idem, *Understanding Church Growth* (Grand Rapids: Eerdmans, 1970).
5. https://www.ijfm.org/PDFs_IJFM/19_4_PDFs/winter_koch_task.pdf.
6. David Garrison, *Church Planting Movements: How God Is Redeeming a Lost World* (Bangalore, India: WIGTake Resources, 2004).
7. Several articles have appeared in *9Marks Journal* critiquing movement principles that flow out of MacGavran's and Garrison's writings. One such article was written by Aubrey Sequeira entitled "A Plea for Gospel Sanity in Missions" (https://www.9marks.org/article/a-plea-for-gospel-sanity-in-missions). In his article, Sequeira argues that "movement thinking" in India has led to an obsession with numbers, an overemphasis on the supernatural, and overeager contextualization. While Sequeira's article argues from what he says are the unintended results of such thinking, Jackson Wu developed an in-depth article critiquing the exegesis that he says influences such an approach to missions. His article can be found at http://ojs.globalmissiology.org/index.php/english/article/view/1711. Note: This author advocates "movement thinking," but not without critical thinking. In fact, I was serving as assistant editor of *Global Missiology Online Journal* and asked Wu to write and submit his article to help me and those who agree with me to think better.

narrative as the apostles embraced the mission of Jesus. Though we are not operating from Jerusalem as our center today, we can certainly learn from the principle of what Jesus was sending the early church out to do. The following table provides a means for evaluating strengths and weaknesses in your own personal or church-based missions strategy. Note that as you move from left to right and from top to bottom, the commitment level is increased.

The Acts 1:8 Strategy Assessment

		Target Area			
		Jerusalem	Judea	Samaria	Ends of the Earth
Level of Involvement	Prayer & Advocacy				
	Projects				
	Partnerships				
	Adoption				

Going Farther Out (Target Areas Defined):

- *Jerusalem* = Any location within the daily sphere of influence of your church

- *Judea* = Any location outside of the daily sphere of influence of your church, but which shares a common worldview

- *Samaria* = Any location outside of the daily sphere of influence of your community of faith that has a slightly differing worldview, but shares some commonalities

- *Ends of the Earth* = Any location outside of the daily sphere of influence of you or your church that is geographically distant and has a radically differing worldview

Going Deeper In (Level of Involvement Defined):

- *Prayer and Advocacy* = Any activity of promotion through education, prayer, or financial commitment

- *Project* = Any on-site activity with predetermined, mutually agreed upon goals that are completed in a single visit

- *Partnership* = Any ongoing activities for the achievement of a specified set of goals shared between your church and other Great Commission Christians in the area. Upon completion of these shared goals the partnership may be redefined or dissolved.

- *Adoption* = A lifelong commitment to a specific location or people involving (but not limited to) any predetermined, mutually agreed upon goals

One way that you could implement this approach is to identify key leaders within your church who will lead each target group. For example, your church could have a "Jerusalem Team," a "Judea Team," and so forth. The responsibility of each team would be to identify ways in which your church is already involved in their target area and move the church toward growth and multiplication in that area. Begin where you are and move outward, and soon you will be spreading a biblical vision for the Great Commission throughout your church!

Summary

This chapter discusses how Scripture in general, and the Great Commission in particular, should shape and drive our missions strategies. Referring back to Jesus and the apostle Paul's examples, we learned that the "core missionary task" is something that is transculturally relevant and that we should be focusing on today. We looked briefly at how missiologists have brought a corrective exhortation back to the way we approach missions strategy. And finally, we looked at Acts 1:8 and how it can help us to go further out and deeper in with our personal and church-based missions commitment. If we are to take the Great Commission seriously, we need to develop a vision and strategy to accomplish the task of reaching the nations. The No Place Left movement was referenced as an example of an army of people around the world who are being mobilized with that kind of laser-focused vision and strategy.

REFLECTION QUESTIONS

1. In what ways has Scripture shaped your understanding of what missionaries should be trying to accomplish?

2. Do you agree with the basic elements of the "core missionary task" as outlined in this chapter? Why or why not?

3. After working through the Acts 1:8 table, how are you and your church doing with regard to your level of commitment to the Great Commission?

4. What needs to change in your life in order for you to have both a Great Commission vision and strategy?

5. What needs to change in your priorities and planning in order to achieve a comprehensive Acts 1:8 strategy in your local church?

Is It Possible to Overemphasize the Great Commission?

The irony of this question is that it is clearly a much greater problem that churches and individuals tend to underemphasize the Great Commission. When the average evangelical church allots between 70 and 90 percent of their budget for maintaining the facilities and ministering to people who are already believers, it is evident that overemphasis of the Great Commission is rarely an issue.[1] Missionary C. T. Studd once said, "The light that shines the farthest shines the brightest at home."[2] Studd had Great Commission churches in mind and was responding to the apathy toward missions in his own time. What is at stake when the Great Commission becomes central to the church's identity? What is at stake when it is peripheral?

When the Great Commission Is Central

"Missions exists because worship does not."[3] Nearly two decades ago pastor John Piper penned those words in his highly influential book, *Let the Nations Be Glad*. In doing so, he was reminding Christians everywhere that there are places in this world where gospel-centered, Christ-honoring worship is altogether absent. Yet, for some reason churches had lost sight of the fact that their reason for existence was to spread worship to the ends of the earth. It is far too easy to lose sight of that when the scorecard for success in churches has produced a consumer mentality among congregants. There are still places in this world where true worship doesn't exist because

---

1. Evangelical Christian Credit Union, "2013 Church Budget Allocations, Learning Priorities, and Quarterly Financial Trends," https://danieldailey.files.wordpress.com/2015/07/eccu_2013_church_budget_trends.pdf.

2. Janet and Geoff Benge, *C.T. Studd: No Retreat* (Seattle: YWAM, 2005), n.p.

3. John Piper, *Let the Nations Be Glad: The Supremacy of God in Missions*, 3rd ed. (Grand Rapids: Baker Academic, 2010), 35.

those places are hard to get to or the people are hardened and resistant. Piper sounded a clarion call that if the gospel is to ever reach and penetrate those people and places, then churches are going to have to focus intently on that goal and change their scorecard for success from consumer-driven to Great Commission-focused. Piper went on to say that one day, "mission will be no more. It is a temporary necessity. But worship abides forever."[4] While worship is the end goal, missions *is*, in fact, indispensable and to be prioritized until Christ returns.

Organizations work meticulously to develop mission statements that then provide a way to plan and function, as well as a means to evaluate success. Many churches develop mission statements for the same reason. Unfortunately, those churches are missing the fact that their mission statement was actually given to them by Jesus and that the church was, in fact, designed for the purpose of fulfilling that mission.

Jesus's Last Command as the Church's First Priority

All four Gospel accounts end with some version of the Great Commission (Matt. 28:18–20; Mark 16:15–16; Luke 24:45–48; John 20:21; see Question 20). The entire Bible ends with this mission being fulfilled. John records, "After this I looked, and behold, a great multitude that no one could number, from every nation, from all tribes and peoples and languages, standing before the throne and before the Lamb, clothed in white robes, with palm branches in their hands, and crying out with a loud voice, 'Salvation belongs to our God who sits on the throne, and to the Lamb!'" (Rev. 7:9–10).

These passages of Scripture together emphasize the global and enduring mission of God through his church. There is no need to come up with our own mission statement or our own scorecard for success. God has designed and commissioned his disciples and the local church to fulfill his mission of gathering worshipers for Jesus from all peoples. Therefore, we would be wise to make his last command our first priority. To make the Great Commission peripheral to our lives or the mission of the church is not only unwise, but tyrannical.

When the Great Commission Is Peripheral

When missions is relegated to a part of what the church does rather than permeating all that it does, the Great Commission has become peripheral. While having a missions pastor on staff at a local church may sound like a good thing, it may actually be an indicator that missions has become one priority among many that compete for time, attention, and resources. In order to keep the Great Commission central to the church's identity and purpose, it is crucial that the lead pastor also be viewed as the lead evangelist,

---

4. Ibid.

disciple-maker, and mission advocate. This doesn't mean that he needs to be the most gifted in these areas. But because he is the most visible, the Great Commission needs to permeate all that he says and does. When the lead pastor delegates missions, evangelism, and disciple-making to other persons in order to remove them from his list of responsibilities, he is communicating that those Great Commission activities are peripheral to his role, and thereby to the church. What gets celebrated gets done. Therefore, those in leadership in local churches should celebrate all aspects of the Great Commission by keeping them central and the top priority.[5]

God-centered vs. Man-centered Witness

There are times when we run the risk of a flawed, man-centered understanding of the Great Commission. When we approach this task in a man-centered way, aspects of the Great Commission can be overemphasized. Hearkening back to Piper's quote and its meaning, missions must be radically God-centered because, "God is ultimate, not man."[6] Some churches and missions organizations have inadvertently espoused such a man-centered approach to the Great Commission by focusing on physical needs to the exclusion of the spiritual, or by altering the message in order to make it more palpable. Following is a helpful list by Will Metzger highlighting the stark contrast between a God-centered versus man-centered approach to the gospel, all of which have Great Commission implications:[7]

Man-centered	God-centered
View of God	
Point of contact with non-Christians is love (God loves you). Therefore, God's authority is secondary.	Point of contact with non-Christians is creation (God made you). Therefore, God has authority over your destiny.
Love is God's chief attribute.	Holiness and love are equally important attributes of God.
God is impotent before the sinner's will.	God is able to empower the sinner's will.

---

5. For a compelling example, see Pastor John Piper's last message to his church as he bequeathed, not the church, but the mission of the church to his successor. See https://www.desiringgod.org/messages/missions-exists-because-worship-doesnt-a-bethlehem-legacy-inherited-and-bequeathed.

6. Piper, *Let the Nations Be Glad*, 35.

7. The content of this table can be found in chapter 3 of Will Metzger's excellent book, *Tell the Truth: The Whole Gospel Wholly by Grace Communicated Truthfully and Lovingly*, 4th ed. (Downers Grove, IL: InterVarsity, 2012), 94.

Man-centered	God-centered
View of God	
The persons of the Trinity have different goals in accomplishing and applying salvation.	The persons of the Trinity work in harmony—salvation accomplished for and applied to the same people.
God is a friend who will help you.	God is a king who will save you.
View of Humanity	
Fallen, yet has the ability (or potential) to choose the good	Fallen, and will not come to God by own willpower
Seeks truth but lacks correct facts	Mind at enmity with God; none seek God
Needs love, help, friendship	Needs new nature (mind, heart, will), regeneration
Makes mistakes, is imperfect, needs forgiveness	Rebels against God, has a sinful nature, needs reconciliation
Needs salvation from the consequences of sin—unhappiness, hell	Needs salvation from guilt and the power of sin
Humanity is sick and ignorant.	Humanity is dead and lost.
View of Christ	
Savior from selfishness, mistakes, hell	Savior from sin and sinful nature
He exists for our benefit.	He exists to gather a kingdom and receive honor and glory.
His death was more important than his life.	His death and his life of obedience were equally important.
Emphasizes his priestly office—Savior	Emphasizes his priestly, kingly, prophetic offices
An attitude of submission to Christ's lordship is optional for salvation.	An attitude of submission to Christ's lordship is necessary for salvation.
View of Response to Christ	
Invitation waiting to be accepted now	Loving command to be obeyed now
Our choice is the basis for salvation—God responds to our decision.	God's choice is the basis for salvation—we respond to God's initiative.
We give mental assent to truths of the gospel—decision.	We respond with our whole person (mind, heart, will)—conversion.

Man-centered	God-centered
View of Response to Christ	
Appeal is made to the desires of the sinner	Truths are driven home into the conscience of the sinner
Saved by faith alone—repentance omitted, for it is thought of as "works"	Saved by faith alone—saving faith always accompanied by repentance
Assurance of salvation comes from a counselor using the promises of God and pronouncing the new believer saved.	Assurance of salvation comes from the Holy Spirit applying biblical promises to the conscience and effecting a changed life.
Sinners have the key in their hands.	God has the key in his hand.

It is not hard to see that a man-centered approach to the gospel will quickly make the Great Commission peripheral to the church, if not altogether absent. By keeping Christ's mission for the church central, rather than peripheral, and keeping gospel ministry God-centered, rather than man-centered, we honor God and give appropriate emphasis to the Great Commission.

Conclusion: Keep the Main Thing, the Main Thing

Ultimately, it would be oxymoronic for Christ's church to overemphasize what he seemed to emphasize. Because the lost world isn't showing up to our church business and planning meetings, their needs are often not as pressing as issues internal to our congregations. Christ knew that the urgency and perseverance that it would take to complete his mission would become peripheral to his church given our self-serving tendencies. However, his kingdom-ethic demands that we consider others above ourselves. When Christians realize that the worship we experience inside the church is to extend outward into a world in need of the gospel, we will find that mission is, in fact, one of the most worshipful things we can do. Returning to Piper's thesis, he adds, "Worship is both the fuel and goal of missions."[8] When we worship Christ rightly, we will value what he values, thereby thrusting us on mission with him. And when we are on mission with Christ making disciples of the nations, we foment an ever-growing multitude of worshippers for Christ. He alone is worthy, and we were made for this.

---

8. Piper, *Let the Nations Be Glad*, 35.

REFLECTION QUESTIONS

1. In what ways has Christ's Great Commission been marginalized in your life and in your church?

2. What needs to change in your life and church to make Christ's last command your top priority?

3. How might a man-centered approach to the gospel affect your approach to the Great Commission?

4. In what ways might a God-centered approach to the gospel fuel your Great Commission obedience?

5. Do you think it is possible to overemphasize the Great Commission? Why or why not?

How Should We Preach the Great Commission?

In previous questions we have explored Great Commission responsibilities for individuals, local churches, and for churches that associate together for doctrinal or strategic purposes.[1] Jesus modeled that mobilization is inherent to the Great Commission when he commanded all of his followers to make disciples of all nations. He delivered that commission to his original disciples in a message that had sermonic overtones that are easily replicated. So how should we preach the Great Commission to ensure that Christ-followers are mobilized for mission? Following is a simple, reproducible expositional outline of Jesus's famous last words as recorded in the "classic" Great Commission text, Matthew 28:18–20. The main points of the text make plain Jesus's power, plan, and presence—all of which are central to our living on mission with God and making his last words our top priority.

"Famous Last Words"

Sir Isaac Newton was a mathematician, physicist, astronomer, and theologian. Perhaps most well-known for his theory of gravitation, his last words were astoundingly modest. Newton reportedly said, "I don't know what I may seem to the world. But as to myself I seem to have been only like a boy playing on the seashore and diverting myself now and then in finding a smoother pebble or a prettier shell than the ordinary, whilst the great ocean of truth lay all undiscovered before me."[2] One of the most intelligent and accomplished men of his time acknowledged how little he actually knew. Likewise, Leonardo da Vinci, the great artist and inventor, was also overly modest in his

---

1. See Appendix B for a sample sermon on the Great Commission by Daniel Akin.
2. William B. Brahms, *Last Words of Notable People: Final Words of More Than 3500 Noteworthy People Throughout History* (Haddonfield, NJ: Reference Desk Press, 2010), 451.

last words, reportedly saying, "I have offended God and mankind because my work did not reach the quality it should have."[3] Perhaps he felt that the Mona Lisa wasn't good enough. Regardless, he knew that he had hardly skimmed the surface of ideas and art.

Not everyone is remembered for their last words. Consider pioneer missionary William Carey, who inspired by Jesus's last words, sailed from England to India in 1793 after forming the Baptist Missionary Society. Prior to becoming a missionary, Carey faced both apathy and opposition toward his desire to obey the Great Commission. In response, Carey said, "Expect great things from God. Attempt great things for God."[4] For more than two hundred years, a long line of missionaries has taken Carey's inspiring, and more importantly, Christ's empowering last words to heart and have expected that God provide all they needed as they took the gospel to the difficult places of the world. Why do we send missionaries? Because of Jesus's last words found in Matthew 28:18–20. This is the very text that motivated William Carey nearly 1,800 years after they were uttered.

Jesus's Power Proclaimed through His Famous Last Words

All Authority in Heaven and on Earth Has Been Given to Me

After Jesus was baptized by John in the Jordan to "fulfill all righteousness," the Father spoke from Heaven and said, "This is my beloved Son, with whom I am well pleased" (Matt. 3:15–17). Then the Spirit descended upon Jesus in the form of a dove and immediately led him out into the wilderness where he would be tempted by the devil. Three times the devil tried to get Jesus to distrust the words he had heard forty days earlier at his baptism—"If you are the Son of God . . . ." Each time Jesus trusted God the Father and conveyed that by responding by quoting from the Old Testament. In that final temptation (Matt. 4:8–9) the devil "took him to a very high mountain and showed him all the kingdoms of the world and their glory. And he said to him, 'All these I will give you, if you will fall down and worship me.'" Think of the absurdity! The devil was offering to Jesus something that was made by Jesus and for him (Col. 1). The devil was offering Jesus all authority on earth—something that he didn't possess to give. He was offering Jesus a cross-less kingdom—a shortcut to power. But Jesus would have none of it for he knew that the Father had sent him to fulfill all righteousness and that meant that he would have to die. And he did! But that wasn't the end.

---

3. Da Vinci's last words have been disputed for centuries. The original source for the quotation is Giorgio Vasari's 1568 collection of biographies, *The Lives of the Most Excellent Painters, Sculptors and Architects* (New York: Scribner's, 1896), 44.

4. Timothy George, *Faithful Witness: The Life and Mission of William Carey* (Downers Grove, IL: InterVarsity, 1992], 32. The words "from God" and "for God" were added to capture the intended meaning.

When preaching to mobilize for the Great Commission it is best to begin where Jesus finished—communicating that mission is made possible not merely because of our involvement, but because of his own power. David Platt notes, "Jesus' authority is the basis for everything else that follows in this text. His authority over heaven and earth means that Jesus is not just the personal Lord and Savior over us. . . . [H]e is exalted at the Father's right hand as the Lord over all creation."[5] The fulfillment of the Great Commission is both possible and promised because Jesus is both willing and able. Jesus certainly demonstrated his power through his life and ministry. Yet, the most potent display of his power was his ability to conquer death. The resurrection of Jesus should give hope and confidence to his followers that what he promised and commands, he will see through.

Observe the comprehensiveness of what Jesus said: "*All authority* in heaven *and* on earth"—that's all authority everywhere. It was through the crucible of the cross that Jesus was given the kingdom. Because Jesus did not take the fraudulent shortcut offered to him by the devil, but instead accomplished all the Father sent him to do, he has been given all authority everywhere to empower us as we fulfill our part in his mission. What then is our part in God's mission?

Jesus's Plan Conveyed through His Famous Last Words

Go Therefore

Our competence and confidence to join God's mission is rooted in the authority of the one who commissioned us. Based upon the fact that Jesus didn't take the shortcut and inherit a cross-less kingdom, based upon the fact that he did in deed fulfill all righteousness, and based on the fact that now all authority in heaven and on earth has been given to him, we are armed with his authority to work his plan! And his plan doesn't allow for us to sit idly by and do nothing. We have been commissioned to "Go!" Not just go anywhere and do anything. Jesus tells us explicitly in his last words where to go and what to do.

And Make Disciples

In the Greek language, this phrase is an imperative. That means this is the root and base command of the entire Great Commission—the top priority. But how does one make disciples? The other three verbs in the verse, which are participles, unpack that for us. We make disciples by going to unbelievers everywhere, baptizing those who surrender to Christ's lordship through our communication of the gospel, and then patiently teaching them a faith-fueled obedience to everything Jesus taught. This is the role of the church in the

---

5. David Platt, *Christ-Centered Exposition Commentary: Exalting Jesus in Matthew* (Nashville: B&H Academic, 2013), 371.

world. Making disciples of Jesus is our part in God's mission. The church does lots of good things, but if it ceases to prioritize this one thing, it ceases to be Christ's church. You might even say that we were made for this.

Of All Nations

Jesus gives us the prioritization of what to do and here we learn where, or more specifically, to whom we should go. The word used here is *ēthne*, which is where we get our word for ethnicities. Jesus was commanding his disciples, who were Jews, not simply to make disciples of people who are like them. Rather, he was commissioning them to go to all of the ethnicities of the world and make disciples among them too. Why make disciples of all nations? Because all nations belong to Jesus. He has authority over them because he is their Creator and Redeemer. Anything less than an emphasis on all nations reduces God to some sort of tribal deity whose lordship only extends as far as one's ethnocultural borders. Jesus's authority extends over and is worthy of all nations.

From a practical standpoint, many argue that there are plenty of lost people around us so there's no need to go elsewhere until all who are near come to faith. While there may in fact be many nearby that are not yet disciples of Jesus, it is clear that Paul and the other disciples interpreted Jesus's commission to thrust them further out to "bring about the obedience of faith for the sake of his name among all the nations" (Rom. 1:5; cf. 16:26). Currently more than half of the world's nearly twelve thousand distinct "people groups" have little or no gospel witness among them at all. Unless churches mobilize all Christ-followers to join in this mission, the nations that Jesus spoke of will never know the hope of the rescue that Jesus provides.

Baptizing Them in the Name of the Father and of the Son and of the Holy Spirit

When obedient Christ-followers go to the nations in the authority of Jesus, what must be done to make disciples among them? The gospel of grace demands a response of repentance and faith, both of which are exemplified in the subsequent act of baptism. Baptism is a public and visible identification with what Christ has accomplished for us. To be baptized in the name of the Holy Trinity is to display for the world that what God has accomplished was for us. Thus, making disciples of all nations involves both proclamation of and response to the gospel. In other words, we don't merely announce the gospel and move on. Implicit within the proclamation is a call to surrender. And that inward surrender is made outward and visible through baptism.

Teaching Them to Observe All That I Have Commanded You

Reaching the nations with the gospel message is just the beginning. In order to make disciples we must teach them to obey—not us—but Jesus.

Therefore, disciple-making must necessarily involve not merely the teaching of content, but also the application of that content to the disciple's life. One must know Christ's commands in order to teach them. And one must be living a life of faith-fueled obedience to the commands of Christ in order to teach others to observe them.

Disciple-making is inherently relational. It involves a "withness" that Jesus himself modeled in his own teaching of the Twelve. This means that Great Commission obedience requires more than getting the gospel out geographically. It requires getting the gospel "in" relationally. In order to make disciples of all nations, we must cultivate relationships with them. This entails learning languages and cultures—all of which is made possible through the indwelling Spirit. There is no barrier to Great Commission obedience that Christ has not accounted for and overcome. We can and must teach those who respond to the gospel by walking alongside them teaching them obedience to all Christ commanded using both our words and our actions.

Jesus's Presence Is Promised in His Famous Last Words

"And behold, I am with you always, to the end of the age." We who make Christ's last command their first priority are promised the comforting presence of our loving Savior—the One who possesses all authority in heaven and on earth. The "withness" necessary to make disciples of all nations is made available to us through the indwelling Spirit. Jesus's promised presence is not merely a platitude. In ways more profound than we can imagine, he is *with* those who are living on mission with God. He guides, empowers, comforts, and enables disciples to make disciples. We were made for this!

Preaching Outline for Mark 16:15

And he said to them, "Go into all the world and proclaim the gospel to the whole creation."

Main Idea of the Text: Jesus intends to redeem all of his creation through sending all of his disciples to proclaim the gospel all over his world.

1. The command to all of Jesus's disciples is to "Go!"

2. The context for Jesus's disciples to go is "all the world."

3. The commission for all Jesus's disciples is to "proclaim the gospel."

4. The context for Jesus's redemptive claim is "the whole creation."

Preaching Outline for Luke 24:45–49

> *Then he opened their minds to understand the Scriptures, and said to them, "Thus it is written, that the Christ should suffer and on the third day rise from the dead, and that repentance for the forgiveness of sins should be proclaimed in his name to all nations, beginning from Jerusalem. You are witnesses of these things. And behold, I am sending the promise of my Father upon you. But stay in the city until you are clothed with power from on high."*

Main Idea of the Text: The same Scriptures that promised Christ's crucifixion and resurrection ensure the application of his sacrifice to reach our neighbors and the nations through our Spirit-empowered witness.

1. The Scriptures point to the risen Christ.

2. The Savior promised the gospel would be proclaimed to all nations.

3. Those saved are to be his witnesses among their neighbors and the nations.

4. The Spirit is given to enable us to fulfill the Savior's mission.

Preaching Outline for John 20:21–23

> *Jesus said to them again, "Peace be with you. As the Father has sent me, even so I am sending you." And when he had said this, he breathed on them and said to them, "Receive the Holy Spirit. If you forgive the sins of any, they are forgiven them; if you withhold forgiveness from any, it is withheld."*

Main Idea of the Text: Our Triune God is committed to sending and empowering for the fulfillment of his mission.

1. The Father sent the Son to redeem.

2. The Son is sending us to proclaim.

3. The Spirit is promised to empower us for mission.

Preaching Outline for Acts 1:8

> *But you will receive power when the Holy Spirit has come upon you, and you will be my witnesses in Jerusalem and in all Judea and Samaria, and to the end of the earth.*

Main Idea of the Text: Our witness begins with Spirit empowerment, and extends so that Christ is made famous both near and far.

1. The power for mission is the Holy Spirit.

2. Our purpose on mission is to bear witness to Jesus.

3. Our place of mission is both near and far.

Summary

In conclusion, Jesus's famous last words contain a simple, but sacrificial command to make disciples of every kind of people in every place. But he couches that command between two very precious and powerful promises: (1) we join God on mission empowered by Jesus's all-encompassing authority; (2) we join God on mission comforted by Jesus's never-ending presence. Having just conquered death as he promised he would, Jesus's commission to his followers and the claims embedded within should provide us with tremendous confidence. This is a message that demands to be preached. Why? Because Jesus himself preached it. Like Jesus, we must make sure that our preaching on the Great Commission is backed by a lifestyle of living it out and inviting others to join us on that journey. I'm sure glad Jesus did that and that his disciples listened and obeyed! Let's do the same.

REFLECTION QUESTIONS

1. If you were preparing a sermon or Bible study on the Great Commission, what would you use as your primary text?

2. How would you preach these texts? Would your main points differ from the ones in this chapter?

3. In what ways have you seen the main idea of these texts lived out? What illustrations might you pull from those observations?

4. What are some pitfalls you need to avoid when preaching these texts?

5. How might you call for a response when preaching these texts? What would you ask your listeners to do?

Select Bibliography

Akin, Daniel L. *10 Who Changed the World*. Nashville: B&H, 2012.

Dever, Mark. *Understanding the Great Commission*. Nashville: B&H, 2016.

Goheen, Michael W. *A Light to the Nations: The Missional Church and the Biblical Story*. Grand Rapids: Baker, 2011.

Köstenberger, Andreas J. and Peter. T. O'Brien. *Salvation to the Ends of the Earth*. New Studies in Biblical Theology. Downers Grove, IL: InterVarsity, 2001.

Piper, John. *Let the Nations Be Glad! The Supremacy of God in Missions*. Grand Rapids: Baker, 1993.

Plummer, Robert L. and John Mark Terry, eds. *Paul's Missionary Methods: In His Time and Ours*. Downers Grove, IL: IVP Academic, 2012.

Schnabel, Eckhard. *Early Christian Mission. Volume 1: Jesus and the Twelve*. Downers Grove, IL: InterVarsity, 2004.

_____. *Early Christian Mission. Volume 2: Paul and the Early Church*. Downers Grove, IL: InterVarsity, 2004.

Tucker, Ruth A. *From Jerusalem to Irian Jaya: A Biographical History of Christian Missions*. 2nd ed. Grand Rapids: Zondervan, 2004.

_____. *Guardians of the Great Commission: The Story of Women in Modern Missions*. Grand Rapids: Zondervan, 1994.

Winter, Ralph D. and Steven C. Hawthorne. *Perspectives on the World Christian Movement: A Reader*, 4th ed. Pasadena, CA: William Carey Library, 2013.

Wright, Christopher J. H. *The Mission of God: Unlocking the Bible's Grand Narrative*. Downers Grove, IL: InterVarsity, 2006.

_____. *The Mission of God's People: A Biblical Theology of the Church's Mission*. Grand Rapids: Zondervan, 2010.

Appendix A[1]

	6 Seasons of God's Kingdom Strategy	
Task	**Jesus (Luke 8–11)**	**Paul (Acts 13–14)**
Entry	8:1—"town to town" 8:4—"large crowd gathering" 8:12–15—Hearts of people equated to soils: "path, rocky, thorns, good soil" 8:19—"crowd, mother, brothers" 8:22, 26—"other side of the lake ... Gerasenes" 8:27—"man living among the tombs" 8:34—"those tending the pigs" 8:39—"all over town" 8:40—"returned to Galilee ... crowd" 8:42—"on his way" (to Jairus's home) 8:47—"presence of all the people" 8:51—"House of Jairus"	13:4–6 **Cyprus** "Synagogues" & "who Island" 13:14–15, 44—**Pisidian Antioch** "Synagogue," "Entire city" & "Gentiles" 14:1—**Iconium** "Synagogue" "people of the city" "Jews & Gentiles" 14:6, 8–10—**Lystra** "Lycaonian people" 14:6, 20—**Derbe** "city"
	9:1, 4—"Sent them out" "Whatever house you enter" 9:6—"So they set out and went from village to village." 9:11—"... crowds followed him. He welcomed them." 9:27—"when they came down the mountain, a large crowd met them." 9:52–53—"And he sent messengers on ahead, who went into a Samaritan village to get things ready for him; but the people there did not welcome him."	
	10:1, 3—"After this the Lord appointed 72 others and sent them two by two ahead of him to every town and place where he was about to go. 'Go! I am sending you.'" 10:3–12—Specific instruction on entering the harvest field 10:38—"As Jesus and his disciples were on their way, he came to a village where a woman named Martha opened her home to him."	
	11:29—"As the crowds increased..." 11:37—"When Jesus had finished speaking, a Pharisee invited him to eat with him; so he went in and reclined at the table."	

---

1. The following chart was developed by Carter Cox. Scripture quotations are from the NIV.

	6 Seasons of God's Kingdom Strategy	
Task	**Jesus (Luke 8–11)**	**Paul (Acts 13–14)**
Evangelism	8:1—"proclaiming the good news" 8:11—"The Seed is the word of God" 8:39—"man went away and told all over town how much Jesus had done for him" 8:47—"she told why she touched Jesus…"	13:5, 12—**Cyprus** "proclaimed" & "teaching" 13:16–41, 44–46, 49—**Pisidian Antioch** "said," "saying," "speak," "spread" 14:1—**Iconium** "spoke," "speaking boldly" 14:7, 9, 15–17—**Lystra** "continued to preach" "speaking" 14:7, 20—**Derbe** "continued to preach," "preached" 14:25—**Perga** "preached the word"
	9:1—"sent them out to proclaim the kingdom of God…" 9:3–6—Specific instruction on what to do, not do when proclaiming the kingdom. 9:6—"Proclaiming the good news and healing people…" 9:11—"… spoke to them about the kingdom of God" 9:23–26—"Whoever wants to be my disciple must deny themselves and take up their cross daily and follow me." 9:57–62—Jesus has hard sayings for those on the road desiring to follow him.	
	10:3–12—Specific instruction on entering and proclaiming the gospel in the harvest field and finding a person of peace. 10:25–37—Jesus answers a teacher of the law who is seeking eternal life by giving him a hard saying.	
	11:17–26—Jesus rebukes a crowd accusing him of driving out Satan by Satan. Gives them a hard saying, "Whoever is not with me is against me, and whoever does not gather with me scatters." 11:29–32—Jesus proclaims to crowds that they should repent, and points them to the sign of Jonah. 11:33–35—Jesus teaches the crowds a parable about a lamp lighting a room being like eyes which are the light of the body. 11:39–52—Jesus proclaims the hypocrisy of the Pharisees while he is inside a Pharisee's home who invited him to eat.	

	6 Seasons of God's Kingdom Strategy	
Task	**Jesus (Luke 8–11)**	**Paul (Acts 13–14)**
Discipleship	8:1—"the 12 were *with* him" 8:9—"disciples asked meaning" 8:15—Jesus describes the good soil person: "hear the word, cling to it, bear fruit" 8:21—"hear God's word, put it into practice" 8:22—"let *us* go," "*they* got in" 8:25—Jesus rebukes disciples: "Where is your faith?" 8:35—Former demon-possessed man: "sitting at Jesus' feet, dressed, in right mind" 8:39—Jesus commands former demoniac: "return home and tell how much God has done for you." 8:48—Jesus says to former bleeding woman: "Your faith has made you well, go in peace" 8:50—Jesus says to Jairus: "don't be afraid, believe" 8:51—Jesus did not let anyone go into Jairus's house except Peter, John, and James. 8:56—"ordered them not to tell what happened" 9:1–2—"called the 12 *together*" "sent *them* out" 9:4—"stay in that house until you leave town" 9:10—"Then he took *them* with him and they withdrew by *themselves*." 9:13–14—"You give them something to eat... Have them sit down in groups of fifty each." 9:18, 20—"Jesus was praying in private and his disciples were *with* him.... 'Who do the crowds say I am?'... 'Who do you say I am?'" 9:21—"The son of man must suffer many things, be killed, raised to life." 9:23–26—"Whoever wants to be my disciple must deny themselves and take up their cross daily and follow me." 9:28—"Jesus took Peter, John and James *with* him up onto a mountain to pray." 9:35—"A voice came from the cloud saying, 'This is my Son, whom I have chosen: listen to him.'" 9:41—"You unbelieving and perverse generation, how long shall I stay with you and put up with you? Bring your son here."	13:12—**Cyprus** "teaching" 13:43, 52; 14:21–22—**Pisidian Antioch** "urged to continue..." "disciples" "strengthen & encourage" 14:3—**Iconium**; 14:21–22 "considerable amount of time" "strengthen & encourage" 14:20; 14:21–22—**Lystra** "disciples gathered" "strengthen & encourage" 14:21—**Derbe** "made disciples" 14:28—**Antioch Syria** "stayed a long time with the disciples."

6 Seasons of God's Kingdom Strategy		
Task	**Jesus (Luke 8–11)**	**Paul (Acts 13–14)**
Discipleship	9:44—"Jesus said to his disciples, 'Listen carefully to what I am about to tell you: The Son of Man is going to be delivered into the hands of men.'" 9:48—"For it is the one who is least among you who is the greatest." 9:49–50—"'Master,' said John, 'we saw someone driving out demons in your name and we tried to stop him, because he is not one of us.' 'Do not stop him,' Jesus said, 'for whoever is not against us is for you.'" 9:55–56—"Jesus turned and rebuked them, then he and his disciples went to another village." 9:57–62—Jesus has hard sayings for those on the road desiring to follow him. 10:2—"The harvest is plentiful, but the workers are few. Ask the Lord of the harvest, therefore, to send out workers into his harvest field. Go! I am sending you." 10:3–12—Specific instruction on staying with and investing in God-prepared person of peace. 10:16—"Whoever listens to you listens to me; whoever rejects you rejects me; but whoever rejects me rejects him who sent me." 10:17–20—"The seventy-two returned with joy…he replied, 'I saw Satan fall like lightning from heaven…do not rejoice that spirits submit to you, but rejoice your names are written in heaven.'" 10:23—"Then he turned to his disciples and said privately…" 10:38—"As Jesus and his disciples were on their way, he came to a village where a woman named Martha opened her home to him." 10:39—"She had a sister called Mary, who sat at the Lord's feet listening to what he said." 10:41–42—"'Martha,' the Lord answered, 'you are worried about many things, but few things are needed—or indeed only one. Mary has chosen what is better, and it will not be taken from her.'"	

	6 Seasons of God's Kingdom Strategy	
Task	**Jesus (Luke 8–11)**	**Paul (Acts 13–14)**
Discipleship	11:1—"One day Jesus was praying in a certain place. When he finished, one of his disciples said, 'Lord, teach us to pray, just as John taught his disciples.'" 11:2–13—Jesus's instructions on how his disciples should pray. 11:17–26—Jesus rebukes a crowd accusing him of driving out Satan by Satan. Gives them a hard saying, "Whoever is not with me is against me, and whoever does not gather with me scatters."	
Gathering	8:1–3—"the 12 were *with* him & also some women…" 8:20—"standing *outside*" 8:22—"let *us* go" "*they* got in" (boat) 8:51—"House of Jairus"	13:1–3—**Antioch Syria** (sent) "in the church" 14:21–23—**Pisidian Antioch** "every church" 14:21–23—**Iconium** "every church" 14:20–23—**Lystra** "every church" 14:26–28—**Antioch Syria (return)** "gathered the church"
	9:1–2—"called the 12 *together*… sent *them* out" 9:4—"stay in that *house* until you leave town" 9:10—"When the apostles returned, *they* reported to Jesus…" "Then he took *them* with him and *they* withdrew by themselves." 9:14—"Have *them* sit down in groups of fifty each." 9:18—"Jesus was praying in private and his disciples were *with* him." 9:28—"Jesus took Peter, John and James with him up onto a mountain to pray." 9:57—"As *they* were walking along the road."	
	10:3–12—Specific instruction on staying in the *home* of the person of peace, not moving from house to house. 10:23—"Then he turned to his disciples and said privately…" 10:38—"As Jesus and his disciples were on *their* way, he came to a village where a woman named Martha opened her *home* to him."	
	11:1—"One day Jesus was praying in a certain place. When he finished, one of his disciples said, 'Lord, teach us to pray, just as John taught his disciples.'" 11:37—"When Jesus had finished speaking, a Pharisee invited him to eat with him; so he went in and reclined at the table."	

6 Seasons of God's Kingdom Strategy		
Task	**Jesus (Luke 8–11)**	**Paul (Acts 13–14)**
Leadership Development	8:1—"the 12 were with him" 8:9—"disciples asked meaning" 8:22—"let *us* go" "*they* got in" 8:45–46—Jesus teaching Peter 8:51—"Peter, John, James" only ones allowed in Jairus's house	13:1–3—Leaders ("**prophets & teachers**") from Antioch send out Paul & Barnabas 14:21–23—Returned to Lystra, Iconium, Pisidian Antioch to strengthen & encourage disciples & "*appoint elders* in every church." (16:1–5)—Timothy joins
	9:13–14—"You give them something to eat.... Have them sit down in groups of fifty each." 9:16—"Then he gave them to the disciples to distribute to people." 9:18—"Jesus was praying in private and his disciples were with him." 9:28—"Jesus took Peter, John and James with him up onto a mountain to pray." 9:57–62—Jesus has hard sayings for those on the road desiring to follow him.	
	10:1—"After this the Lord appointed 72 others and sent them two by two ahead of him to every town and place where he was about to go." 10:17–20—"The seventy-two returned with joy...he replied, I say Satan fall like lightning from heaven...do not rejoice that spirits submit to you, but rejoice your names are written in heaven." 10:23—"Then he turned to his disciples and said privately..."	
	11:1—"One day Jesus was praying in a certain place. When he finished, one of his disciples said, 'Lord, teach us to pray, just as John taught his disciples.'" 11:2–13—Jesus's instructions on how his disciples should pray.	

6 Seasons of God's Kingdom Strategy		
Task	Jesus (Luke 8–11)	Paul (Acts 13–14)
Partnership & Exit	8:1—"town to town" (implies he didn't set up shop in just one) 8:22—He "set out" from where they were. 8:37—"Got in boat and left" (to Gerasenes) 8:40—"Returned" (to Galilee)	13:3—**Antioch Syria** "sent off" for "**the work**" 13:13—**Cyprus** "Sail from" (no persecution) 13:50-51—**Pisidian Antioch** "expelled / shook dust from" (persecution)
	9:4–5—"stay in that house until you *leave* town" "shake dust from your feet if you are not welcome." 9:10—"When the apostles *returned*, they reported to Jesus…" 9:49–50—"'Master,' said John, 'we saw someone driving out demons in your name and we tried to stop him, because he is not one of us.' 'Do not stop him,' Jesus said, 'for whoever is not against us is for you.'" (on partnerships) 9:51—"As the time approached for him to be taken up to heaven, Jesus resolutely set out for Jerusalem."	14:6—**Iconium** "fled" (persecution) 14:20—**Lystra** "left" (persecution) 14:23-26—Returned to **Lystra, Iconium, Pisidian Antioch** to strengthen & encourage disciples & "*appoint elders* in every church." Returned to Syrian Antioch church after "**the work**" was "**completed**."
	10:3–2—Specific instruction on leaving a city where you are not welcome 10:17—"The seventy-two returned with joy."	

Appendix B

Sermon on Matthew 28:16–20
The Great Commission & William Carey:
A Passionate Global Vision[1]

William Carey may have been the greatest missionary since the time of the apostles. He rightly deserves the honor of being known as "the father of the modern missions movement." Carey was born in 1761, and he left England in 1793 as a missionary to India. He would never return home again, instead dying in 1834 among the people he had given his life to.

William Carey was poor, with only a grammar school education, and yet he would translate the Bible into dozens of languages and dialects. He established schools and mission stations all over India. Timothy George (dean of Beeson Divinity School) described Carey as a "lone, little man. His resume would have read: Education—minimal. Degrees—none. Savings—depleted. Political influence—nil. References—a band of country preachers half a world away. What were Carey's resources? Weapon—love. Desire—to bring the light of God into the darkness. Strategy—to proclaim by life, lips, and letters the unsearchable riches of Christ."[2]

William Carey understood Matthew 28:16–20. It was his farewell text to his church at Harvey Lane before departing to India. Though he had been rebuked earlier by the respected minister John Ryland Sr., Carey was undeterred. Ryland had told him, with his now-infamous words, "Young man, sit down. When God pleases to convert the heathen, he will do without your aid or mine."[3] Despite this, he would powerfully proclaim, "Expect great things. Attempt great things." (Later tradition would add "from God" and "for God," though this is undoubtedly what he meant.)[4]

He would publish his famous *An Enquiry into the Obligations of Christians to Use Means for the Conversion of the Heathens.*[5] Here he would pen searing words for the church of his day, as well as our own. Commenting on the Great Commission text, found in Matthew 28:16–20, Carey wrote:

---

1. This sermon was originally published in Daniel L. Akin, *10 Who Changed the World* (Nashville: B&H, 2012), 1–12. Used by permission, all rights reserved.
2. Timothy George, *Faithful Witness: The Life and Mission of William Carey* (Downers Grove, IL: InterVarsity, 1992), 93.
3. Ibid., 53.
4. Ibid., 32.
5. William Carey, *An Enquiry Into the Obligations to Use Means for the Conversion of the Heathens* (Dallas: Criswell Publication, 1988).

This commission was as extensive as possible, and laid them under obligation to disperse themselves into every country to the habitable globe, and preach to all the inhabitants, without exception, or limitation. They accordingly went forth in obedience to the command, and the power of God evidently wrought with them. Many attempts of the same kind have been made since their day, and which have been attended with various success; but the work has not been taken up, or prosecuted of late years (except by a few individuals) with that zeal and perseverance with which the primitive Christians went about it. It seems as if many thought the commission was sufficiently put in execution by what the apostles and others have done; that we have enough to do to attend to the salvation of our own countrymen; and that, if God intends the salvation of the heathen, he will some way or other bring them to the gospel, or the gospel to them. It is thus that multitudes sit at ease, and give themselves no concern about the far greater part of their fellow sinners, who to this day, are lost in ignorance and idolatry.[6]

Carey would later add, "I question whether all are justified in staying here, while so many are perishing without means of grace in other lands."[7]

The words found in Matthew 28 constitute the last words of Jesus in this gospel. They are intended to be lasting words and the final marching orders for Christ's followers until he returns. I once heard Adrian Rogers in a sermon say that in this passage we find "the heartbeat of the Son of God." Here we are told that, "We are all to bring all men by all means to Jesus by any cost."

Acknowledge He Has All Power (Matt. 28:16–18)

The eleven disciples minus Judas go north to Galilee "to the mountain where Jesus had told them to go" (v. 16, NIV). The scene is reminiscent of the setting of the Sermon on the Mount (Matt. 5:1). It is interesting to note that the climatic temptation (Matt. 4:8–11), the Sermon on the Mount (Matt. 5–7), the transfiguration (Matt. 17:1), the Olivet Discourse prophecy (Matt. 24–25), and now the Great Commission of the Great King all took place on a mountain.

Suddenly they see the resurrected, risen Lord. What transpires is instructive for our careful consideration and response.

---

6. Ibid., 4.
7. Ibid., 56.

Worship Him (v. 17)

Seeing him the people worship. Amazingly though, some still doubt. Did they have doubts as to whether or not they should worship this man? Perhaps. Were their doubts confusion about the whole thing? Perhaps. Did the people doubt because they did not know how to respond given their past failures and track record? Almost certainly.

Even in the midst of their doubts, worship is the wise and right thing to do. Even when I may not understand all he is doing in my life, *worship*. If I am confused, unsure, and hesitating, *worship*. When I am sorrowful, heartbroken, and crushed, *worship*. Am I discouraged, depressed, and in utter despair? *Worship*. Even when I am at death's door? *Worship!*

On his deathbed, Carey breathed to the Scottish missionary Alexander Duff, "When I am gone, say nothing about Dr. Carey. Speak about Dr. Carey's Savior."[8] Jesus is the Savior, so worship him.

Hear Him (v. 18)

Jesus said, "All authority in heaven and on earth has been given to me." Satan offered Jesus an earthly kingdom, but His Father planned so much more (Matt. 4:8–11). The words echo the great Son of Man text where the Bible declares of this heavenly, divine Man, "Then to Him was given dominion and glory and a kingdom, that all peoples, nations, and languages should serve Him. His dominion is an everlasting dominion, which shall not pass away, and His kingdom the one which shall not be destroyed" (Dan. 7:14, NKJV). John Piper gets to the heart of these words and says,

> Here we see the *peak of power*. Notice verse 18. Jesus says, "All authority in heaven and on earth has been given to me." If you gathered all the authority of all the governments and armies of the world and put them in the scales with the authority of the risen Christ, they would go up in the balance like air. *All authority* on earth has been given to the risen Christ. *All* of it! The risen Christ has the right to tell every man, woman, and child on this planet today what they should do and think and feel. He has absolute and total authority over your life and over cities and states and nations. The risen Christ is great— greater than you have ever imagined.
>
> Here is our witness to the world: The risen Christ is your king and has absolute, unlimited authority over your life. If you do not bow and worship him and trust him and obey him, you commit high treason against Christ the King, who is God

---

8. George, *Faithful Witness*, xii.

over all. The resurrection is God's open declaration that he lays claim on every person and tribe and tongue and nation. . . . "All authority on earth is mine." Your sex life is his to rule; your business is his to rule; your career is his to rule; your home is his; your children are his, your vacation is his, your body is his; He is *God!* So if you resist his claim, feel no admiration for his infinite power and authority, and turn finally to seek satisfaction from thrills that allow you to be your own master, then you will be executed for treason in the last day. And it will appear so reasonable and so right that you should be executed for your disloyalty to your Maker and Redeemer that there will be no appeals and no objections. Your life of indifference to the risen Christ and of half-hearted attention now and then to a few of his commandments will appear on that day as supremely blameworthy and infinitely foolish, and you will . . . weep that you did not change.[9]

Obey His Authoritative Plan (Matt. 28:19–20)

Commenting on Matthew 28:19, John Calvin wrote, "Now the wall is pulled down and the Lord orders the ministers of the gospel to go far out to scatter the teaching of salvation throughout all the regions of the earth."[10] Tragically many in Carey's day, as well as our own, have imbibed the spirit of the eighteenth-century anti-missions hymn: *Go into all the world, the Lord of old did say. But now where he has planted thee, there thou shouldst stay.*[11]

Carey would have no part of this spiritually bankrupt and impotent thinking. Rather, having his heart gripped by the words of our Savior, he said, "I care not where or how I lived, or what hardships I went through, so that I could but gain souls for Christ. While I was asleep I dreamed of these things, and when I awoke the first thing I thought of was this great work. All my desire was for the conversion of the heathen, and all my hope was in God."[12]

The imperative or command of verse 19 is "make disciples." The "therefore" links the command to the "all authority" declaration of verse 18. Further, wed to an imperative, the three participles—going, baptizing, and teaching— receive the force and thrust of imperatives. Thus Jesus charges us, commands us to make disciples by going, make disciples by baptizing, and make disciples by teaching.

---

9. John Piper, "Worship the Risen Christ," *desiringgood.org*, April 3, 1983, http://www.desir-inggod.org/resource-library/sermons/worship-the-risen-christ.
10. Quoted in George, *Faithful Witnesses*, 39.
11. Ibid.
12. Ibid., 45.

Make Disciples by Going (v. 19)

There is no need to pray and ask God if we should go and take the gospel to the nations. We have been told to go. Again, John Piper says:

> So there you have the word of God from the mouth of Jesus. The lofty claim: "All authority is given to me." The loving comfort: "I am with you always, even to the end of the age." The last command: "Go make disciples among all the peoples of the world." What is clear from this final word of Jesus is that he is trying to move us to act. He not only says, "Go make disciples." He also gives us a warrant for doing it so that we can know it is a legitimate and right thing to do: All authority in heaven and on earth is his. He gives us tremendous encouragement and comfort and strength to go, with the promise that he would go with us and never leave us. Jesus ended his earthly life with these words because he wanted us to respond. He was motivating us to act.[13]

Do you need a reason to go? No! You need a reason to stay! Some 1.6 billion people have yet to hear the name of Jesus.

R. T. France captures the theological thrust of Jesus's command to go when he says, "Jesus' vision of the future heavenly enthronement of the Son of Man in Matthew 24:30 led naturally into a mission to gather his chosen people from all over the earth (24:31). . . . But the agents of this ingathering are not now to be angels . . . but those who are already Jesus' disciples."[14]

Go and make more followers, more disciples of Jesus. Where? All the nations.

In his journal entry on March 29, 1794, Carey wrote, "O what is there in all this world worth living for but the presence and service of God—I feel a burning desire that all the world may know this God and serve Him."[15]

Go and make disciples.

Make Disciples by Baptizing (v. 19)

Here is the badge of being a disciple. Here is where biblical profession of faith takes place. Here is my unashamed identification with Jesus as my Lord by public declaration.

Baptism—immersion, plain and clear.

Name—singular.

13. John Piper, "The Lofty Claim, the Last Command, the Loving Comfort," *desiringgod. org*, November 1, 1998, http://www.desiringgod.org/resource-library/sermons/the-lofty-claim-the-last-command-the-loving-comfort.

14. R. T. France, *Matthew*, NICNT (Grand Rapids: Eerdmans, 2007), 1114.

15. William Carey, *The Journal and Selected Letters of William Carey*, ed. Terry G. Carter (Macon, GA: Smyth & Helwys, 2000), 21.

Father, Son, and Holy Spirit—Father, Savior, and Comforter, the Triune God.

What joy to initiate new believers into the church of the Lord Jesus as they identify themselves with Christ in death, burial, and resurrection. And that they would be found in every nation and from all the peoples of the earth! What a gospel! What a mission! What an assignment!

Closing his *Enquiry* with a word of missionary encouragement Carey wrote, "What a heaven will it be to see the many myriads of poor heathens . . . who by their labors have been brought to the knowledge of God. Surely a 'crown of rejoicing' (1 Thess. 2:19) like this is worth aspiring to. Surely it is worth while to lay ourselves out with all our might in promoting the cause and kingdom of Christ."[16]

Make Disciples by Teaching (v. 20)

We do not make converts. We are called to make disciples, "little Christs," who observe all His teachings. James Boice well says, "Robust disciples are not made by watered-down teaching."[17] A "hit and run" approach to missions and ministry will fail to accomplish this. Short-term endeavors, though commendable and valuable, are no substitute for those who give years, even the rest of their lives, to teach others who can teach others who can teach others.

Baptism is preschool enrollment into a school of learning that one never graduates from! But someone must go and teach them.

Trust His Amazing Promise (Matt. 28:20)

William Carey was a great man, but he was a man. Life brought him many tragedies. Francis Wayland said of him, "Like most of the master minds of all ages, Carey was educated in the school of adversity."[18] There were times when his soul was plunged to the depths of depression. He would bury two wives, with his first, Dorothy, sorrowfully, going insane. He would bury three children, and certain others disappointed him. He lost most of his hair due to illness in his early twenties, served in India for forty-one years never taking a furlough, fought back dysentery and malaria, and did not baptize his first Indian convert, Krisha Pal, until his seventh year on the field! What kept him going? What promise of God did he claim again and again in the face of discouragement and defeat? He had asked his friend John Williams in 1801, "Pray for us that we may be faithful to the end."[19] He was! How? This promise: "And lo, I am with you always, even to the end of the age" (Matt. 28:20, NKJV).

---

16. Carey, *Journal and Selected Letters*, 65.
17. James M. Boice, *The Gospel of Matthew* (Grand Rapids: Baker, 2006), 649.
18. Quoted in George, *Faithful Witness*, 94.
19. Ibid., 154.

Two aspects to this amazing promise sustained Carey, and they will sustain us as well wherever the Lord might send us.

He will be with you constantly ("always"). He will be with you continually ("to the end of the age"). Knowing God was with him constantly and continually saw Carey through those valleys of the shadow of death, "dungeons of despair," and feelings of total inadequacy. In a letter to his father he wrote concerning his call:

> I see more and more of my own insufficiency for the great work I am called to. The truths of God are amazingly profound, the souls of men infinitely precious, my own ignorance very great and all that I do is for God who knows my motives and my ends, my diligence or negligence. When I (in short) compare myself with my work, I sink into a point, a mere despicable nothing.[20]

In his journal entry dated Aug. 27–31, 1794, Carey wrote:[21]

August 27
Nothing new, my Soul is in general barren and unfruitful; Yet I find a pleasure in drawing near to God; and a peculiar sweetness in His Holy Word. I find it more and more to be a very precious treasure.

August 28–30
Nothing of any importance except to my shame, a prevalence of carnality, negligence, and spiritual deadness; no heart for private duties, indeed everything seems to be going to decay in my soul, and I almost despair of being any use to the heathen at all.

August 31
Was somewhat engaged more than of late in the things of God, felt some new devotedness to God, and desired to live entirely to him, and for his glory; O that I could live always as under his eye, and feel a sense of his immediate presence, this is life and all besides this is death to my soul.

G. Campbell Morgan was reading Matthew 28:20 to an eighty-five-year-old saint. Finishing the verse he said, "That is a great promise." She looked

---

20. Ibid., 25.
21. Carey, *Journal and Selected Letters*, 39.

up and said sharply, with the light of sanctified humor in her eyes, "That is not a promise at all, that is a fact. Oh, if the church of God could remember that fact!"[22]

Conclusion

Matthew 28 begins with a resurrection and ends with a commission. These final words of our Lord are weighty, heavy, and not easily digested. They do not need an adrenalin response. They need a cardiac response, a heart response. They need a response that has carefully considered the King who speaks them, and the kind of servant who obeys them. Once more hear the words of William Carey, who heard and heeded his Master's call.

> A Christian minister is a person who is "not his own" (1Cor. 6:19); he is the servant of God, and therefore ought to be wholly devoted to him. By entering on that sacred office he solemnly undertakes to be always engaged as much as possible in the Lord's work, and not to choose his own pleasure or employment, or pursue the ministry as something that is to subserve his own ends or interest, or as a kind of sideline. He engages to go where God pleases, and to do or endure what he sees fit to command or call him to in the exercise of his function. He virtually bids farewell to friends, pleasures, and comforts, and stands in readiness to endure the greatest sufferings in the work of the Lord, his Master. It is inconsistent for ministers to please themselves with thoughts of numerous congregations, cordial friends, a civilized country, legal protection, affluence, splendor, or even an income that is sufficient. The slights and hatred of men, and even pretended friends, gloomy prisons, and tortures, the society of barbarians of uncouth speech, miserable accommodations in wretched wildernesses, hunger and thirst, nakedness, weariness, and diligence, hard work, and but little worldly encouragement, should rather be the objects of their expectation.... I question whether all are justified in staying here, while so many are perishing without means of grace in other lands.... On the contrary the commission is a sufficient call to them to venture all, and, like the primitive Christians, go everywhere preaching the gospel.[23]

---

22. G. Campbell Morgan, *The Gospel according to Matthew* (New York: Fleming H. Revell Co., 1929), 320–21.

23. Carey, *Journal and Selected Letters*, 55–56.

On his seventieth birthday, three years before his death, Carey would give his own humble evaluation of his life and ministry. Herein we discover something of the man that made him great for God. In a letter to his son Jabez he wrote:

> I am this day seventy years old, a monument of Divine mercy and goodness, though on a review of my life I find much, very much, for which I ought to be humbled in the dust; my direct and positive sins are innumerable, my negligence in the Lord's work has been great, I have not promoted his cause, nor sought his glory and honor as I ought, notwithstanding all this, I am spared till now, and am still retained in his Work, and I trust I am received into the divine favor through him. I wish to be more entirely devoted to his service, more completely sanctified and more habitually exercising all the Christian graces, and bringing forth the fruits of righteousness to the praise and honor of that Savior who gave his life a sacrifice for sin.[24]

After he died on June 9, 1834, these simple words would be inscribed on the stone slab that marked his grave in Serampore, India: "A wretched, poor, and helpless worm, on thy kind arms I fall."[25] Would to God that he would raise up from among us an army of such wretched, poor, and helpless worms. The world needs them. Jesus deserves them. Our churches should provide them.

---

24. George, *Faithful Witness*, 155.
25. Ibid., 168.

Scripture Index

Genesis

1 ....208, 209
1:1 ....219, 270
1:25–26 144
1:26 208
1:26–27 271
1:26–28 208
1:28 ....144, 216, 219, 220, 271
1:31 271
1–2 207
1–11 ....220, 224
2 208
2:7 194
2:16 211
2:17 210
2:25 212
3 ....210, 212, 213, 219, 271
3:1 210
3:6 211
3:7 212
3:14–19 211
3:15 ....213, 219, 272, 278
3–11 ....219, 220
4:8 219
6:5 219
8:21 219
10 145
11 145
11:4 219
12 ....220, 224
12:1–3 ....219, 220
12:3 ....219, 272
26:24 169
27:13 149
28:15 169
33:14–15 219
37:14 150
49:8–12 272

Exodus

3:12 170
4:12 170
5:18 150
12:32 150
15:18 233
34 221
34:6–7 ....219, 221

Leviticus

19:18 37
19:33–34 305

Numbers

23:21 233

Deuteronomy

5:1–11:32 38
6:4–5 ....37, 38
6:5 38
20:4 170
31:6 170
33:5 233

Joshua

1:1 170
1:5 170
1:9 170

Judges

6:12 170
6:16 170

1 Kings

8 226

2 Kings

2:16 150
17:13 248
19:15 233

1 Chronicles

22:1–16 229

Psalms

16:10 185
19:1 271
22:1 184
22:6–7 184
22:27 223
22:27–28 233
29:10 233
31:5 184
31:13 184
33:8–9 219

Isaiah

46:10 223
47:2 233
66 223
66:1 223
67 223
67:1–2 223
67:3 120
72:17 220
90:2 270
96:3 223
96:10 ....223, 233
97:1 233
99:1–4 233
103:19 233
108:5 223
110:1 185
117 223
117:1 223
145:11 233
150:6 223

Isaiah

2:3 186
6:5 233
7:1–9:7 228
7:14 ....228, 272
8:12–13 263
9 128
9:1–2 ....128, 227
9:2 222
9:6 272
13–23 221
19:24–25 220
24:23 233
32:15 188
33:22 233
40:28 222
41:5 222
41:9 222
41:10 170
42:6 ....185, 222
42:6–7 ....219, 221
42:7 222
42:10 222
42:19–20 222
43:5 170

43:6...............................222
43:8...............................222
43:10.............................187
43:15.............................233
44:3...............................188
44:8...............................187
44:18–19......................222
45:20–24......................222
48:20.............................222
49:6........185, 202, 219, 222
52:7...............................233
52:13.............................237
53:1–12.........................272
53:5...............................192
53:7–8..........................184
60:3...............................193
61:1–2....................231, 290
62:1–3..........................272

Jeremiah
1:1–10...........................229
1:8...............................170
4:2...............................220
46:18.............................233
46–51...........................221

Ezekiel
25–32............................221
37:9...............................194
39:29.............................188

Daniel
2:44...............................233
7:14..........30, 131, 227, 345

Hosea
6:2...............................185

Joel
2:1...............................186
2:28–29.........................188
2:32...............................186

Amos
1:2–2:16................219, 221

Jonah
4:2...............................221

Micah
4:2...............................186
5:2...............................226
7:12...............................193

Nahum
1:3...............................221

Habakkuk
2:14...............................120

Zephaniah
2:1–3:5.........................221
3:15...............................233

Haggai
1:13...............................170

Zechariah
8:13...............................220
14:9...............................233

Matthew
1:1..........213, 220, 226, 227
1:3–5.............................227
1:20...............................228
1:21...............................20
1:23............130, 171, 228
2:1–12...........................227
2:2...............................226
2:6...............................226
2:8...................149, 150, 226
2:11...............................226
2:13........................149, 151
2:20...............................151
3...............................157
3:11...............................158
3:15–17.........................326
3:16–17.........................158
4:8–9.............................326
4:8–11.............21, 344, 345
4:10...............................130
4:12–17.........................227
4:15...............................137
4:15–16..................128, 227
4:17........................162, 231
4:19........162, 166, 278, 287
4:23........................158, 231
4:23–24..................130, 226
5:1...............................344
5:1–2.............................128
5:2...............................158
5:7–8.............................165
5:10...............................299
5:12...............................162
5:13...............................292
5:14–16.........................292
5:16...............................163
5:17...............................159
5:17–18.........................166
5:18–19.........................159
5:21–22.........................163

5:22...............................163
5:24...............................151
5:24–25.........................163
5:27–28.........................163
5:29–30.........................162
5:31–32.........................164
5:37...............................163
5:38–39.........................163
5:38–42.........................163
5:44........163, 165, 227, 299
5:48...............................163
5–7...........21, 158, 227, 344
6:1–4.............................165
6:5–6.............................165
6:9...............................164
6:9–10...........................234
6:9–13...........................164
6:19–20.........................165
6:32........................137, 142
6:33...............................163
7:1–3.............................163
7:6...............................166
7:7–8.............................165
7:12........................163, 228
7:13–14.........................162
7:15...............................166
7:21...............................234
7:24...............................159
7:24–27.........................227
7:28–29.........................226
7:29........................130, 158
8...............................130
8:5–13...........................227
8:9...............................130, 226
8:10...............................227
8:11–12.........................234
8:18–22.........................228
8:28–34.........................227
8:29–32..................130, 226
9:1–8.............................236
9:5–8.............................226
9:6...............................130, 151
9:13...............................150
9:35..............130, 158, 226
9:37–38.........................296
9:38........................165, 279
10...............................158, 227
10:1........................130, 226
10:5..............137, 138, 142
10:5–6...........137, 138, 227
10:6...............................138

10:7 151
10:16 166
10:18 137
10:23 138
10:26 164
10:28 164
11:1 158
11:4 .... 149, 150, 151
11:7 151
11:11 234
11:20–24 265
11:27 .... 130, 158, 226
11:28–30 119
11:29 .... 134, 162
12:18 137
12:21 142
12:22 .... 130, 226
12:28 .... 158, 234
12:28–29 233
12:31 164
13 .... 158, 227
13:3–8 234
13:12 .... 165, 166
13:24–30 234
13:31–32 233
13:33 233
13:34 158
13:39 172
13:40 172
13:41 .... 130, 226
13:44 234
13:45–46 234
13:47–50 234
13:49 172
13:52 .... 134, 228, 253
13–28 276
14:3 128
14:31 129
14:33 226
15:4 164
15:6 166
15:21–28 227
15:29 128
16:6 166
16:18 .... 26, 141
16:27 158
17:1 .... 21, 344
17:1–3 128
17:18 .... 130, 226
17:27 .... 149, 150
18 .... 158, 227

18:10 166
18:15 .... 164, 228
18:17 141
18:19 228
18:20 228
18:21–22 164
19:6 164
19:16–22 228
19:17 159
19:28 226
20:1–16 234
20:19 137
20:20–23 226
20:25 .... 137, 142
20:26–28 164
21 212
21:2 151
21:4 164
21:6 152
21:9 226
21:12 226
21:14 226
21:15 226
21:19 212
21:23 158
21:23–27 .... 130, 227
21:43 142
22:1–4 233
22:15 152
22:19–21 165
22:37 39
22:37–38 164
22:37–39 163
22:37–40 .... 37, 227
22:38 39
22:39 .... 37, 164
23:3 159
23:23 166
23–25 158
23–27 166
24 .... 48, 239, 244
24:1–35 48
24:3 .... 172, 240
24:3–4 129
24:4–6 166
24:4–13 .... 240, 245
24:4–14 240
24:4–35 242
24:7 .... 137, 142
24:9 .... 137, 142
24:13–14 172

24:14 .... 47, 48, 137, 142,
            239, 240, 241,
            242, 243, 244
24:30 347
24:31 347
24:36 158
24:36–25:46 48
24:36–51 242
24:42–44 243
24–25 .... 21, 227, 344
25:1–13 234
25:13 243
25:16 152
25:29 165
25:31 226
25:31–46 .... 234, 292
25:32 .... 46, 137, 142
26:14–15 152
26:26–28 164
26:30 129
26:32 128
26:41 165
26:55 158
27:54 227
27:57 .... 134, 228, 253
27:66 152
28 .... 17, 45, 46, 66,
          159, 180, 224, 228,
          251, 344, 350
28:7 .... 127, 128, 151
28:9 .... 130, 226
28:10 .... 127, 128, 151
28:11 151
28:16 .... 23, 24, 127, 180
28:16–17 127
28:16–18 .... 127, 344
28:16–20 ...... 18, 21, 25, 56,
          68, 127, 132,
          148, 180, 225,
          229, 236, 343
28:17 .... 129, 169, 226,
            276, 345
28:18 .... 30, 127, 130, 131,
          139, 172, 224, 227,
          345, 346
28:18–19 18
28:18–20 .... 9, 19, 21, 63,
          64, 65, 66, 67, 69,
          99, 177, 215, 275,
          320, 325, 326

28:19.......... 40, 46, 47, 127,
              128, 131, 134,
              137, 147, 148, 149,
              151, 153, 157, 162,
              166, 181, 220, 227,
              228, 239, 253, 256,
              257, 346, 347
28:19–20 .... 63, 133, 165,
              181, 182, 219,
              228, 247, 258, 346
28:20 .... 25, 46, 48, 131,
              136, 166, 169, 170,
              172, 216, 228, 258,
              348, 349

Mark
1:15 .... 162, 231, 234, 265
2:1–12 236
2:7 196
2:10 236
2:17 232
2:18–20 233
2:22 233
3:7–12 234
4:3–8 234
5:20 236
6:53–56 234
6:56 235
9:1 234
9–20 179
10:46–52 236
10:52 236
11:7 142
11:17 142
12:29–31 37
12:30 39
12:31 39
13:8 142
13:10 .... 21, 64, 142, 180
14:9 ....21, 180
14:22–24 164
14:25 234
15:40 179
15:47 179
16 ....17, 67
16:1 179
16:7 179
16:8 179
16:9 ....179, 180
16:9–11 179
16:9–20 .... 21, 178, 179,
              181, 182

16:11 179
16:12 180
16:12–13 179
16:14 ....17, 180
16:14–18 64
16:15 ....65, 66, 180,
              181, 182, 329
16:15–18 ....177, 182
16:15–20 21
16:16 181
16:17 181
16:18 181

Luke
1:35 188
1:44 235
1:47 235
1:79 232
2:10 235
2:32 .... 142, 186, 202, 235
4:5 241
4:14 188
4:14–15 232
4:14–30 231
4:16–30 232
4:18–19 ....231, 290
4:39 236
4:43 231
5:17 188
5:17–26 236
6:20 232
6:23 235
6:38 165
7:5 142
7:21–22 232
7:22 232
7:36–50 162
8:2 179
8:39 236
8–11 313
9:1–6 187
9:23 162
9:51 187
10:1–12 187
10:2 296
10:19 181
10:24–27 37
10:25–37 163
10–20 235
11:2 234
12:15 165
12:16–21 234

12:29–30 142
12:54–56 233
13:13 236
13:33 187
14:12–14 164
14:16–24 233
14:28–32 234
14:33 279
15:11–32 ....162, 234
16:1–9 234
16:1–16 165
16:19–31 234
17:11–19 236
17:20–21 234
18:1–8 164
18:9–14 162
18:31 187
19:6 235
19:37 235
21:3 232
21:10 142
21:24 142
21:26 241
22:7–20 164
22:19 164
22:19–20 164
23:2 142
24 188
24:1–11 187
24:11 179
24:13–15 183
24:13–35 179
24:26 213
24:36–49 187
24:41 235
24:44–49 64
24:45–49 330
24:46–47 .... 184, 185, 202
24:46–49 ....21, 177,
              183, 200
24:47 .... 138, 142, 200
24:48 ....200, 202
24:49 .... 162, 188, 200
24:51 179
24:52 235

John
1:12–13 193
1:14 192
1:29 192
1:32 193
3:3 193

3:5 193
3:7 162
3:16–17 235
3:17 192
3:18 181
3:34 193
3:35 30
3:36 181
4:4–42 166
4:34 .... 192, 193
4:53 236
5:19 193
5:23–24 192
5:30 192
5:36–38 192
6:27 193
6:29 192
6:38–39 192
6:44 192
6:57 192
7:16 192
7:18 192
7:28–29 192
7:33 192
7:39 .... 194, 195
8:16 192
8:18 192
8:26 192
8:29 192
8:42 192
9:4 192
9:35 236
9:38 236
10:36 .... 192, 193
11:42 192
11:48 142
11:50–52 142
11:51–53 237
11:52 143
12:32 237
12:33 237
12:44–45 192
12:49 192
13:16 192
13:20 192
13:24 192
13:31 195
13:34 164
13:34–35 39
14:2–3 31
14:5 31

14:6 31
14:12 .... 181, 194
14:15 .... 40, 164, 166
14:16–17 172
14:16–18 194
14:25–26 .... 173, 194
14:27 191
14–16 .... 193, 196
14–17 188
15:9–12 39
15:19 192
15:21 192
15:25–26 194
15:26–27 .... 192, 195
16:5 192
16:7 .... 173, 195
16:8–11 194
16:12–15 194
17:2 30
17:3 192
17:4 193
17:5 195
17:6 166
17:8 192
17:17 193
17:18 .... 192, 193
17:21 192
17:23 192
17:25 192
18:35 142
18:36 233
20 194
20:11–18 179
20:17 193
20:19 .... 191, 196
20:19–23 .... 21, 64
20:20 191
20:21 .... 20, 30, 42, 177,
                 192, 193, 196,
                 303, 320
20:21–23 .... 191, 330
20:22 .... 162, 194
20:23 .... 196, 197
20:24–29 276
20:26 195
20:31 .... 31, 236
21:1–3 195
21:15–16 166
21:15–19 276
21:25 161

Acts
1:1 199
1:4 200
1:6 .... 199, 200, 203
1:7 199
1:7–8 64
1:8 .... 21, 23, 31, 56,
                 68, 71, 87, 178,
                 181, 186, 187,
          188, 200, 202, 222,
          248, 283, 287, 314,
          315, 316, 317, 331
1:9 179
1:21–22 .... 201, 202
1:22 187
2 .... 34, 88, 194,
                       201, 250
2:1–4 21
2:4 .... 181, 188
2:5 142
2:8–11 34
2:17–18 .... 188, 248
2:23–24 188
2:27 185
2:32 .... 187, 188, 201, 202
2:34 185
2:36–47 161
2:37 157
2:37–39 162
2:38 .... 157, 158, 181,
                       200, 249
2:40–41 163
2:42 .... 164, 166, 202,
                       250, 287
2:42–43 165
2:42–46 165
2:42–47 163
2:44–47 202
2:46 164
2:46–47 166
2:47 287
3 .... 250, 290
3:8 248
3:15 .... 187, 188, 201, 202
3:26 248
4 .... 30, 248, 249
4:2 .... 30, 188, 202
4:3 248
4:8 188
4:10 .... 188, 202
4:12 31

4:17....................................202
4:17–18 30
4:18....................................248
4:19–20 31
4:21....................................248
4:30–31 202
4:31............... 188, 248, 249
4:32–37 165
4:33....................188, 202
5:12....................................181
5:20....................................202
5:21–22 202
5:25....................................202
5:28....................................202
5:30....................................188
5:32........187, 188, 201, 202
5:42....................................202
6:2......................................202
6:4......................................202
6:7......................................202
6:10....................................188
7..287
7:7......................................142
7:54–60 249
8....................................24, 287
8:1–3...................................249
8:9......................................142
8:12–13 249
8:16....................................158
8:26–39 163
8:29....................................188
8:32–33 184
8:35–36 249
8:38....................................249
8:39....................................188
8–18....................................301
9:12....................................181
9:15....................................142
9:15–16 247
9:17....................................181
9:18....................................249
9:31......................................23
10:19..................................188
10:22..................................142
10:35..................................142
10:36..................................227
10:38....................232, 236
10:39............. 187, 201, 202
10:41....................187, 188
10:44..................................188
10:44–48 250

10:46..................................181
10:48..................................158
11:2–3 249
11:12..................................188
11:19–26 88
11:28..................................241
12:24..................................202
13..............................26, 250
13:2–4 188
13:4–5 299
13:6–9 299
13:10–12 300
13:12..................................300
13:13..................................300
13:14–15 300
13:16–47 300
13:19..................................142
13:30–37 188
13:31....................187, 201
13:35..................................185
13:46..................................142
13:47......142, 186, 202, 222
13:48..................................300
13–14 .... 24, 299, 313
13–28 23
14:1–2 300
14:3....................................301
14:4–18 301
14:16..................................142
14:19–20 301
14:21..................................134
14:21–23 ....251, 301
14:22....................251, 259
14:24–28 301
14:27–28 26
15....................................33, 250
15:7....................................142
15:14..................................142
15:16–17 142
15:17..................................143
15:23..................................142
15:40....................................24
15:41..................................259
16:3......................................24
16:7....................................172
16:14–15 250
16:16–18 249
16:18..................................181
16:22–23 249
16:23–24 249
16:32..................................250

16:32–33 250
16:33..................................250
17..250
17:3....................................188
17:5....................................249
17:16....................................34
17:18....................88, 188
17:22–34 247
17:23–24 34
17:26....................142, 143
17:30..................................247
17:31..................................188
18:2–3 24
18:6....................................142
18:8....................................250
18:11..................................259
18:22..................................259
18:24–27 24
18:26..................................248
18–19 72
19:5....................158, 250
19:6....................................181
19:8....................................248
19:20..................................202
19:27..................................241
19:29..................................249
20..250
20:18–20 259
20:27..................................259
20:31..................................259
21:11..................................142
21:32..................................249
22..250
22:15....................187, 201
22:16....................158, 249
22:20..................................187
22:21..................................142
24..250
24:2....................................142
24:10..................................142
24:17..................................142
26..250
26:4....................................142
26:16..................................187
28:3–6 181
28:8....................................181
28:11..................................259
28:19..................................142
28:22..................................249
28:31..................................250

Romans

1 35
1:5 .... 142, 167, 328
1:8 87
1:11 259
1:16 138
1:17 187
1:18–32 215
1:20 35
1:21–25 211
2 35
3:23 271
3:39 142
4:5 214
4:17–18 142
5:12 212
5:19 214
6:3 158
6:3–4 ....157, 257
6:4 257
8:9 172
8:28–30 215
9:24 142
10:9–17 34
10:13 256
10:13–15 256
10:14–15 256
10:16 ....167, 256
10:18 ....138, 241
12 150
12:2 215
15:9–12 142
15:11 ....143, 223
15:14 259
15:14–21 254
15:16 142
15:18–24 241
15:19 .... 144, 187, 241,
                       242, 254
15:20 ....49, 254
15:23 ....254, 313
15:24 23
15:24–25 72
16:19 87
16:26 .... 142, 167, 241

1 Corinthians

1:13 257
1:13–17 256
1:17 257
1:21 34

4:16 22
6:19 350
9:19–22 262
9:20 138
9:22 255
9:23 ....255, 262
12:12–31 25
12:13 ...... 157, 250, 257, 258
14:36 255
15:3–4 ....278, 292
15:45–54 215
15:49 215
16:5–9 259
16:9 72
16:15 257

2 Corinthians

1:15–16 259
2:14–16 292
3:18 215
4:4 215
4:4–6 298
5:19 207

Galatians

2:9 142
3:8 ....142, 143
3:14 142
3:27 .... 157, 158, 257
4:6 172

Ephesians

1:20 172
1:20–21 131
1:20–22 30
4 286
4:5 .... 157, 257, 258
4:11–12 ....254, 283
4:11–16 254
4:12–16 260
4:13 254
4:15 259
6:18–20 249

Philippians

1:19 172
1:27 262
2:9–10 30
2:16 22
3:20–21 215

Colossians

1 326
1:3–5 39

1:5–7 255
1:6 241
1:10 262
1:15–24 213
1:23 87
1:25 254
1:28 .... 254, 258, 259
2:10 30
2:11–12 ....157, 257
2:23 257
3:1 ....172, 257
3:16 259

1 Thessalonians

1:3 39
1:5 255
1:8 ....22, 87, 256
2:12 262
2:13–14 256
2:17–20 259
2:19 348
5:1–2 243
5:1–11 199
5:6 243

2 Thessalonians

1:8 167
3:1 256
3:15 259

1 Timothy

2:3 98
2:5 31
2:12 287
3:2 260
3:15 260
5:17 260

2 Timothy

2:2 260
3:6–17 312
4:2 260
4:17 142

Titus

1:9 260
2:3–4 287

Philemon

6 39

Hebrews

1:3 172
9:26 172
10:12 172
10:32–34 264

10:32–39 299
12:2................................172
13:3................................299

James
1:26................................291
1:27................................291

1 Peter
1:11................................172
2:5–9..............................285
2:9..................................142
2:17.........................39, 263
3:1..................................262
3:1–2..............................265
3:2..................................263
3:14................................263
3:14–16 263
3:15................................263
3:15–16 263
3:18................................272
3:22................................172
4:14................................264
4:16................................264
4:17................................167
5:8..................................298

2 Peter
1:20–21 248
3:1–10 265
3:9...........................239, 265
3:10................................243
3:11–12 ....239, 244

1 John
2:2..................................264
2:17................................264
3:2..................................215
3:8..................................213
4:9..................................264
4:11..................................39
4:14................................264
4:19..................................38
4:20..................................39
5:19................................264

3 John
1 261
5 ....261, 262
5–6................................261
5–8................................261
6 ....261, 262
6–8................................261

7 262
7–8................................262

Revelation
5 145
5:7....................................22
5:9 ....47, 142, 143, 145
5:9–10 ....217, 237
7:9....................................47
7:9–10 ....311, 320
11:9................................142
12:5........................142, 143
13:7................................142
14:6.........................47, 142
14:18...............................142
15:4..................47, 142, 143
16:15...............................243
16:19...............................142
17:14.................................30
19:15–20:8 142
21:3–4 273
21:5–6 207
21:24...............................142
22:8–9 130